Non fiction Gift Aid L14
£ 4.00

0 031140 029972

REF ADM 17/24

CW00704623

DIVINE STYLE

Divine Style

Walt Whitman and the King James Bible

F. W. Dobbs-Allsopp

https://www.openbookpublishers.com

©2024 F. W. Dobbs-Allsopp

This work is licensed under an Attribution-NonCommercial 4.0 International (CC BY-NC 4.0). This license allows you to share, copy, distribute and transmit the text; to adapt the text for non-commercial purposes of the text providing attribution is made to the author (but not in any way that suggests that they endorse you or your use of the work). Attribution should include the following information:

F. W. Dobbs-Allsopp, *Divine Style: Walt Whitman and the King James Bible*. Cambridge, UK: Open Book Publishers, 2024, https://doi.org/10.11647/OBP.0357

Copyright and permissions for the reuse of the images included in this publication may differ from the above. This information is provided in the captions and in the list of illustrations.

Further details about CC BY-NC licenses are available at http://creativecommons.org/licenses/by-nc/4.0/

All external links were active at the time of publication unless otherwise stated and have been archived via the Internet Archive Wayback Machine at https://archive.org/web

Any digital material and resources associated with this volume will be available at https://doi.org/10.11647/OBP.0357#resources

ISBN Paperback: 978-1-80511-101-6
ISBN Hardback: 978-1-80511-102-3
ISBN Digital (PDF): 978-1-80511-103-0
ISBN Digital ebook (EPUB): 978-1-80511-104-7
ISBN XML: 978-1-80511-106-1
ISBN HTML: 978-1-80511-107-8
DOI: 10.11647/OBP.0357

Cover image: Copy of an engraving of Walt Whitman from Codex Ms263. The codex contains the holograph original of Whitman's late essay, "The Bible as Poetry." Although the engraving is not credited in the manuscript, it appears to be a copy of one done by Samuel Hollyer in April 1888, based on a photograph of Whitman by Jacob Spieler at the Charles H. Spieler Studio, ca. 1876.

Background Image: "The Bible as Poetry," Codex Ms263. Both images courtesy of the Hanna Holborn Gray Special Collections Research Center, University of Chicago.
Cover design by Jeevanjot Kaur Nagpal

for Les, always —
"the woman that loves me, and whom I love more than my life"
LG 1860, 289

Contents

Acknowledgements   ix

Abbreviations   xiii

Prefatory Note on Links   xvii

Introduction   1

1. Whitman on the Bible   11
   Whitman on the Bible: A Retrospective   11
   "The Bible as Poetry"   23
   The Bible and the Birth of (Whitman's) Free Verse 43

2. The Bible in Whitman: Quotation, Allusion, Echo   63
   Some Preliminary Observations   64
   "No Quotations": The 1850 Poems   73
   The Bible in Whitman's Prose from 1850–53   80
   Biblical Echoes in the Early Notebooks and Unpublished Poetry
   Manuscripts   86

3. Whitman's Line: "Found" in the KJB?   111
   The Development of Whitman's Long Line: A Chronology 112
   G. W. Allen, Parallelism, and the Biblical Poetic Line 123
   The Verse Divisions of the KJB and Whitman's Line 136
   The KJB Mediated Otherwise   201
   Conclusions   217

4. Parallelism: In the (Hebrew) Bible and in Whitman   223
   The Politics of Parallelism   223
   Lowth's Idea of Parallelism and Its Modern Reception 230
   Whitman and Biblical Parallelism: Line-Internal Parallelism 241
   A Note on Chronology   268
   Whitman's Parallelism   273

5. "The <u>Divine Style</u>": An American Prose Style Poeticized   285

    "Plate-glassy style"   286

    (Some) Biblical Elements of Whitman's Plain Style   292

    Formatting of Attributed Speech   321

    Prose into Poetry   327

    "Walt Whitman, an American"   330

Afterword   337

Selected Bibliography   351

    I. Works Published by Walt Whitman   352

    II. Collected Writings of Walt Whitman, Special, and Translations   354

    III. Other Literature   355

List of Figures   371

Index   375

Acknowledgements

This is a work of philological and literary-critical scholarship, and yet it is suffused with much love and affection for the subject matter, which, after all, is the heartbeat of all good philology (etymologically, the literal "love of words"). My love for Walt Whitman and his poetry, in the first place, came from my mother Gladys "Ginger" Smith, an English professor who grew up in Huntington, Long Island and attended Walt Whitman High School. She loved Whitman and taught his poetry regularly; in fact, my brother, David Allsopp, wrote a paper on Whitman for one of her classes. My own adult reawakening to Whitman came as a doctoral student when I bought a used copy of *Leaves of Grass*. I was just then beginning to think seriously about biblical Hebrew poetry and as I began (re)reading *Leaves* I could not help but hear and feel the biblical undercurrents in Whitman's verse. Maybe already here is the planting of the seed for what would become this project. More certainly, Whitman would eventually help me figure out how to conceptualize the decidedly non-metrical verse of the Hebrew Bible. The introductory sub-section of a chapter on my understanding of the free rhythms (free verse) of biblical poetry is entitled, "Through Whitman's Eyes." As the sub-section tipped over eighty pages, I knew I had to find another outlet for my thoughts on Whitman and the Bible. It was then that this book was truly born.

As with most of my writing projects, I owe much to many, most of whom I cannot individually acknowledge here. But I am deeply grateful to all who helped me with one aspect or another of this project. Thank you all. There are some I must mention. In the first place, I owe a huge debt of gratitude to my Hebrew Bible/Old Testament colleagues, both here at the Seminary and across the field, who have indulged my insistence on reading papers on Whitman in venues not accustomed to such topics. In particular, I thank the following: the University of Chicago Divinity School where I presented my first public presentation on Whitman—Simi Chavel was my host and Rick Rosengarten served as the respondent; on another trip to Chicago Simi Chavel and Jaime Zamparelli Abramov helped me work through Codex Ms263, Whitman's holograph manuscript of"The Bible as Poetry" essay; Vanderbilt Divinity School and my host Leong Seow and his students, where we discussed all manner of things including Whitman—there is a bit of Leong's history of consequences project ghosting through this book; the American Church in Paris, where my wife Leslie and I were hosted by our good friend and former classmate Scott Herr and which afforded me the opportunity to learn about Whitman's impact on French *vers libre* and much also about the art of the readymade; the Columbia Hebrew Bible Seminar, which has been a hospitable scholarly home for me for my entire career; and the Old Testament Research Colloquium at Princeton Seminary, where I presented twice on Whitman and both were consequential for this book: in the first Mark Smith insisted that I could not write a book on Whitman and the Bible without a chapter on parallelism; and in the second Elaine James equally firmly insisted that my re-reading of Lowth needed to appear in a more Bible-centric publishing venue—the chapter does exist (Chapter Four) and is a little lighter and more readable for my having placed the more detailed reading of Lowth in the *Journal of Hebrew Scriptures*, https://jhsonline. org/index.php/jhs/article/view/29586.

On the Whitman side, thanks to the two reviewers of the manuscript for Open Book Publishers (https://www.openbookpublishers.com/), both for their critical insights about aspects of my argument and for their affirmation of the project as a whole. I also am appreciative of the early encouragement from Ken Price and Ed Folsom. The *Walt Whitman Archive* (https://whitmanarchive.org/) has matured over the course of this project and has become one of the premier digital repositories in the humanities. Both as a non-specialist and as a visually disabled academic, it is impossible for me to imagine completing this project without the existence of this archive. Thanks to the editors and all who have worked on the Archive. This book is at least one tangible example of what can be done when primary sources and quality scholarship are made easily and freely available. And whether or not the builders of this fabulous resource had print disabled users in mind as they created the Archive, it is a great boon for us, for (giving us) the capacity to continue doing primary research on such a rich textual corpus. Thank you. If ever there was a publisher well positioned to match the ideas and values that animate the *Walt Whitman Archive*, it is Open Book Publishers, with their commitments to Open Access publishing, publishing high quality scholarship, and exploring how digital technologies can expand and enhance the academic monograph. Alessandra Tosi and her colleagues have been a joy to work with. I am honored and excited to be publishing with OBP—thanks to my colleague Elaine James for bringing OBP to my attention and encouraging me to explore the possibility of publishing with them. Matt Green served as my research assistant this year and has worked as hard on the final manuscript as anyone. Having lost my ability to read print in the last few years, this manuscript would not have made it to publication without Matt's contribution. And even more crucially, Matt has helped me learn to lean on others' eyes. And thanks to Princeton Theological Seminary for being my academic home for almost twenty-five years and whose sane teaching load and generous sabbatical policy means that faculty have time to research and write. Last but never least, I thank Leslie Dobbs-Allsopp, my wife, my lover, and my best friend. My scholarship has always only emerged in her company. This book is no different, except I think we both agree that our journey with Walt—from Camden to New York, to Paris and back— has been by far the most enjoyable. I am a little sad that this particular journey has come to a close, but most happy that Les and I still have yet many roads to travel together. And no doubt Walt Whitman will be one of our perennial companions—

I bequeath myself to the dirt to grow from the grass I love,

If you want me again look for me under your bootsoles.

...

Failing to fetch me me at first keep encouraged,

Missing me one place search another,

I stop somewhere waiting for you (*LG*, 56)[1]

---

1   I cite these famous lines from the end of what would later be called "Song of Myself" in the version of that first edition of *Leaves of Grass* (1855). There are two probable mistakes in these lines—the philologist in me, of course, loves the untidiness of the material artifact: the doubly written "me" in the third line quoted and the lack of a period at the end of the final line. Both are corrected in succeeding editions. But I very much like, mistake or not, how the refusal of sentential closure (no period) wonderfully ramifies the never-ending nature of the promise Whitman is here making to his readers, then and for all time to come.

Abbreviations

ANET –Ancient Near Eastern Texts Relating to the Old Testament. Edited by J. B. Pritchard. 3d ed. Princeton, 1969

ASV – American Standard Version (1901)

BDB – F. Brown, S. R. Driver, and C. A. Briggs. *A Hebrew and English Lexicon of the Old Testament*. Oxford, 1907

BHS – Biblia Hebraica Stuttgartensia. Edited by K. Elliger and W. Rudolph. Stuttgart, 1983

CAT – The Cuneiform Alphabetic Texts from Ugarit, Ras Ibn Bani and Other Places. Edited by M. Dietrich, O. Loretz, and J. Sanmartin. 3rd enlgd. ed. Munster: Ugarit-Verlag, 2013

CEB – Common English Bible

Conj – conjunction

CPW – Walt Whitman, *The Complete Prose Works*. Philadelphia: David McKay, 1892,
https://whitmanarchive.org/published/other/CompleteProse.html

CW – The Complete Writings of Walt Whitman. Edited by Richard Maurice Bucke, Thomas Biggs Harned, Horace Traubel, and Oscar Lovell Triggs. New York: G. P. Putnam's Sons, 1902

DBN – Daybooks and Notebooks. Ed.William White. 3 vols. New York: New York – University Press, 1978 (ACLS Humanities E-Book)

DO – direct object

Drum-Taps – Walt Whitman. *Drum-Taps*. New-York, 1865,
https://whitmanarchive.org/published/other/DrumTaps.html

EPF – *The Early Poems and the Fiction*. Ed. T. L. Brasher. New York: New York – University, 1963

Folsom, "Whitman" – A collection of early, fragmentary manuscript drafts for "I celebrate myself" (later "Song of Myself"), http://bailiwick.lib.uiowa.edu/whitman/

HALOT – Koehler, L., W. Baumgartner, and J. J. Stamm. *The Hebrew and Aramaic Lexicon of the Old Testament*. Translated and edited under the supervision of M. E. J. Richardson. 5 vols. Leiden, 1994–2000

IBHS – *An Introduction to Biblical Hebrew Syntax*. B. K. Waltke and M. O'Connor. Winona Lake, 1990

Inf Abs – infinitive absolute

KJB – King James Bible (1611)

LG – Walt Whitman. *Leaves of Grass*. Brooklyn, New York, 1855, https://whitmanarchive.org/published/LG/1855/whole.html

LG 1856 – Walt Whitman. *Leaves of Grass*. Brooklyn, New York, 1856, https://whitmanarchive.org/published/LG/1856/whole.html

LG 1860 – Walt Whitman. *Leaves of Grass*. Boston: Thayer and Eldridge, 1860–61, https://whitmanarchive.org/published/LG/1860/whole.html

LG 1867 – Walt Whitman. *Leaves of Grass*. WM. E. Chapin & Co, Printers, 24 Beekman – Street, New York, 1967, https://whitmanarchive.org/published/LG/1867/whole.html

LG 1871-72 – Walt Whitman. *Leaves of Grass*. Washington D. C. 1871, https://whitmanarchive.org/published/LG/1871/whole.html

LG 1881 – Walt Whitman. *Leaves of Grass*. Boston: James R. Osgood and Copany, 1881–82, https://whitmanarchive.org/published/LG/1881/whole.html

LG 1891-92 – Walt Whitman. *Leaves of Grass*. Philadelphia: David McKay, 1891–92, https://whitmanarchive.org/published/LG/1891/whole.html

LGCRE – *Leaves of Grass, Comprehensive Reader's Edition*. Ed. Harold W. Blodgett and Sculley Bradley. New York: New York University Press, 1965

ms – masculine singular

MT – Masoretic text (the textus receptus of the Hebrew Bible)

Neg – negative particle

NJV – New Jewish Version (Jewish Publication Society)

NP – noun phrase

NPEPP – *The New Princeton Encyclopedia of Poetry and Poetics*. Eds. A. Preminger and T. V. F. Brogan. Princeton: Princeton University, 1993

NRSV – New Revised Standard Version

NUPM – *Notebooks and Unpublished Prose Manuscripts*. Ed. Edward F. Grier. 6 vols. New York: New York University Press, 1984 (ACLS Humanities E-Book)

O/Obj – object

OED – *Oxford English dictionary*, https://www.oed.com

PEPP – *The Princeton Encyclopedia of Poetry and Poetics*. Edited by Stephen Cushman, et al. Princeton: Princeton University Press, 2012 (Kindle edition)

PN – personal name

Prep – preposition

PP – prepositional phrase

PW – Walt Whitman, *Prose Works 1892*. Ed. F. Stovall. 2 vols. New York: New York University, 1963–64

RV – Revised Version (1885)

S/Subj – subject

Sequel – Walt Whitman. *Drum-Taps* and *Sequel to Drum-Taps*. New-York/ Washington, 1865/1865–66, https://whitmanarchive.org/published/other/DrumTapsSequel.html

sf – suffix

TAD – *Textbook of Aramaic documents from ancient Egypt*. Edited by B. Porten and A. Yardeni. Winona Lake: Eisenbrauns, 1986

UPP – *The Uncollected Poetry and Pose of Walt Whitman*. Edited by E. Holloway. 2 vols. Garden City: Doubleday, 1921

V/Vb – verb

VP – verb phrase

WWA – *The Walt Whitman Archive*, https://whitmanarchive.org

WWWC – H. Traubel. *With Walt Whitman in Camden*. 9 vols. 1906–96, https://whitmanarchive.org/criticism/disciples/traubel/index.html

Prefatory Note on Links

Unless noted otherwise, the editions of Walt Whitman's many unpublished writings (e.g., notebooks, unpublished poetry manuscripts, letters) used in this study are those found on the Walt Whitman Archive (https://whitmanarchive.org/). These are referenced by title only in the body of the text (without supporting bibliography in an effort to reduce some of the clutter in the footnotes), so readers are directed to the appropriate sections of the Archive (e.g., In Whitman's Hand, https://whitmanarchive.org/manuscripts/index.html) for critical editions (transcriptions, images, references to supporting secondary literature) of these texts. Links to the Walt Whitman Archive (and other publicly accessible repositories with Whitman holdings) for Whitman's writings are provided whenever possible. My preference throughout is to link to specific page images, since this allows for a more precise reference to the passage in view. More general links to the various digital editions of Whitman's writings are provided in the List of Abbreviations, Selected Bibliography, and, as a rule, upon first mention in each chapter. Therefore, in many cases, readers will be able to easily access both page images and the critical transcriptions of individual texts. Digital object identifiers (DOIs) are provided (where they exist) in the Selected Bibliography. There, too, I link to books and articles made accessible on the Walt Whitman Archive, viz. Select Criticism, https://whitmanarchive.org/criticism/current/index.html.

Introduction

"The interior & foundation quality of the man [Walt Whitman] is Hebraic, Biblical, mystic"

— Walt Whitman, "Introduction to the London Edition" (1867)

"Suppose the comparative method applied to such ~~an order~~ a theory & practice of poetry as Walt Whitman's, and ~~a new~~ floods of light are forthwith thr own on what would otherwise be puzzling & dark"

— Walt Whitman, "Is Walt Whitman's Poetry Poetical?" (1874)

Having recently celebrated the 400th anniversary of the King James Bible (2011) and the 200th anniversary of Walt Whitman's birth (2019), it is fitting to take a fresh look at what has been one of the oldest preoccupations of Whitman scholarship: the nature and extent of the KJB's influence on Whitman and his mature style, especially as manifested in the early editions of *Leaves of Grass*. Whitman was an inveterate collagist of outside writing, an appropriator of found language, extracting "phrases and lines that attracted him, and in the process of moving them from their initial sources into new contexts, he filtered and changed their tone and meaning."[1] His sources are manifold and diverse, ranging from an ornithological guidebook to newspaper reports of Civil War battles, Ralph Waldo Emerson's lectures and essays, George Sand's *The Countess of Rudolstadt*, and Jules Michelet's *The People* and *The Bird*, to cite some of the better documented examples.[2] It is therefore no surprise that the English Bible, which Whitman counted among the finest poetry of the world ("I don't know but the deepest

---

1   Matt Miller, *Collage of Myself* (Lincoln: University of Nebraska, 2010), 86; see also Paul Zweig, *Walt Whitman: The Making of the Poet* (New York: Basic Books, 1984), 151–52.

2   See Miller, *Collage of Myself*, 26, 79–103; Zweig, *Walt Whitman*, 143–63; and esp. Floyd Stovall, *The Foreground of Leaves of Grass* (Charlottesville: University Press of Virginia, 1974).

©2024 F. W. Dobbs-Allsopp, CC BY-NC 4.0   https://doi.org/10.11647/OBP.0357.01

and widest")[3] and which he noted he "went over thoroughly" during "summers and falls" at "Long Island's seashores," should be for him another source of found language, imagery, themes, rhythm, and style to mine and mold and mobilize into *Leaves*. Indeed, it may well be, as G. W. Allen states, that "no book is more conspicuous in Walt Whitman's 'long foreground' than the King James Bible."[4]

It has certainly become a common trope among Whitman scholars and biographers to reference summarily some vague and probably unconscious influence of the Bible on Whitman's writing. Matt Miller's version of the trope is typical: "That Whitman was aware that his line seemed biblical is undeniable, and he was surely influenced, even if only unconsciously, by English translations of the Bible's Hebraic rhythms."[5] Such statements are usually prefaced by the intimation of a prolonged history of discussion—implicit justification for the abbreviated comment—and are often accompanied by expressions of dissatisfaction with the overall thesis or its implications ("But the Bible of course must have always been present as a potential influence in Whitman's mind, so....").[6] However, aside from Allen's two groundbreaking essays from the early 1930s, "Biblical Analogies for Walt Whitman's Prosody" (1933) and "Biblical Echoes in Whitman's Works" (1934), and T. E. Crawley's initial statement on the "Christ-Symbol" in *Leaves* in a chapter of his *The Structure of Leaves of Grass*

---

3   *CPW*, 379.

4   *A Reader's Guide to Walt Whitman* (Syracuse: Syracuse University, 1970), 24.

5   *Collage of Myself*, 25. Already in 1933 Allen can summon an early version of the trope: "Many critics have ventured opinions on the influence of the Bible on Whitman's versification...." ("Biblical Analogies for Walt Whitman's Prosody," *Revue Anglo-Americaine* 6 [1933], 490–507, at 490). And again in his *The Solitary Singer: A Critical Biography of Walt Whitman* (rev ed; New York: New York University, 1967 [1955]), 144), though now only requiring parenthetical notice: "In his early free verse experiments he may have used several literary sources (certainly including the King James Bible), but...." Stovall offers yet another version of the trope: "There is abundant evidence that Whitman was familiar with the Bible both as a young man and later" (*Foreground*, 56).

6   Miller, *Collage of Myself*, 25. C. Carroll Hollis is even more dismissive: the language that was formational for the early *Leaves*, he maintains, was not "that of the Bible, which he [Whitman] seems to have venerated or even studied only in old age, when he touted the Bible to pick up a little credit for *Leaves* by a sort of cultural back-formation" (*Language and Style in Leaves of Grass* [Baton Rouge/London: Louisiana State University, 1983], 205).

(1970), there has been no substantive published treatment of the general topic.[7]

The subject is an old one, dating at least as far back as 1860 where an unsigned review in the Boston *Cosmopolite* remarks, "In respect of plain speaking, and in most respects, *Leaves* more resembles the Hebrew Scriptures than do any other modern writings."[8] Other brief notices in contemporary reviews followed.[9] Whitman himself, as just noted, makes explicit meta-references to the Bible (more on this in Chapter One). Beginning with Bliss Perry in 1906, Whitman's many biographers have routinely noticed his knowledge and use of the Bible.[10] Finally, a

---

7   Allen, "Biblical Analogies," 490–507; "Biblical Echoes in Whitman's Works," *American Literature* 6 (1934), 302–15; T. E. Crawley, *The Structure of Leaves of Grass* (Austin: University of Texas, 1970), esp. 27–49, 50–79.

8   4 August 1860 (page number unknown), https://whitmanarchive.org/criticism/reviews/lg1860/anc.00037.html; reprinted in Richard Maurice Bucke, *Walt Whitman* (Philadelphia: David McKay, 1883), 200–01; and also in Milton Hindus, *Walt Whitman* (New York/London: Routledge, 1997), 103–04; cf. Kenneth Price, *Walt Whitman: The Contemporary Reviews* (Cambridge: Cambridge University, 1996), 108. There is also a slightly earlier passing notice of Whitman as "too Hebraic to be polite" by his friend G. S. Phillips ("Literature. Leaves of Grass— by Walt Whitman," *New York Illustrated News* 2 [26 May 1860], 43, https://whitmanarchive.org/criticism/reviews/lg1860/anc.01068.html; reprinted in Walt Whitman, *A Child's Reminiscence* [T. O. Mabbott and R. G. Silver, eds.; Seattle: University of Washington, 1930], 33.

9   William D. O'Connor, "Walt Whitman," *The New York Times* (2 December 1866), 2, https://whitmanarchive.org/criticism/reviews/lg1867/anc.00064. html. O'Connor, of course, by this time had become a close friend of Whitman's and one of his staunch defenders, and thus his notice of the poet's similarities to "the poetic diction of the Hebraic muse" strongly implies Whitman's own conscious awareness of the same); Robert Buchanan, *David Gray and Other Essays* (London, 1868), 207; William Michael Rossetti, "Prefatory Notice" in Poems by Walt Whitman (London: John Camden Hotten, Piccadilly, 1868), 6, https://whitmanarchive.org/published/books/other/rossetti.html; George Saintsbury, "Review of Leaves of Grass (1871)," *The Academy* 6 (10 October 1874), 398–400, https://whitmanarchive.org/criticism/reviews/lg1871/anc.00076.html; Anonymous, "Walt Whitman, a Kosmos," *The Springfield Sunday Republican* (13 November 1881), 4, https://whitmanarchive.org/criticism/reviews/lg1881/anc.00208.html; G. E. M., "Whitman, Poet and Seer," *The New York Times* (22 January 1882), 4, https://whitmanarchive.org/criticism/reviews/lg1881/anc.00216.html; R. L. Stevenson, *Familiar Studies of Men and Books* (London: Chatto and Windus, 1882), 106, 120–21; R. M. Bucke, *Walt Whitman* (Philadelphia: David McKay, 1883), 103, 119, 185; W. Harrison, "Walt Whitman's 'November Boughs'," *The Critic* n.s. 11 (19 January 1889), 25, https://whitmanarchive.org/criticism/reviews/boughs/anc.00123.html; Oscar Wilde, "The Gospel According to Walt Whitman," *The Pall Mall Gazette* (25 January 1889), 3, https://whitmanarchive.org/criticism/reviews/boughs/anc.00124.html.

10   *Walt Whitman: His Life and Work* (New York: Houghton, Mifflin and Company, 1906).

number of briefer notices of various sorts (e.g., specific allusions to the Bible in Whitman, Whitman's prophetic voice) have been published over the years. But this is about the sum of it. In general, scholarship on the topic of the Bible and Whitman is actually rather thin and, even at its best—as in Allen's early articles and in his several restatements over the course of his career—often problematic. In fact, M. N. Posey in his 1938 dissertation comes essentially to the same conclusion: general assertions of Whitman's debt to the English Bible, though multiple and varied, "have not usually been followed by careful investigation and massing of evidence."[11] I cannot see that things have changed greatly in the intervening eighty years since Posey's statement. My impression is that this remains a subject that would repay the kind of detailed philological treatment that Posey calls for (and in part delivers) and which has been paid to the question of the English Bible in other writers (e.g., Shakespeare, Melville).[12]

My own ambition for what follows is more modest and framed explicitly from the perspective of an outsider, that of a biblical scholar and not a Whitman specialist. Biblical and Whitman specialists have much in common (e.g., how they read texts, the diachronic orientation of their research). Both also curate disciplinary-specific knowledge that is difficult for the non-specialist to assimilate fully, no matter how patient and persistent the research. Here I seek to leverage the field-specific knowledge of a biblicist in querying Whitman's literary debt to the KJB. No (Hebrew) Bible scholar can read *Leaves of Grass* and fail to hear and feel its familiar rhythms, style, and, at times, even manner of phrasing.[13] My aim will be to give these impressions some more precise articulation and illustration. In the end, I think Allen's strong intuition, however much he hedges in the name of scholarly propriety, that Whitman's debt to the KJB is substantial and significant is correct.

---

11   "Whitman's Debt to the Bible with Special Reference to the Origins of His Rhythm" (unpubl. Ph.D. dissertation, University of Texas, 1938), 1.

12   E.g., Ilana Pardes, *Melville's Bibles* (Berkeley: University of California, 2008); H. Hamlin, *The Bible in Shakespeare* (Oxford: Oxford University, 2013).

13   The Israeli poet Shin Shalom refracts this same sensibility when he states, "Whitman's pioneering is very close to us, and so are his Biblical rhythms. To translate him into Hebrew is like translating a writer back into his own language" (*New York Herald Tribune Book Review* [26 March 1950], 3).

My efforts here are offered in the spirit of Allen's own project, to the same end, and in admiration of his perceptions.

Since the post-1995 re(dis)covery of some of Whitman's lost notebooks, scholars have been able to narrow the timeframe for the emergence of Whitman's mature style to the early 1850s.[14] With the aid of the notebooks and early poetry manuscripts, exciting glimpses of this new style can be seen evolving on the page. Still, what provoked these writing experiments that would culminate in the 1855 *Leaves* remains as ever a mystery, perhaps not entirely by accident. It is nonetheless the case, in anticipation of the conclusions reached in what follows and stated most positively, that those aspects most reminiscent of the English Bible—Whitman's signature long lines, the prevalence of parallelism and the "free" rhythms it helps create, his prosiness and tendency towards parataxis, aspects of diction and phrasing, and the decidedly lyrical bent of the entire project—are all characteristics of the style that begin to emerge in the immediate run-up to the 1855 *Leaves* and come into full bloom in that volume (and the succeeding two editions of the *Leaves*), but which are either entirely absent or not prominent in Whitman's earlier writings (prose and poetry). And what is more, in almost every instance, as far as I can tell, what Whitman takes from the Bible he reshapes, recasts, extends, molds, modifies—even contorts and warps, such that it becomes his own. That is, this is the kind of collaging that Miller notes is "essential" to Whitman's "writing process," and thus by its nature such taking—in many instances at least—often requires the sense and sensibility of a Hebraist for its detection and (fuller) appreciation. Whitman's use of the English Bible cannot of its own fully account for the genius of his mature style, but it seems to me to be an impactful force in shaping key aspects of this style.

* * *

Chapter One provides a preliminary brief for Whitman's familiarity with the Bible. While there is a longstanding consensus among Whitman scholars on this issue, it nevertheless seems appropriate to begin with the "massing of evidence" called for by Posey. The ensuing survey is

---

14   A.L. Birney, "Missing Whitman Notebooks Returned to Library of Congress," *WWQR* 12 (1995), 217–29.

somewhat eclectic (e.g., connecting Whitman with known or currently extant bibles) but it focuses in the main on Whitman's own meta-discourse about the Bible and features an extended look at his late and under-appreciated essay, "The Bible as Poetry" (1883).[15] In particular, I seek to discern what of the sentiments expressed about the Bible in this essay (e.g., Whitman's awareness of the lack of rhyme in biblical poetry) may be traced back to the germinal period of *Leaves'* inception. In the process, I begin identifying aspects of Whitman's style that may be indebted (to varying degrees) to the Bible (e.g., his preference for lyric). I close the chapter by spotlighting the coincidence of Whitman's breaking into free verse in 1850 while writing three biblically inflected poems. And though I do not elaborate on this free verse or Whitman's proclivity for the lyric, that both offer substantial links to the Bible should not go unnoticed. Whitman collages all manner of language material, especially those aspects of form and structure that are not oversaturated with semantic uptake.

Chapter Two takes up the topic of biblical quotations, allusions, and echoes in Whitman's writings, albeit with a very specific end in view. Allen pioneered this line of research in his "Biblical Echoes," which remains the single largest published collection of biblical quotations, allusions, and echoes in Whitman.[16] This sampling alone establishes Whitman's knowledge and use of the Bible, and the direct quotations from the Bible make clear Whitman's use of the KJB translation in particular. Allen also ably emphasizes the "elusive" nature of Whitman's allusive practice in *Leaves* as it pertains to the Bible.[17] My own point of departure is the (modest amount of) research carried out on this topic since Allen's foundational study. I begin by elaborating a number of general observations that entail from these more recent studies, not a few of which contrast with emphases placed by Allen (e.g., the prominence of the Hebrew Bible/Old Testament in Whitman's collages from the Bible). The chapter's principal focus is on the important period from 1850–55. A survey of Whitman's writings

15   *The Critic* 3 (3 February 1883), 57; later collected in *November Boughs* ([Philadelphia: David McKay, 1888], 43–46) and in *CPW*, 379–82).

16   "Biblical Echoes," 302–15.

17   Allen, "Biblical Echoes," 303; cf. B. L. Bergquist, "Walt Whitman and the Bible: Language Echoes, Images, Allusions, and Ideas" (unpubl. Ph.D. dissertation, University of Nebraska, 1979), 81, 133. "Elusive" is his term.

(both poetry and prose) from this period reveals a plethora of biblical language, imagery, themes, characters, and imitations of all sorts, and this allusive practice turns out to be a very tangible way of tracking one dimension of Whitman's evolving poetic theory—"no quotations." At the time of the three free-verse poems from the spring and summer of 1850, Whitman could still freely embed quotations from the Bible in his poems. But by the time of the early notebooks and poetry manuscripts, and then in the 1855 *Leaves*, Whitman's new poetics is firmly in place: no more direct quotations, a concerted trimming away of some biblical trappings, and a tendency to work-over allusions to the point that they become, as B. L. Bergquist says, "more 'elusive,' more hidden."[18] The survey includes close scrutiny of Whitman's prose writings (mostly journalistic in nature) from 1850–53 and the early pre-*Leaves* notebooks and unpublished poetry manuscripts.

The question of the origin of Whitman's signature long line remains shrouded in mystery. The renewed attention paid to the early notebooks and poetry manuscripts has enabled scholars to see much more clearly the emergence of that line and to have a better idea of its rough chronology. But what of this line's inspiration? Its animating impulse? Where does it come from? And why? The evidence at hand does not permit conclusive answers to these and related questions. Still, in Chapter Three I probe the possibility that the KJB played a role in shaping Whitman's ideas about his emerging line. In particular, I build on an insight of George Saintsbury who, in a review of the 1871(–72) edition of *Leaves*, calls attention to the likeness of Whitman's line to "the verse divisions of the English Bible, especially in the poetical books."[19] A number of aspects of Whitman's mature line (e.g., its variability, range of lengths, typical shapes and character, and content), I argue, become more clearly comparable to the Bible when thought through in light of Saintsbury's appreciation of the significance of the actual "verse divisions of the English Bible." Along the way I sketch the chronological development of Whitman's line, emphasizing the poet's break with meter as key to opening the possibility for a longer line, and consider other possible means by which knowledge about the Bible beyond direct

---

18 "Whitman and the Bible," 81.
19 Saintsbury, "Review of Leaves of Grass (1871)," 398–400.

readerly encounters may have been mediated to Whitman, such as in the poetry of James Macpherson and Martin Farquhar Tupper.

Galway Kinnell observes that Whitman is "the greatest virtuoso of parallel structure in English poetry."[20] Allen's early essay, "Biblical Analogies," successfully establishes the presence and significance of parallelism in Whitman, especially as it bears upon the poet's underlying prosody, and the likelihood that the Bible is an important source of Whitman's knowledge of parallelism. In that analysis, parallelism is understood primarily through Robert Lowth's biblical paradigm.[21] Unfortunately, that paradigm was already much belated in 1933, then a full 180 years after Lowth's initial exposition of it. Moreover, Allen's own explication of the paradigm—mediated at second- and third-hand—is flawed in various ways. And compounding these problems is the fact that the understanding of parallelism in Whitman scholarship more broadly appears to be essentially that of Allen (with a few exceptions), and thus is dated and shot through with problematic assumptions. The overriding ambition of Chapter Four, then, is to re-situate the study of parallelism in Whitman. The initial part of the chapter is dedicated to explicating Lowth's paradigm and its critical reception in modern biblical scholarship. I do this because of the foundational role which the biblical paradigm has played in Whitman scholarship and because Hebrew Bible is one of the few disciplines of textual study where parallelism as a literary phenomenon has been robustly theorized. The analytics of parallelism, regardless of its originating textual source, is portable, as Allen rightly perceived. The main body of the chapter, building on the foregoing overview, seeks to discern more precisely what may have devolved from the Bible in Whitman's understanding and use of parallelism. The final section of the chapter features exploratory observations about how Whitman moves beyond the biblical paradigm he inherits and molds parallelism to suit his own poetic ends.

---

20   "'Strong is Your Hold': My Encounters with Whitman" in *Leaves of Grass*: *The Sesquicentennial Essays* (eds. S. Belasco and K. M. Price; Lincoln: University of Nebraska, 2007), 417–28.

21   *Lectures on the Sacred Poetry of the Hebrews* (2 vols.; trans. G. Gregory; London: J. Johnson, 1787; reprinted in *Robert Lowth (1710–1787): The Major Works*, vols. 1–2 [London: Routledge, 1995]).

In the book's last chapter, I turn to an examination of stylistic elements in Whitman's verse that derive (ultimately) from the plain style of the KJB's prose. My point of departure is Robert Alter's *Pen of Iron: American Prose and the King James Bible,* in which the author argues for the existence of an "American prose style" among major American novelists that descends from the KJB.[22] Whitman as a poet is not considered by Alter, and yet, there are ways in which the style of Whitman's poetry, especially in the early editions of *Leaves,* shares much with the prose style charted by Alter, albeit in a nonnarrative mode and with a decidedly political bent—an American prose style poeticized and politicized. The chapter begins by tracing Whitman's self-denominated "plate-glassy style" back, first, to the plain style of the KJB and, ultimately, to William Tyndale (d. 1536), the first to translate the Hebrew and Greek of the Bible into English and the primordial source of the stylistic distinctiveness of the KJB's prose. The main body of the chapter surveys leading elements of Whitman's style that may be tied to the KJB, including his use of parallelism, parataxis, the periphrastic *of*-genitive, and the cognate accusative. I also stress the important difference of poetry in how and what is inherited from the prose tradition of the KJB and how that inheritance may manifest itself. What Whitman helps to illuminate, in light of Alter's identification of an American prose style devolved from the KJB, is the possibilities for that style beyond the narrative mode. Next, I reflect on the place of prose in Whitman's poetry and argue that Whitman may be viewed properly as participating in the prose tradition that Alter identifies, even if in the end Whitman's poetic style diverges, strikingly in places, from that of the novelists in the tradition. I close by emphasizing Whitman's political investment in his style. For Alter the term "American" in the subtitle of his book serves chiefly as a descriptor of nationality and to delineate a style of written prose characteristic of novelists with this nationality. For Whitman, by contrast, "American" as a descriptor is always thoroughly politicized. As the poet culls stylistic elements from the prose of the KJB and reinscribes them in his "great psalm of the republic" (*LG,* iv), he saturates them with political "stuff" such that upon reading (and rereading) they are themselves political acts of consequence and incitements toward still other such acts. Indeed,

---

22 Princeton: Princeton University, 2010.

throughout the volume I notice how frequently Whitman's gleanings from the Bible (e.g., parallelism, free verse, parataxis, end-stopping) are infused with and give expression to the political. The poet's biblical borrowings are part and parcel of the political alchemy that charges his "barbaric yawp."

* * *

The main aim of this study is to measure the KJB's impact on Whitman's poetic style, especially as it is developing in the immediate run-up to the 1855 *Leaves* and during the period of the first three editions more generally. The style of Whitman's later poems shifts dramatically in places (e.g., shorter lines, more conventional punctuation, less aversion to stock phrases) and a full accounting of the stylistic debt Whitman owes to the English Bible would require an equally substantial engagement with these later materials. In my brief closing "Afterword" I gesture toward this fuller accounting to come through a reading of Whitman's late (and posthumously published) "Death's Valley" (1889),[23] a poem simultaneously provoked by George Inness's painting, "The Valley of the Shadow of Death" (1867)[24] and the psalm of the latter's inspiration, including that most mesmerizing of the KJB's mistranslations, "the valley of the shadow of death," which Whitman deftly (and unbiblically) rephrases in his title.

---

23   *Harper's New Monthly Magazine* 84 (April 1892), 707–09, https://whitmanarchive.org/published/periodical/poems/per.00028.

24   http://emuseum.vassar.edu/objects/59/the-valley-of-the-shadow-of-death.

1. Whitman on the Bible

No true bard will ever contravene the Bible. Coming steadily down from the past, like a ship, through all perturbations, all ebbs and flows, all time, it is to-day his art's chief reason for being
— Walt Whitman, "The Bible as Poetry" (1883)

Most of what I want to say about aspects of Walt Whitman's evolving style and their debt to the King James Bible (KJB) will involve drawing inferences from Whitman's writings. Here I offer, in summary fashion, a preliminary brief for Whitman's familiarity with the Bible, on which there is a longstanding scholarly consensus. The survey features a look at Whitman's late but telling "The Bible as Poetry,"[1] the final sentences of which I use as the chapter's headnote. I conclude by spotlighting the coincidence of Whitman's breaking into free verse in 1850 while writing three biblically inflected poems.

Whitman on the Bible: A Retrospective

"Americans in the nineteenth century," writes P. Zweig, "were probably the most bookish people on earth,"[2] and therefore it is hard to imagine as avid a reader as Whitman having missed out on reading what, in his own terms, was the "Book of Books," the Bible, and in the translation that dominated the century until the 1880s, the King James version. And Whitman himself, not always the most trustworthy informant, tells

---

1 *The Critic* 3 (3 February 1883), 57; later collected in *November Boughs* ([Philadelphia: David McKay, 1888], 43–46) and in *CPW*, 379–82).
2 *Walt Whitman: The Making of the Poet* (New York: Basic Books, 1984), 144. Cf. D. Daniell, *The Bible in English: Its History and Influence* (New Haven: Yale University, 2003), 580–81, 701, fig. 37.

©2024 F. W. Dobbs-Allsopp, CC BY-NC 4.0 https://doi.org/10.11647/OBP.0357.02

us (albeit belatedly) in "A Backward Glance o'er Travel'd Roads"(*LG* 1891–92, 425–38) of his early reading of the Bible:

> Later, at intervals, summers and falls, I used to go off, sometimes for a week at a stretch, down in the country, or to Long Island's seashores—there, in the presence of outdoor influences, I went over thoroughly the Old and New Testaments, and absorb'd... Shakspere, Ossian, the best translated versions I could get of Homer, Eschylus, Sophocles, the old German Nibelungen, the ancient Hindoo poems, and one or two other masterpieces, Dante's among them.[3]

H. Traubel often mentions coming upon Whitman "reading the Bible," as on one evening (8 November 1888) not long after "A Backward Glance" was first published in *November Boughs*.[4] R. M. Bucke, Whitman's confidant, disciple, and first biographer (1883), reprints as an appendix W. D. O'Connor's (another Whitman disciple) *The Good Gray Poet: A Vindication*,[5] which includes the following characterization of Whitman: "He is deeply cultured by some of the best books, especially those of the Bible, which he prefers above all other great literature...."[6]—I cite this later version in particular because Whitman had a large hand in shaping the content and phrasing of this first biography about him, and thus O'Connor's characterization may be presumed to have met with Whitman's approval.[7] Whitman's high estimate of the Bible and its well-suitedness to American democratic values is apparent in a selection from *Democratic Vistas* (1871):

> While of the great poems of Asian antiquity, the Indian epics, the book of Job, the Ionian Iliad, the unsurpassedly simple, loving, perfect idyls of the life and death of Christ, in the New Testament, (indeed Homer and the Biblical utterances intertwine familiarly with us, in the main,) and along down, of most of the characteristic, imaginative or romantic relics of the continent, as the Cid, Cervantes' Don Quixote,

---

3   In *November Boughs*, 5–18, here 12–13; also included in *LG* 1891–92, 425–38. Cf. Whitman's late poem, "Old Chants" (*Truth* 10 [19 March 1891], 11, https://whitmanarchive.org/published/periodical/figures/per.00048.001.jpg; reprinted in *Good-Bye My Fancy* [1891]).
4   *WWWC*, 3:50; cf. 1:421; 2:351, 410; 3:80, 165, 332.
5   (New York: Bunch & Huntington, 1866).
6   *Walt Whitman* (Philadelphia: David McKay, 1883), 103.
7   In a letter to O'Connor from 19 February 1883 Whitman expresses his deep satisfaction with the *Good Gray Poet* generally, https://whitmanarchive.org/biography/correspondence/tei/nyp.00475.html.

&c., I should say they substantially adjust themselves to us, and, far off as they are, accord curiously with our bed and board to-day, in New York, Washington, Canada, Ohio, Texas, California—and with our notions, both of seriousness and of fun, and our standards of heroism, manliness, and even the democratic requirements—those requirements are not only not fulfilled in the Shaksperean productions, but are insulted on every page.[8]

From an earlier period, Whitman records his routine reading of Scripture to the sick and wounded he visited during the war.[9] Somewhat differently but no less telling is the fact that the 1860 edition of *Leaves of Grass* (the third edition), in particular, was imagined by Whitman as a "New Bible,"[10] and, indeed, with its individually numbered poems and sections, is reminiscent of the English Bible's numbered chapters and verse divisions; it looks like a Bible (Fig. 1).[11] The initial leaf of

---

8   Walt Whitman, *Democratic Vistas* (Washington, D.C., 1871), 81. Cf. G. W. Allen, "Biblical Echoes in Whitman's Works," *American Literature* 6 (1934), 302–15, here at 312.

9   *PW*, I, 56, 73–74.

10   *NUPM* 1, 353. P. C. Gutjahr notes that "by the 1850s a wide variety of fiction was winning acceptance among Protestants as a viable means for people to become imaginative participants in the Bible's narrative" (*An American Bible: A History of the Good Book in the United States, 1777–1880* [Stanford: Stanford University, 1999], 147)—a trend that aspects of *Leaves* would seem to answer well to. Bucke calls *Leaves of Grass* "the bible of Democracy" (*Walt Whitman*, 185). he American public's Bible buying frenzy was precisely at its height at mid-century, though the Bible market in America was bullish throughout the whole century (Daniell, *Bible in English*, esp. fig. 37; cf. chs. 31 and 38). And the appetite was not limited to bibles alone. This period also saw much interest in fictionalizations of the Bible, one of the most successful of which was Joseph Smith's *The Book of Mormon* (Gutjahr, *American Bible*, 143–78; Daniell, *Bible in English*,726–33; M. Robertson, "'New-Born Bard[s] of the Holy Ghost': The American Bibles of Walt Whitman and Joseph Smith" in *Above the American Renaissance* [eds. H. K. Bush and B. Yothers; Amherst: University of Massachusetts, 2018], 140–60). Whitman's early short story "Shirval: A Tale of Jerusalem" (first published in *The Aristidean*, March, 1845, https://whitmanarchive.org/published/fiction/shortfiction/per.00337.html), which paraphrases and expands the plot of Luke 7:11-16, is an example of the latter and shows that Whitman's "biblicizing" impulse did not begin with the 1860 edition of *Leaves*. At any rate, the great publishing success of bibles throughout the nineteenth century would have been enough to catch the eye of the bookmaker in Whitman, especially one who wanted so much to be absorbed by the American public. For potential Romantic influence on Whitman's conception of the "New Bible," see E. S. Culler, "Romanticism" in *Walt Whitman in Context* (eds. J. Levin and E. Whitley; Cambridge: Cambridge University, 2018), 654–71 esp. 663–65 (Google Play edition).

11   J. Stacy, Introduction to *Leaves of Grass, 1860: The 150th Anniversary Facsimile Edition* (ed. J. Stacy; Iowa City: Iowa University, 2009), xx. William Blake was one

Whitman's personal copy of this edition of *Leaves* (known as the "Blue Book" because it was bound in blue paper wrappers) compares the number of words in that edition (150,500) to the number of words in the Bible (895,752, excluding the Apocrypha) and in the New Testament (212,000); he also tallies counts for the *Iliad, Aeneid*, Dante's *Inferno*, and *Paradise Lost*)—clearly indicating that the Bible even figures (as a measure) at a macro-level in Whitman's thinking about *Leaves*—though as E. Folsom observes, "an impressive amount of verbiage, but still quite a ways from overtaking his ancient rival."[12]

In one of the post-1856 notebooks ("made largely of end papers from the 1856 edition of Leaves of Grass"), entitled "Notebook Intended for an American Dictionary," there is a clipping (see Fig. 2) from a printed source which tells in brief the story of the KJB.[13] The clipping itself bears the title, "King James' Bible" and the account ends by noting (correctly) that the translation "was not immediately received with the unanimity for which James had hoped"—perhaps explaining, given the initial, mostly unfavorable reception of *Leaves*, (at least part of) Whitman's interest in the clipping. But regardless of the motivation, the clipping itself, and that it was clipped in the first place and then saved by Whitman, makes clear his conscious awareness of the KJB. Also, the notebook contains a page in Whitman's hand labeled, *Words of the Bible*:

---

of the first poets to mimic the Bible in this way, e.g., *The Book of Urizen* (1794; cf. J. J. McGann, *Social Values and Poetic Acts: A Historical Judgment of Literary Work* [Cambridge: Harvard University, 1988], 153).

12　https://whitmanarchive.org/published/1860-Blue_book/images/leaf002v. html For discussion of these tallies, see E. Folsom and K. M. Price, *Re-Scripting Walt Whitman: An Introduction to his Life and Work* (Blackwell, 2005), ch. 2,; E. Folsom, *Whitman Making Books/Books Making Whitman: A Catalog and Commentary* (Obermann Center for Advanced Studies; Iowa City: University of Iowa, 2005), fig. 17 and discussion On the "Blue Book" in general, see A. Golden, "Walt Whitman's Blue Book" in *Walt Whitman: An Encyclopedia* (eds. J. R. LeMaster and D. D. Kummings; New York: Garland Publishing, 1998). K. Price, "Love, War, and Revision in Whitman's Blue Book," *Huntington Library Quarterly* 73/4 (2010), 679–92.

13　The notebook is a part of the Charles E. Feinberg Collection of the Papers of Walt Whitman in the Library of Congress (*DBN* III, 675). Many thanks to Alice L. Birney of the Manuscript Division of the Library of Congress for directing me to this notebook, especially in reference to Whitman's entry about the *Words of the Bible* (email of 7 January 2011).

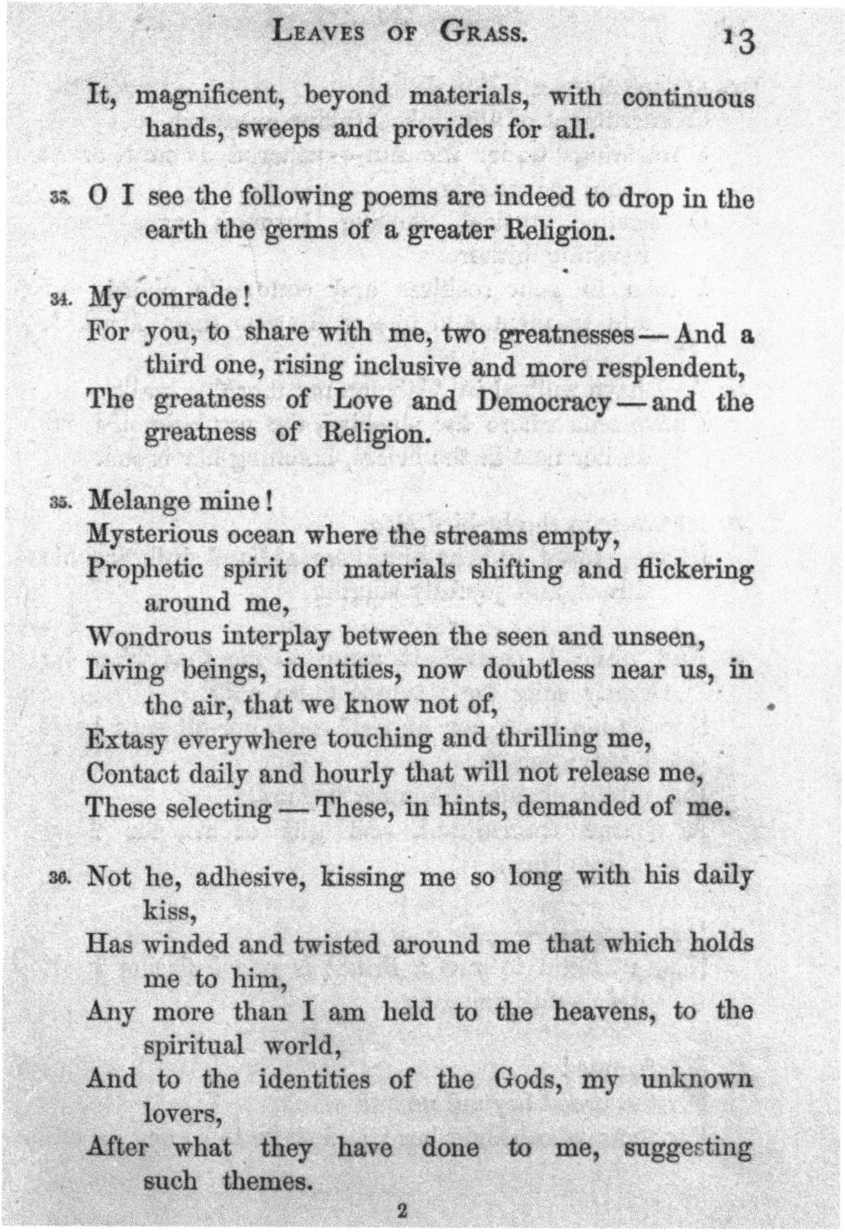

It, magnificent, beyond materials, with continuous
 hands, sweeps and provides for all.

33. O I see the following poems are indeed to drop in the
 earth the germs of a greater Religion.

34. My comrade!
For you, to share with me, two greatnesses — And a
 third one, rising inclusive and more resplendent,
The greatness of Love and Democracy — and the
 greatness of Religion.

35. Melange mine!
Mysterious ocean where the streams empty,
Prophetic spirit of materials shifting and flickering
 around me,
Wondrous interplay between the seen and unseen,
Living beings, identities, now doubtless near us, in
 the air, that we know not of,
Extasy everywhere touching and thrilling me,
Contact daily and hourly that will not release me,
These selecting — These, in hints, demanded of me.

36. Not he, adhesive, kissing me so long with his daily
 kiss,
Has winded and twisted around me that which holds
 me to him,
Any more than I am held to the heavens, to the
 spiritual world,
And to the identities of the Gods, my unknown
 lovers,
After what they have done to me, suggesting
 such themes.

2

Fig. 1: P. 13 from the 1860 *Leaves of Grass* (Boston: Thayer and Eldridge, 1860–61, https://whitmanarchive.org/published/LG/figures/ppp.01500.021.jpg). Public domain. Shows section numbers in "Proto-Leaf." Section 34 also mimes the "graded number sequence" of the Bible.

Words of the Bible

Bible Literature

What powerful and quite indefinable words have been contributed by
the proper nouns of the Old Testament—the names of the Deity—of
Hell, of Heaven—of the great persons—[14]

Whatever more may be made of this entry, it again provides eloquent
testimony to the consciousness of the Bible in Whitman's thinking.

From a still earlier period, one of the book notices Whitman placed
in the *Daily Eagle* (21 October 1846) references what is at least one Bible
that we can both identify and know for certain that Whitman read:
"'Bible, The Holy,' Harper's Illuminated Edition. It is almost useless
to say that no intelligent man can touch the Book of Books with an
irreverent hand." And it is precisely the kind of publication that would
appeal to Whitman's "printerly eye." P. C. Gutjahr describes the Harper
and Brothers' *Illuminated Bible* (1846) as "a sort of urtext for the large
family bibles of the nineteenth century" and one of the century's more
spectacular publishing events (Fig. 3).[15] Weighing in at over thirteen
pounds, it featured the finest quality paper, over sixteen hundred
illustrations (where no previous American-made bible contained more
than a hundred), and was the first volume in America printed with
the new technology of electrotyping.[16] It was billed by the Harpers as
"the most splendidly elegant edition of the Sacred Record ever issued."[17]
Some 75,000 copies were printed, an unprecedented number for the
time. The translation of the "Sacred Record," of course, was that of
the KJB, set in its familiar bi-columnar page layout (Fig. 4). As noted,
the KJB was the English Bible of the nineteenth century. Its primacy in
America and Britain would not begin to be seriously challenged until
the publication of the Revised Version in the 1880s. It was the KJV that
Whitman would have read throughout his life, and in the *Illuminated
Bible* we have one small but sure way of tying Whitman directly to the
KJB—and as will be seen later, his many quotations and allusions to the
Bible confirm this (see Chapter Two).

---

14   *DBN* III, 682.
15   *American Bible*, 70.
16   See Gutjahr, *American Bible*, 70–76; Daniell, *Bible in English*, 655–58. "Electro-
     plating" appears in the 1856 *Leaves* and "electrotyping" then in the 1860 edition.
17   Gutjahr, *American Bible*, 70–76. esp. 70.

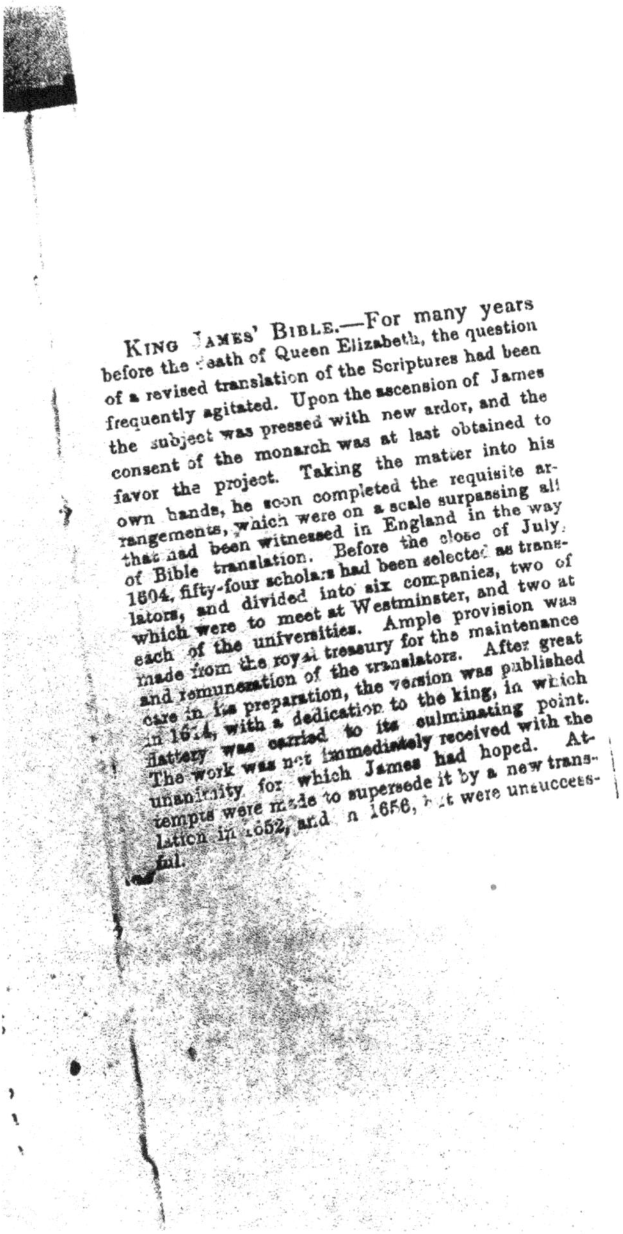

KING JAMES' BIBLE.—For many years before the death of Queen Elizabeth, the question of a revised translation of the Scriptures had been frequently agitated. Upon the ascension of James the subject was pressed with new ardor, and the consent of the monarch was at last obtained to favor the project. Taking the matter into his own hands, he soon completed the requisite arrangements, which were on a scale surpassing all that had been witnessed in England in the way of Bible translation. Before the close of July, 1604, fifty-four scholars had been selected as translators, and divided into six companies, two of which were to meet at Westminster, and two at each of the universities. Ample provision was made from the royal treasury for the maintenance and remuneration of the translators. After great care in its preparation, the version was published in 1614, with a dedication to the king, in which flattery was carried to its culminating point. The work was not immediately received with the unanimity for which James had hoped. Attempts were made to supersede it by a new translation in 1652, and in 1656, but were unsuccessful.

Fig. 2: Clipping entitled "King James' Bible" from the "Notebook Intended for an American Dictionary" (*DBN* III, 675). Courtesy of the Library of Congress.

Photograph by F. W. Dobbs-Allsopp.

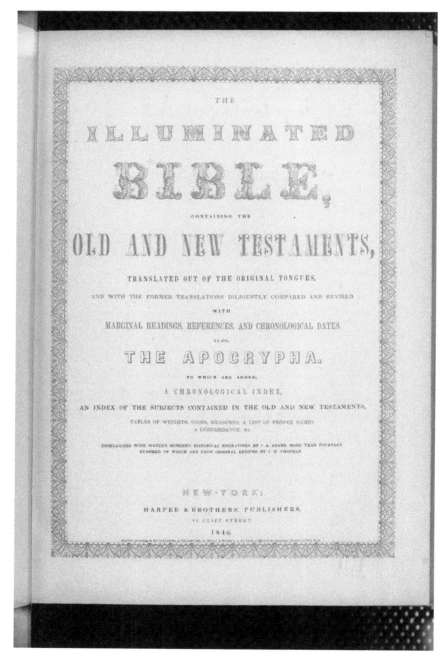

Fig. 3: Harper and Brothers *Illuminated Bible* (1846), title page. Public domain.

Fig. 4: Gen 32:21–34:1 from Harper's *Illuminated Bible,* showing bicolumnar page layout common to the KJB. Public domain.

There are a handful of other known bibles that may be connected directly to Whitman. K. Molinoff describes a Whitman family bible, which at the time of Molinoff's writing (1941) was in the possession of Whitman's grandniece, Mrs. Tuthill.[18] It has recently reappeared and was donated to the Walt Whitman Birthplace (Fig. 5).[19] This bible registered births, marriages, and deaths, which Whitman's sister, Mary Elizabeth Van Nostrand, had requested of Whitman in a letter ("copy our family record").[20] The bible is inscribed on a pasted-in white slip of paper in Whitman's hand and even contains a bit of verse.[21] The bible is large (measuring "about 14 and 5/8 ins. x 11 and 1/2 ins. x 4 and 3/4 ins.), typical for family bibles of the time, and is an edition of the KJB.

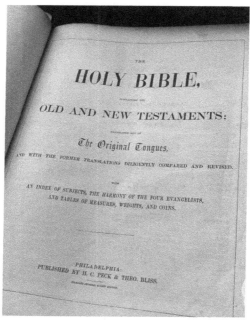

Fig. 5: Walt Whitman's Family Bible. Image courtesy of the Walt Whitman Birthplace.

---

18 *Some Notes on Whitman's Family* (Brooklyn: Comet, 1941), 6–8.
19 Margaret Guardi, the Curator at the Whitman Birthplace, confirmed the identity of the bible for me in an email (19 February 2021). An image of the bible appears in J. Loving's *Walt Whitman: A Song of Himself* ([Berkeley: University of California, 1999], illustration after p. 208).
20 Letter from 16 March 1878, https://whitmanarchive.org/biography/correspondence/tei/duk.00755.html.
21 From "Beyond," a popular poem by Mrs. J. E. Akers (according to Guardi).

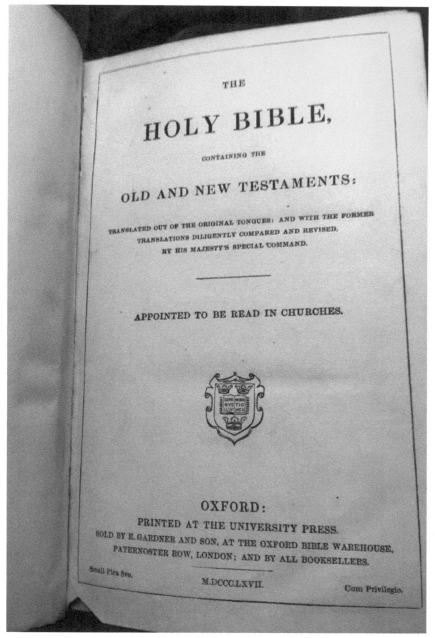

Fig. 6: Family Bible (published in 1867) that Whitman gave to William and Ellen O'Connor (January 1, 1871). Its translation is that of the KJB. Feinberg Collection of the Library of Congress. Photograph by Leslie Dobbs-Allsopp.

Fig. 7: A copy of the edition of *Leaves of Grass* published in celebration of Whitman's 70th birthday, modeled on a little "Oxford Bible" (with thin "Oxford Bible" paper, black leather cover, wraparound flap). On display at Grolier Club, "'Poet of the Body': New York's Walt Whitman" (May 15–July 27, 2019). Photograph by Leslie Dobbs-Allsopp.

The Library of Congress has in its collections another bible that Whitman had owned (Fig. 6), which he also inscribed as a gift: "To William and Ellen O'Connor and their daughter Jeannie. from Walt Whitman 1 January 1871."[22] Not surprisingly, like the Illuminated Bible and the family bible Whitman gave his sister, it is an edition of the KJB. There is also the little "Oxford Bible" on which Whitman modeled his 70th birthday edition of Leaves (Fig. 7)[23] and "a Bible" the poet lists in "More Books" among his books at 328 Mickle Street in 1885. Finally, in the Feinberg Collection there is a manuscript entitled "Books of WW" (date: "Between 1890 and 1892") which records in part: "Copies, evidently often read, of the Bible, Homer and Shakspere."[24] In total, then, at least six known bibles (some physically extant) may be associated directly with Whitman.

In sum, even on such a cursory review—of Whitman's published statements about the Bible, the opinions of close associates, actual bibles that can be connected to the poet—Whitman's familiarity with and high opinion of the Bible may be stipulated.

"The Bible as Poetry"

Whitman's most extensive meta-comment on the Bible is an essay entitled "The Bible as Poetry," first published in 1883. Critics have rarely paid attention to the short essay, except to note that it once more registers

---

22   References courtesy of Dr. Alice L. Birney, Cultural Manuscript Historian, Manuscript Division, Library of Congress; Clark Evan, RBSCD (email, 7 January 2011). Whitman references this bible ("the new year's Bible") in a letter to Ellen O'Connor (8 June 1871), https://whitmanarchive.org/biography/correspondence/tei/nyp.00297.html. Elmer E. Stafford, in a letter to Whitman (11 January 1878), https://whitmanarchive.org/biography/correspondence/figures/loc_jc.00373_large.jpg, writes that "I have received my bible," perhaps referencing another gift of a Bible from Whitman.

23   Several notices for March 1889 in WWWC 4 (295, 300, 328–29) mention a little "Oxford Bible" which Traubel shows Whitman as a model for the "pocket edition" of the 1881 Leaves of Grass (fourteenth printing) that would be printed in celebration of Whitman's 70th birthday. Whitman admires the narrow margins of the Oxford Bible and the high quality of the paper (especially its thinness) that is used. And indeed the resulting little volume with its "'Oxford Bible paper' and a fancy Biblical black leather cover" (the first batch even fitted out with a "wraparound tongued flap") very much has the look and feel of a Bible (see Folsom, Whitman Making Books, esp. Figs. 78–80).

24   https://whitmanarchive.org/manuscripts/marginalia/annotations/loc.03426.html. Image: https://whitmanarchive.org/manuscripts/marginalia/figures/loc_nhg.00170.jpg

Whitman's admiration of the Bible, much like his statements in both *Democratic Vistas* and "A Backward Glance."[25] But the admiration is worth underscoring: "it is to-day," says Whitman in the closing sentence that he eventually omitted in the version re-published in *November Boughs*, the bard's "chief reason for being."[26] Indeed, the opening sentence of that final paragraph, "No true bard will ever contravene the Bible," shares something of the same sentiment with the much earlier book notice quoted above, "It is almost useless to say that no intelligent man can touch the Book of Books with an irreverent hand." This I do not think is coincidental. What is remarkable about the late "The Bible as Poetry" is just how his description of the Bible—and especially the "Hebrew Bible"[27]—answers to the poetic theory Whitman was evolving in the early 1850s in particular. In summary fashion, Whitman's emerging new American poetics aspired to be simple—"a perfectly transparent plate-glassy style"; shorn of unnecessary "ornaments" and "the stock 'poetical' touches"; rhythmical but without "arbitrary or rhyming meter"; refusing to "go into criticism or arguments"—a "language of ecstasy," as Zweig says; and filled with ideas or notions that are democratic, that relate "to American character or interests."[28] In "The Bible as Poetry," the Bible is projected very much as the archetype of Whitman's new poetics, a paradigm of not only "what the office of poet was in primeval times," but also what it "is yet capable of being anew, adjusted entirely to the modern."[29] The Bible has "nothing at all, of the mere esthetic," and its "spinal supports" are "simple and meager." There is "nothing of argument or logic," but is surpassing in proverbial wisdom, "religious ecstasy," daring metaphors, and "the lawless soul" and "thick-studded with human emotions"—"nowhere else the simplest human emotions conquering the gods of heaven." Whitman notes, on the

---

25   One exception is T. E. Crawley, who does give some notice to the essay (*Structure*, 25–26).

26   *November Boughs*, 46.

27   Anne Gilchrist in a letter to Whitman (https://whitmanarchive.org/biography/correspondence/tei/loc.05697.html) from 6 May 1883 confirms that she had read and prized "the article on the Hebrew Scriptures," about which Whitman had inquired in an earlier letter (23 February 1883), https://whitmanarchive.org/biography/correspondence/tei/loc.02154.html.

28   Zweig, *Walt Whitman*, esp. 143–63; Miller, *Collage of Myself*, 41–42, 44.

29   All quotations are from the original 1883 rendition, unless otherwise noted. The holograph of Whitman's manuscript for the essay is in the Special Collections at the University of Chicago, https://www.lib.uchicago.edu/e/scrc/findingaids/view.php?eadid=ICU.SPCL.MS263

authority of Frederick de Sola Mendes, that "rhyming" and "meter" were not "characteristic of Hebrew poetry at all." For Whitman, the Bible is the very antipathy of the European and classical poetic traditions or "our Nineteenth Century business absorption": "no hairsplitting doubts, no sickly sulking and sniffling, no 'Hamlet' no, 'Adonais,' no 'Thanatopsis,' no 'In Memoriam.'" This riff is very much to the same end as this from the 1856 "George Walker" notebook: "Avoid all the 'intellectual subtleties,' and 'withering doubts' and 'blasted hopes' and 'unrequited loves,' and 'ennui,' and 'wretchedness' and the whole of the lurid and artistical and melo-dramatic effects."[30] Whitman recognizes in the Bible many of his own cherished themes—"the glow of love and friendship,"[31] "the fervent kiss," "suggestions of mortality and death, man's great equalizers," "the finest blending of individuality with universality," and "projecting cosmic brotherhood, the dream of all hope." He notices that it is "the *old man*," a favored Whitmanian persona (as in "The bodies of men and women engirth me"), who is the leading figure in the East, a cultural pattern, he implies, that is illustrated in the "oldest Biblical narratives." Indeed, without the Bible, writes Whitman, "this America of ours, with its polity and essentials, could not now be existing."

Unmistakably, "The Bible as Poetry" shows that by the early 1880s Whitman was able to frame his understanding of the Bible in terms of the poetic aesthetic that he had evolved over the course of his career and to see the Bible very much as a forerunner of that aesthetic. Whether or not this is a fair representation of Whitman's thinking about the Bible from earlier periods is harder to tease out positively. I am inclined to think that it is, however. His easy and knowing use of the Bible—especially evident in his many quotations of it and allusions to it at all periods of his life (see Chapter Two)—suggests, as B. L. Bergquist says, "a constantly used resource and stimulus to intellectual and spiritual growth" that was "returned to again and again."[32] His high esteem for the Bible is

---

30   See discussion in Miller, *Collage of Myself*, 43.
31   This is a theme Whitman had long associated with the Bible. Hearing the chanting of Hebrew during a synagogue service reminds Whitman of "the same tones which Jonathan and Saul used in their beautiful friendship" ("A Peep at the Israelites," *New York Aurora* (28 March 1842), 2. Reprinted in *Walt Whitman's Selected Journalism* (eds. D. A. Nover and J. Stacy; Iowa City: University of Iowa, 2014), 196–98, 197.
32   "Walt Whitman and the Bible," 77.

effectively registered early on in the "Book of Books" comment from the 1846 book notice, a comment, moreover, as noted, that anticipates the closing statement in the later "The Bible as Poetry." Indeed, this image of the "true bard" able to absorb the biblical traditions through himself and adjust them to the modern is also very much in the spirit of a passage Whitman clipped and underscored from a British literary magazine in 1849 (or early 1850):

> As a thousand rivulets are blended in one broad river, so the countless instincts, energies, and faculties, as well as associations, traditions, and other social influences which constitute national life, are reconciled in him whom future ages are to recognize as the poet of the nation.[33]

And everything about Whitman's use of the Bible is consistent with the poetics he starts articulating in his early notebooks. But, as Miller observes, "the notebooks don't offer much evidence either way about the Bible."[34] True enough. Though not "much," the notebooks (and unpublished prose manuscripts) do offer *some* evidence about the Bible. Explicit mention of the Bible is made in the "Notebook Intended for an American Dictionary," as noted above. A selection of other similar instances include:

> "O Bible!" say I "what nonsense and folly have been supported in thy name!"
>
> "Autobiographical Data" (1848–1855/56)[35]

> Hebrew [:] The ethereal and elevated Spirituality—this seems to be what subordinates all the rest—the Soul—the spirit—rising in vagueness—
>
> "Egyptian religion" (soon after 1855)[36]

> Verse was the first writing of all we know—Greeks—Old Testament.
>
> "Speaking of literary style" (1854/55)[37]

---

33 Clipped from an article entitled "Modern Poetry and Poets" from *Blackwood's* (October 1849). As quoted in Allen, *The Solitary Singer*, 1967 [1955]), 132.

34 *Collage of Myself*, 26.

35 https://whitmanarchive.org/manuscripts/notebooks/loc.05935/images/leaf004r. html Cf. A. C. Higgins, "Wage Slavery and the Composition of *Leaves of Grass*: The 'Talbot Wilson' Notebook," *WWQR* 20/2 (2002), 76, n. 35.

36 https://whitmanarchive.org/manuscripts/marginalia/figures/duk.00198.001.jpg. *NUPM* VI, 2028, cf. p. 2025.

37 https://whitmanarchive.org/manuscripts/figures/nyp_jc.00019.jpg. *NUPM* I, 162; cf. p. 81.

The florid rich, first phases of poetry, as in the Oriental Poems—the Bible—.... The primitive poets, their subjects their style, all assimilate.— Very ancient poetry, of the Hebrew prophets, of Ossian, of the Hindu fathers [*illg.*] singers and extatics... all resemble each other

"The florid rich" (1855–60)[38]

Taking en-masse, what is called literature... with but here and there, as accident has had it, a little sample specimen put in record... —A few Hebrew canticles....

"Taking en-masses" (post 1856)[39]

Whatever Theological inferences once thought and orthodox may be demolished by the scientific and historical inquiries of our times, but the Bible collect of the Bible as a traditional poem so various in its sources and times, still remains at [illeg] to perhaps the most [illeg] instructive, suggestive, even artistic memorial of the past

"Theological inferences" (presumably early)[40]

Names. The Biblical poets—David, Isaiah, the Book of Job—etc. Also the New Testament writers....

"Names. The Biblical poets"[41]

—the Syrian canticles, the Book of Job and the other books & emerging from them the idylls of the life of C[42]

"Poets—Shakespeare" (1860s)[43]

---

38 https://whitmanarchive.org/manuscripts/marginalia/figures/duk.00673.001.jpg. *NUPM* IV, 1555.

39 *NUPM* IV, 1562; see also V, 1620 ("Literature [:] Iliad, Bible,....").

40 An undated manuscript note from the Trent Collection, Duke University (quarto 35). I have found notices to it in E. F. Frey, *Catalogue of the Walt Whitman Collection in the Duke Library* (Durham: Duke University Library, 1945), 28, no. 40; Crawley, *Structure*, 58 (he reads the last word erroneously as "East"); M. Moon, *Disseminating Whitman: Revision and Corporeality in Leaves of Grass* (Cambridge: Harvard University, 1993), 236–37, n. 3. An image of the holograph may be viewed at: http://library.duke.edu/rubenstein/scriptorium/findaids/images/whitmaniana/whitman2023/index.htm. The top of page has an asterisk with the following underscored: "To the ## poet, [illeg] surpasses all else."

41 *NUPM* IV, 1564. For Whitman, "Syria" was a modern geographical designation for the lands of the Bible, especially that of ancient Israel and Judah: "You Jew journeying in your old age through every risk to stand once on Syrian ground!" (LG 1856, 118).

42 *NUPM* IV, 1572, n. 10: "Presumably Christ."

43 *NUPM* IV, 1572.

—Yet in religion & poetry the old Asiatic land dominates to this day until above the world shall arise peaks still higher than the Hebrew Bible, the Ionian Iliad, & the psalms & great epics of India.

"—How different" (late 1860s)[44]

The Bible Shakespere Homer....

"The Bible Shakespere" (not earlier than 1873)[45]

The Hebraic poems—(the Bible) with readings—the Book of Job dominating

"On Poems" (1860s/70s)[46]

The sense of Deity is indispensable in grand poems—this is what puts [inserted: the book of Job & much of] the Old Hebrew Bible with the Book of Job—and also the plays of Eschuylus ahead of all poetry we know.

"Emerson uses the Deific" (1872)[47]

The divine immortal Hebraic poems—Homer's, Virgil's, and Juvenal's compositions—Dante's, Shakspeare's and even Tennyson's—

"Is Walt Whitman's Poetry Poetical?" (1874)[48]

Several observations may be offered in regard to these notices of the Bible in Whitman's notebooks and prose manuscripts. First, they date from the early 1850s through the 1870s, and thus show that Whitman's late statement in "The Bible as Poetry" has various points of contact with his earlier thinking. Second, there is considerably more here than Miller's not "much evidence either way" might suggest—and this is by no means an exhaustive listing and does not include passages with biblical characters, allusions, echoes, or the like (see Chapter Two). Third, the manner of the references is significant. The emphasis here, as in "The Bible as Poetry," is often explicitly on the "Hebrew Bible"—viz. "Old Testament," "Hebrew," "Oriental Poems," "Hebrew prophets," "Hebrew canticles," "Syrian canticles," "Hebrew poems." This squares with T. E. Crawley's broader finding that "the religious spirit of *Leaves of Grass* is basically Hebraic"[49]

---

44   *NUPM* IV, 1574. Note here Whitman clearly articulates his aspiration to be one of these "peaks"; cf. *NUPM* I, 111; V, 1752–53.
45   *NUPM* IV, 1578.
46   *NUPM* V, 1804.
47   E. Folsom, "Whitman's Notes on Emerson: An Unpublished Manuscript," *WWQR* 18/1 (2000), 60–62 (image on back cover).
48   *NUPM* IV, 1519.
49   *Structure*, 57, cf. 57–63—he points to over seventy references in Whitman's prose to support this contention (228).

and with Whitman's own explicit self-description in the never published "Introduction to the London Edition" cited earlier as a headnote to the Introduction—"the interior & foundation quality of the man is Hebraic, Biblical, mystic."[50] There is no doubting the deep impress that Christianity—and especially "the crucifixion scenes of the Christ-drama" in the Gospels—had on Whitman and his poetry, but G. W. Allen's early impression that Whitman "drew most of his biblical inspiration from the New Testament" requires modification.[51] The Hebrew Bible is every bit as influential on Whitman as the New Testament, and in some respects (as detailed below) it is far more influential.

Fig. 8: P. 2 (obv) of "The Bible as Poetry." Codex Ms263. Shows clipping containing ideas attributed to Frederick de Sola Mendes. Image courtesy of the Hanna Holborn Gray Special Collections Research Center, University of Chicago, https://www.lib.uchicago.edu/e/scrc/findingaids/view.php?eadid=ICU.SPCL.MS263

---

50 *NUPM* IV, 1501.
51 "Biblical Echoes," 302; cf. J. Loving, "The Political Roots of *Leaves of Grass*" in *A Historical Guide to Walt Whitman* (ed. D. S. Reynolds; New York/Oxford: Oxford University, 2000), 102.

The terminology is noteworthy also because it is not confessional in origin. Again this is in keeping with Whitman's late essay. More importantly, this suggests that Whitman's familiarity with the Bible is not solely dependent on personal or casual reading (however early and often) but derives in part from secondary discussions (of various sorts) of the Bible. This is not surprising since Whitman was a voracious reader and engaged in an intense period of self-directed reading during the late 1840s and early 1850s in particular.[52] A number of these sources can even be identified. Whitman often clipped articles from newspapers, magazines, and books and pasted them into his homemade notebooks. A number of these clippings are on the Bible, including several that were annotated or scored by Whitman: "Divisions of the Bible," "Books Mentioned in the Bible Now Lost or Unknown," "The Holy Land," "The Psalms," "The Unity of the Bible," "Errors in Printing Bible," "King James' Bible" (see above), and a clipping of a note on the underlying Hebrew and Greek of "woman" and "women" in the English Bible.[53] Whitman also explicitly references a number of authorities, including, for example, a "discourse on 'Hebrew Poets'" by De Sola Mendes,"[54] "William H. Seward" and "his travels in Turkey, Egypt, and Asia Minor,"[55] "Prof Wines' Commentary on the Hebrew Law,"[56] "'Ancient Hebrews,' by Abm. Mills A. S. Barnes & Co.,"[57]

---

52   See F. Stovall, "Notes on Whitman's Reading," *AL* 26/3 (1954), 337–62"; *The Foreground of Leaves of Grass* (Charlottesville: University Press of Virginia, 1974), 140–51.

53   All except the final two clippings are listed by Bucke in *Notes & Fragments* IV (nos. 80, 103, 205, 337, 407, and 491), *CW* X, 69, 70, 76, 84, 88, 93. For the "King James' Bible" and the translation clippings, see *DBN* III, 675, 707.

54   "The Bible as Poetry." This, too, is actually from a clipping. The original manuscript of the essay (Codex Ms263), now in the Special Collections of the University of Chicago Library, shows two pasted-in clippings containing the language attributed to de Sola Mendes (Fig. 8). The second clipping (with slightly wider spacing between lines of text) is an indirect description of de Sola Mendes' views (viz. "Dr. Mendes said that....."), not a direct quotation as Whitman punctuates it in *The Critic* ("Dr. Mendes said 'that....'"). De Sole Mendes was a rabbi and founding faculty of the Jewish Theological Seminary.

55   "The Bible as Poetry." On the travels of William H. Seward and Edward John Trelawney to the Orient, see Gutjahr, *American Bible*, 60–69.

56   This from an early notebook (*DBN* III, 778), dated to 1856. On the flyleaf, there is a reference to E. C. Wines, *Commentaries on the Laws of the Ancient Hebrews* (New York: G. P. Putnam, 1853), which is listed in the Astor Library's holdings from 1861 (*Catalogue or Alphabetical Index of the Astor Library in Two parts. Pt. 1, Authors and Books*, Q-Z [New York: R. Craighead, 1861], 2084)

57   In the same early notebook as the Wines' reference (*DBN* III, 778): Abraham Mills, *The Ancient Hebrews* (New York: A. S. Barnes, 1856).

"De Vere's Comparative Philology 1853,"[58] "Bunsen,"[59] and "Volney."[60]

58 In a manuscript scrap entitled "Even now Jasmund", probably dating between 1856 and 1858 (see C. C. Hollis, "Whitman and William Swinton: A Co-operative Friendship," *AL* 30 [1959], 436), Whitman quotes from M. Schele de Vere's *Outlines of Comparative Philology: With a Sketch of the Languages of Europe, Arranged upon Philologic Principles, and A Brief History of the Art of Writing* (New York: Putnam, 1853): "—'Even now Jasmund, the people's poet, prefers to sing in Provencal'" (taken from p. 324, with the grammar slightly adjusted by Whitman). A copy which was owned originally by William Swinton was in Whitman's library at his death (C. E. Feinberg [ed], *Walt Whitman: A Selection of the Manuscripts, Books, and Association Items Gathered by Charles E. Feinberg. Catalogue of an Exhibition Held at the Detroit Public Library, Detroit, Michigan, 1955* [Detroit Public Library, 1955], 126, no. 377). The volume is also referenced in Swinton's *Rambles Among Words: History and Wisdom* (New York: Charles Scribner, 1859), which Whitman may have contributed to (see *NUPM* V, 1651). And some of Whitman's annotations in "Old theory started" (*NUPM* V, 1894) may come from de Vere as well. Indeed, Whitman's sense of how ancient history—especially ancient "Asian" history—informs and feeds the present is much the same as expressed by de Vere.

59 Whitman references C. K. J. Bunsen in four notations: "Resume—(from Bunsen)" (*NUPM* V, 1916—citing p. 231 from volume 1 of *Outlines of the Philosophy of Universal History Applied to Language and Religion* [London: Longman, Brown, Green, and Longmans, 1854]); "(Bunsen)" (*NUPM* V, 1917—notes made from the same volume, see Stovall, "Notes on Whitman's Reading," 338); "Lecture" "law" "lex" (*NUPM* VI, 2031—"(Bunsen) Abrahamic movement [:] 28th or 29th Century before Christ," which Stovall says could derive either from Bunsen's *Outlines* (I, 229) or from his *Egypt's Place in Universal History: An Historical Investigation in Five Books* ([London: Longman, Brown, Green, and Longmans, 1859], III, 351), which Whitman also knew, cf. Stovall, *Foreground*, 164, n.14; and "Religion—Gods" (*NUPM* VI, 2025). There is also a clipping entitled "Bunsen's Chronology" (Bucke, *Notes & Fragments* IV, no. 104 [*CW* X, 70]). Bunsen is also prominently mentioned in "Notebook Intended for an American Dictionary" (e.g., on Semitic languages, *DBN* III, 720).

60 Cited explicitly by Whitman in "Religions-Gods" (*NUPM* VI, 2026), referencing C.-F. Volney, *Ruins: Or, Meditation on the Revolutions of Empires* (Boston: C. Gaylord, 1835), see D. Goodale, "Some of Walt Whitman's Borrowings," *AL* 10/2 (1938), 202–13. Whitman "quotes" Volney (p. 163; Goodale does not catch this; Grier says, "Source not identified"): "Talmud (of Jerusalem) very old 'sybilline verses among the ancients' always looking for 'a great mediator, a judge, god, [lover,] legislator, friend of the poor and degraded, conqueror of powers." The words are clearly Volney's, but even with quotation marks Whitman is already massaging—or as E. Holloway and R. Adimari put it in their prefatory comments to Whitman's essay, "The Egyptian Museum," Whitman read history "creatively" (*New York Dissected* [New York: R. R. Wilson, 1936], 27). In Volney the "Talmud of Jerusalem" is mentioned in a footnote on p. 162. The "sybilline verses so celebrated among the ancients" comes from a footnote on p. 163, following the list in the body of p. 163: "a great mediator, a final judge, a future savior, a king, god, conqueror, and legislator"—this last in reference to the hope after the 586 destruction of Jerusalem for such a deliverer to restore the empire of David, which Volney characterizes as a sacred and mythological tradition that had "spread through all Asia." Importantly, Whitman is already weaving Volney's language to serve his own purpose, especial in his addition of "lover" to this list. Note also Whitman's play on Hab 2:2 ("Write the vision, and make it plain upon tablets, that he may run that readeath it") at

Most of Whitman's collaging from his reading goes uncredited, though scholars over the years have been able to identify many of the poet's sources. Whitman read fairly extensively in ancient history and religion (esp. that pertaining to ancient Egypt, Mesopotamia, Persia, Greece, India),[61] many of the sources for which F. Stovall has illuminated.[62] Some of these sources (e.g., de Vere, Bunsen, Volney) could have furnished Whitman with some of the factual information about the Bible that he writes down (e.g., dates). A case in point is Whitman's notation, "Moses born in 1571 B.C.," which as Stovall remarks comes out of J. G. Wilkinson's *Manners and Customs of the Ancient Egyptians* ("Moses born, 1571"), a book Whitman was very familiar with.[63] More importantly, even when sources cannot be identified, factual information of this kind implicates more than a casual, readerly knowledge of the Bible. And there are quite a lot of these kinds of entries in Whitman's notebooks (and other manuscript scraps).

One striking example by way of illustration. It comes from an undated manuscript (Grier: "before 1885"), "(For words)": "The word Jehovah weaves the meaning of the past, present and future tenses—personalizes Time, as it was, is, and ever shall be."[64] This appears to reflect some of the speculation during the nineteenth century on the formation of the Tetragrammaton used throughout the Hebrew Bible as one name for the God of Israel—*YHWH*. Whitman (from an early period, Grier: "probably 1855") once instructed himself (after a brief description of the god Mithras): "Look at a theological dictionary [1855

the beginning of "The Egyptian Museum": "Some of these lessons are so plain that they who walk may read" (see Holloway and Adimari, *New York Dissected*, 204, n. 8).

61   Cf. *NUPM* V, 1915–29; VI, 2019–2107.
62   Esp. *Foreground*, 161–83.
63   (new ed.; London: J. Murray, 1878 [1837]), I, 34; cf. Stovall, "Notes on Whitman's Reading," 356. The references in this manuscript ("Moses of course was born," https://whitmanarchive.org/manuscripts/marginalia/annotations/ duk.00066.html) and in "Immortality was realized," https://whitmanarchive. org/manuscripts/marginalia/annotations/mid.00018.html, supplied a lot of the information in the chronological synopsis in Whitman's "Egyptian Museum" essay (pp. 33–34), see Holloway and Adimari's note 11 on pp. 204–05; cf. Stovall, "Notes on Whitman's Reading," 347, 356. Cf. *DBN* III, 719–23 (where Bunsen is the source).
64   *NUPM* V, 1699.

Walt Whitman]."[65] Consulting the entries for "Jehovah" from five such dictionaries from the period reveals that all associate the deity's name with the Hebrew verbal root *hyh* "to be, exist," taking their cue above all from the play on that root in Exod 3:13–15, and most reference Rev 1:4, 8 as well. Samuel Green, in *A Biblical and Theological Dictionary*, says, in language very close to Whitman's: "That its grammatical form is a compound of the past, the present, and the future."[66] Richard Watson, whose *Biblical and Theological Dictionary* is listed among the Astor Library's holdings for 1851,[67] though more round-about gets at the same point: "...that is, always existing; whence the word eternal appears to express its import; or, as it is well rendered, 'He who is and also was, and who is to come,' Rev 1:4."[68] John Eadie in his *Biblical Cyclopaedia* is very similar, citing both Exod 3:14 and Rev 1:4 and also offers the gloss, "Him 'who was, and is, and is to come.'"[69] Patrick Fairbairn in *The Imperial Bible-Dictionary* is more sophisticated. He grounds his explanation explicitly in the imperfective (or "future") form of the verb, which the divine name resembles (the kind of folk etymology at play in Exod 3:14): "the so-called future in Hebrew differs widely from our future..., expressing as it does what has been wont to be in the past as well as what will be in the future—the ongoing of being or action (as opposed to its completion) in whatever sphere of time."[70] William Smith in his detailed discussion agrees that the basic etymology from the verb *hyh* "to be" is correct and that Exod 3:14 is "key to the whole mystery" (of the meaning of the Tetragrammaton), but the assertion that the name "embraces past, present, and future" based on Rev 4:8 and the

---

65   *NUPM* VI, 2030. In 1850, in a letter to the editor of the *National Era* ([21 November 1850], 187; reprinted in R. G. Silver, "Whitman in 1850: Three Uncollected Articles," *American Literature* 19/4 [1948], 314), Whitman also references "commentators on the Bible," showing he certainly knows of, and likely had read, some secondary literature about the Bible.

66   (London: Elliot Stock, 1867).

67   *Alphabetical Index to the Astor Library* (New York: R. Craighead, 1851), 421 (compiled by J. Cogswell).

68   *A Biblical and Theological Dictionary* (rev. Am. ed; New York: Lane and Scott, 1851 [1832]), 505. Cf. *Calmet's Dictionary of the Holy Bible* (eds. C. Taylor; E. Robinson; Rev. American ed; Boston: Crocker and Brewster, 1832), 549–50 (the 8th edition of the *Dictionary* [1841, in 5 volumes] is listed in the holdings of the Astor Library (*Catalogue or Alphabetical Index* [A-Z, 1857], 215),

69   (12th. ed; London: Charles Griffin and Company, 1870 [1848]), 354–55.

70   (London: Blackie and Sons, 1866), I, 855—he is referencing the fact that verbs in Hebrew are marked morphologically for aspect and not tense.

like (i.e., that the name "was compounded of the Present Participle, and the Future and the Praeterite tenses of the substantive verb") lacks solid grammatical warrants.[71]

Whitman need not have consulted any of these specific volumes. I cite them because they give a fair representation of the kind of thought that lies behind Whitman's jottings in "(For words)." That he could have come across such information on Jehovah would seem a good possibility in light of his reminder to check a "theological dictionary."[72] He then massages the image towards the "Father Time" ("personalizes Time") figure of the "Ancient of days" (Aram. ʿatfiq yômayyāʾ) of Daniel 7 (vv. 7, 13, 22). The image strongly resembles that of the "Father Time" figures in the opening section of "Chanting the Square Deific" (*Sequel*, 15):

> CHANTING the square deific, out of the One advancing, out of the sides;
>
> Out of the old and new—out of the square entirely divine,
>
> Solid, four-sided, (all the sides needed)...from this side JEHOVAH am I,
>
> Old Brahm I, and I Saturnius am;
>
> Not Time affects me—I am Time, modern as any;

It is hard not to see in Whitman's "JEHOVAH am I" an allusion to Exod 3:14, "I AM THAT I AM" (capitalized in the KJB) and "I AM hath sent me unto you" (a similar capitalization figures in several of the dictionary discussions as well)—and in fact in an 1842 article from the *Aurora* Whitman himself references the "great I AM upon the mountain of clouds" (Exodus 19–20).[73] Here Whitman adopts the

---

71 W. Smith, *A Dictionary of the Bible* (vol 1; Boston: Little, Brown, and Company, 1860), 952–59, quotations from p. 955. The volume is listed in the Astor Library's holdings from 1861 (*Catalogue or Alphabetical Index* [Q–Z, 1861], 1818).

72 There is an interesting mention of "Jah" in the early "Talbot Wilson" notebook ("If I walked with Jah in Heaven...," https://whitmanarchive.org/manuscripts/figures/loc.00141.062.jpg; cf. "myths of Jah" in "The genuine miracles of Christ," https://whitmanarchive.org/manuscripts/transcriptions/loc.01019.html), which is referenced in many of these dictionary entries (e.g., Watson, *Biblical and Theological Dictionary*, 500: "one of the names of God"; cf. *Calmet's Dictionary*, 543). Otherwise the shortened form only occurs once in Ps 68:4 (of the KJB)—with reference to "him that rideth upon the heavens." Regardless, no mistaking the ultimate source for this designation, the KJB.

73 "A Peep at the Israelites," 2, https://whitmanarchive.org/published/periodical/journalism/tei/per.00418.html. The article records Whitman's visit to Crosby Street synagogue.

KJB's capitalizations, as they mimic the Tetragrammaton of the Hebrew Bible—*YHWH* (Exod 6:3; Ps 83:18; Isa 12:2; 26:4).[74]

A final characteristic to note about Whitman's manner of phrasing in these manuscripts is his emphasis literally on the Bible *as poetry*. There is a generic sense in which the Bible as a whole often got characterized as "poetry" during the nineteenth century, and this can be glimpsed with Whitman at times, for example, when in "Names. The Biblical poets" he also includes "the New Testament writers"—there is very little actual poetry (verse) in the New Testament. By contrast, however, almost a third of the Hebrew Bible is verse. The KJB, of course, is a prose translation of the Bible, with no formatting distinction made for verse (a point I come back to in Chapter Three). Yet certainly by the time of "The Bible as Poetry" essay Whitman is well aware that the Hebrew Bible contains poetry (viz. his referencing of de Sola Mendes' opinion).[75] As the manuscript notations quoted above show, this awareness goes back into the 1850s at least, viz. "verse... Old Testament," "very ancient poetry, of the Hebrew prophets," "a few Hebrew canticles," "the Biblical poets—David, Isaiah, the Book of Job," "the Syrian canticles," "the Hebraic poems."[76] This reemphasizes Whitman's privileging

---

74 "Jehovah" results from a misunderstanding of the nature of the "perpetual *qere*" involving the Tetragrammaton in the Masoretic manuscripts of the Hebrew Bible (e.g., Gen 3:14 in B19a). Instead of reading the *qere* *ᵓădōnāy* (lit. "my Lord") in place of the unpronounceable written form (the *ketib*) of the name of the deity, *yhwh* (cf. Jerome's translation of Exod 6:3, Adonai), it combines the consonants of the Tetragrammaton with the vowel points of *ᵓădōnay*, yielding the non-existent"Jehovah." The *OED* credits P. Galatinus with the earliest such rendering, in Latin ("Iehoua," 1518 CE). Tyndale introduces the new coinage into English in 1530 (e.g., "Iehouah" in Gen 6:3; cf. Wycliffite: "Adonay" [after the Vulgate], *OED*), which then spreads into the English vernacular through succeeding Bible translations, especially that of the KJB.

75 From the same period comes Whitman's essay on Emerson ("Emerson's Books, (The Shadows of Them.)," *Boston Literary World* [22 May 1880] = *Specimen Days & Collect* [1882] [*CPW*, 319–21]), in which he writes: "At times it has been doubtful to me if Emerson really knows or feels what Poetry is at its highest, as in the Bible, for instance, or Homer or Shakspere"—a similar sentiment is contained in Whitman's notes for the essay, which date back to 1872 (see E. Folsom, "Whitman's Notes on Emerson: An Unpublished Manuscript," *WWQR* 18/1 [2000], 60–62).

76 Whitman reports attending his first synagogue service in "A Peep at the Israelites" (2, https://whitmanarchive.org/published/periodical/journalism/tei/per.00418. html). He is clearly aware of Hebrew as the original language of the Hebrew Bible/Old Testament—"the tones and the native language of the holy Psalmist."

of the Hebrew Bible (especially its poetic portions) and the strong likelihood of his having benefited from outside sources for some of this awareness—that is, it is an awareness again that would not necessarily be obvious to a casual reader of the Bible in an English prose translation. Stovall even comments on the peculiarity of Whitman's language about the Bible *as poetry*: "As a boy in Sunday School and under the usual influences of a Protestant Christian home, he had absorbed much of the Old and New Testaments, but so far as I can discover, he never thought of the Hebrew Bible as poetry until 1850 or later."[77] Certainly, his early notebooks reveal him having already come to this new appreciation of poetry in the (Hebrew) Bible. One theme in particular, that all early writing was in verse, can be traced back into the early 1850s. It appears in both "The florid rich" (1855–60) and "Speaking of literary style" (1854/55), specifically associated with the Bible. And the same theme is also present in the best known of Whitman's early notebooks, the "Talbot Wilson" notebook (1854[78]), albeit without explicit connection to the Bible: "In the earliest times... everything written at all was poetry.... Therefore history, laws, religion, war ^{were} all in the keeping of the poet.— He was literature.— It was nothing but poems."[79] The theme is the same, and as I illustrate below, there are biblical connections with this notebook as well.

But what is possibly Whitman's earliest mention of "Biblical poetry" comes among comments annotating a clipping about Ossian from Margaret Fuller's "Things and Thoughts on Europe. No. V" (*New York Tribune*, 30 September 1846).[80] Grier dates the manuscript to the time of Fuller's article, 1846, "since it is reasonable to assume that WW made these notes at the time the clipping... was published."[81] Stovall, more

His later line from the "Poem of Salutation"—"I hear the Hebrew reading his records and psalms" (*LG* 1856, 106)—likely reflects such lived experiences.

77   *Foreground*, 184.
78   On the date, see esp. A. Birney, "Missing Whitman Notebooks Returned to Library of Congress," *WWQR* 12 (1995), 217–29; E. Shephard, "Possible Sources of Some of Whitman's Ideas in *Hermes Mercurius Trismegistus* and Other Works," *MLQ* 14 (1953), 67n; E. F. Grier, "Walt Whitman's Earliest Known Notebook," *PMLA* 83 (1968), 1453–1456; Higgins, "Wage Slavery," 53–77; Miller, *Collage of Myself*, 2–5.
79   https://whitmanarchive.org/manuscripts/figures/loc.00141.117.jpg
80   "An Ossianic paragraph," https://whitmanarchive.org/manuscripts/marginalia/figures/mid.00016.001.jpg
81   *NUPM* V, 1806.

cautious, says, "the clipping was doubtless made in 1846, but the note seems to be of later date"[82]—though he does not speculate on how much "later." Either way "An Ossianic paragraph" is early. In the annotation Whitman queries the possible source of Ossian's poetry: "?Can it be a descendant of the Biblical poetry?—Is it not Isaiah, Job, the Psalms, and so forth, transferred to the Scotch Highlands? (or to Ireland?)." And then added in pencil (like the parenthetical query about Ireland): "? The tremendous figures and ideas of the Hebrew poems,—are they not *original?*—for they are certainly great—(Yes they are original." This is a fascinating quote for a variety of reasons (not least of which is that Whitman's instinct was correct, Ossian turned out to be the creation of poet James Macpherson who was indeed influenced by the Bible[83]). For the moment what is to be accentuated is Whitman's clear awareness of the fact of "Biblical poetry"—"Hebrew poems," "Isaiah, Job, the Psalms, and so forth," and at an early date—entirely consistent with the kind of reading and note-taking that typified his intense period of self-study from 1845–52.[84]

That Whitman would gravitate to the "poetry" of the Hebrew Bible during the very period when he was coming to his identity as a poet is perhaps natural enough (at least in hindsight). It is also worth stressing that the kind of poetry one finds in the Hebrew Bible is almost entirely nonnarrative in nature, mostly lyric and didactic, with a large block of prophetic verse that often combines a mix of genres and generally lacks strong fixed forms.[85] There is no true epic verse whatsoever in the Bible (doubtless Hebrew epics were performed in antiquity, but they did not get written down). Whitman, of course, is mainly a lyricist in the early *Leaves*. As Allen reminds readers about that first rendition of

---

82 Stovall, *Foreground*, 115.
83 Stovall, *Foreground*, 117.
84 Whitman's quotations and allusions to the Bible in editorials and such from 1846–47 as editor of the *Brooklyn Daily Eagle*, which on Bergquist's count amounts to 67 in total (Allen finds 25 specific allusions or quotes), alone show that he was certainly reading and referencing the Bible at the beginning of this period of self-study.
85 See F. W. Dobbs-Allsopp, "The Idea of Lyric Poetry in the Bible" in *On Biblical Poetry* (Oxford/New York: Oxford University, 2015), 178–232. For the general resemblance between Whitman's verse and the free forms of biblical prophecy, see K. Renner, "Tradition for a Time of Crisis: Whitman's Prophetic Stance" in *Poetic Prophecy in Western Literature* (eds. J. Wojcik and R.-J. Frontain; Rutherford, N.J.: Fairleigh Dickinson University, 1984), 119–30, esp. 120–21.

"Song of Myself," its "final effect... is lyrical, and it is as a lyric it should
be judged."[86] And then this further characterization, which is just as
accurate a descriptor of biblical poetry as it is of "Song of Myself" (and
Leaves more generally): "It has passages which present dramatic scenes,
but it has no plot; such narration as it has is episodic, and this only in
a few spots."[87] Whitman himself remarks specifically on the lack in
Leaves of conventional "plots of love or war" and "no legend, or myth, or
romance."[88] The latter is the stuff of "objective, epic" poetry—"of other
persons"—which Whitman explicitly contrasts with the "subjective"—
"out of the person himself"—"or lyric" nature of his own verse: "'Leaves
of Grass,' must be called *not* objective, but altogether *subjective*."[89] The
"great psalm of the republic," according to the 1855 Preface (*LG*, iv), is
"to be indirect and not direct or descriptive or epic."[90] Direct address, as
J. P. Warren notes, is an important feature of Whitman's style in the early
Leaves.[91] An "I" addressing a "you" is the prototypical pronominal shape
of lyric discourse generally and characteristic of much nonnarrative
verse in the (Hebrew) Bible. And lyric's capacities to enfold multiple
and even opposing voices, viewpoints or ideas turns out to be crucial
to Whitman's politics of inclusion, what D. S. Reynolds describes as
Whitman's "long-term strategy" of "resolving thorny political issues

---

86 *Solitary Singer*, 164; cf. Crawley, *Structure*, 79 ("it is fundamental... to remember
    that he [Whitman] was a lyric poet").
87 Allen, *Solitary Singer*, 164. K. M. Price identifies "A Child's Reminiscence" (1859;
    later, "Out of the Cradle Endlessly Rocking") as Whitman's first poem "based on a
    narrative structure" (*Whitman and Tradition* [New Haven: Yale University, 1990], 63).
88 *CW*, III, 45.
89 The pastiche of quotations comes from *CW* IX, 228 and *NUPM* IV, 1432—the latter
    is from a manuscript scrap that Grier dates between 1856 and 1858.
90 T. J. Rountree explains one part of Whitman's "indirect expression" as his attempt
    "to make the reader become active by *reciprocating to his poems*" ("Walt Whitman's
    Indirect Expression and Its Application to 'Song of Myself,'" *PMLA* 73/5 [1958],
    550–51; cf. B. Erkkila, (*Whitman the Political Poet* (New York/Oxford: Oxford
    University, 1989]), 90–91). In R. Greene's analysis this is lyric's ritual dimension in
    which the auditor turns collaborator, lyric's capacity "to superpose the subjectivity
    of the scripted speaker on the reader" (*Post-Petrarchism: Origins and Innovations
    of the Western Lyric Sequence* [Princeton: Princeton University, 1991], 5–6; for
    his analysis of Whitman, see pp. 133–52). It also seems possible that indirect
    as opposed to direct and epic should be glossed as subjective, i.e., not a direct
    statement of objective fact but an observation "out of the person" for consideration
    by other persons.
91 "Style" in *A Companion to Walt Whitman* (ed. D. D. Kummings; London: Blackwell,
    2006), 377–91, esp. 382.

by linguistic fiat."[92] So famously, "Do I contradict myself?/ Very well then…. I contradict myself;/ I am large…. I contain multitudes" (*LG*, 55). And such capacities are well exploited by biblical poems (e.g., "We have transgressed and have rebelled: thou hast not pardoned," Lam 3:42).[93] The very genres that populate *Leaves of Grass*, then, are perhaps not happened upon entirely innocently, as they are also very much the kinds of poetry one finds in "Isaiah, Job, the Psalms"—and in another late essay Whitman even references "the Hebrew lyricists."[94] Indeed, as B. Perry remarks, in the English Bible Whitman found "precisely that natural stylistic variation between the 'terrific,' the 'gentle,' and the 'inferior' parts" that he so desired, and there, too, "were lyric fragments, of consummate beauty, embedded in narrative or argumentative passages."[95]

The period of the "New Bible" provides yet additional evidence for the influence of the Bible on Whitman's ever evolving conception of *Leaves of Grass*, especially of the 1860 edition.[96] An 1859 unpublished manuscript reads as follows:

> [illeg.] The greatest thing is to make a nation's poems.— The grand true making of the Poems of a nation would combine all those that has belongs to the Iliad of Homer and the Jewish ^Hebrew^ Canticles called the

---

92 "Politics and Poetry: *Leaves of Grass* and the Social Crisis of the 1850s" in *The Cambridge Companion to Walt Whitman* (ed. E. Greenspan; Cambridge: Cambridge University, 1995), 70.

93 The second clause (the second line of the original Hebrew couplet) is strongly disjunctive (viz. "*but* thou…."). The conventional theology of the day presumed that once wrongs are confessed the deity should forgive (or "pardon"), and thus the second clause is uttered in complaint, critical of Yahweh's failure to grant such "pardon." For details, see F. W. Dobbs-Allsopp, *Lamentations* (IBC; Louisville: Westminster-John Knox, 2002), 122–25. On lyric's congenial disposition to sponsoring contradictory voicings, see broadly Dobbs-Allsopp, "Idea of Lyric," esp. 178–214 (with references to other literature); "Poetic Discourse and Ethics" in *Dictionary of Scripture and Ethics* (eds. J. Green et al. Grand Rapids, Baker, 2011), 597–600; and on Lamentations specifically, Dobbs-Allsopp, *Lamentations*, 12–20, 24–27.

94 "Poetry To-day in America" in *PW* II, 486 (originally published as "The Poetry of the Future," *NAR* 132 [1881], 195–210).

95 *Walt Whitman*, 96. Earlier Perry reports that Whitman "frequently" noted "his interweaving of lyric with descriptive passages" (and compared this to the "alternating aria and the recitative of an oratorio," p. 86).

96 H. J. Levine offers a compelling reading of the 1855 "I celebrate myself" in light of Whitman's own articulated "New Bible" aspirations ("'Song of Myself' as Whitman's American Bible," *Modern Language Quarterly* 48/2 [1987], 145–61).

Bible and of S̶k̶hakespear's delineation of feudal heroism and personality and would carry ^all the influences o̶f̶ b̶o̶t̶h̶ and all that branches from them for thousands of years.—[97]

The aspiration articulated here, that Whitman's "Poems of a nation" should include all that belongs to the "^Hebrew Canticles," correlates well with the opening sentiment of "The Bible as Poetry":

> If the time ever comes when Iconoclasm does its extremest in one direction against this Book, the collection must still survive in another, and dominate just as much as hitherto, or more than hitherto, through its divine and primal poetic structure. To me, that is the living and definitive element-principle of the work, evolving everything else. Then the continuity; the oldest and newest Asiatic utterance and character, and all between, holding together, like the apparition of the sky, and coming to us the same. Even to our Nineteenth Century here are the fountain heads of song.[98]

Here Whitman clearly articulates his sense of carrying on the biblical tradition through his own poetry, the kind of combining he writes about in the 1859 "Poems of a nation" manuscript—"Could there be any more opportune suggestion, to the current popular writer and reader of verse, what the office of poet was in primeval times—and is yet capable of being, anew, adjusted entirely to the modern?"[99] And then toward the end of "The Bible as Poetry," the image of "all that branches from them [the Bible, etc.] for thousands of years" gets "resolved into" a related image, that of "a collection of old poetic lore [the Bible], which, more than any one thing else, has been the axis of civilization and history through thousands of years—and except for which this America of ours, with its polity and essentials, could not now be existing."

---

97 Entitled, "Poems of a nation," now in the Charles E. Feinberg Collection of the Papers of Walt Whitman, Library of Congress (Notes and Notebooks, 1847–1891 mss18630, box 40; reel 25, https://www.loc.gov/item/mss1863001283). Thanks to Amanda Zimmerman from the Rare Books and Special Collections Division of the Library of Congress for tracking down this manuscript fragment for me.

98 In a slightly edited form, this is shifted to the end of the essay in *November Boughs* (45–46).

99 This is also a sentiment that Whitman poeticizes in the late poem, "Old Chants" (*Truth* 10 [19 March 1891], 11), viz. "(Of many debts incalculable,/ Haply our New World's chiefest debt is to old poems.)" (lines 6–7).

Both the 1859 "Poems of a nation" manuscript and "The Bible as Poetry" also seem to have in common Whitman's resistance to the notion of originality, "at least in the superficial sense." Miller explicates Whitman's understanding with reference to a draft of what was perhaps a self-review of *Leaves of Grass*, though the manuscript apparently is now lost.[100] Whitman explains, in reference to his poems, that "there is nothing actually new only an accumulation or fruitage or carrying out these new occasions and requirements."[101] Miller even suggests that Whitman "seems to be thinking here of something like Ecclesiastes' claim that there is no new thing under the sun."[102] Miller is perhaps nearer the mark than he supposes. The language, as I assume Miller means to imply, is close to the KJB of Eccl 1:9 ("and there is no new thing under the sun"). But what is more, in *Specimen Days & Collect* (1882) Whitman entitles a paragraph-long section "Little or Nothing New, After All," again an apparent allusion to Eccl 1:9.[103] And the paragraph elaborates yet another rendition of Whitman's notion of originality:

> How small were the best thoughts, poems, conclusions, except for a certain invariable resemblance and uniform standard in the final thoughts, theology, poems, &c., of all nations, all civilizations, all centuries and times. Those precious legacies—accumulations! They come to us from the far-off—from all eras, and all lands—from Egypt, and India, and Greece, and Rome—and along through the middle and later ages, in the grand monarchies of Europe—born under far different institutes and conditions from ours—but out of the insight and inspiration of the same old humanity—the same old heart and brain—the same old countenance yearningly, pensively, looking forth. What we have to do to-day is to receive them cheerfully, and to give them ensemble, and a modern American and democratic physiognomy.[104]

The Bible is not mentioned explicitly here but it is surely implied, viz. "from all eras, and all lands." As Zweig observes, Whitman's famous catalogues in general are highly symbolic statements as well: "a random list is, by definition, merely a sample of an unspoken list

---

100 *Collage of Myself*, 87–88. The manuscript is cited by Miller as printed in *CW* 9:12.
101 Miller, *Collage of Myself*, 87. Cf. *LG*, 24: "These are the thoughts of all men in all ages and lands, they are not original with me."
102 Ibid., 88.
103 See Bergquist, "Walt Whitman and the Bible," 285.
104 *CPW*, 336.

containing everything."[105] And by way of confirmation, the paragraph itself is formed from parts of two paragraphs that were originally a part of a series of connected paragraphs in *Two Rivulets* (1876), gathered under the general heading, "Thoughts for the Centennial."[106] Not two paragraphs later in *Two Rivulets* "the holy Bible itself" is included in a long list of literary contributions from "foreign countries," ancient as well as contemporary, in which "each has contributed after its kind, directly or indirectly, at least one great undying Song, to help vitalize and increase the valor, wisdom, and elegance of Humanity, from the points of view attain'd by it up to date."[107] The emphasis here is slightly different but the underlying sensibility is the same as Whitman's other variations on his theme of originality.[108] And Miller himself shows that this take on originality can be traced back into the Preface to the 1855 *Leaves* (e.g., "The greatest poet forms the consistence of what is to be from what has been and is," *LG*, vi) and perhaps even earlier.[109] One of the chief bequests of nineteenth-century philology was a greatly increased appreciation for history and the present's ineluctable debt to the past, which Whitman's sense of "originality" (as Miller develops it) must grow out of and which Whitman will have absorbed from among other sources his reading of Bunsen, Schele de Vere, and the like.[110] And the notebooks show that his catalogues of literary and religious

---

105 *Walt Whitman*, 248–49.

106 (Camden, New Jersey: Author's Edition, 1876), 15–22.

107 *Two Rivulets*, 16. The two paragraphs relevant here are reprinted in a slightly reedited form in *Specimen Days* under the section title, "Lacks and Wants Yet" (*PW*, II, 533–34).

108 A similar list appears in the late poem "Old Chants," only with explicit mention of the Bible: "The Biblic books and prophets, and deep idyls of the Nazarene," (line 11). Note also the inclusion of "Syria's" in this rejected line from another late poem, "Death's Valley" (a response to a painting about Ps 23:4): "Syria's, India's, Egypt's, Greece's, Rome's" (from a manuscript entitled "Aye, well I know 'tis ghastly to descend," http://hdl.loc.gov/loc.mss/ms004014.mss18630.00626. Here, too, there is no question of the Bible's (at least belated) inclusion in Whitman's mind among "the ancientest humanity."

109 *Collage of Myself*, 88–90.

110 For example, here is Schele de Vere: "With these great religions, Europe owes to Asia every one of those mighty impulses, that, from time to time, have given fresh life to sinking empires, or new hopes to despairing nations" (*Outlines of Comparative Philology*, 94). Cf. Whitman's reference to the "comparative method" in *NUPM* IV, 1519.

forebears routinely include the Bible. This outline for a "Poem of Wise Books" from the "Dick Hunt" notebook (1856/57) is typical:

Poem of Wise Books

Poem of the Library—(bring in all about the few leading books.

Literature of Egypt,

Assyria

Persia

Hindostan

Palestine

Greece—Pythagoras Plato—Socrates—Homer—Iliad Odyssey

Rome,—Virgil

Germany—Luther

Christ   Bible   Shakespeare   Emerson Rousseau—("Social Contract")

So here is another place where there is confidence that the perspective of "The Bible as Poetry" is not (only) a late, retrospective (re)framing, but reflects a perception long held by Whitman.

The Bible and the Birth of (Whitman's) Free Verse

I close with some reflections on what may be Whitman's most startling revelation in "The Bible as Poetry," his awareness of the unmetered and unrhymed nature of biblical Hebrew poetry via de Sola Mendes, to whom he attributes the following: "rhyming was not a characteristic of Hebrew poetry at all. Metre was not a necessary mark of poetry. Great poets discarded it; the early Jewish poets knew it not."[111] I describe this awareness as "startling" because even though there were nineteenth-century biblical scholars (as also in previous eras) who thought of biblical poetry as unmetered, the question continued to be debated

---

111 Cf. Posey, "Whitman's Debt," 151, n. 24.

throughout the twentieth and now into the twenty-first century.[112] R. Lowth in his field-founding *Lectures on the Sacred Poetry of the Hebrews* from the middle of the eighteenth century frankly admits his inability to reconstruct Hebrew meter, but he presumes its presence nonetheless since he could no more imagine poetry without meter than a world older than what the Bible represented.[113] He does end up stretching received notions of meter such that later scholars (e.g., J. G. Herder) can begin to imagine the idea of biblical poetry being nonmetrical. Allen's understated reminder (some fifty years after Whitman's own comment) with regard to the putative newness of Whitman's "free" rhythms (i.e., his free verse)—namely, that "the truth of the matter" is that these rhythms "are not new, since they are, to go no farther back, at least as old as Hebrew poetry"[114]—was a position on biblical poetry that would not

---

112 E.g., M. Stuart, *A Hebrew Chrestomathy* (Andover: Codman Press, 1829), 193–94 (Stuart's *Chrestomathy* was eventually included [minus the Hebrew text] at the end of his translation of the *Hebrew Grammar of Gesenius* (ed. Roediger; trans. M. Stuart; Andover: Allen, Morrill, and Wardwell, 1846], 352). George Wither (1588–1667 CE) is an outstanding example of a premodern who recognized the nonmetrical nature of biblical verse: "The *Hebrews* are full of variety in their *Numbers*, and take great liberty in their *Verses*. For as *Marianus Vićlorius* reports, they are not always measured out by the same Number or quality of Syllables, as the *Greeke* or *Latine Verses* are" (*A Preparation to the Psalter* [London: Nicholas Okes, 1619], 59). For a recent overview of the question of meter in biblical poetry, see D. R. Vance, *The Question of Meter in Biblical Hebrew Poetry* (Lewiston: Edwin Mellen, 2001).

113 R. Lowth, *Lectures on the Sacred Poetry of the Hebrews* (2 vols.; trans. G. Gregory; London: J. Johnson, 1787; reprinted in *Robert Lowth (1710–1787): The Major Works*, vols. 1–2 [London: Routledge, 1995]).

114 *American Prosody*, 220; cf. G. W. Allen, "Biblical Analogies for Walt Whitman's Prosody," *Revue Anglo-Americaine* 6 (1933), 490–507, at 491; Posey, "Whitman's Debt," 151, 168; Hartman, *Free Verse*, 90. The truth, of course, is that such "free" rhythms—nonmetrical verse—are attested even earlier than the Bible, as they are characteristic of ancient Levantine (e.g., Ugaritic), Mesopotamian, and Egyptian poetry as well (e.g., D. Wesling and E. Bollobaś, "Free Verse" in *NPEPP*, 425; G. B. Cooper, "Free Verse" in *PEPP*). Allen also stresses in his comments here that Whitman's verse (and by extension free verse more generally) is not entirely "free" either. Here it will suffice to direct readers to B. H. Smith's discussion of free verse in which she too emphasizes the common misapprehension of freedom when directed at nonmetrical verse (*Poetic Closure: A Study of How Poems End* [Chicago: University of Chicago, 1968], 84–95). As she observes, "the distinction between metrical verse and free verse is a relative, not an absolute, one" (p. 87).

be explicitly theorized by biblical scholars for another thirty years.[115] It is above all the conscious eschewing of rhyme and meter in a dominantly parallelistic type of verse that has most suggested to Whitman scholars over the years the poet's prosodic debt to the KJB, an English prose translation of the Bible that manifestly lacks rhyme and meter. The presumption is most conveniently tracked in the many biographies of Whitman, from Perry to Loving. Loving's statement is both summative and illustrative:

> Probably Bliss Perry, like Allen a biographer of Whitman, was right when he determined that Whitman's main model for his new prosody was the English Bible. "Here," Perry wrote, "was precisely the natural stylistic variation between the 'terrific,' the 'gentle,' and the 'inferior' parts, so desired by William Blake.... The parallelism which constituted the peculiar structural device of Hebrew poetry gave the English of the King James version a heightened rhythm without destroying the flexibility and freedom natural to prose. In this strong, rolling music, the intense feeling, these concrete words expressing primal emotions in daring terms of bodily sensations, Whitman found the charter for the book he wished to write."[116]

The earliest published reference linking Whitman's rhyme-less rhythm to the (English) Bible is made by R. Buchanan in 1867: "In about ten thousand lines of unrhymed verse, very Biblical in form, and showing indeed on every page the traces of Biblical influence, Walt Whitman professes to sow the first seeds of an indigenous literature...."[117] Around the same time W. M. Rossetti was in the process of putting together a volume of selections from Whitman's

---

115 B. Hrushovski [Harshav], "On Free Rhythms in Modern Poetry" in *Style in Language* (ed. T. Sebeok; 1960), 173–90; cf. "Prosody, Hebrew" in *Ecy Jud* (1971–72), 13: 1200–03. And now see in detail, F. W. Dobbs-Allsopp, "The Free Rhythms of Biblical Hebrew Poetry" in *On Biblical Poetry*, 95–177 (note esp. the opening section entitled, "Through Whitman's Eyes," 95–99).

116 Loving, *Song of Himself*, 197. Loving is quoting B. Perry, *Walt Whitman: His Life and Work* (Boston: Houghton Mifflin, 1906), 96. Posey surveys the earliest scholarship on this question, citing no less than eighteen different reviewers/scholars (including Perry) who call attention to the rhythmic kinship between Whitman and the Bible prior to Allen's first study ("Whitman's Debt," 142–47).

117 "Walt Whitman," *The Broadway* 1 (November 1867), 188—5, https://whitmanarchive.org/criticism/reviews/drum/anc.00065.html. Cf. R. Buchanan, *David Gray and Other Essays* (London, 1868), 207.

poems for a British audience.[118] In his "Prefatory Notice" to the volume, Rossetti observes that "a certain echo of the old Hebrew poetry may even be caught" in Whitman's *Leaves*.[119] W. D. O'Connor in an earlier review of the 1867 *Leaves* referenced "the poetic diction of the Hebraic muse."[120] And Whitman himself in a never-published manuscript he offered to Rossetti to use as the "Introduction" to the latter's volume—passing it off as O'Connor's work—immediately calls attention to the "the form of these verses, not only without rhyme, but wholly regardless of the customary verbal melody & regularity so much labored after by modern poets," and then some pages later also refers to himself as a "man" whose "interior & foundation quality... is Hebraic, Biblical, mystic."[121] Triangulating from these several observations, it seems likely that already by 1867 (well before "The Bible as Poetry" essay from 1883) Whitman was aware of biblical poetry's leading prosodic characteristics, namely, its lack of rhyme and meter.

In fact, Whitman was hyper-conscious of his decision to elaborate a rhythmical style free of "arbitrary and rhyming meter" and the break with the poetic norms of the day that this entailed. He argued repeatedly and explicitly throughout his life on behalf of his own unrhymed and unmeasured "new American poetry." This begins already in the immediate aftermath of his first trial experiments with such rhyme-less poetry. In an 1850 letter to the editor of the *National Era*, Whitman notes that "poetry exists independent of rhyme."[122] His

---

118 See letters 161, 167, and 169 collected in W. M. Rossetti, *Rossetti Papers: 1862–1870* (London: Sands & Co., 1903); Allen, *Solitary Singer*, 382–87; *NUPM* IV, 1497. Rossetti's edition came out in 1868: Poems by Walt Whitman (London: John Camden Hotten, Piccadilly, 1868), https://whitmanarchive.org/published/books/other/rossetti.html.

119 Poems by Walt Whitman, 6.

120 "Walt Whitman," *The New York Times* (2 December 1866), 2., https://whitmanarchive.org/criticism/reviews/lg1867/anc.00064.html.

121 *NUPM* IV, 1498, 1501. The same ideas co-occur a few years later (February, 1874), though in closer proximity, on leaves 7 and 8 of an unpublished article Whitman wanted Burroughs to publish under his name ("Is Walt Whitman's Poetry Poetical?", *NUPM* IV, 1518, 1519): "discarding exact metre and rhyme, (not discarding rhythm rhythm at all" and "The divine immortal Hebraic poems."

122 The letter appeared on 21 November 1850 (reprinted in Silver, "Whitman in 1850," 314).

early notebooks contain similar notices (e.g., "a perfectly transparent plate-glassy style, artless, with no ornaments"[123]), and this aspiration for a non-rhyming kind of verse is made explicit in the following lines from "I celebrate myself":

> Loafe with me on the grass.... loose the stop from your throat,
>
> Not words, not music or rhyme I want.... not custom or lecture, not even the best,
>
> Only the lull I like, the hum of your valved voice. (*LG*, 15)

It is also articulated in the 1855 Preface ("poetic quality is not marshaled in rhyme or uniformity or abstract addresses to things," *LG*, v; cf. iii, vi) and its later poeticized versions (e.g., "Rhymes and rhymers pass away," *LG* 1856, 194), for example. One of Whitman's most explicit statements on the topic comes in *Two Rivulets* (1876): "the truest and greatest poetry, (while subtly and necessarily always rhythmic, and distinguishable easily enough,) can never again, in the English language, be expressed in arbitrary and rhyming meter, any more than the greatest eloquence, or the truest power and passion."[124] The page layout in *Two Rivulets* features poems on the top half of the page and prose on the bottom half, the two being separated by a wavy horizontal line. In this instance the two poems, "Wandering at Morn" and "An Old Man's Thought of School" (presented on the top halves of pp. 28 and 29; see Fig. 9), exemplify the kind of "always rhythmic" but nonmetrical verse for which Whitman is advocating.

---

123 From "Rules for Composition", https://whitmanarchive.org/published/books/other/rossetti.html; cf. *NUPM* I,132–33 (from "I know a rich capitalist," https://whitmanarchive.org/manuscripts/notebooks/transcriptions/nyp.00129.html). This aesthetic is consistent with Whitman's art (e.g., Silver, "Whitman in 1850," 305–06) and music (e.g., Silver, "Whitman in 1850," esp. 304–05, 314–16) theory from the early 1850s.

124 (Camden, New Jersey, 1876), 29.

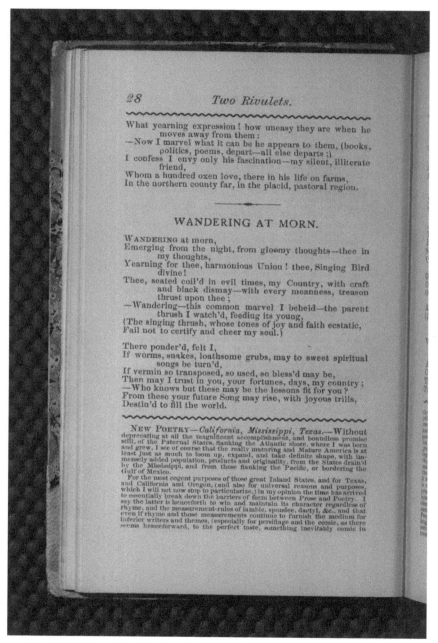

Fig. 9: P. 28 from *Two Rivulets* (Camden, New Jersey, 1876). Showing poetry and prose divided by a wavy line running across the middle of the page. Public domain.

The statement in "The Bible as Poetry," then, is of a piece with Whitman's thinking about his free verse since the early 1850s. In emphasizing the kindred nature of biblical poetic prosody in that essay, Whitman's chief aim was to lend authority to his own prosodic practice and not so much to identify the Bible as a source for that practice. That the latter is also probable, as noted, has been widely observed from early on, with parallelism and the reiterative play that parallelism sponsors and stages being among the readiest signs of this rhythmic debt.[125] Stovall ties Whitman's ideas about "the free growth of metrical laws" (*LG*, v; and one might add, the very form of his free verse itself) to Emerson's contention in "The Poet" that "it is not metres, but a metre-making argument that makes a poem."[126] Emerson read Lowth as an undergraduate and does not find his way to unclogging the "free step" of unrhymed and unmetered verse without having encountered Lowth.[127] And thus whatever the Emersonian influence on Whitman's prosodic theory and practice, this, too, ultimately derives (in part) from Lowth and the Bible. And in the case of the Bible's lack of rhyme, more specifically, there is no question that Whitman also knew this, and knew it fairly early. In a marginal note to a clipping about John Milton from "the summer of 1849" (or later), there is the following: "What is in the Bible had better not be paraphrased. The Bible is indescribably

---

125 Even for a scholar like B. Erkkila, who (rightly in my view) thinks there is more to Whitman's prosody than biblically-based parallelism and repetition (*Political Poet*, 332, n. 26), nevertheless recognizes the important role of parallelism and repetition in Whitman's free-verse prosody (*Political Poet*, esp. 87–91). For a general characterization of the place of iteration and recurrence—parallelism is essentially a trope of iteration—in free-verse prosodies more broadly, see Dobbs-Allsopp, *On Biblical Poetry*, esp. 109–10 (with bibliography).

126 Stovall, *Foreground*, 298. R. W. Emerson, "The Poet" in *The Complete Essays and Other Writings of Ralph Waldo Emerson* (ed. B. Atkinson; New York: Modern Library, 1950), 319–41, at 323.

127 See R. D. Richardson, *Emerson: The Mind on Fire* (Berkeley: University of California, 1995), 11–14; J. Engell, "Robert Lowth, Unacknowledged Legislator" in *The Committed Word: Literature and Public Values* [University Park: Pennsylvania State University, 1999], 119–40, at 124–25. Another likely source of inspiration was Wordsworth, also influenced by Lowth (Engell, "Robert Lowth," 124, 131–32, 135), who famously pushed against the idea of a hard and fast difference between verse and prose, see esp. G. Schmidgall, "Wordsworth and Whitman" in *Containing Multitudes: Walt Whitman and the British Literary Tradition* (Oxford/New York: Oxford University, 2014), 200–51—Wordsworth also speaks prominently about "the Poet" in his famous Preface to the *Lyrical Ballads*.

perfect—putting it in rhyme, would that improve it or not?"[128] The presumption here must be that the Bible is unrhymed in Whitman's view.[129]

The timing of Whitman's break with the metrical tradition can be identified precisely. It happens on 22 March 1850 when he published "Blood-Money" in a supplemental issue of the *New York Daily Tribune*.[130] This is one of four poems Whitman writes in the spring and early summer of 1850. All are political poems (as is so much of Whitman's mature poetry), giving vent to his ire over the Compromise of 1850 that included passage of a Fugitive Slave law, permitted slavery into portions of the newly acquired western territories, and generally left the slavery issue itself unsettled. Whitman's resort to poetry is curious. No doubt the impetus is multifaceted. Klammer, for example, notices that Whitman lacked ready access to an editorial venue at the time, and thus could not fallback on his familiar journalistic mode of discourse (apparently he was not freelancing either).[131] Many see Emerson's ideas throughout the first edition of *Leaves of Grass*, especially in the form of his essay, "The Poet."[132] Loving points out that Emerson's second visit

---

128 The clipping is from: "Christopher under Canvas," *Edinburgh Magazine* 65 (1849), 763–66, https://whitmanarchive.org/manuscripts/marginalia/transcriptions/ duk.00015.html; image: tps://whitmanarchive.org/manuscripts/marginalia/ figures/duk.00015.002.jpg. Whitman emphasizes his perspective in another comment: "The difference between perfect originality and second-hand originality is the difference between the Bible and Paradise Lost," https://whitmanarchive. org/manuscripts/marginalia/figures/duk.00015.004.jpg. Stovall discusses the clipping and note in *Foreground*, 127–28. He concludes that Whitman's annotations are from that summer or "probably later."

129 Many of the early reviews connected Whitman's long, unmetered and unrhymed line with that of Martin Farquhar Tupper (see M. Cohen, "Martin Tupper, Walt Whitman, and the Early Reviews of Leaves of Grass," *WWQR* 16/1 [1998], 23–31)." That Tupper modeled his line on the Bible is and was widely acknowledged, and as a consequence an early awareness on Whitman's part of the unmetered nature of biblical verse may be posited on the basis of the association with Tupper's poetry. One early reviewer explicitly likens Whitman's "wild, irregular, unrhymed, almost unmetrical" lines to those of Tupper's "or some of the Oriental writings" (George Eliot, "Transatlantic Latter-Day Poetry," *The Leader* 7 [7 June 1856], 547–48, https://whitmanarchive.org/criticism/reviews/lg1855/anc.00027.html). Whitman reprinted this review in the second issue of the 1855 *Leaves* and again in the 1856 edition (381-83) (Stovall, *Foreground*, 256).

130 P. 1, https://whitmanarchive.org/published/periodical/poems/per.00089.

131 *Emergence*, 75.

132 Esp. Stovall, *Foreground*, 296–303. Whitman could have heard Emerson's lecture on "The Poet" as early as 5 March 1842 (in New York City; see Stovall, *Foreground*,

to lecture in the New York City area coincided with the publication of Whitman's two March 1850 poems.[133] And certainly Emerson featured among the readings perused during Whitman's intense period of self-study (1845–52 in particular), as did other materials from leading British literary magazines and journals (especially focused on poetry), and even some modest bits of biblical scholarship.[134] It also has become more apparent that in the early 1850s Whitman (however consciously) was experimenting with various forms and genres of written discourse. As the early notebooks make clear, the form that *Leaves* would eventually take (poetry) was not decided on until relatively late. Those same notebooks include, for example, notes towards lectures of various sorts, one of Emerson's favored modes of discourse.[135] Whitman's brother, George, remembered that in the early 1850s Whitman "had an idea he could lecture" and wrote what Whitman's mother called "'barrels' of lectures."[136] If so, most have not survived—though there is his lecture, "Art and Artists," given on 31 March 1851 before the Brooklyn Art Union.[137] He also takes up again his occasional freelancing in 1851 (e.g., the several "Letters from Paumanok"). Loving reports on Whitman's efforts, in 1850, to sell a serialized novel ("The Sleeptalker"), which evidently was rejected,[138] and now Z. Turpin has recovered the serialized novella, "Life and Adventures of Jack Engle," which was published anonymously by Whitman in six installments from 14 March to 18 April

---

284–85; Loving, *Song of Himself*, 59–60. And he had certainly encountered the essay by the time (1854) he penned the passage entitled "The Poet" in the "Poem incarnating the mind" notebook, https://whitmanarchive.org/manuscripts/figures/loc_jc.01674.jpg.

133 Loving, *Song of Himself*, 156–60; and more broadly, J. Loving, *Emerson, Whitman, and the American Muse* (Chapel Hill: University of North Carolina, 1982).

134 Stovall, *Foreground*, esp. 184–88, 265–81; 282–305. Whitman himself remembered this general period (1847–54) as the expanded run-up to the 1855 *Leaves* (*CPW*, 278).

135 C. C. Hollis emphasizes the "oratorical impulse" in *Leaves* in his study, *Language and Style in Leaves of Grass* (Baton Rouge/London: Louisiana State University, 1983).

136 H. L. Traubel et al (eds.), *In Re Walt Whitman* (Philadelphia: David McKay, 1893), 35.

137 Printed afterwards in the Brooklyn *Daily Advertiser* (3 April 1851). *UPP* I, 241–47.

138 Loving, *Song of Himself*, 162–64; cf. Z. Turpin, "Introduction to Walt Whitman's 'Life and Adventures of Jack Engle,'" *WWQR* 39/3 (2017), 225, 227–28. Whitman's letter to the editors of the *New York Sun* is dated to a time (17 June 1850) between the appearances of the summer poems from 1850, "The House of Friends" and "Resurgemus," which emphasizes, among other things, the variability of Whitman's writing projects at the time.

1852 in the Manhattan newspaper, the *Sunday Dispatch*.[139] And, of course, Whitman had published poetry before, as recently as the spring of 1848.[140]

The first of the four 1850 poems, "Song for Certain Congressmen" (2 March 1850),[141] like all of his other "juvenile" verse,[142] is entirely conventional—metered and apportioned in (twelve) rhymed stanzas:

> Beyond all such we know a term
>
>   Charming to ears and eyes,
>
> With it we'll stab young Freedom,
>
>   And do it in disguise;
>
> Speak soft, ye wily Dough-Faces—
>
>   That term is "compromise."

Then just twenty days later appears "Blood-Money":

> Of olden time, when it came to pass
>
> That the Beautiful God, Jesus, should finish his work on earth,
>
> Then went Judas, and sold the Divine youth,
>
> And took pay for his body.

The break from conventional metered poetry—and with all of Whitman's previous verse—could not be plainer. There is no meter or rhyme—this, as Loving notices, "is probably Whitman's first free-verse poem."[143] And

---

139 "Life and Adventures of Jack Engle: An Auto-Biography," *WWQR* 34/3 (2017), 262–357, https://whitmanarchive.org/criticism/wwqr/; cf. Turpin, "Introduction," 225–61. Whitman's notes for the story contained in a red notebook ("A schoolmaster," https://whitmanarchive.org/manuscripts/notebooks/transcriptions/loc.04588.html; *NUPM* I, 97–99; Grier dates the notebook to "as late as 1852" based on a clipping from the "Tribune" from March 1852) establish his authorship, see Turpin, "Introduction," 228–30.

140 "Mississippi at Midnight," *New Orleans Daily Crescent* (6 March 1848), 2, hive.org/published/periodical/poems/per.00063. Revised as "Sailing the Mississippi at Midnight," *CPW*, 374; *EPF*, 42–43.

141 *New York Evening Post* (2 March 1850), 2, https://whitmanarchive.org/published/periodical/poems/per.00004.

142 Cf. *UPP* I, 1–25, 30–31; *EPF*, 3–35, 42–43, 49–53.

143 Loving, *Song of Himself*, 153. The equivocation ("probably") is perhaps no longer required since the chronology of most of the early notebooks is now better understood, see Chapter Three.

the resulting *mis-en-page* is completely different (see Fig. 10)—the sixfold use of indentation to continue the longer, nonmetrical lines not only is contrary to conventional poetic practice but anticipates the "hanging indentation" that signals verse in the holographs of Whitman's notebooks and poetry manuscripts.[144] The poem is thematized around a biblical passage, Matthew 26–27, and is even provided with a close version of 1 Cor 11:27 ("Guilty of the Body and Blood of Christ") as an epigraph, as if to underscore the biblical turn taken in the poem—and here again strikingly different from the epigraph from *Webster's Dictionary* used in "Song for Certain Congressmen." And the poem is signed "Walter Whitman" (and not "Paumanok" or some other pseudonym), the same name the poet used in the copyright notice for the 1855 *Leaves* (*LG*, ii) and belatedly unveiled later in the volumes first poem ("Walt Whitman, an American," *LG*, 29).[145] The two poems that follow in the early summer of 1850, "The House of Friends" (14 June)[146] and "Resurgemus" (21 June),[147] are of a kind with "Blood-Money." The style of the three poems is still not that of the more mature "Walt" (*LG*, 29) Whitman of the 1855 *Leaves*. For example, the lines, though not metrical, remain mostly confined in length (though occasionally stretching beyond eight words),[148] enjambment is prevalent, and the rhythmic exploitation of parallelism is still nascent

---

144 This would seem to be a practice that emerges out of the mechanics of fitting type to the columns of newspapers. When the poem is reprinted in the New York Evening Dispatch ([30 April 1850], 1, http://nyshistoricnewspapers.org/lccn/sn83030390/1850-04-30/ed-1/seq-1/—even though the width of the column is essentially the same as initially, several new indentations are needed (lines 10, 13), and in one more words are included in the indented line (line 24). Zweig remarks that in these 1850 poems "Whitman is still a voice from the press" (*Walt Whitman*, 120). It is certainly true that part of the poet he becomes, down to the mechanics of setting type, owes something to his printerly sensibility.

145 Interestingly, when Whitman reprints the poem in *Specimen Days* he (intentionally?) misdates it (April, 1843) and signs it "Paumanok" (*CPW*, 372–73). And he needs no indentations since the wider page layout can comfortably accommodate the length of the lines, i.e., transposed from the narrow columns of a newspaper layout.

146 *New York Daily Tribune* (14 June 1850), 3, https://whitmanarchive.org/published/periodical/poems/per.00442.

147 *New York Daily Tribune* (21 June 1850), 3, https://whitmanarchive.org/published/periodical/poems/per.00088.

148 For example, the three lines in "Resurgemus" that contain more than eight words are taken into the 1855 *Leaves* without being combined with other material (*UPP* I, 27–30; ll. 1, 38, 46). In the 1855 *Leaves*, the sweet spot in terms of line-length is from eight to sixteen words per line (lines of these lengths each occur more than a *hundred* times, see Fig. 21 and discussion in Chapter Three).

(e.g., "Look forth, Deliverer,/ Look forth, First Born of the Dead,/ Over the tree-tops of Paradise," "Blood-Money," lines 15–17). And yet that these poems are the beginning that anticipates that style of a few years later nevertheless would seem to be equally obvious, especially now that the chronology of the early notebooks containing trial lines for the 1855 *Leaves* is better understood. The prominence in these poems of biblical themes, imagery, language, tropes, and characters has been well observed.[149] And yet perhaps what still needs emphasizing is the coincidence of Whitman's breaking into free verse while writing such highly biblicized poems and what this may imply about the impetus for such an "auspicious change."[150]

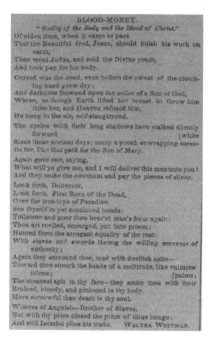

Fig. 10: "Blood-Money," the *New York Daily Tribune* (March 22, 1850), p. 1, https://whitmanarchive.org/published/periodical/poems/per.00089. Whitman's first nonmetrical poem. Cropped image courtesy of The Walt Whitman Archive, https://whitmanarchive.org/

149 E.g., Zweig, *Walt Whitman*, 117–21, 150–51; Erkkila, *Political Poet*, 54–59; Klammer, *Emergence*, esp. 77-83; Loving, *Song of Himself*, 152–60.
150 Loving, *Song of Himself*, 153.

Not unexpectedly, Allen comes closest to the diagnosis I have in mind, albeit offered in the name of parallelism and still confounded by the early (1847) (mis)dating of the "Talbot Wilson" notebook. He says of "Blood-Money" that Whitman "was already fumbling" for his "technique" of parallelism, the "basic verse structure" of *Leaves*, "but here [i.e. in 'Blood-Money'] he was paraphrasing both the thought and the prose rhythm of the New Testament (Matthew 26–27)."[151] Indeed, a close version of Matt 26:15 is distributed across lines 12–14 of the poem. Parallelism *per se* is at best embryonic in "Blood-Money," as Allen's follow-up comment clarifies: "He [Whitman] is experimenting with phrasal or clausal units; not yet 'thought rhythm' [i.e., parallelism]. But his arrangement of the verse is a step in that direction."[152] What I find acutely perceptive in Allen's comment here is his awareness that Whitman is "fumbling" after his style (broader than just his use of parallelism) as he collages language from the Bible, viz. "paraphrasing both the thought and the prose rhythm of the New Testament," and then massages it into the language of his poem, viz. "Again goes one, saying,/ What will ye give me...." That is, the "fumbling" consists of the adoption and adaptation of biblical language, style, and rhythm.

In fact, Allen's analysis may be sharpened by recalling the political dimension of this poem, as it is the combustible mixture of Bible and politics (in this specific instance) that join to ignite Whitman's fumbling toward a new rhymeless and meterless style of verse. "Blood-Money" is an angry poem. It is a direct response to Daniel Webster's famous "Seventh of March" address in the Senate in which the senator spoke against legislation prohibiting the extension of slavery into the western territories and in favor of a fugitive slave act.[153] The poem works in two movements (lines 1–8, 9–30). The first is shorter and dedicated to Whitman's poeticized (and much abbreviated) rendition of the story of Judas' betrayal of Jesus (Matthew 26–27). Time shifts to the present at the beginning of the second movement (lines 9–11) and another "Iscariot" (see line 30) looks to betray another man, a

---

151 *The New Walt Whitman Handbook* (New York: New York University, 1986), 219; cf. Loving, *Song of Himself*, 153.

152 Allen, *New Walt Whitman Handbook*, 219.

153 See Erkkila, *Political Poet*, 54–55; Klammer, *Emergence*, 76–79.

"Brother of Slaves" (line 28).[154] Whitman uses a close rendition of Matt 26:15 (lines 12–14) to emphasize the biblical paradigm as he redeploys it. Jesus, as "a Son of God" (line 6) and "First Born of the Dead" (line 16), is evoked as "Deliverer" (line 15) and "Witness" (line 28), on the one hand, and, on the other, is imagined as incarnate—the literal second coming so much proclaimed in the New Testament (e.g., John 14:3)—in a "hunted" fugitive slave: "thou bare'st man's form again" (line 19). This anticipates the poet's more famous embodiment of the "hounded slave" ("I am the hounded slave," *LG*, 39) and ventriloquism of black "Lucifer" in the 1855 *Leaves* (*LG*, 74).[155] The Christ-slave is hunted, imprisoned, and beaten (lines 20–27), leveraging imagery and language from the biblical story. The new "Iscariot" who "still... plies his trade" (line 30) in the last line of Whitman's political allegory is above all Webster, but also anyone who thinks and acts like Webster.

The reading of Matthew 26–27 elaborated in "Blood-Money" is avowedly political, informed by the politics of the Gospel story itself—"Not with thy price closed the price of thine image" (line 29). The break with conventional rhyme and meter is of a piece with this biblically inflamed politics. It comes literally out of the Bible— no rhyme, no meter there—and at the same time follows from the poet's biblically inspired political commitments. The connection between Whitman's poetics and politics has been astutely observed by B. Erkkila. Of "Whitman's free verse," she writes generally, it "originated from a similar desire to release humanity from the fetters

---

154 In the Hebrew Bible kinship language (e.g., son, father) often gets used with extended senses, e.g., "I am a brother to dragons," Job 30:29. Whitman plays on the Hebrew name Ahimoth (1 Chron 6:25) in "Resurgemus," where he glosses it as "brother of Death" (l. 4). He may also have Phil 2:7 in mind here: "and [Jesus] took upon him the form of a servant [Greek. δούλου], and was made in the likeness of men."

155 "How he informs against my brother and sister and takes pay for their blood" (*LG*, 74) even echoes the language ("brother") and larger theme of "Blood-Money." Also note the similarity between "they smite thee with their palms" and "they beat me violently over the head with their whip-stocks" (*LG*, 39). Whitman makes his poetic logic explicit a few lines later: "I do not ask the wounded person how he feels.... I myself become the wounded person,/ My hurt turns livid upon me as I lean on a cane and observe" (*LG*, 39). And there are many allusions to the Passion narratives of the Gospels (e.g., *LG*, 43).

of external form, political or artistic."[156] Whitman himself in the 1855 Preface makes explicit the potent "defiance" that might advance from "new free forms": "Of the traits of the brotherhood of writers savants musicians inventors and artists nothing is finer than silent defiance advancing from new free forms" (*LG*, vii). This is specifically true of "Blood-Money." Whitman's unmetered and unrhymed lines, as they break with convention, perform poetic acts of liberation that Webster's politics sought to foreclose. They are the poem's most tangible tokens of freedom. The breaking free from "yet continued bonds," whether those that bind the "hunted" (fugitive) slave or his "Brother," is enacted time and again across the surface of the poem in Whitman's free(d) verse(s).

Another outstanding example of this kind of biblical collage comes roughly a year later in Whitman's "Art and Artists" lecture, only this time the language is a paraphrastic riff on the creation narrative from Genesis 1:

> When God, according to the myth, finished Heaven and Earth — when the lustre of His effulgent light pierced the cold and terrible darkness that had for cycles of ages covered the face of the deep — when the waters gathered themselves together into one place and made the sea — and the dry land appeared with its mountains and its infinite variety of valley, shore and plain — when in the sweetness of that primal time the unspeakable splendor of the sunrise first glowed on the bosom of the earth — when the stars hung at night afar off in this most excellent canopy, the air, pure, solemn, eternal — when the waters and the earth obeyed the command to bring forth abundantly, the beasts of the field, the birds of the air and the fishes of the sea — and when, at last, the superb perfection, Man, appeared, epitome of all the rest, fashioned after the Father and Creator of all — then God looked forth and saw everything that he had made, and pronounced it good. Good because ever reproductive of its first beauty, finish and freshness. For just as the Lord left it remains yet the beauty of His work.[157]

This is prose, of course. Yet as Loving observes it is also "almost a free-verse poem."[158] To ramify just how much this "looks and sounds like

---

156 Erkkila, *Political Poet*, 86; cf. Loving, *Song of Himself*, 196.
157 *UPP* I, 242; cf. Allen, "Biblical Echoes," 306; Posey, "Whitman's Debt," 208; Bergquist, "Whitman and the Bible," 288.
158 Loving, *Song of Himself*, 171.

something belonging to the first *Leaves of Grass*" Loving even lineates
a portion of the paragraph, taking his cues from Whitman's dashes.[159]
Loving's last lined version of Whitman's phrasing is an incredibly close
rendition of Gen 1:31:

> Then God looked forth and saw everything that he had made, and
> pronounced it good. (Loving lineating Whitman)

> And God saw every thing that he had made, and, behold, it was very
> good. (Gen 1:31)

This is not an overly fanciful exercise on Loving's part. Whitman
collaged just as much (if not more) language material for his poems
from the prose of his early notebooks as from the trial verse lines
they also contained.[160] In fact, many prose sources were mined in this
fashion. And quite famously Whitman reworks the similarly rhythmic
and highly parallelistic prose of the 1855 Preface into verse starting
already with the 1856 "Poem of Many In One" (*LG* 1856, 181–201;
later "By Blue Ontario's Shore"). In fact, Allen in his assessment of
Whitman's "evolving" prosodic style specifically calls attention to
the 1855 Preface. Despite being "arranged as prose," Allen notes,
"the thought-units"—"often separated by periods"—and their
"rhythmical effect" are patent.[161] He cites the following passage as
emblematic:

> He sees eternity less like a play with a prologue and a denouement...
> he sees eternity in men and women... he does not see men and women
> as dreams or dots. Faith is the antiseptic of the soul... it pervades the
> common people and preserves them... they never give up believing and
> expecting and trusting. (*LG*, v)

Though a small slice, its kinship to the paragraph from the "Art and
Artists" lecture (absent the latter's biblical theme and using suspension
points instead of long dashes) is obvious. And some of this prose
Whitman does eventually turn into verse:

---

159 Ibid.
160 See esp. Miller, *Collage of Myself*, and Chapter Three below.
161 Allen, *New Walt Whitman Handbook*, 219–20.

He sees eternity less like a play with a prologue and denouement,

He sees eternity in men and women—he does not see men and women
as dreams or dots. (*LG* 1856, 189)

Interestingly, Whitman ends his "Art and Artists" lecture by quoting
a selection of lines from "Resurgemus," the maturest of the three
nonmetrical 1850 poems and the only one which (after revision) he
includes in the 1855 *Leaves* ("Suddenly out of its stale and drowsy lair,"
LG, 87). The poem in general well evidences Whitman's incipient use
of a biblical-styled parallelism. From the quoted lines alone several
sets of parallel lines stand out, all eventually get combined and recast
into longer, internally parallel lines of the kind that come to typify the
1855 *Leaves*:

"Resurgemus":	Those martyrs that hang from the gibbets,
	Those hearts pierced by the grey lead
=> *LG* (88):	Those martyrs that hang from the gibbets.... those hearts pierced by the gray lead
"Resurgemus":	They were purified by death, They were taught and exalted
=> *LG* (88):	They were purified by death.... They were taught and exalted[162]
"Resurgemus":	Not a grave of those slaughtered ones,
	But is growing its seed of freedom
=> *LG* (88):	Not a grave of the murdered for freedom but grows seed for freedom

In these instances, the language is not biblical (though plenty of
biblicisms abound in the poem, see Chapter Two), but the trope—
parallelism—is (see Chapter Four). The first two examples are

---

162 Notice that Whitman even retains the capitalization from the 1850 version, which
by the 1881 edition is normalized (p. 212).

of the synonymous variety of parallelism ubiquitous in *Leaves*, as Allen observed early on—"no one can doubt the parallelism of the synonymous form."[163] More significant, perhaps, because it is comparatively rarer in *Leaves*, is the final example, which exemplifies the antithetic "species" of parallelism, what Lowth originally described as obtaining "when a thing is illustrated by its contrary being opposed to it."[164] Such parallelism is especially prominent in the Bible's wisdom poetry, e.g., "The wise shall inherit glory: but shame shall be the promotion of fools" (Prov 3:35).

The coincidence of Whitman's breaking into free verse and "fumbling" (in prose and poetry) towards a prominently parallelistic and iterative rhythm while collaging and massaging biblical language and tropes is noteworthy and suggestive of the importance of the Bible—and no doubt also of Whitman's (secondary) reading about the Bible (recall Stovall dates Whitman's use of language specifically about "Hebrew poetry" to 1850 or thereabouts)—in this development. This is not to ignore, undervalue, or dismiss other significant contributing factors to the evolution of Walt Whitman as the poet of *Leaves of Grass*, whether it is his imbibing of Emerson (and other thinkers and artists), his ever hyper-political sensibility, especially focalized in 1850 on the issue of slavery, his writerly temperament, or the visual orientation of his printerly eye. To the contrary, such other factors were always impactful for Whitman's holistic sensibility. But the place of the Bible, at least in this one respect, his turn to a form of verse free of meter and rhyme—that is, to free verse, seems paramount. Or to put it more provocatively, it is difficult to imagine the specifically unrhymed, free-verse poetry of the 1855 *Leaves* evolving absent some kind of originary, mediating (and maybe also mediated) encounter with the Bible—"Blood-Money," after all, is "a sustained use of biblical allusion and line."[165] Like preference for the lyric, Whitman's evolution of a nonmetrical form of verse is among "those autochthonic bequests of Asia" that the poet seizes upon and

---

163 "Biblical analogies," 493.
164 *Lectures*, II, 45.
165 Erkkila, *Political Poet*, 55.

adjusts "entirely to the modern."[166] The chapters that follow attempt to flesh out still further dimensions of Whitman's poetic style that appear to bear the imprint of the Bible, especially in the build-up to the 1855 *Leaves*.[167]

---

166 Whitman, "The Bible as Poetry," 57.

167 Interestingly, the German free verse tradition also is indebted to biblical poetry's meter-less prosody. The German term *freie Rhythmen* (lit. "free rhythms") was coined to describe the poetry of Friederich Gottlieb Klopstock from the 1750s, which was very much influenced by the Bible, and especially the Psalms (see. K. M. Kohl, *Rhetoric, the Bible, and the Origins of Free Verse: The Early "Hymns" of Friedrich Gottlieb Klopstock* [Berlin/New York: de Gruyter, 1990]). And in France, *vers libre* first emerges at the end of the nineteenth century with a direct assist from Whitman. The birth date of *vers libre* is quite specific, 1886, when in a quick succession of issues of *La Vogue* edited by Gustave Khan are published Arthur Rimbaud's *Illuminations*, Jules Laforgue's translations from *Leaves* (e.g., from "Inscriptions," "O Star of Franc," and "A Woman Waits for Me") and ten of Laforgue's own free-verse poems (including "L'Hiver qui vient"), and Kahn's series "Intermède" (C. Scott, "Vers Libre" in *NPEPP*, 1344; B. Erkkila, *Whitman Among the French: Poet and Myth* [Princeton: Princeton University, 1980], 49–94). Indeed, Rimbaud's two earliest *vers-libre* poems, "Marine" and "Mouvement," likely date to 1874 and were directly influence by the translated selections of Whitman's verse published in two critical essays on Whitman from 1872 by E. Blémont ("La Poésie en Angleterre et aux Etats-Unis, III, Walt Whitman," *Renaissance Artistique et Littéraire* 7 [June 1872], 54–56; 11 [July 1872], 86–87; 12 [July 1872], 90–91) and T. Bentzon ("Un Poète américain, Walt Whitman; 'Muscle and Pluck Forever,'" *Revue des Deux Mondes* [1 June 1872], 565–82).

2. The Bible in Whitman: Quotation, Allusion, Echo

> In writing, give no second hand articles—no quotations—no authorities
> — Walt Whitman, "med Cophósis"notebook (ca. 1852–54)

In a 1934 article, G. W. Allen pioneered research into Walt Whitman's biblical quotations and allusions and to date his collection of a hundred and sixty "specific" biblical allusions, echoes, and quotations in Whitman's writings (prose and poetry), as well as an equally large number of more "general or inclusive allusions" to the Bible, remains the single largest published collection of its kind.[1] Articles published since Allen have added to the list of possible biblical allusions, as well as T. E. Crawley's more in-depth survey of Christ-Symbol imagery in *Leaves of Grass* (which Allen anticipates),[2] and there are several unpublished dissertations on the topic, which (among other things) tally hundreds of more possibilities, especially in *Leaves*, for which Allen counts less than two dozen echoes of Scripture. After offering preliminary observations made in light of scholarship on the topic since Allen, the chapter is dedicated to documenting Whitman's allusive practice in the immediate run-up to the 1855 *Leaves*, from the three unmetered 1850 poems through to the early notebooks and preliminary drafts of lines for the 1855 *Leaves*. At many points my discussion finds its way from these preparatory materials into the 1855 (and later editions of) *Leaves*.

---

1   "Biblical Echoes in Whitman's Works," *American Literature* 6 (1934), 302–15.
2   *The Structure of Leaves of Grass* (Austin: University of Texas, 1970). Crawley's "Appendix" (pp. 227–29) registers references (general and specific) to the Bible and the Christ-symbol in Whitman's writings, inclusive of some of the materials from the notebooks and unpublished manuscripts.

©2024 F. W. Dobbs-Allsopp, CC BY-NC 4.0   https://doi.org/10.11647/OBP.0357.03

Some Preliminary Observations

A number of observations may be offered already in light of the scholarship on biblical allusions in Whitman since Allen. There is much more to assessing and appreciating the allusive texture of an author's writing than just quantity, but the numbers are not insignificant either. Allen's sampling alone is warrant enough of Whitman's knowledge and use of the Bible, even allowing for contested interpretations. In point of fact, however, Allen misses as many allusions, echoes, and quotations as he identifies. The larger counts of M. N. Posey and B. L. Bergquist, who lists a hundred and forty-three biblical allusions in *Leaves* alone, for example, again allowing for disagreements (e.g., Posey's and Bergquist's lists agree only roughly half the time), are surely nearer the mark, and at the very least ramify the Bible's importance to Whitman. That is, the numbers alone argue the importance of the Bible as a source (of inspiration, language, imagery, etc.) for Whitman.

Second, the direct quotations from the Bible make clear Whitman's use of the KJB translation. This corroborates what may be inferred from the KJB's dominance in America during the nineteenth century and what is known from the bibles that can be tied directly to Whitman. And how Whitman quotes is of interest as well. As Bergquist notices there are times when it is clear that Whitman must have a Bible open before him, but just as often Whitman is content to paraphrase (and massage) from memory.[3] As an example of the former, Bergquist cites a Christmas editorial from the *Daily Eagle* which includes multiple exact quotes from the Christmas story in Luke (2:14; 2:10; 1:79).[4] In another example, the full quotation of Zech 13:6 (with citation noted) is offered as the headnote to "The House of Friends" (1850): "'And one shall say unto him, What are these wounds in thy hands? Then he shall answer, Those with which I was wounded in the house of my friends.'—Zechariah, xiii. 6."[5] An interesting example of Whitman's tendency to paraphrase comes in the version of Gen 1:31 (the "spinal meaning of the Scriptural text,")

---

3   "Whitman and the Bible," 106; cf. Posey, "Whitman's Debt," 37.
4   Bergquist, "Whitman and the Bible," 106–07.
5   *New York Daily Tribune* (14 June 1850), 3, https://chroniclingamerica.loc.gov/lccn/ sn83030213/1850-06-14/ed-1/seq-3/. KJB has "thine" where Whitman has "thy," an understandable mistake, if not already in some editions of the KJB, given the archaism of the second person pronouns (already archaic in 1611!).

in "A Memorandum for a Venture" from *Specimen Days*: "*God overlook'd all that He had made*, (including the apex of the whole—humanity—with its elements, passions, appetites,) *and behold, it was very good*"[6]—the last exact. Of interest is that Whitman revised the phrase "God overlook'd all that He had made" from an earlier "God weighed all that He had made,"[7] though (apparently) not going to the KJB to get the wording exactly right: "And God saw everything that he had made." What is significant here is Whitman's bent toward revision and tinkering, a characteristic that is amply manifested in the notebooks and unpublished poetry manuscripts and in Whitman's lifelong revision of *Leaves of Grass*. Most scholars do not deny the Bible's influence on Whitman, and yet there seems to be a strong want to emphasize the unconscious nature of the influence.[8] But everything that is known about Whitman's writing process, especially evident in the notebooks, is that conscious deliberation is integral to it—"a deliberate effort of construction."[9] Surely the Bible did exert unconscious influence on Whitman, perhaps a great deal. But most of what can be tracked, contrary to the impression, is Whitman's *conscious* use of the Bible (even when such consciousness leads Whitman to erase the biblical lineaments).

Another preliminary observation concerns Bergquist's statistical overview. Even if only taken heuristically, it is telling. Roughly the same amount of allusive referencing of the Bible appears in *Leaves* as in Whitman's other writings and does not vary so markedly chronologically or across genres—all trends contrary to Allen's impressions.[10] There is rough continuity across the writings as well in the uses to which Whitman puts his allusive discourse. Emblematic of this is the poet's proclivity (across all genres) to read the Bible as much against the grain of its meaning as with it.[11] Bergquist cites an example from one of Whitman's

---

6   *PW*, II, 497; cf. Bergquist, "Whitman and the Bible," 112–13.
7   See *PW*, II, 496, n. 181.
8   E.g., G. W. Allen, *A Reader's Guide to Walt Whitman* (Syracuse: Syracuse University, 1970), 167; M. Miller, *Collage of Myself* (Lincoln: University of Nebraska, 2010), 25.
9   Zweig, *Walt Whitman*, 206; cf. Posey, "Whitman's Debt," 22; Allen, *Reader's Guide*, 159.
10   Bergquist, "Whitman and the Bible," 78–83. Posey, too, sees less of a chronological disparity than Allen ("Whitman's Debt," esp. 23–24, n. 7). Cf. Allen, "Biblical Echoes," 302–03.
11   A similar point is stressed by E. S. Zitter, "Songs of the Canon: *Song of Solomon* and 'Song of Myself,'" *WWQR* 5 (1987), 8–15, 8; cf. Posey, "Whitman's Debt," 40, 54.

editorials ("American Workingmen, versus Slavery") in which "what is interesting" is that Whitman takes an obvious allusion to Gen 3:19 and "manipulates it so that the traditional 'curse of Adam' sounds like a most desirable aspect of our human heritage."[12] In *Leaves* Whitman famously and wonderfully reads "Lucifer" (from the Vulgate, *lucifer*; Hebrew *hêlēl* lit. "shining one")[13] against the mocking thrust of Isaiah's parody of a dirge for the king of Babylon (Isa 14:12). For Isaiah the figure is meant to be belittling, the fall from heaven (to the underworld—"to hell") symbolizing the king of Babylon's fall from favor (cf. Lam 2:1).[14] The conventional "how" of lament (Hebrew *ʾēk*) is turned into a mocking, gleeful gloat: "How art thou fallen from heaven, O Lucifer, son of the morning! how art thou cut down to the ground, which didst weaken the nations!" Whitman, however, redeems the figure of Lucifer, associating it with rebellion and admiring the "resistance to the all-powerful God."[15]

---

12 "Whitman and the Bible," 91—although Whitman's reading is probably closer to the "grain" of the original text than either he or Bergquist realizes, since one large ambition of the material in Genesis 1–11 more generally is to offer up mythic "explanations" as to why life and the world are the way that the Israelites and Judahites had come to know them to be (cf. M. S. Smith, *The Genesis of Good and Evil in the Garden of Eden* [Louisville: Westminster John Knox, 2019). Indeed, Whitman's trusting of his intuitive sensibilities about what he finds attractive in the Bible often makes his own interpretations both interesting and relevant contemporarily.

13 Traditionally rendered "Day Star" or the like (e.g., NRSV; cf. *HALOT*, 245), presuming the reference is to the planet Venus.

14 On the fallen-god myth, see H. R. Page, *The Myth of Cosmic Rebellion: A Study of Its Reflexes in Ugaritic and Biblical Literature* (SVT LXV; Leiden: Brill, 1996). Most recently, L. Quick ("*Hêlēl ben-Šaḥar* and the Chthonic Sun: A New Suggestion for the Mythological Background of Isa 14:12–15," *Vetus Testamentum* 68 [2018], 129–48) has argued that it is the nightly journey of the "sun" to the underworld that stands behind Isaiah's critique of Mesopotamian royal ideology in which the king was associated with the rising sun. Cf. Posey, "Whitman's Debt," 202.

15 See esp. E. Folsom, "Lucifer and Ethiopia: Whitman, Race, and Poetics Before the Civil War and After" in *A Historical Guide to Walt Whitman* (ed. D. S. Reynolds; Oxford/New York: Oxford University, 2000), 46–96, esp. 47–53; "Erasing Race: The Lost Black Presence in Whitman's Manuscripts" in *Whitman Noir: Black Americans and the Good Grey Poet* (ed. I. G. Wilson; Iowa City: University of Iowa, 2014), 20–49, esp. 24, 28–31 (Google Play); K. M. Price, "Whitman in Blackface" in *To Walt Whitman, America* (Chapel Hill: University of North Carolina, 2004), 9–36; M. Klammer, *Whitman, Slavery, and the Emergence of Leaves of Grass* (University Park: Pennsylvania State University, 1995), 95–100. Also see E. Folsom's online treatment of "The Sleepers," with special emphasis given to the material related to the poem in Whitman's notebooks (Folsom, "Whitman").

This is made clear, as E. Folsom notes, in a reference from the early and never published "Pictures":[16]

> And this black portrait—this head, huge, frowning, sorrowful,
>   ~~I think it~~—is Lucifer's portrait—the denied God's portrait,
>
> (But I do not deny him—though cast out and rebellious, he is my God
>   as much as any;)[17]

"Black Lucifer" is one of Whitman's most powerful and evocative images of slavery and one of the earliest instances in American poetry, according to Folsom and K. M. Price,[18] where a white poet gives over the narrative voice of a poem to a black character:

> Now Lucifer was not dead.... or if he was I am his sorrowful terrible
>   heir;
>
> I have been wronged.... I am oppressed.... I hate him that oppresses me,
>
> I will either destroy him, or he shall release me.
>
>
> Damn him! How he does defile me,
>
> How he informs against my brother and sister and takes pay or their
>   blood,
>
> How he laughs when I look down the bend after the steamboat that
>   carries away my woman.
>
> Now the vast dusk bulk that is the whale's bulk.... it seems mine,
>
> Warily, sportsman! though I lie so sleepy and sluggish, my tap is death.
>   (*LG*, 74)

---

16 "Lucifer and Ethiopia," 48–49.

17 *NUPM*, IV, 1300.

18 Folsom, "Lucifer and Ethiopia," 49, 51; "Erasing Race," 28; Price, *To Walt Whitman*, 17; cf. E. Folsom and K. M. Price, *Re-Scripting Walt Whitman: An Introduction to His Life and Work* (London: Blackwell, 2005), 17–40. Folsom also notes the play on "lucifer-matches" (or "loco-focos" as they were also known), providing a knowing incendiary understanding to Whitman's use of "Lucifer" ("Lucifer and Ethiopia," 49)—though the biblical lineage is primary ("I am a hell-name," *NUPM* IV, 1300, n. 80; Isa 14:15: "thou shalt be brought down to hell [Hebrew šĕʾôl].").

In a preliminary version of these lines, Whitman verbalizes his intent: "~~You~~ You ~~He~~ cannot speak for ~~your~~ ^him self, ~~slave,~~ ^negro —I lend ~~you~~ ^him my own ~~mouth~~ tongue."[19] And also in the "Poem incarnating the mind" notebook, after a section of writing that eventually gets worked into Whitman's sketch of the "hounded slave" (*LG*, 39), there is a canceled reference to Lucifer: "~~What Lucifer felt~~ ^cursed when ~~tumbling from Heaven~~."[20] In the material that precedes this comment the ventriloquizing is made visible as Whitman can be seen revising the voice of his discourse from third to first person (e.g., "~~His blood~~ ^My gore"). It perhaps merits underscoring that it is an image from that most un-racial (literally before race) of books, the Bible, that provokes Whitman's racial crossing in this instance and the compellingly humanitarian and empathetic portrayal of a black person ("Black Lucifer") that results.[21] And yet even when the biblical source informing Whitman's language is not in doubt, as with the figure of Black Lucifer, other potential influences are often also detectable. Whitman's collaging frequently involves imbrications of multiple resource materials. In this case, the impulse to use a biblical figure to animate the lived experiences of enslaved African-Americans is shared with the evocation of Black Samson in Henry Wadsworth Longfellow's poem "The Warning" (viz. "The poor, blind Slave,.../... There is a poor, blind Samson in this land," lines 11–13), and is likely not accidental.[22] The latter was widely noticed after its initial publication.[23]

---

19 "I am a curse," http://whitmanarchive.org/manuscripts/figures/uva.00256.001. jpg. For a transcription, see Folsom, "Whitman."

20 https://whitmanarchive.org/manuscripts/figures/loc_jc.01660.jpg. Cf. Klammer, *Emergence*, 99–100.

21 K. M. Price emphasizes the importance of such racial crossings for the construction of Whitman's masculinity ("Whitman in Blackface") and Klammer appreciates what Whitman accomplishes in passages like the Lucifer passage ("Slavery and Race" in *A Companion to Walt Whitman* [ed. D. D. Kummings; London: Blackwell, 2006], 101–21), and both are mindful as well of Whitman's complicated and problematic attitudes on race and slavery, which become increasingly "painful to encounter," especially after the Civil War (so Folsom, "Erasing Race," 31). That the Bible does not entangle itself in race, of course, has not stopped its readers, especially in America, from reading race into it.

22 Henry Wadsworth Longfellow, *Poems on Slavery* (2d ed; Cambridge: John Owen, 1842), 30–31. The first two stanzas of the poem date back to 1834 and the image of Samson was not originally associated by Longfellow with an African-American slave, see T. G. Bartel, "The Origin of Longfellow's 'The Warning,'" *Notes and Queries* 65/3 (2018), 377–78. The same impulse appears in Whitman's "Blood-Money" (1850).

23 Esp. N. Junior and j. Schipper, *Black Samson: The Untold Story of an American Icon* (New York/Oxford: Oxford University, 2020), 11–22.

Whitman, early and late, was an admirer of Longfellow,[24] and crucially he reviewed Longfellow's *The Poems of Henry Wadsworth Longfellow* in the *Brooklyn Daily Eagle* in 1846, a volume that includes "The Warning" (and Longfellow's other "Poems on Slavery").[25]

A subtler example comes from the beginning of what would become section 19 of the "Song of Myself":

> This is the meal pleasantly set.... this is the meat and drink for natural hunger,
>
> It is for the wicked just the same as the righteous.... I make appointments with all,
>
> I will not have a single person slighted or left away,
>
> The keptwoman and sponger and thief are hereby invited.... the heavy-lipped slave is invited.... the
>
> venerealee is invited,
>
> There shall be no difference between them and the rest. (*LG*, 25)

Folsom and C. Merrill begin their commentary on this section of (the later) "Song of Myself" by calling attention to the "meal table," which in most cultures provides "sacred space, an intimate place that gathers family and friends—those that we select out from the multitude."[26] However, the table fellowship tradition this passage most obviously echoes is the Lord's supper tradition of the gospels and Paul (Matt 26:26–29; Mark 14:22–25; Luke 22:14–22: 1 Cor 11:17–34) (and its regular instantiations in Christian liturgy).[27] Whitman's opening line in particular mimics the rhythm of the Lukan version: "This is my body

---

24   J. A. Rechel-White, "Longfellow, Henry Wadsworth (1807-82)" in *Walt Whitman: An Encyclopedia* (eds. J. R. LeMaster and D. D. Kummings; New York: Garland, 1998); cf. K. M. Price, *Whitmand Tradition: The Poet in His Century* (New Haven: Yale University, 1990), 72–73, 82–83, 86–87; J. A. Rechel-White, "Longfellow's Influence on Whitman's 'Rise' from Manhattan Island," ATQ 6 (1992), 121–129.

25   Henry Wadsworth Longfellow, *The Poems of Henry Wadsworth Longfellow* (New York: Harper, 1846) ["The Warning" appears on p. 56]. Whitman's review appears as a part of "The Literary World," *The Brooklyn Daily Eagle* (12 October 1846), 2 (column 3). Cf. *UPP*, I, 133–34; Stovall, *Foreground*, 121. In the review Whitman quotes from Longfellow's poem "Rain in Summer" (*Poems*, 103).

26   Walt Whitman, *Song of Myself: With a Complete Commentary* (eds. E. Folsom and C. Merrill; Iowa City: University of Iowa, 2016), 71–72.

27   Cf. Bergquist, "Whitman and the Bible," 289. The "bits of the eucharist" are mentioned towards the end of "Come closer to me" (*LG*, 64).

which is given for you: this do in remembrance of me" (Luke 22:19; cf. 1 Cor 11:14)—the deictic "this" is remarkable, and especially important to the larger section in Whitman's poem.[28] "Meat and drink" (Rom 14:17)[29] and the "wicked" and the "righteous" (155x together in the KJB) are biblical tropes. Whitman is intent, of course, on overturning the heavenly or otherworldly thrust of the biblical tradition (esp. Matt 26:29; Mark 14:25; Luke 22:16, 18) in favor of satisfying "natural hunger" and emphasizing the democratic nature of the meal his poem means to "equally set" (as in the later "Song of Myself").[30] Indeed, Whitman may well have perceived Jesus's meal with "the twelve apostles" (Luke 22:14) as epitomizing anti-democratic intimacy. Yet Paul, like Whitman, appears to emphasize the inclusivity of the invitation to the table (esp. 1 Cor 11:17–18, 33).

Finally, not only does Whitman read the Bible against the grain of its plain meaning, but often his collaging results in new poetic creations that echo, vary, or supplement the biblical source materials while overwriting them. This is not so much allusion as that quintessential anxiety of influence in response to a strong literary antecedent.[31] This general pose toward the Bible is perhaps made most explicit during the preparation of the 1860 edition of *Leaves* as the "New Bible"—the very conceptualization of which signals Whitman's responsive and competitive aspirations. But it is also evident earlier, as made manifest in Whitman's great commandment about organic fluency from the 1855 Preface:

> Who troubles himself about his ornaments or fluency is lost. This is what you shall do: Love the earth and sun and the animals, despise riches, give alms to every one that asks, stand up for the stupid and crazy, devote your income and labor to others, hate tyrants, argue not concerning God, have patience and indulgence toward the people, take off your hat to nothing known or unknown or to any man or number of men, go freely with powerful uneducated persons and with the young and with the mothers of families, read these leaves in the open air every season of

---

28   Folsom and Merrill, *Song of Myself*, 72.
29   Whitman would have relished emphasizing the naturalness of "meat and drink," which the Romans passage sets as the antithesis of the "kingdom of God."
30   Cf. Folsom and Merrill, *Song of Myself*, 71–72.
31   Cf. H. Bloom, *The Anxiety of Influence: A Theory of Poetry* (New York/Oxford: Oxford University, 1997 [1973]).

every year of your life, re examine all you have been told at school or church or in any book, dismiss whatever insults your own soul, and your very flesh shall be a great poem and have the richest fluency not only in its words but in the silent lines of its lips and face and between the lashes of your eyes and in every motion and joint of your body. (*LG*, v–vi)

The set-up, "This is what you shall do," is composed of (modernized) biblical phrasing: "thou shalt do" occurs twenty-four times in the KJB and "what thou shalt do" three times, including "and he will tell thee what thou shalt do," Ruth 3:4; cf. 1 Sam 10:8; 2 Sam 16:3). The long length of what the poet's addressee "shall do" with its thirteen imperatives obscures its scriptural inspiration, first, in the Mosaic injunction to love God (Deut 6:4–9) and neighbor (Lev 19:18), and then in Jesus' own riffing on and replaying of these great commandments, especially in Matt 5:43-45 (cf. Matt 22:36–40; Mark 12:28–34; Luke 10:25–28).[32] While the long catalogue of imperatives is quintessential Whitman, there are a number of intriguing Pauline forerunners that anticipate this Whitmanian stylistic tick. 1 Thess 5:14-23 reads as follows:

> Now we exhort you, brethren, warn them that are unruly, comfort the feebleminded, support the weak, be patient toward all *men*. See that none render evil for evil unto any *man*; but ever follow that which is good, both among yourselves, and to all *men*. Rejoice evermore. Pray without ceasing. In every thing give thanks: for this is the will of God in Christ Jesus concerning you. Quench not the Spirit. Despise not prophesyings. Prove all things; hold fast that which is good. Abstain from all appearance of evil. And the very God of peace sanctify you wholly; and *I pray God* your whole spirit and soul and body be preserved blameless unto the coming of our Lord Jesus Christ.

---

32 Cf. Crawley, *Structure*, 69. And Emerson is also likely an influence here. Toward the end of "The Poet" (in *The Complete Essays and Other Writings of Ralph Waldo Emerson* [ed. B. Atkinson; New York: Modern Library, 1950], 339–40) Emerson addresses the poet directly ("O poet") in a related way, as noticed by Stovall (*Foreground*, 303). Significantly, Emerson also uses biblical style to authorize his injunction. He switches to using the archaic second person pronouns ("thee," "thy," "thou"), and in particular "thou shalt" (840x in KJB) and "thou shalt not" (240x in KJB)—contrast Whitman's modernized version of the biblicism, "you shall," though he closes the paragraph with a sequence of "shall"s and "shall not"s. Emerson also references "a Noah's ark" and that "God wills" in this material, pointing up the biblical inspiration for the archaizing style here.

And Rom 12:9-21:

> *Let* love be without dissimulation. Abhor that which is evil; cleave to
> that which is good. *Be* kindly affectioned one to another with
> brotherly love; in honour preferring one another; Not slothful in
> business; fervent in spirit; serving the Lord; Rejoicing in hope;
> patient in tribulation; continuing instant in prayer; Distributing
> to the necessity of saints; given to hospitality. Bless them which
> persecute you: bless, and curse not. Rejoice with them that do
> rejoice, and weep with them that weep. *Be* of the same mind one
> toward another. Mind not high things, but condescend to men of
> low estate. Be not wise in your own conceits. Recompense to no
> man evil for evil. Provide things honest in the sight of all men.
> If it be possible, as much as lieth in you, live peaceably with all
> men. Dearly beloved, avenge not yourselves, but *rather* give place
> unto wrath: for it is written, Vengeance *is* mine; I will repay, saith
> the Lord. Therefore if thine enemy hunger, feed him; if he thirst,
> give him drink: for in so doing thou shalt heap coals of fire on
> his head. Be not overcome of evil, but overcome evil with good.

Matt 5:44 contains its own run of four such imperatives ("Love," "bless,"
"do good," and "pray") and is followed in the next verse by a purpose or
result clause ("That ye may be...," v. 45), which in function is not unlike
Whitman's final clause, "and your very flesh shall be...." The structural
logic of the whole is the same in both cases, and Matt 4:43 makes it
apparent that Jesus acknowledges the old commandment while doing it
one better, or perhaps more charitably, while updating and applying it
to his own time and place. That is, the gospel passage gives Whitman the
idea for his own hermeneutic when it comes to the Bible, viz. "adjusted
entirely to the modern."[33]

Interestingly, Whitman's commandment feels at times like the
expanded exegesis of some Targums—the Targums were early Jewish
translations of the Hebrew Bible into Aramaic.[34] Some Targums are

---

33   "Bible as Poetry," 57. Wendell Berry's "Manifesto: The Mad Farmer Liberation.
     Front" (from *The Country of Marriage* [New York: Harcourt Brace Jovanovich,
     1973], https://cales.arizona.edu/~steidl/Liberation.html) likely riffs on both
     Whitman and his biblical forerunners (viz. "Love the Lord./ Love the world. .../
     Love someone who does not deserve it").
34   For a readable and informative introduction to the Targumim, see P. S. Alexander,
     "Targum, Targumim" in the *Anchor Bible Dictionary* (eds. D. N. Freedman et al;
     New York: Doubleday, 1992), VI, 320–31.

expansive. An example of an expanded reading appears in Targum Pseudo-Jonathan's rendering of the love of God command in Deut 6:5: "Moses the prophet said to the people, the House of Israel, 'Go after the true worship of your fathers, and love the Lord your God with the two inclinations of your mind, even if your life and all of your money are taken from you.'" The underlying Hebrew text is still visible even in such an expanded and highly interpretive rendering. In Whitman's Preface the opening command to "Love" with its triple object ("the earth and sun and the animals") mimes the rhythm and feel of the love command in the Shema, "And thou shalt love the LORD thy God with all thine heart, and with all thy soul, and with all thy might" (Deut 6:5).[35] The command to "read these leaves" responds to the biblical instruction to memorize, teach, and write down the words of the Shema (Deut 6:6, 7, 9). Instead of binding the words "upon thine hand" and "as frontlets between thine eyes" (Deut 6:8), as Moses urges, Whitman's promise for all who obey his own charge is that "your very flesh shall be a great poem and have the richest fluency not only in its words but in the silent lines of its lips and face and between the lashes of your eyes and in every motion and joint of your body." This latter is especially redolent of its biblical model.[36]

The principal intent in the foregoing example, again, is not to allude in any strong way to the biblical commandments, but rather to respond to them, to carry forward their "autochthonic bequests… adjusted entirely to the modern" and adapted to the needs of American democracy. The chief effect is that of an echo, an oblique resounding at a distance both familiar and distinct.

"No Quotations": The 1850 Poems

Where there is a difference between the allusions in *Leaves of Grass* (especially in the 1855 edition) and the rest of Whitman's writings is in the nature of the allusions. In *Leaves* there are no extended quotations

---

35 Note also the rhythmic echo in "go freely with… and with… and with…."
36 When Whitman culls lines from this material for the "Poem of Many In One" (*LG* 1856, 196), the biblical echoes are entirely expunged. The setup ("Who troubles… This is what you shall do") and overarching structure are exploded, the final clause is dropped, and the Bible-miming imperatives are replaced by first person finite forms in the past tense (e.g., "I have loved").

of biblical passages ("You shall no longer take things at second or third hand.... nor look through the eyes of the dead.... nor feed on the spectres in books" (*LG*, 14), and allusions "become more 'elusive,' more hidden."[37] Exemplary is Whitman's central image of "grass" in "I celebrate myself," which owes a debt to the Bible, as Zweig notices: "All flesh is grass, laments Isaiah in a passage [Isa 40:6–8] Whitman surely knew; after a season, it dies. But the grass grows again; and leaves of grass—those 'hieroglyphics' of the self, that book not a book, of poems that are not poems—they, too, will grow again, if the reader will stoop to gather them up."[38] Whitman, of course, as is often his want, massages the image to suit his own ends. In this case, he takes the biblical image of grass as signifying human transience ("the grass withereth," Isa 40:8) and molds it into a sign of optimism and democratic equality,[39] that which is always emerging anew from the very realm of death ("the beautiful uncut hair of graves," *LG*, 16). Not only does Whitman's language at the beginning of what becomes section 6 of "Song of Myself" mime that of the anonymous prophet of the exile ("A voice said"// "A child said"; "What shall I cry?"// "What is the grass?"), but Whitman even provides his own kind of "hieroglyphic" pointing to his source—"it is the handkerchief of the Lord" (*LG*, 16).[40] And at the end of the poem, referencing the speaker's mortality, Whitman retrieves the biblical sense of grass as a cypher of human transience, not to lament but to celebrate and luxuriate in:

> I effuse my flesh in eddies and drift it in lacy jags.
>
> I bequeath myself to the dirt to grow from the grass I love,
>
> If you want me again look for me under your bootsoles. (*LG*, 56)

Like so many of the echoes of Scripture in *Leaves*, this one serves Whitman's present-oriented poetic ends and does not flaunt its biblical lineage.

---

37   Bergquist, "Walt Whitman and the Bible," 81.
38   *Walt Whitman*, 252; cf. Bergquist, "Whitman and the Bible," 177–80.
39   Esp. M. C. Nussbaum, "Democratic Desire: Walt Whitman" in *A Political Companion to Walt Whitman* (ed. J. E. Seery; Lexington: University Press of Kentucky, 2011], 113–15; M. Edmundson, *Song of Ourselves: Walt Whitman and the Fight for Democracy* (Cambridge: Harvard University, 2021), Part I (Bookshare).
40   Cf. Loving, *Song of Himself*, 192.

The lack of quotations in *Leaves* follows from the aesthetic sensibility that Whitman was evolving in the early 1850s, as Allen well recognizes specifically with reference to the Bible: "Of course, it must be remembered that the use of literary allusions was against the avowed poetic doctrines for *Leaves of Grass*."[41] The sentiment is most explicitly articulated in a manuscript fragment known as the "Rules for Composition," conjectured to date from sometime in the early 1850s. One portion of the "Rules" reads as follows:

> Take no illustrations whatever from the ancients or classics, nor from the mythology, nor Egypt, Greece, or Rome—nor from the royal and aristocratic institutions and forms of Europe.—Make no mention or allusion to them whatever, except as they relate to the new, present things—to our country—to American character or interests.—Of specific mention of them, even infor these purposes, as little as possible.—[42]

The Bible is not explicitly mentioned in the "Rules for Composition" fragment, although there is the intriguing canceled notation at the bottom of the leaf, "~~Mention God not at all~~." This "~~God~~" is above all the God of the Bible (capitalized appropriately) who does in the end get mentioned quite often in the 1855 *Leaves* (e.g. "As God comes a loving bedfellow," *LG*, 15). Regardless, that the Bible falls under the purview of the "Rules" is perhaps one implication to be drawn from the canceled comment. And the Bible is also likely assumed in the catch-all references to "the ancients." The list that follows is of the kind, as noted earlier, where Whitman has included the Bible, which is after all exemplary and not comprehensive in nature.[43]

---

41   "Biblical Echoes," 303, n. 8. Allen's comment is offered to justify the paucity of biblical allusions he finds in *Leaves*. As noted, more recent scholarship has turned up the likelihood of a good deal more than the two dozen or so (specific) allusions to the Bible Allen identifies. Still, his comment is on mark more generally, as biblical allusions or echoes remain relatively few in *Leaves* and highly burnished and elusive.

42   https://whitmanarchive.org/manuscripts/figures/2095_010.jpg. Cf. Miller, *Collage of Myself*, esp. 42.

43   The Bible is frequently characterized as "ancient" by Whitman, e.g., "the great poems of Asian antiquity," "the oldest… Asiatic utterance," "autochthonic bequests of Asia" ("Bible as Poetry"), and from the notebooks and unpublished manuscripts: the Old Testament is used to exemplify early writing in "verse" ("Speaking of literary style," *NUPM* I, 162;), the poetry of the "Hebrew prophets" is said to be "very ancient" ("The florid rich," *NUPM* IV, 1555.), the Hebrew Bible is listed among the "poetry" of "the old Asiatic land" ("—How different," *NUPM*

In this case, what Whitman explicitly theorizes can also be tracked in his poetic practice. The three unmetered 1850 poems—"Blood-Money,"[44] "The House of Friends,"[45] "Resurgemus"[46]—begin to anticipate Whitman's mature poetry in important ways. So much so that P. Zweig says of "The House of Friends" in particular, of that poem's "angry rhythm" and its suggestion of Whitman's later line, that "here, maybe, is the very dividing line between the two styles"—between the style of the "juvenile" poems and the style that characterizes the 1855 *Leaves*.[47] The three poems do indeed constitute something of a dividing line on many aspects, including the use of quotations—"in writing, give no second hand articles—no quotations—no authorities" ("med Cophósis" notebook).[48] "The House of Friends," as already mentioned, cites Zech 13:6 in whole, with quotation marks and citation, as its epigraph, and the title itself is a slightly adjusted (as in l. 3) quote (KJB: "the house of my friends").[49] Whitman either did not completely understand the context of Zech 13:2–6[50]—and admittedly the context (and content) is not so obvious, especially in the KJB translation—or, as likely, was attracted mainly to the image of the speaker wounded in the house of his friends. The latter is used by Whitman to allude to the betrayal (in his view) of the North in the debates over slavery and the

---

IV, 1574.), and the "Old Hebrew Bible" ("Emerson uses the Deific," see E. Folsom, "Whitman's Notes on Emerson: An Unpublished Manuscript," *WWQR* 18/1 [2000], 60–62). One of the books Whitman notes in "An Early Notebook," Mills's *The Ancient Hebrews* (1856), not only has "ancient" in its title, but begins in the Preface by speaking about "the Ancients" in a way that is obviously inclusive of the Bible" (*DBN* III, 778)· In another early notebook, the "I know a rich capitalist" notebook (1854), Whitman records finding "pleasure" in the "sayings and doings" of various peoples dating "thirty centuries ago," including those "of wandering Jewish tribes."

44   *New York Daily Tribune*, Supplement (22 March 1850), 1, http://whitmanarchive. org/published/periodical/poems/per.00089..

45   *New York Daily Tribune* (14 June 1850), 3, http://chroniclingamerica.loc.gov/lccn/ sn83030213/1850-06-14/ed-1/seq-3/.

46   *New York Daily Tribune* (21 June 1850), 3, https://whitmanarchive.org/published/ periodical/poems/per.00088.

47   Zweig, *Walt Whitman*, 119; cf. 114–21; Miller, *Collage of Myself*, 7–9—though Miller places more accent on the differences between the 1850 poems and the emergence of Whitman's more mature style beginning around 1854.

48   https://whitmanarchive.org/manuscripts/figures/loc.00005.003.jpg. For the dating of this notebook (1852–54), see Miller, *Collage of Myself*, 11–15.

49   Allen, "Biblical Echoes," 305.

50   So Klammer, *Whitman, Slavery, and Leaves of Grass*, 80, n. 56.

Compromise of 1850. The opening lines contain a few biblicisms ("thou art," "thy," and "house of friends," which is a close version of the Bible's "house of my friends") and the poem closes with the admonition to the "young North" to "Arise" and "fear not," both commonplaces, especially in the prophetic literature. Indeed, the serial apostrophes to the various states (e.g., "Virginia, mother of greatness," "Hot-headed Carolina") even faintly recall the famous pattern (poetic) oracle against the nations in Amos 1:3–2:16 (e.g., "For three transgressions of Damascus, and for four," Amos 1:3).

Similarly, "Blood-Money" features an epigraph citing a close version of 1 Cor 11:27, also set apart in quotation marks (though no explicit citation): "Guilty of the Body and Blood of Christ" (compare KJB: "guilty of the body and blood of the Lord").[51] Whitman's change from "Lord" (Greek *kyriou*) to "Christ" is perhaps a clarifying gesture, and the added capitalization for emphasis. The title itself alludes to Matt 27:6, as Bergquist maintains ("Then went Judas, and sold the Divine youth,/ And took pay for his body").[52] Whitman even quotes from the Bible (Matt 26:15) within the body of the poem itself (lines 12–14):

> Again goes one, saying,
>
> What will ye give me, and I will deliver this man unto you?
>
> And they make the covenant and pay the pieces of silver.

Here, too, I have the sense that Whitman's diversions from KJB ("And said unto them, What will ye give me, and I will deliver him unto you? And they covenanted with him for thirty pieces of silver.") are mostly contextual adjustments. This is certainly the case with the change from "him" to "this man," since the quote has been lifted out of its immediate narrative context where the identities of the characters are clear. The dropping of the specific sum ('thirty") may be in deference to the new "cycles" where the "fee" need only be "like that paid for the Son of Mary." Also, however, such deviations become characteristic of how Whitman collages. Once finding a bit of readymade language of interest (as in the Bible), he shapes it to suit his poetical ends.

---

51   Allen, "Biblical Echoes," 305.
52   "Whitman and the Bible," 120, 281.

Of the three poems, "Resurgemus" is the most mature, exhibiting the "rhythmical instinct" that will characterize Whitman's later poetry, and is the only one to be included (albeit in revised form) in the 1855 *Leaves* (*LG*, 87–88). "Resurgemus" exhibits no direct quotations from the Bible, though the Bible's imprint on the poem remains palpable in the mention of "God" (first word in the second stanza) and of a biblical figure ("Ahimoth, brother of Death," cf. 1 Chron 6:25),[53] allusions (e.g., "And all these things bear fruits, and they are good," cf. Gen 1:12, 31),[54] and even in aspects of Whitman's diction (e.g., "thee," "lo" [followed by comma—"lo,"—as throughout the KJB], "locusts," "seed").[55] Of these, the direct reference to "God," "Ahimoth," the biblical figure of "locusts," and the twofold use of "thee" in the final stanza are excised in the 1855 version of the poem—all no doubt in violation of the poetic theory that Whitman had by then evolved.[56] However, the allusions stay,

---

53 Cf. Posey, "Whitman's Debt," 223. Significantly, Whitman's gloss of the name, "brother of Death," is very close to an over-literal gloss of the Hebrew ʾăḥîmôt "my brother is death" (BDB, 27)—Whitman's version construes the component nouns as a construct chain, the biblical Hebrew genitival construction. As this is not information given in the biblical text of the KJB, it must mean that Whitman's knowledge here reflects some secondary source (e.g., W. Smith, *A Dictionary of the Bible* [Boston: Little, Brown, and Company, 1860], I, 51).

54 Bergquist, "Whitman and the Bible," 122. Not to try to parse too closely, nevertheless, the image in Gen 1:12 of the fruit bearing trees (and their "seed") that are pronounced "good" (but not "very good," as in v. 31) is likely what is in Whitman's mind here, viz. "And the earth brought forth grass, and herb yielding seed after his kind, and the tree yielding fruit, whose seed was in itself, after his kind: and God saw that it was good."

55 Biblical Hebrew *zeraᶜ* "seed" also has the extended meaning of "offspring." In the Bible human perpetuity is achieved chiefly through one's offspring. Whitman trumps (as he plays on) this idea by suggesting that it is the idea of "freedom" (as entombed in the graves of "the murderd") that will "bear seed" and "live elsewhere with unslaughter'd vitality." For a discussion of the biblical resonances of "seed"/"offspring" in Faulkner's *Absalom, Absalom!*, see R. Alter, *Pen of Iron* (Princeton: Princeton University, 2010), 102–05.

56 E. Holloway (*UPP* I, 30, n. 1) makes the following observation in regard to the change of "thee": "This *thee* giving place to the *you* of the 1855 and later editions is an illustration of Whitman's 'getting rid of the stock poetic touches' which appeared in the first drafts of his 'Leaves of Grass.' Observe also the omission of the reference to Ahimoth (l. 4) in the 1855 edition." Holloway is certainly on mark here. There are no *thees* or *thous* in the 1855 edition, though they begin appearing in dramatic fashion in the later editions. One convenient source of these archaic pronouns, of course, is the KJB (see A. McGrath, *In the Beginning: A History of the King James Bible and How It Changed a Nation, a Language, and a Culture* [New York: Anchor], ch. 11). Whitman would have likely inherited this kind of diction both from the Bible and from the English verse tradition more generally,

given their present relevance and their more "elusive," worked over texture. The latter is especially well evidenced in the poem's final lines, which clearly allude to "the coming of the Son of Man," though they have been worked over such that the tracks of the source text have been well covered (see Matt 24:42, 48–50; 25:13; Mark 13:34–35 ["Watch ye therefore: for ye know not when the master of the house cometh"]; Luke 21:36; Acts 20:31):[57]

> Liberty, let others despair of thee,
>
> But I will never despair of thee:
>
> Is the house shut? Is the master away?
>
> Nevertheless, be ready, be not weary of watching,
>
> He will surely return; his messengers come anon.[58]

Therefore, certainly with respect to this one dimension of Whitman's evolving poetic theory—"no quotations"—1850 and the three poems composed during that spring and summer do seem to offer something of a watershed, a "dividing line." At that time, Whitman could still freely embed quotations in his poems. Beginning with "Resurgemus" and by the time of the early notebooks (1852 to 1854)[59] and then in the

---

which remained full of *thees*, *thous*, *thys*, and *thines* (as was Whitman's own early poetry)—and Quakerism, which exerted (some) influence on Whitman, especially in his early years, perhaps was another mediating source for such language (see some of the characters in "Life and Adventures of Jack Engle: An Auto-Biography," *WWQR* 34/3 [2017], 262–357).

57 *UPP*, I, 30, n. 2; Allen, "Biblical Echoes," 305–06; *Solitary Singer*, 105, 168, 555 n. 151; Bergquist, "Whitman and the Bible," 122.

58 The revised version of the poem's ending is only slightly altered—"thee"s are dropped and the shorter lines combined to comport with Whitman's evolving preference for a longer line. The "coming of the Son of Man" allusions remain: Liberty let others despair of you.... I never despair of you. Is the house shut? Is the master away? Nevertheless be ready.... be not weary of watching, He will soon return.... his messengers come anon. (*LG*, 88) The New Testament echoes of the "master" who "will soon return" with "his messengers" leading the way are hard to miss—indeed, "almost" a "paraphrase," as Allen notes (*Solitary Singer*, 268).

59 Most of the early notebooks with trial lines pre-dating the first edition of *Leaves* are mostly dated to 1854. The "med Cophósis"notebook (https://whitmanarchive. org/manuscripts/notebooks/t) is an exception. It dates sometime between 1852 and 1854. There is also the "Autobiographical Data" notebook (https://

1855 *Leaves*, Whitman's new poetics is firmly in place: no more direct quotations, a concerted trimming away of (some) biblical and other literary trappings—those "stock touches," and a tendency to work over allusions to the point that they become, as Bergquist says, "more 'elusive,' more hidden." The latter is already well-evident in the 1850 version of "Resurgemus," and Whitman's revisions of the poem for inclusion in the 1855 *Leaves* reveals still others. It is perhaps no accident that these stylistic developments all start with three poems heavily invested in the Bible. The period corresponds with the point at which Whitman starts referencing the "poetry" of the Hebrew Bible and the time of his self-study, which included (some) secondary literature about the Bible. The poems themselves have their most immediate provocation in the slavery issue and the political machinations leading up to the Compromise of 1850, to which Whitman was adamantly opposed.[60] The biblical quotations, allusions, and phraseology are not incidental, as M. Klammer notes with respect to "House of Friends" in particular, as each side in the slavery debates "attempted to buttress its position with references to the Bible."[61] But at any rate it is with respect to biblical quotations that one can actually track Whitman's theory about writing in his own writing practice.

The Bible in Whitman's Prose from 1850–53

The 1850 poems are the last writings Whitman composed with line breaks until the trial lines of the early notebooks (with their signature "hanging indentations"). However, there is now a goodly amount of prose (mostly journalistic in nature) from the three-plus-year period between the time of the 1850 poems and the late summer of 1853—nearly two dozen separate pieces. This material shows Whitman writing

---

whitmanarchive.org/manuscripts/notebooks/transcriptions/loc.05935.html) that dates as early as 1848, though containing material that may date as late as early 1856. The notebook possibly contains verse (*NUPM* I, 211–12; cf. A. C. Higgins, "Art and Argument: The Rise of Walt Whitman's Rhetorical Poetics, 1838–1855" [unpbl. Ph.D. diss; University of Massachusetts Amherst, 1999], 136–39). Currently, there is no evidence (aside from the latter notebook) that Whitman wrote poems (with line-breaks) between 1850 and 1852 at the earliest.

60   Esp. Klammer, *Whitman, Slavery, and Leaves of Grass*, 75–84.
61   Ibid., 77, n. 51.

abundantly (thinking in particular of the two novelistic contributions, "Sleeptalker" and "Jack Engle"),[62] almost up until the time of the early pre-*Leaves* notebooks. Some of this writing has long been known to Whitman scholars and features in the surveys of biblical allusions by Allen and others. Other material has only recently been recovered (e.g., "Jack Engle"). In general, these prose writings share the same basic attitude to the use of the Bible as is evident in the 1850 poems: the Bible is not prohibited; indeed, as it never appears to be in Whitman's prose writings. This is most explicit in the "Art and Artists" lecture, which besides the two pieces of long fiction, is perhaps the most carefully crafted essay of the period. It is, as R. L. Bohan observes, "studded with quotations from and indirect references to Emerson, the Bible, Carlyle, Ruskin, Rousseau, Shakespeare, Pope, Bryant, Horace, Socrates, and an unnamed Persian poet"[63]—Whitman is clearly not worried about second-hand attributions. In addition to the long, rhythmic paraphrase of Genesis 1 previously discussed (see Chapter One), there is also a riff on the risen Christ's commandment, "And he said unto them, Go ye into all the world, and preach the gospel to every creature" (Mark 16:15): "To the artist, I say, has been given the command to go forth into all the world and preach the gospel of beauty."[64] Here the use of biblical language and form (i.e., a command) is intended to layer Whitman's aesthetic charge with the familiarity and traditional authority of the gospel saying.

Some further examples will illustrate Whitman's practice in this material. Periodic eruptions of stylistic flourishes that will typify (much of) the 1855 *Leaves* are not uncommon, and often are accompanied by (more and less) obvious biblicisms. The editors of the *Walt Whitman Archive* call attention, for example, to the following paragraph from the

---

62 Letter to the *New York Sun* offering to publish a serialized novel entitled "Sleeptalker," an adapted version of a Danish novel, which Z. Turpin, for example, assumes "was almost certainly a completed novel" ("Introduction to Walt Whitman's 'Life and Adventures of Jack Engle,'" *WWQR* 39/3 [2017], 227; "Jack Engle" in the *Sunday Dispatch* (14 March–18 April 1852).

63 *Looking into Walt Whitman: American Art, 1850–1920* (University Park: Pennsylvania State University, 2006), 19. The "Art and Artists" was delivered by Whitman on 31 March 1851 and published subsequently in the *Brooklyn Daily Advertizer* (3 April 1851; reprinted in *UPP* I, 241–47.

64 *UPP* I, 243; cf. Allen, "Biblical Echoes," 306 (though he cites Matt 28:19).

third of the so-called "Paumanok letters" (of 1851),[65] noting how its "tone and style" anticipate "Song of Myself":

> Have not you, too, at such a time, known this thirst of the eye? Have you not, in like manner, while listening to the well-played music of some band like Maretzek's, felt an overwhelming desire for measureless sound—a sublime orchestra of a myriad orchestras—a colossal volume of harmony, in which the thunder might roll in its proper place; and above it, the vast, pure Tenor,—identity of the Creative Power itself—rising through the universe, until the boundless and unspeakable capacities of that mystery, the human soul, should be filled to the uttermost, and the problem of human cravingness be satisfied and destroyed?

The run of rhetorical questions come in for particular comment, reminiscent, as they are, of Whitman's "strategic use" of such questions in *Leaves*, such as in the following passage:

> Have you reckoned a thousand acres much? Have you reckoned the
>   earth much?
>
> Have you practiced so long to learn to read?
>
> Have you felt so proud to get at the meaning of poems? (*LG* 14)

Such questions have a biblical lilt about them. The phrase "have ye not" appears twenty-six times in the KJB, often similarly rhetorical in nature, including this short run from Isa 40:21: "Have ye not known? have ye not heard? hath it not been told you from the beginning? have ye not understood from the foundations of the earth?" The lineation of the *Leaves* passage helps bring out the parallelism (itself a device with a biblical lineage, see Chapter Four) that is present also in Isaiah (a triplet or pair of couplets in the original Hebrew, cf. *BHS*, *NRSV*) and in the journalistic passage.

   An uncollected newspaper column from the *Brooklyn Evening Star* (24 May 1852), entitled "An Afternoon Lounge About Brooklyn," offers another example of writing that anticipates the mature poetry of *Leaves*. This one contains one of those ample and ambling sentences (fifty-three words) that come to characterize Whitman's sentential palette in the early *Leaves*:

---

65   "Letters from Paumanok," *New York Evening Post* (14 August 1851), http://
     whitmanarchive.org/published/periodical/journalism/tei/per.00266.html.

> Brooklyn is especially beautiful as a summer town. The innumerable trees—the elevated grounds—the views of land and water—the hundreds of choice private gardens, with the frequent glimpses, here and there, of the rare collections in the private conservatories of fruits and flowers, all cause the time of the singing of birds to be our city's special season of attraction.[66]

The long dashes are used, much like the suspension points in the 1855 *Leaves*, to provide the undergirding necessary to support Whitman's complex and expansive subject (37 words long, no verbs). And Whitman brings the sentence to a close by lifting a phrase from the Song of Songs' own paean to spring, Song 2:8–17: "the time of the singing of birds" (2:12). The allusion may well be intentional, and yet Whitman is not quoting or citing the biblical text but folding its phrasing into his writing, appropriating its language as his own. Another example comes from one of the long known 1851 "Letters from Paumanok."[67] Here Whitman is reporting an encounter between old "Aunt Rebby" ("she was seventy years old"—"Rebby" is presumably short for "Rebekah") and Whitman's equally biblically named interlocutor, "Uncle Dan'l," whom the old woman at first fails to recognize. When she does recognize him, Whitman writes: "A new light broke upon the dim eyes of the old dame." The trope of "dim eyes" appears eight times in the Bible, mostly in descriptions of the elderly (Gen 27:1 [said of Isaac, Rebekah's husband]; 48:10; Deut 34:7; 1 Sam 3:2; 4:15; cf. Job 17:7; Isa 32:3; Lam 5:17).[68]

The phrase "talents of gold" appears in the last of Whitman's 1850 "Letters from New York" (also signed "Paumanok").[69] The phrasing is straight from the KJB where "talent" is a unit for measuring gold or silver (Hebrew *kikkar*/*kikkārîm*; with gold, 1 Kgs 9:14; 10:10, 14; 1 Chron

---

66   P. 2.

67   "Letters from Paumanok," *New York Evening Post* (28 June 1851), http://
      whitmanarchive.org/published/periodical/journalism/tei/per.00265.html; cf. *UPP*
      I, 252.

68   The coinage is another of Tyndale's (e.g., "and his eyes were dymme," Gen 27:1)
      carried forward by the KJB. The adjective "dim" is only used one time in the KJB
      not associated with the characterization of the eyes of the elderly. In Lam 4:1
      "dim" is used in the description of the loss (dulling) of gold's luster—this dates
      back to Coverdale's rendering from 1535 (*OED*).

69   R. G. Silver, "Whitman in 1850: Three Uncollected Articles," *American Literature*
      19/4 (1948), 302–17 (parenthetical references in this section refer to the pagination
      of Silver).

22:14; 29:4; 2 Chron 8:18; 9:9, 13; with silver, Exod 38:27; 1 Kgs 20:39; 2 Kgs 5:22; 15:19; 1 Chron 19:6; 22:14; 25:6; Ezra 8:26; Est 3:5). Here Whitman's collaging of language is accompanied by his massaging of the meaning toward the more standard connotation of the English, viz. talent as aptitude, ability, facility, gift, knack. So "talents of gold," like Whitman's own parallel coinage, "endowments of silver" (p. 316; echoing the Bible's occasional joining of the two phrases, e.g., 2 Kgs 18:14; 23:33; 2 Chron 36:3), are "the highest order of gifts and blessings" (p. 316). The letter also mentions "commentators on the Bible" (p. 314), God (pp. 315, 317), "tales of Gog and Magog" (cf. Ezek 38:2; Rev 20:8; p. 316), and "leaven" that "leaveneth the whole lump" (1 Cor 5:6;[70] Gal 5:9; p. 317). Other notable examples of collaged biblical phrasing include "light of life" (John 8:12),[71] "Priests of the Sun" (2 Kgs 23:5),[72] and the biblicized "and will satisfy any man that hath eyes to see" (cf. Deut 29:4; Ezek 12:2),[73] all in regard to the new technology of the daguerreotype and all from the summer of 1853.[74]

Given its recent recovery, Whitman's anonymously published novella "Jack Engle" deserves some attention.[75] There are more than thirty obvious biblicisms, including names that derive from biblical characters (e.g., "Ephraim Foster," p. 264; "Rebecca," p. 274; "Isaac Leech," p. 288), biblical language (e.g., "ministered unto," p. 268—22x in KJB; "I say," pp. 271, 332—212x in KJB; "blessed is/are," p. 272—37x and 31x respectively

---

70   As noted by Silver ("Whitman in 1850," 317, n. 41).
71   "An Hour Among the Portraits" (*Brooklyn Evening Star* [7 June 1853], 2: "A thousand faces! They look at you from all parts of the large and sumptuously furnished saloon. Over your shoulders, back, behind you, staring square in front, how the eyes, almost glittering with the *light of life*, bend down upon one, and silently follow his motions" [emphasis added].
72   Ibid. "Success, say we in conclusion, to Photography and the workers in the same. It is a noble art, modern as it is; and from what we have seen from them, the *Priests of the Sun* themselves are worthy of their great vocation—good fellows and worthy to shine in any presence" [emphasis added]. Cf. Peterson, *Chaining the Sun* about Gurney's photography where the same imagery appears.
73   "A Brooklyn Daguerreotypist," *Brooklyn Daily Eagle* (27 August 1853), 2.
74   From an earlier article on art ("Something about Art and Brooklyn Artists," *New York Evening Post* [1 February 1851]; cf. *UPP* I, 236) there is also the highly biblicized English of "to bring light out of the present darkness" (cf. Job 12:22; 2 Cor 4:6; 1 Pet 2:9; cf. Ps 107:14)—allusions obviously intended.
75   Parenthetical references to page numbers are to Turpin's edition. I do not include in my tally the *thees*, *thys*, and the like that are obvious Quakerisms used by Whitman in the dialogue of some of his characters (e.g., Mr. Covert).

in in KJB; "saith," p. 273—1262x in KJB; "O, Lord!" [353x], "brethren" [563x] and "Amen" [78x], pp. 298–99), direct quotations (e.g., "spirit of Christ," (p. 268—Rom 8:9; 1 Pet 1:11; "angel from Heaven," p. 270)—Gal 1:8; "lusts of the flesh," p. 300—2 Pet 2:18; "in the twinkling of an eye," p. 316—1 Cor 15:52), and allusions (e.g., "and wouldn't have taken the name of the Lord in vain," p. 281—Exod 20:7; Deut 5:11; watchmen scene, pp. 321–26—Song 3:1–5; 5:2–8; "as the dove, which went forth from the ark," p. 333—Gen 8:8–12; "sower of seeds that have brought forth good and evil," p. 334—Matt 13:4, 19, 24, 29, 31; Luke 8:5; cf. 2 Cor 9:10; "the serpent has cast his slough," p. 345)—Genesis 3). One of the more remarkable biblical inflections in "Jack Engle" is a close version of 1 Cor 15:52 ("the trumpet shall sound, and the dead shall be raised"), which Whitman lineates as verse: "The trumpet shall sound,/ And the dead shall rise" (p. 335). This comes from one of the epitaphs on a gravestone, some of which Whitman copied out from actual headstones and used in his story.[76] In fact, Whitman has Jack Engle, on his "ramble" through the Trinity Church graveyard, copying down such epitaphs—"I put my pencil and the slip of paper on which I had been copying, in my pocket" (p. 336). Whitman himself loved such rambles and his avid note taking in small handmade notebooks is amply attested. The fictionalized process here is a reflection of one of Whitman's favored modes of composition—collaging—and that he models Jack's ramble on his own habits anticipates Whitman's later move to first-person discourse in *Leaves*. And as significant, this may well offer another concrete example of Whitman literally making verse out of biblical language.[77]

There is nothing especially biblical about "Jack Engle." And yet the thirty odd biblical phrases, echoes, allusions, and adaptations from the novella show Whitman's easy familiarity with the Bible and how ready he is in the spring of 1852 to absorb its language into his own writing.

In sum, although there is no new verse production during this period (aside possibly from the [readymade] versified tombstone inscription of 1 Cor 15:52), Whitman continues to write (in quantity) and continues to evolve and hone a style of writing that will eventually

---

76 Turpin, "Introduction," 258, n. 66.
77 And even if the versified version of 1 Cor 15:52 itself proves to be found (on an actual tombstone), this too is not uninteresting, as it represents a functionalization of Whitman's habitual compositional practice of collage.

come to characterize the nonnarrative poetry of the 1855 *Leaves*.[78] Biblical and biblicized phrasing abounds in this material. Such phrasing is not chiefly citational in orientation but forms part of the collaged language materials that Whitman absorbs into his writing. In these mainly occasional pieces the lifted phrases are mostly left as taken, their biblical patina not yet burnished away, and hence easily recognizable.

Biblical Echoes in the Early Notebooks and Unpublished Poetry Manuscripts

The early notebooks and unpublished poetry manuscripts fill in another part of the gap between the three 1850 poems and the 1855 *Leaves of Grass*. Here I turn, first, to the early (1852–54) notebooks, and then to the never published poem, "Pictures," and a sampling of some of the pre-*Leaves* poetry manuscripts. In this preparatory material leading up to the 1855 *Leaves*, the biblical allusions, echoes, and stylistic borrowings begin to take on the "more 'elusive'" texture of the 1855 *Leaves*, though many are still readily traceable, perhaps because most of this material was not yet (if ever) finalized for publication. Before focalizing this early material, however, I want to consider a later (Grier: "after July 1, 1865") pantomime of an "old Hebrew" prophet in a manuscript scrap entitled, "We need somebody."[79] Here Whitman calls for the making of a national literature (following Emerson and Carlyle, and himself in the 1855 Preface). What is of interest is how he names and then shapes this call as if it were a prophetic utterance from the Bible. He begins: "We need ~~someth~~ somebody or something, whose utterance ~~is~~ ^were^ like ~~that~~ ~~[illeg.] of~~ an Hebrew prophet's, only substituting ^rapt^ Literature instead of ~~the~~ rapt religion." He then gives us the "utterance ~~sh~~ crying aloud":

"Hear, O People! O poets & writers, ~~you~~ ye have ~~supposed your~~ ^made of^ literature ~~as an accompaniment, an adjunct, as if the same~~ ^as the^

---

78 Loving makes a related observation about Whitman expanding his writing in the *Aurora* (in 1842 and following) to include the "essay form." "It is from the essay," Loving writes, "more than anywhere else perhaps, that Whitman's use of free verse came into being" (*Song of Himself*, 60). I take this as a comment on Whitman's developing style as he works towards the kind of poetry that will characterize the 1855 *Leaves*.

79 After *NUPM* IV, 1606; cf. Allen, "Biblical Echoes," 313.

upholstery of your parlors, or the confections of your tables. ^Ye have^
made a mere ornaments, a prettiness . ~you~ Ye have ^feebly^ followed &
feebly multiplied the models of other ^Yet^ lands. ~& put~ Ye are in the midst
of idols, of clay, silver & brass. I come to call you to the ~truth~ knowledge of
the Living God, in writings. ~Its liter~ Its own literature, to a Nation, is the
first of all things. Even its Religion appears only through its Literature,
& as a part of it. Know ye, ^Ye^ may have all other ~things~ possessions but
without your own ~grand~ ^Soul's^ Literature, ye are ~as~ but little better than
an[?] trading prosperous beasts. Aping but others ye are but intelligent
apes. Until ye prove title by productions, remain subordinate, & cease
~those~ ^that perpetual^ windy bragging. Far, far above ~also~ all else, ^in a^
~nation,~ & making ~all~ its ^men^ to move as gods, behold ~in a nation~ ^nation^
~race its orignal own poets~ the bards, orators, & authors, born of the spirit
& body of the ~race~ nation.[80]

This is clearly intentionally over the top and Whitman means to make his own "aping" of a prophetic judgment oracle obvious (e.g., address, complaint and judgment, call for new behavior—the making of the nation's own literature, proclamation of good news—"behold... the bards"). Contrary to his poetic theory,[81] instead of getting rid of stock phrases and unnecessary "ornaments" he puts them in. The King James "ye," for example, occurs a total of nine times. At several points Whitman slips and writes "y/You," cancels it and inserts "y/Ye." He tells us it is like an "old Hebrew prophet's" utterance and then proceeds to litter the passage with phrasal echoes of the Bible, e.g., "Hearken, O people" (1 Kgs 22:28) or "Hear, all ye people" (Mic 1:2); "thou hast moreover multiplied thy fornication in the land of Canaan unto Chaldea" (Ezek 16:29); the famous "image" of Daniel 2 is made up of silver, clay, and brass (esp. vv. 32–33); "I am not come to call the righteous" (Matt 9:13); and in two cases there are actual phrases from the Bible—"Living God," occurring thirty times in total (the capitalization helps to secure readerly attention) and "behold," which appears over a thousand times in the Hebrew Bible alone, most often as a translation of Hebrew *hinnê*. And all, of course, is in prose just like all of the prophetic literature in the rendering of the KJB.

---

80   *NUPM* IV, 1606–07.
81   Whitman's early worries over second-hand quotations and stock phrasing and the like is much relaxed in his later poetry. And of course this is a (later) prose sketch.

I cite this lampoon for two principal reasons. First, it underscores the centrality of the prophetic to Whitman's poetic sensibility, which though widely stipulated is also perhaps too easily (and often) sublimated. No doubt he owes much to Carlyle and Emerson for his conception of the poet-prophet whose voice is heard commanding assent throughout the 1855 *Leaves*.[82] But the idea is ultimately rooted in "old Hebraic anger and prophecy."[83] R. Lowth, and thus the Bible, is the ultimate source for this Romantic conceit—it "runs from Lowth to Blake, to Herder, and to Whitman."[84] Whitman himself acknowledges the biblical source of this Romantic pose in his entry, "The Death of Thomas Carlyle," included in *Specimen Days*, where he writes admiringly of Carlyle, "Not Isaiah himself more scornful, more threatening" and then quotes Isa 28:3–4 (from the KJB): "The crown of pride, the drunkards of Ephraim, shall be trodden under feet: And the glorious beauty which is on the head of the fat valley shall be a fading flower."[85] And his own "dream" about the rise of a future "race of... poets" who are "newer, larger prophets—larger than Judea's, and more passionate."[86] As J. R. LeMaster emphasizes, "That Whitman presented himself as a prophet is beyond doubt."[87] And that his conception of prophecy owes a huge debt to Isaiah and the corpus of prophetic poetry in the Bible is equally beyond doubt—as the early twentieth-century Hebrew poet Uri Zvi Greenberg emphasizes, "Whitman should have written in Hebrew, since he is molded from the same substance as a Hebraic prophet."[88] And thus this is another tell of the Bible's import to Whitman.

---

82   See D. Kuebrich, "Religion and the Poet-Prophet" in *Companion to Walt Whitman*, 197–215, esp. 198–205. For the influence of American Protestantism on Whitman generally and also as it bears on the place of prophecy in his imagination, see B. Yothers, "Nineteenth-Century Religion" in *Walt Whitman in Context* (eds. J. Levin and E. Whitley; Cambridge: Cambridge University, 2018), 524–42.

83   Esp. Crawley, *Structure*, 27–49; cf. Posey, "Whitman's Debt," 6–12.

84   R. D. Richardson, *Emerson: The Mind on Fire* (Berkeley: University of California, 1995), 12; cf. M. Roston, *Prophet and Poet: The Bible and the Growth of Romanticism* (Evanston, Ill.: Northwestern University, 1965).

85   *CW* IV, 305; *CPW*, 169; cf. 253 ("poets... possess'd of the religious fire and abandon of Isaiah").

86   *CW* V, 224; *PW* II, 486; cf. Allen, "Biblical Echoes," 312.

87   "Prophecy" in *Routledge Encyclopedia of Walt Whitman*.

88   As cited in E. Greenspan, "Whitman in Israel" in *Walt Whitman and the World* (eds. G. W. Allen and E. Folsom; Iowa City: University of Iowa, 1995), 386–95, at 388.

Second, the pantomime of an "old Hebrew" prophetic utterance in "We need somebody," in its explicitness and exaggeration, also enables a better appreciation of another dimension of Whitman's debt to the Bible, his mimicry of it. The Bible's influence on Whitman has been measured mostly by the degree to which he can be seen directly engaging the Bible, e.g., through allusion, by borrowing biblical phrases, by referencing it. Yet there are not many direct biblical references in *Leaves*. By far the largest way in which the Bible has influenced Whitman is in his adoption of its manner(s) of phrasing, its rhythms and parallelism, its genres, even its formatting, and then shaping them to suit his own poetry, themes, diction, etc. And so I have gathered some of Whitman's references to biblical prophecy and prophets (e.g., Isaiah), but far more telling is how Whitman himself takes on this persona, this pose—the poet-prophet, and enacts it throughout his mature poetry. There, of course, with few exceptions (e.g., "The dirt receding before my prophetical screams," *LG*, 31), it usually goes un-explicated, un-narrated, un-designated. Hence, the importance of the pantomime. In it we catch Whitman doing what he always does but here the mimicry is intentionally made plain for all to see. Allen's diagnosis of Whitman's adoption and adaptation of biblical parallelism is perhaps the parade example of such mimicry (see Chapter Four). Much of what I have to say about Whitman's line, lyricism, free verse, and prose style is in an effort to locate and unpack the artistry of such mimicry. The difference is, we usually lack a pantomime or some other means of self-explication by which to catch Whitman in the act of imitation, of borrowing, of working and re-working, of writing and re-writing until he makes what he borrows his own. In these instances, I will only be able to triangulate on Whitman's biblical imitations up to a point and then no further. But at least in this case, we may be certain of the ultimate source of his prophetic pose.

* * *

Now to the early notebooks and their biblical inflections. Perhaps the earliest pre-*Leaves* notebook, the "Autobiographical Data" notebook, appears to have been used over an extended period of time (1848–55/56),[89]

---

89   https://whitmanarchive.org/manuscripts/notebooks/transcriptions/loc.05935. html. On the dates of use, see Higgins, "Wage Slavery," 76, n. 35.

and thus only some aspects of its content may be fixed more precisely. Still, the notebook contains a number of general references to the "Bible" and queries rhetorically, "[~~illeg.~~] ^{Why} confine the matter to that part of ~~the~~ it involved in the Scriptures?" There is an echo of the "curse" of humankind from the second creation story in Genesis 2–3 ("Every precious gift to man is linked with a curse—and each pollution has some sparkle from heaven")—the immediately following line/sentence mentions "angels," "heaven," and "serpents." And then there is an extremely ugly reference to "Mordecai the Jew" (cf. Est 2:5: "there was a certain Jew, whose name was Mordecai").

In the "Med *Cophósis*"[90] notebook (1852–54) there is a set of three proverbial sayings that though unbiblical in content (with no specific allusions) imitate biblical diction:

> Can a man be wise without he get wisdom from the books?
>
> Can he be religious and have nothing to do with churches or prayers?
>
> Can he have great style, without being dressed in fine clothes and without any name or fame?[91]

These sayings appear to be in prose—or at least they do not exhibit the kind of "hanging indentation" that typifies Whitman's written verse in these notebooks (and eventually replicated in print in *Leaves*). The rendering in fact looks very much like the similarly prosaized proverbial sayings in the KJB.[92] The use of such rhetorical questions is characteristic of the Bible's proverbial wisdom (e.g., Job 6:6; 22:2; 36:29; Prov 6:27–28; 20:24; Mark 8:4; John 3:4). And indeed Prov 6:27–28 contains a short run of verses that sound very much like Whitman's notations, though with different subject matter:

> Can a man take fire in his bosom, and his clothes not be burned?
>
> Can one go upon hot coals, and his feet not be burned?

---

90   https://whitmanarchive.org/manuscripts/notebooks/transcriptions/loc.00005.html.

91   https://whitmanarchive.org/manuscripts/figures/loc.00005.003.jpg.

92   Indeed, the indentation (i.e., each of the three "Can" sayings begin on a new indented line), as it opposes Whitman's later custom, is especially reminiscent of the KJB's practice of versification (see Figs. 14–19).

In fact, the second verse could be translated even more literally ("Can a man," JPS), as the Hebrew repeats גֶּבֶר "man" from v. 27, which the KJB translators have altered (for stylistic and grammatical reasons) to "one." There is also the run of "Canst thou" headed lines in the Yahweh speeches from Job (38:31–35; 39:1–2, 10, 20; 40:9; 41:1–2, 7).[93] The pair "wise (man)"// "wisdom" appears nineteen times in the KJB (e.g., "Wisdom strengthens the wise," Eccl 7:19).

From the "Poem incarnating the mind" notebook (1854),[94] there is this trial line: "And ~~wrote~~ chalked on a ~~great~~ board, <u>Be of good cheer, we will not desert you</u>, and held it up ~~as they to against the~~ and did it."[95] The line is voiced by the "captain" of a rescue ship and is addressed to survivors of a ship wrecked by a storm. The phrase "Be of good cheer" is lifted directly from the gospels, Jesus's words, also in the middle of a storm, "<u>Be of good cheer</u>; it is I; be not afraid" (Matt 14:27; Mark 6:50; cf. Matt 9:2; John 16:33).[96] There is a reference to Adam and Eve and several to God, and then a more serious kind of imitation, or better, exaltation, where Whitman admits that "Yes Christ was Great large ~~so was~~ and Homer ^{was great}" and then affirms, "I know that I am ~~great~~ large and strong as any of them." And: "Not even ~~that dread~~ God is so great to me as ~~m~~Myself is great to me.— Who knows but that I too shall in time be a God as pure and prodigious as any of them."[97] The reference to "~~that dread~~ God" (preceded by mention of Christ who "brings the perfumed bread") makes clear that it is the biblical God that Whitman has chiefly

---

93   By way of partial confirmation of my interpretation, I note that Martin Farquhar Tupper, who is quite explicit about the biblical models for his *Proverbial Philosophy* (London: Joseph Rickerby, 1838), has many similarly shaped lines, e.g., "Can a cup contain within itself the measure of a bucket?" (p. 26);"Can the Unchangeable be changed, or waver in his purpose?" (p. 95); Canst thou measure Omnipotence, canst thou conceive Ubiquity (p. 126). For more on Tupper and Whitman, see Chapter Three.

94   https://whitmanarchive.org/manuscripts/notebooks/transcriptions/loc.00346.html.

95   https://whitmanarchive.org/manuscripts/figures/loc_jc.01673.jpg.

96   Even Whitman's added phrase, "we will not desert you," mimics the cadence of the gospel passages which add a phrase following the verb θαρσεω (which is often translated nowadays more etymologically, i.e., be courageous, take heart (cf. NRSV), e.g., "thy sins be forgiven thee" (Matt 9:2). The whole line is slightly revised and goes into the 1855 *Leaves*: "And chalked in large letters on a board, Be of good cheer, <u>We will not desert you</u>" (*LG*, 39). Cf. Posey, "Whitman's Debt," 280; Bergquist, "Whitman and the Bible," 158.

97   https://whitmanarchive.org/manuscripts/figures/loc_jc.01676.jpg.

in mind here. In "You know how" notebook ("before 1855"),[98] there are also a few obvious biblical allusions: "the god that made the globe," "reliable[?] ~~sure~~ as immortality ~~pure as Jesus~~," and "clear and fresh as the Creation."[99]

In several of the 1854 notebooks distinct "echoes" of the Bible's manner of saying things are heard. For example, in the "Memorials" notebook there is a sequence of didactic conditional statements in which the protasis and apodosis feature the same lexeme, viz. "If the general has a good army..., he has a good army," "If you are rich... you are rich," "If you are located... you are well located," "If you are happy... you are happy."[100] The same trope shows up in *Leaves*, from both 1855 ("If the future is nothing they are just as surely nothing," *LG*, 65) and 1856 ("If one is lost, you are inevitably lost," *LG* 1856, 18). Compare Prov 9:12, "If thou be wise, thou shalt be wise for thyself," and 1 Cor 14:38, "But if any man be ignorant, let him be ignorant." And there is this analogous run from 1 Esdras (4:7–9):

> ...if he command to kill, they kill; if he command to spare, they spare; If he command to smite, they smite; if he command to make desolate, they make desolate; if he command to build, they build; If he command to cut down, they cut down; if he command to plant, they plant.

Also in the fourth of Whitman's conditionals appears a typical Whitman tick: "but I tell you..." (e.g., "If you carouse at the table I say I will carouse at the opposite side of the table," *LG*, 58). "I tell you" or "I say" commonly occur in the KJB (e.g., Isa 36:5; Ps 27:14; Eccl 6:3; Matt 5:18,20, 22, 26, 8; Luke 4:25; 13:3, 5, 27), and thus Whitman in (sarcastic) pantomime: "'O Bible!' say I 'what nonsense and folly have been supported in *thy* name!'"[101] And in "I know a rich capitalist" (1854)[102] Whitman registers

---

98   https://whitmanarchive.org/manuscripts/notebooks/transcriptions/loc.00142. html. Cf. Higgins, "Wage Slavery," 74, n. 14.

99   https://whitmanarchive.org/manuscripts/figures/loc.00142.009.jpg.

100 *NUPM* I, 146. In Whitman's letter to Emerson a prosaicized version of this trope (minus the conditional) appears: "he who travels... travels straight for the slopes of dissolution" (*LG* 1856, 350–51).

101 "Autobiographical Data." For the inverted word order ("say I"), see esp. Matt 21:43, 1 Cor 9:8, 10:19, and Gal 1:9—in each case the manner of translation goes back ultimately to Tyndale's 1526 New Testament, though curiously there does not appear to be any obvious impetus for the inversion in the Greek (perhaps here the influence is from Luther's German, viz "sage/rede ich").

102 https://whitmanarchive.org/manuscripts/notebooks/transcriptions/nyp.00129.html.

the following (complaint?): "Be ~~thou~~ you like the grand powers."[103] The phrase "be thou" appears some sixty-two times in the KJB, including, "be thou like a roe or a young hart" (Song 2:17).[104] Here, too, Whitman can be seen scrubbing the archaic "thou" out of the phrase.

The "Talbot Wilson" notebook[105] has a fair number of (possible) biblical echoes. It is littered with archaic diction (e.g., "thither," "beget"/"begat"), for which the KJB would have been one readily available source. The syntax of much of the verse recorded here is beginning to take on the highly paratactic profile of the 1855 *Leaves*, another feature shared with the KJB (see Chapters Three and Five). And Whitman's manner of phrasing often has a biblical ring to it. An example of the latter occurs in the following set of lines that appear by themselves on a single leaf:

> ~~Do~~ ^{Have} you supposed it beautiful to be born?
>
> I tell you, ~~it~~ ^{I know}, it is more ^{just as} beautiful to die;
>
> For I take my death with the dying
>
> And my birth with the new-born ^{babes} [106]

The phrase "have ye" occurs some eighty-three times in the KJB, and "hast thou" some 147 times (both especially common in rhetorical questions), with this passage from Matthew being especially close to the sound, rhythm, and logic of Whitman's lines:

> Or have ye not read in the law, how that on the sabbath days the priests in the temple profane the sabbath, and are blameless? But I say unto you, That in this place is one greater than the temple.... For the Son of man is Lord even of the sabbath day. (Matt 12:5–6, 8)[107]

---

103 https://whitmanarchive.org/manuscripts/figures/nyp.00129.004.jpg.
104 Even more common in the Bible is the negative imperative idiom, "be not...," as in "Be not desirous of his dainties" (Prov 23:3), or "Be not afraid of them that kill the body" (Luke 12:4), which will have provided Whitman with one model for the phrasing of his line in the 1855 version of "I celebrate myself": "And I call to mankind, Be not curious about God" (*LG* 54)—and this in a context in which Whitman would appear to be riffing on the *Imago Dei* (e.g., Gen 1:26), viz. "In the faces of men and women I see God." The slightly later "Dick Hunt" notebook has a line with both positive and negative renditions: "Be it the same as if I were with you—Be not too certain but I am with you" (*NUPM* I, 268).
105 https://whitmanarchive.org/manuscripts/notebooks/transcriptions/loc.00141.html.
106 https://whitmanarchive.org/manuscripts/figures/loc.00141.091.jpg
107 Cf. Jer 44:9–13; Ezek 13:7–8; Amos 5:25–272.

Tellingly, the biblical lilt of the notebook lines is entirely jettisoned in their published version:

> Has any one supposed it lucky to be born?
>
> I hasten to inform him or her it is just as lucky to die, and I know it.

> I pass death with the dying, and birth with the new-washed babe....
> and am not contained between my hat and boots (*LG*, 17).

Whitman has removed the biblically sounding "Have you" ("has" [as opposed to "hast"] only occurs four times in the KJB) and "I tell you" and exploded the overall logic (no "For") and rhythm of the lines, as well as their integrity as a distinct unit.

In a similar vein, there is a longish prose passage that is shaped on the underlying substructure of antithetical logic that informs so much of the parallelism in the biblical book of Proverbs: "The world ignorant ^man^ is demented with the madness of owning things—... —But the wisest soul knows that ~~nothing~~ ^no not one^ object ~~in the vast universe~~ can really be owned by one man or woman any more than another.—~~meddlesome[?] fool who who fancies that.~~[108]" Compare, for example, the following from Proverbs:

> The wise shall inherit glory: but shame shall be the promotion of fools. (3:35)
>
> The wise in heart will receive commandments: but a prating fool shall fall. (10:8)
>
> The lips of the righteous feed many: but fools die for want of wisdom. (10:21)
>
> It is as sport to a fool to do mischief: but a man of understanding hath wisdom. (10:23)
>
> The way of a fool is right in his own eyes: but he that hearkeneth unto counsel is wise. (12:15)
>
> Every prudent man dealeth with knowledge: but a fool layeth open his folly. (13:16)

---

108 https://whitmanarchive.org/manuscripts/figures/loc.00141.054.jpg.

The desire accomplished is sweet to the soul: but it is abomination to fools to depart from evil. (13:19)

The heart of him that hath understanding seeketh knowledge: but the mouth of fools feedeth on foolishness. (15:14)

A fool uttereth all his mind: but a wise man keepeth it in till afterwards. (29:11)

Even the biblical binary "wise man"/"fool" is clearly originally in view in Whitman's "wisest soul" and the "meddlesome[?] fool.

Whitman's holistic anthropology is already well developed in these notebook entries. For example, the couplet "I am the poet of the body/And I am the poet of the soul" which will feature in the 1855 *Leaves* (*LG*, 26) makes its first appearance in this notebook.[109] Although Whitman likely will have come to this holistic sensibility from various sources,[110] it is worth stressing that in distinction to the New Testament (and much traditional Christian thought) the Hebrew Bible (like the ancient Semitic world more generally) exhibits a distinctly holistic anthropology as well—body and soul/mind are a unity and not at all dichotomous. Whether Whitman explicitly appreciated this fact is unclear to me,[111] but the compatibility with his own thinking is patent[112] and perhaps helps to

---

109 https://whitmanarchive.org/manuscripts/figures/loc.00141.070.jpg. *NUPM* I, 67.

110 For example, S. J. Tapscott ("Leaves of Myself: Whitman's Egypt in 'Song of Myself,'" *American Literature* 50/1 [1978], 49–73, esp. 62–64) calls attention to Whitman's well-known infatuation with Egypt and wonders whether Egypt does not furnish one set of influences on Whitman's "self-soul split." Whitman is attracted to a phrase he gleans from G. R. Gliddon's *Ancient Egypt* (13–13), "the remedy of the soul" (Whitman, "Egyptian Museum," 32) and Tapscott even hears in Whitman an echo of a now well-known Egyptian wisdom text ("A Dispute over Suicide," *ANET*, 405–07) in which a man contemplates suicide through a dialogue with his own soul ("Leaves of Myself," 63–64). Although as Tapscott notes, knowledge of such a text could have been only conveyed secondarily to Whitman, as translations were only published later ("Leaves of Myself," 63–64, n. 31). Regardless, as noted, there were also analogously staged dialogues with the soul already readily accessible to Whitman in the Bible. For the influence of transcendentalism on Whitman's notion of the soul, see R. Schober, "Transcendentalism" in *Walt Whitman in Context*, 388-405, esp. 390–92, 396–98.

111 Note the intriguing comment at the end of a manuscript leaf ("Egyptian religion") which Grier says likely dates "soon after 1855" (*NUPMS* VI, 2028): "Hebrew [:] The most ethereal and elevated Spirituality—this seems to be the what subordinates all the rest—The soul—the spirit—rising in vagueness—".

112 Bergquist makes a similar point ("Whitman and the Bible," 175–76), though he principally has the New Testament in view, which does not provide as close a fit as

explain Whitman's assimilation of so much from the Hebrew Bible. And yet the KJB's typical, hyper-literal translation of Hebrew *nepeš* as "soul" individuates and animates the concept in ways suggestive of Whitman's many stagings of his "soul."[113] There are differences, of course. The KJB translators can imagine (no doubt because of their own assumptions about a bipartite anthropology) the psalmist in dialogue with his soul (e.g., Ps 3:2; 11:1; 16:2; 35:3; 42:5, 11; 43:5; cf. Luke 12:19), which Whitman mimics ("and I said to my soul When we become the god enfolders....";[114] cf. *LG*, 52) and then eroticizes, imagining his soul having sex with his body (*LG*, 15–16). In fact, there are several biblical inflections in this famous passage from the 1855 *Leaves*.[115] Whitman's soul-lover, who is addressed directly ("you my soul," cf. Ps 16:2), "reached till you felt my beard, and reached till you held my feet" (*LG*, 16), an internally parallelistic and wonderful merism—from bearded head (top) to foot (bottom; cf. Song 5:10–16; 2 Sam 14:25)—that surely also must mean to play on "feet" as a biblical euphemism by which the "Hebrews modestly express those parts which decency forbids us to mention" (e.g., "uncover his feet," Ruth 3:4).[116] The "hand of God" (16x in the KJB; "hand of the LORD," 39x)[117] and the "spirit of God" (26x; "spirit of the LORD," 31x) are common biblical phrases and the release that such handling brings is conveyed so as to echo Paul:[118]

> Swiftly arose and spread around me the peace and joy and knowledge
> that pass all the art and argument of the earth (*LG*, 15)

> And the peace of God, which passeth all understanding, shall keep
> your hearts and minds through Christ Jesus (Phil 4:7)[119]

---

the Hebrew Bible.

113 See G. Kateb's insightful observations about Whitman's dualistic stagings of the body and the soul, "Walt Whitman and the Culture of Democracy" in *Political Companion*, 24.

114 https://whitmanarchive.org/manuscripts/figures/loc.00141.040.jpg.

115 For the larger cultural and religious background of this passage, see Reynolds, *Whitman's America*, 268–70.

116 *Calmet's Dictionary*, 439.

117 "The Hand of the LORD" is an important motif in the mythology of biblical Yahwism (e.g., P. D. Miller and J. J. M. Roberts, *The Hand of the Lord: A Reassessment of the "Ark Narrative" of 1 Samuel* [Baltimore: Johns Hopkins University, 1977]).

118 Posey, "Whitman's Debt," 287; Crawley, *Structure*, 65; Bergquist, "Whitman and the Bible," 177, 289; Folsom and Merrill, *Song of Myself*, 29 ("biblical-sounding passage").

119 Whitman quotes the biblical passage ("*the peace of God that passeth all understanding*") in *Specimen Days* (*CPW*, 161; cf. Allen, "Biblical Echoes," 304;

As for the notebook couplet quoted above, not only is the animating thought characteristically Hebraic, but so too is the formal shaping of the lines—a parallelistic couplet made up of relatively short lines— it eventually is stretched into a typical, elongated and internally parallelistic Whitmanesque line: "I am the poet of the Body and I am the poet of the Soul" (*LG* 1881, 45; see Chapter Four).

More specific allusions abound as well. There is a set of lines in which Whitman's "I" encompasses that of Christ, on the cross and as incarnated in Whitman himself walking the streets of New York and San Francisco these some "two thousand years" later:

> In vain ^{were} nails driven through my hands, ~~and my head my head mocked with a prickly~~
>
> ~~I am here after~~ ^{I remember} my crucifixion and ~~my~~ bloody coronation
>
> The sepulchre and the white linen have yielded me up[120]
>
> ~~The~~ I remember the mockers and the buffeting insults
>
> I am ~~just as~~ alive in New York and San Francisco, ~~after two thousand years~~
>
> Again I tread the streets after two thousand years.[121]

These lines anticipate Whitman's identification with Christ in "I celebrate myself" (*LG*, 43)—viz. "That I could forget the mockers and insults!"; "my own crucifixion and bloody crowning"; "I troop forth replenished"; "We walk the roads of Ohio... and New York... and San Francisco." The allusive texture of the latter again is not as explicit as in the notebook entry, yet still the allusion remains clear.[122]

Dilation is one of Whitman's "spinal ideas"[123] and features prominently in the "Talbot Wilson" notebook. Two passages in that notebook contain trial versions of lines that eventually appear in "I celebrate myself" (*LG*, 45). The scene, as made clear in the first notebook

---

Bergquist, "Whitman and the Bible," 285).

120　Following *NUPM* I, 78, n. 4—line written at top of the page with an arrow suggesting Grier's placement.

121　https://whitmanarchive.org/manuscripts/figures/loc.00141.107.jpg.

122　On the allusion in *Leaves*, see Crawley, *Structure*, 64; Bergquist, "Whitman and the Bible," 182–85; Levine, "Whitman's American Bible," 156.

123　See Miller, *Collage of Myself*, 101–60.

rendition, is intended as an extended metaphor to show Whitman as "the poet of Strength and Hope,"[124] whose poetry is life giving and restorative. The speaker rushes to the house of a dying man, seizes him, and raises "him with resistless will." The speaker invites the "ghastly man," to "to press your whole weight upon me" and "With tremendous ~~will~~ breath," the speaker says, "I force him to dilate." The latter line gets further revised to "I [illeg.] dilate you with tremendous breath [illeg.],/ I buoy you up," [125]which is made into a single line in the 1855 *Leaves*: "I dilate you with tremendous breath…. I buoy you up" (*LG*, 45). Bergquist, commenting on the *Leaves* passage, recognizes that the Bible provides a number of striking parallels "where divine 'breathing' is said to fill with the power of life."[126] In particular, he cites Elisha's restoring of the child of the Shunammite woman (2 Kgs 4:18–37), in which the prophet stretches himself on the boy's body, puts "his mouth upon" the boy's mouth and the boy "sneezes seven times" and opens "his eyes." He also points to Gen 2:7: "And the LORD God formed man of the dust of the ground, and breathed into his nostrils the breath of life; and man became a living soul."[127] There are other potential parallels as well (e.g., John 11; cf. Ezek 37:5, 9–10).[128] It seems likely, in fact, that Whitman is not here alluding to one particular passage but has an amalgam of such scenes in mind.[129] If the specific mention of the "house of any one dying" and the image of "pressing" in the first notebook passage are especially suggestive of the Kings passage, the phrase "bafflers of hell" in the second notebook passage is more reminiscent of Luke 16:20–31, which involves the deaths of the beggar Lazarus and a rich man and is set in

---

124 https://whitmanarchive.org/manuscripts/figures/loc.00141.071.jpg. Cf. Miller, *Collage of Myself*, 148.

125 https://whitmanarchive.org/manuscripts/figures/loc.00141.086.jpg.

126 Bergquist, "Whitman and the Bible," 188.

127 Whitman alludes to this verse as well elsewhere, see *UPP*, I, 109, 257; *CW*, II, 296; V, 66; VI, 157; cf. Posey, "Whitman's Debt," 195, 208, 215, 217, 229.

128 Cf. H. Aspiz, *So Long! Walt Whitman's Poetry of Death* ([Tuscaloosa and London: University of Alabama, 2004], 63.

129 One also thinks of Luke 7:11–18, the story of the raising of the widow's son at Nain, which though not involving "dilation" as such was certainly well known to Whitman, as the inspiration for his short story, "Shirval: A Tale of Jerusalem," https://whitmanarchive.org/published/fiction/shortfiction/per.00337.html; cf. Bergquist, "Whitman and the Bible," 115–16. See also this allusion to this passage by Whitman from an 1842 editorial: "with which the widow's son, who was dead, and brought to life again, gladdened his desolate mother's heart" ("A Peep at the Israelites," 2).

hell—where the rich man stays. And the revised version of this line, "bafflers of graves," makes better sense in light of that other Lazarus in John 11, who is restored to life specifically out of a grave (vv. 17, 38, 43). At any rate, the notebook passages, with their more obvious biblical inflections (e.g., "Lo!", "I say^tell you") and even a canceled out mention of God (viz. "God and I have^embraced you, and henceforth possess you all to our^myselves"), would appear to support Bergquist's intuition about the Bible supplying Whitman with the basic inspiration for the scene. Besides, as Miller observes, mouth-to-mouth resuscitation, which might seem to the modern reader an obvious starting point for Whitman's imagery, was not yet practiced at the time these lines were drafted in the notebook, and thus Miller, like Bergquist, references the Elisha story from the Bible.[130]

A last example comes near the end of the notebook on two successive leaves:

> vast and tremendous is the scheme! It involves no less than constructing a ~~state~~ nation of nations.—a ~~state whose integral~~ state whose grandeur and comprehensiveness of territory and people make the mightiest of the past almost insignificant—and[131]

And:

> Could we imagine such a thing—let us suggest that before a manchild or womanchild was born it should be suggested that a human being could be born—imagine the world in its formation—the long rolling heaving cycles—can man appear here?—can the beautiful ~~animal~~ vegetable and animal life appear here?[132]

The second of the passages features a typically "elusive" allusion to the creation stories in Genesis. This is cast within the century's growing understanding of the Earth's great age and so demythologized to some extent (esp. "the long rolling heaving cycles"). But the shift to first person plural voice ("could we," "let us"), the gender inclusivity (esp. Gen 1:27: "male and female created he them"), "beautiful" as a descriptor, and the mention of "vegetable and animal life" all echo the creation accounts, especially in Genesis 1, and are prominent in other echoes of

---

130 Miller, *Collage of Myself*, 149.

131 https://whitmanarchive.org/manuscripts/figures/loc.00141.118.jpg.

132 https://whitmanarchive.org/manuscripts/figures/loc.00141.119.jpg.

this material in Whitman's writings, including in the 1855 *Leaves*.[133] For example, in "I celebrate myself" occurs an echo of the Priestly writer's closing assessment of God's creation, *ṭôb mĕʾōd* "very good" (Gen 1:31): "The earth good, and the stars good, and their adjuncts all good" (*LG*, 17; cf. *LG*, 69—"what is called good is perfect"). And in "Who learns my lesson complete? (*LG*, 92) Whitman speaks of "this round and delicious globe, moving so exactly in its orbit forever and ever" (the latter phrase appears 46x in the KJB), of which he says, "I do not think it was made in six days." This is clearly an allusion to the Priestly version of creation in Genesis 1 (cf. "Nor planned and built one thing after another"). Whitman immediately goes on to mention the Bible's trope of "seventy years" for the typical length of a well-lived life.

I wonder whether even the language of "manchild" and "womanchild" in the notebook passage, though chosen perhaps because of the resonance with "man" and "human being" elsewhere in the passage and because of the species emphasis of Whitman's thought here, does not owe a debt to biblical diction. The former occurs some ten times in the KJB, including Job 3:3 ("Let the day perish wherein I was born, and the night in which it was said, There is a man child conceived"), a passage rich with cosmological imagery.[134] The phrase "nation of nations" at the beginning of the first notebook passage certainly mimes the use of the periphrastic genitive made popular by William Tyndale in his intentionally close English renditions of the Hebrew superlative construction (a construct chain in Hebrew, viz. "God of goddes," "lorde of lordes"; cf. Whitman's "Book of books," etc.; see Chapter Five for details)—a clear bit of biblicized English diction.[135]

---

133 Bergquist ("Whitman and the Bible," 127), for example, underscores the frequency with which Whitman alludes to the Bible's creation stories. Of particular note is another riff on the creation theme (first in prose and then as verse, viz. "Out of the vast, first Nothing") in the "I know a rich capitalist" notebook, a version of which eventually shows up in *Leaves* (*LG*, 50).

134 The KJB translators muddle things here. The Hebrew is *geber* "man." One never literally conceives a man but only a child or baby, this much the KJB perceives. The change-up in vocabulary is intentional on the part of the Joban poet, who is telegraphing the fact that he intends his curse ("let the day perish") to have cosmological ramifications. Not only does he wish for the erasure of his own birthday, but also for the uncreating of the creation itself.

135 Also "Love is the cause of causes" (https://whitmanarchive.org/manuscripts/figures/nyp.00129.011.jpg) in "I know a rich capitalist" in a passage with creation imagery.

Whitman's unpublished poem, "Pictures,"[136] which most date to sometime around 1855,[137] fits well into the trajectory of the poet's development leading up to the 1855 *Leaves*. As with the three 1850 poems and the verse experiments in the early notebooks, Whitman's rhythms in this poem are distinctly non-metrical.[138] His lines are consistently longer (as in the 1855 *Leaves*) than in the other pre-1855 poetic materials, and they are written here with Whitman's characteristic "hanging indentation" (Fig. 11) as in the notebooks. No biblical quotations, but there are references to biblical figures and characters (e.g., Adam, Eve, Hebrew prophets, Christ, Lucifer). The two lines immediately preceding the line dedicated to Adam and Eve (from the second creation story in Genesis) focus day and night alluding to the first creation story in Genesis:

Whitman: "There is represented the Day" and "And there the Night"[139]

Genesis 1: "Let there be light: and there was light" (v. 3) and "And God called the light Day, and the darkness he called Night" (v. 5)

Whitman keeps the capitalization of the KJB to highlight the allusion and the biblical sequence of the two creation accounts (first the Priestly account of Gen 1:1–2:4a and then that of the Yahwist (or the non-Priestly source), the garden of Eden story of Genesis 2–3) is even emulated. Other specific scriptural allusions include those to the crucifixion narratives in the gospels ("the divine Christ" "en-route to Calvary")[140] and to Isa 14:12 ("the black portrait" of "Lucifer"),[141] both allusions that Whitman makes elsewhere as well. The sequence of references in leaves 37–38 of "Pictures"—Adam and Eve, Egyptian temple, Greek temple, Hebrew prophets, Homer, Hindu sage, Christ, Rome, Socrates, Athens—represents the same basic litany of admired figures from antiquity discussed previously (in Chapter One), and is well evidenced in the early notebooks. There are even lines reminiscent of material from the early notebooks. For example, the image of Lucifer's "black portrait" in

---

136 https://brbl-dl.library.yale.edu/vufind/Record/3521996.

137 For example, Grier: "at the earliest" (*NUPM* IV, 1296).

138 Allen (*Solitary Singer*, 145) and Zweig (*Walt Whitman*, 206) emphasize how Whitman's rhythm here is still very close to the rhythm of prose.

139 *NUPM* IV, 1297.

140 *NUPM* IV, 1297.

141 *NUPM* IV, 1300.

"Pictures" (*NUPM* IV, 1300) appears again in a fragment cited by R. M. Bucke ("I am a hell-name and a curse:/ Black Lucifer was not dead"),[142] both of which are preparatory for the related image in the 1855 *Leaves* (*LG*, 74; see discussion above). The trinitarian line about the "heads of three other Gods" ("The God Beauty, the God Beneficence, and the God Universality," *NUPM* IV, 1301) has a striking parallel in the "I know a rich capitalist" notebook: "Yes I believe in the Trinity—God Reality— God Beneficence or Love—God Immortality or Growth."[143] And the language of "Hebrew prophets, chanting, rapt, ecstatic" (*NUPM* IV, 1297) is echoed in the "Poem, as in" manuscript fragment: "Poem, as in a rapt and prophetic vision."[144] "Pictures," thus, patterns well with the early, pre-1855 notebooks and unpublished poetry manuscripts, demonstrating Whitman's ongoing interest in and handling of the Bible.

"Pictures" is Whitman's first long poem. As Allen notes, what Whitman needed at the time "was an adequate form, a literary vehicle,"[145] and the long poem would become one of his chief poetic vehicles, especially in the earlier editions of *Leaves*. The poem itself conceptualizes Whitman's mind and memory as a kind of picture gallery (the daguerreotype gallery then fashionable),[146] a "(round) house" of images, personal and otherwise, stored up over a lifetime on whose "walls hanging" are "portraits of women and men, carefully kept" (*NUPM* IV, 1296), some of which (those with biblical allusions or characters) I have just briefly reviewed. The long poem—which aspires "to achieve epic breadth by relying on structural principles inherent in lyric rather than in narrative modes"[147]—is mostly a modern phenomenon. Indeed, Whitman's "Song of Myself" is often credited as one of the more influential early instantiations of the modern genre.[148] The surpassing length that characterizes such poems was expressly enabled by writing. The biblical

---

142 *Notes & Fragments*, 19 (I, no. 40).
143 https://whitmanarchive.org/manuscripts/figures/nyp.00129.013.jpg. *NUPM* I, 131.
144 *NUPM* IV, 1347.
145 *Solitary Singer*, 144.
146 See esp. Bohan, *Looking*, 23–26; Zweig, *Walt Whitman*, 203–06; Reynold, *Whitman's America*, 277–305. Note Whitman's own account of a visit to such a "saloon" in "An Hour Among the Portraits," *Brooklyn Evening Star* (7 June 1853), 2—Whitman even collages language from the essay into "Pictures," viz. "And here," "And there."
147 T. Gardner, "Long Poem" in *PEPP* (Kindle ed.) (quoting C. Altieri).
148 T. Gardner, "Modern Long Poem" in *NPEPP*, 791.

poetic tradition emerges out of a predominantly oral culture,[149] and therefore has no true long nonnarrative poems—Psalm 119, which is the most obvious exception (containing 176 verses), is itself an explicitly written poem, as the alphabetic acrostic that structures the psalm is a scribal trope, patterned after a common scribal practice genre, the abecedary. So there is no question of Whitman finding the long poem *as such* in the Bible.

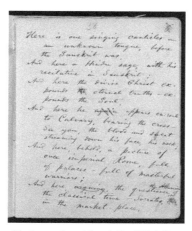

Fig. 11: From "Pictures," holograph notebook (leaf 38r). Image courtesy of the Walt Whitman Collection. Yale Collection of American Literature, Beinecke Rare Book and Manuscript Library, https://collections.library.yale.edu/catalog/2007253.

However, this is not to discount totally the possibility of the Bible's impress on Whitman even here. If there are no genuine long poems in the Bible for Whitman to imitate, nevertheless, the Bible (or portions thereof), especially in the prose translation of the KJB, could certainly be read in a fashion that could give rise to the idea of a long poem. One of the peculiarities of the page layout of the KJB (which it inherits in the main from the Geneva Bible) is that each verse (whether prose or poetry) is numbered separately and begins on a new indented line (see Figs. 4, 12). One consequence of such formatting is to occlude the distinction between the prose and poetry of the underlying Hebrew (in the Old Testament). From their look on the page one simply cannot tell the two apart (cf. Figs. 4, 13–17). As a practical matter, this uniformity

---

149 See F. W. Dobbs-Allsopp, "An Informing Orality: Biblical Poetic Style" in *On Biblical Poetry* (New York/Oxford: Oxford University, 2015), 233–325.

at the "outer surface of Scripture,"observes R. G. Moulton (writing at
the end of the nineteenth century), means that "the successive literary
works appear joined together without distinction, until it becomes the
hardest of tasks to determine in the Bible, exactly where one work of
literature ends and another begins."[150]

Fig. 12: Job 2:2–3:26 from the Harper *Illuminated Bible*. In the prose and page
layout of the KJB it is often difficult to discern the shift from prose to poetry in the
original Hebrew—Job 1–2 is prose, while Job 3 is poetry.

In the prose sections of the Bible (e.g., in the Torah) narrative prevails.
But in long sections of the Bible's nonnarrative poetry (e.g., Isaiah
40–55, Song of Songs) there is no narrative logic and no clear way
to tell where individual poems begin and end, or even if there are
individual poems. Which is to say that this poetry in the translation
of the KJB can be read as large singular wholes, long runs of singular
indented verses (of varying lengths)—so Whitman: "All its history,
biography, narratives, etc., are as beads, strung on and indicating the
eternal thread of the Deific purpose and power."[151] Intriguingly, Levine

---

150 *The Literary Study of the Bible* (2d ed; Boston, 1899 [1895]), v–vi. The chief aim of
     this work is to make clear that the Bible is made up of various forms of literature—
     "epics, lyrics, dramas, essays, sonnets, philosophical works, histories and the like"
     (v), a fact that is generally obscured by the (KJB) uniformity in formatting—the
     Bible is "the worst-printed book in the world" (45).

151 "Theological inferences,", https://library.duke.edu/rubenstein/scriptorium/
     findaids/images/whitmaniana/whitman2023/index.htm, an undated manuscript
     note from the Trent Collection, Duke University (quarto 35).

posits the Yahweh speeches from Job 38–41 as the "biblical prototype" for Whitman's "list"-like catalogues of the "Song of Myself."[152] I might add, on the one hand, that the scale of the Joban poems (presumably the products of written composition) are themselves (individually and collectively) well matched to the scale of Whitman's early catalogues; and, on the other hand, that the survey of human history from a single person's perspective in "Pictures," which offers a starkly contrasting perspective to that reported "out of the whirlwind," epitomizes the post-Christian, secular antitype to biblical divinity revealed in Levine's reading of "Song of Myself."

Whether the KJB played a role in Whitman's discovery of the long poem as his "literary vehicle" of choice, as exemplified embryonically in "Pictures," is impossible to say. What is certain is that the KJB (a literary source well known to Whitman), because of its prosaic nature and genre-leveling page layout, contains page after page of runs of indented verse divisions in narrow columns that lend themselves (especially visually) to being read stichicly (as verse)—the look and feel are remarkably similar to the page layout of a typical nineteenth-century newspaper or even the visual display conveyed by the covered wall space in a daguerreotype gallery. Moreover, the fifty-two line-initial "And"s offer (collectively) another important pointer to the Bible, and especially to the prose portions of the Bible where they dominate especially in verse-initial position (because of the prominence of the main underlying Hebrew narrative form, the so-called *wayyiqtol* form, see Chapters Three and Five for details) and where the individual verses routinely stretch out in Whitmanesque proportions. Consider Gen 30:1–13 in the rendering of the KJB (Figs. 13–14). Twelve of the thirteen verses begin with "And" and are very reminiscent of several of the leaves from "Pictures," which are also dominated by runs of line-initial "And"s (see Fig. 11). Note that it is Whitman's use of the conjunction in "Pictures" that distinguishes his poetic renderings from his similarly posed journalistic descriptions of portraits in a daguerreotype gallery.[153] Allen even notices that the "rhythms" in

---

152 "Whitman's American Bible," 154.
153 E.g., "Here is an aged man, with long hair, white as silver. His eyes, although taken down by time and trouble, are yet clear and form. What a patient, manly,

"Pictures" are "simply those of prose."[154] Such prosiness is sensible from several angles, but especially if the source of inspiration, whether in the Bible or Whitman's own journalism, is itself prosaic in nature (see further Chapter Five). In short, read holistically and grossly in the English translation of the KJB, the Bible (especially in certain stretches) looks very much like a Whitmanian long poem (or "cluster" of such long poems).

Fig. 13: Gen 29:5–30:3 from the Harper *Illuminated Bible*.

---

benevolent expression!" ("An Hour Among the Portraits," *Brooklyn Evening Star* [7 June 1853], 2). Compare these lines from "Pictures" (*NUPM* IV, 1296):

—Here! Do you know this? This is cicerone himself;

And here, one after another, see you, my own States—and there there the world itself, rolling bowling through the air;

And there, on the walls hanging, portraits of women and men, carefully kept,

Bohan and others have recognized in the catalogue in "Pictures" in particular—the first extended experiment with one of Whitman's most distinctive poetic devices—a "transformation" into writing of the kind of visual exhibition experience Whitman describes in "An Hour Among the Portraits" (Bohan, *Looking into Walt Whitman*, 24; cf. Reynolds, *Whitman's America*, 287). But he also adopts the very same pose of the latter written description, only now the speaker of the poem is touring the gallery of "pictures" in his own mind—"many pictures hanging suspended," "hundreds and thousands" (*NUPM* IV, 1296)). And even more striking, as briefly illustrated here, the same rhetorical strategy is used for staging the individual pictures, though now the vignettes are somewhat abbreviated and lined out as verse—"each verse presenting a picture of some scene, event, group or personage" (*NUPM* IV, 1294).

Fig. 14: Gen 30:4–39 from the Harper *Illuminated Bible*.

There are a number of surviving preliminary drafts of lines (or blocks of lines) for *Leaves* that stand between the trials of the early notebooks and the versions published in 1855. On occasion these, too, reveal biblicisms. Some examples by way of illustration may be offered from proto-versions of "I celebrate myself."[155] In "I call back blunders," there is this line that Whitman never publishes: "I give strong meat in place of panada."[156] The "strong meat" is the KJB's translation of Greek στερεὰ τροφή from Heb 5:12 and 14, which references solid food (as opposed, for example, to milk, or as Whitman has it, "panada"—a kind of bread soup). In both of the biblical verses the image is applied figuratively as a trope for teaching, knowledge, the capacity to reason—very much akin to Whitman's usage. In a manuscript leaf from Duke University, "I know

---

154 *Solitary Singer*, 145.

155 Folsom has collected a number of the holographs that anticipate "I celebrate myself" from several university collections ("Whitman," http://bailiwick.lib. uiowa.edu/whitman/). These are accessible at *WWA*. Unless otherwise noted, I reference these manuscripts as transcribed and edited by Folsom.

156 https://whitmanarchive.org/manuscripts/figures/uva.00250.001.jpg.

as well as you that Bibles are divine revelation," Whitman references "~~God~~" (3x), "the Lord," "Jehovah," and possibly "~~Adonai~~."[157] These are all quite specifically references to the God of the Bible, and especially the Hebrew Bible (or Old Testament). "Jehovah" and "Adonai" are each used once in *Leaves*, in the section the manuscript leaf appears to be working towards (*LG*, 45). The phrase "the Lord"—with definite article and capitalization—appears twice in *Leaves* (*LG*, 15, 84). And "God"—capitalized and not canceled—occurs fully twenty-four times in *Leaves* (*LG*, v, vi, viii, xi, 15 [2x], 16, 29, 34, 38, 45, 50, 51, 53, 54 [9x], 95). And there are a number of phrases, like the "hand of God" and "spirit of God" discussed earlier, that are either biblical or sound biblical: "By God!" (*LG*, 29, 45) when swearing an oath (Mark 5:7; cf. Gen 21:23; 1 Sam 30:15; 2 Chron 36:13; Neh 13:25; also frequently "by the Lord," e.g., 1 Kgs 1:30); "orchards of God" (*LG*, 38) sounds very much like a play on and broadening of the idea of Eden, the "garden of God" (Ezek 28:13; 31:8, 9); "And I call to mankind, Be not curious about God" (*LG*, 54)—this has the feel, shape, and even punctuation (manner of embedding direct discourse) of a saying of Jesus (e.g., "Then said Jesus unto them, Be not afraid," Matt 28:10) or a prophet (e.g., "And Isaiah said unto them, Thus shall ye say unto your master, Thus saith the LORD, Be not afraid of the words...," Isa 37:6);[158] "In the faces of men and women I see God" (*LG*, 54)—"yet in my flesh shall I see God" (Job 19:26); and "before God" (*LG*, 95; 48x in KJB). From the Duke University manuscript, "a revelation ~~of God~~" is close to similar New Testament idioms, such as "revelations of the Lord" (2 Cor 12:1) or "revelation of Jesus Christ" (Gal 1:12; 1 Pet 1:13; Rev 1:1). And the mention of "~~the~~ Bibles," capitalized and pluralized with the canceled definite article, shows Whitman in the process of deconstructing (and democratizing) the otherwise very particular connotation of this term in English (i.e., "THE BOOK... the sacred volume, in which are contained the revelations of God," Webster, *American Dictionary* [1852], 102) and

---

157 http://whitmanarchive.org/manuscripts/figures/duk.00051.001.jpg. The latter can be read as "Adonis" (so Folsom).

158 The explicit deconstruction of the God-centeredness of the Bible makes the use of biblical style here, now in service to Whitman's democratic, anthropocentric creed (cf. Levine, "Whitman's American Bible," 158), all that more effective.

anticipating his twofold usage of "bibles" (generalized, pluralized, and not capitalized) in the 1855 *Leaves* (*LG*, 29, 60).

Another Duke manuscript ("There is no word in any tongue")[159] contains draft ideas about God that eventually get worked into "I celebrate myself." Many of the phrases have a biblical feel to them. There is "the scope and purpose of God" that may descend ultimately from Rom 9:11: "(For the children being not yet born, neither having done any good or evil, that the purpose of God according to election might stand, not of works, but of him that calleth;)." Whitman uses the biblical "Lo" once. The phrase "Of God I know not," though itself not biblical, the subject is certainly the biblical "God" and the inverted syntax of "know not" comes straight out of the KJB (71x). Gen 1:26–27 likely lurks somewhere in the background of "Mostly this we have of God: we have Man": "And God said, Let us make man in our image, after our likeness... So God created man in his own image, in the image of God created he him...." (Gen 1:26–27). Creation imagery is drawn on as well in another Duke manuscript scrap: "My ~~Soul~~ ^Spirit^ ~~was [illegible words] sped back to the~~ ^sped [illegible] back to the^ ~~beginning~~ times when the earth was forming mist."[160] The inserted (and capitalized) "Spirit" is perhaps intended to counterpoint the "Spirit of God" that moves over the surface of the waters in the Bible's first creation account (Gen 1:3; cf. *LG*, 16), and Whitman's language at the end of the line, "^the^ ~~beginning~~ times when the earth was forming mist," is a slight re-shaping of language from the beginning of the second creation story: "But there went up a mist from the earth" (Gen 2:6).

* * *

In sum, the early notebooks and poetry manuscripts and "Pictures" help fill in some of the gap between the three 1850 poems and the 1855 *Leaves*. They evidence Whitman's continued engagement with the Bible and show him beginning to abide more scrupulously by his evolving poetic theory as it pertains to no second-hand quotations. In general, even in this pre-*Leaves* material Whitman is more advanced than in the 1850 poems or the prose writings from 1850–53—there are no direct

---

159 http://whitmanarchive.org/manuscripts/figures/duk.00018.001.jpg.
160 https://whitmanarchive.org/manuscripts/figures/duk.00262.001.jpg.

quotes. But it is often the case when this preparatory material shows up in *Leaves* the allusions or echoes have been further sanitized. This is simply to emphasize that the early notebooks and unpublished poetry manuscripts provide yet further evidence of Whitman's taste for collage and tendency to erase all signs of his sources. But they also show that Miller's strong assertion that "the notebooks don't offer much evidence either way about the Bible" to be overstated.[161] Even in the early notebooks (and early unpublished poetry manuscripts), where Whitman is already committed to his poetic theory of providing no second-hand quotations, the poet's use of biblical ideas, language, themes, figures, and tropes is still trackable.

---

161 *Collage of Myself*, 26.

3. Whitman's Line: "Found" in the KJB?

Perhaps the likeness which is presented to the mind most strongly is that which exists between our author and the verse divisions of the English Bible, especially in the poetical books

> — G. Saintsbury, review of 1870–71 *Leaves of Grass* (1874)

"Since *Leaves of Grass* was first published," observes M. Miller, "readers have often assumed that Whitman developed his line from the Bible."[1] This is a startling observation. Yes, there has been a long-running interest in the more general topic of Whitman and the Bible, but the line only very rarely comes in for specific comment. For example, R. Asselineau in *The Evolution of Walt Whitman: An Expanded Edition* does remark that Whitman's long verses "recall above all the Bible," though without further elaboration or substantiation.[2] And I return below to one of the early reviews of *Leaves* and what is perhaps the most probative perception about Whitman's line as it relates to the Bible. But in fact such observations specifically about Whitman's line are not so numerous, and nothing overly detailed, let alone evidence for a continuous and incisive scholarly debate on the topic. In the chapter that follows, then, I propose to undertake such an inquiry, a probing of the proposition that "Whitman developed his line from the Bible." Once focused on the principal site of textual encounter, the King James Bible, I point to a number of ways in which that Bible may have played a role in shaping Whitman's ideas about his mature line, its length(s), familiar shapes,

---

1   *Collage of Myself: Walt Whitman and the Making of Leaves of Grass* (Lincoln/London: University of Nebraska, 2010), 25.
2   (Iowa City: University of Iowa, 1999 [1960, 1962]), II, 240. Cf. J. P. Warren, "Style" in *A Companion to Walt Whitman* (ed. D. D. Kummings; London: Blackwell, 2006), 377–91, at 383.

©2024 F. W. Dobbs-Allsopp, CC BY-NC 4.0   https://doi.org/10.11647/OBP.0357.04

contents, and even in places its very staging. Yet as with so much of Whitman's collaging, the finding is only part of the art. Here, too, what (of the line) Whitman finds is typically worked and reworked such that the finding itself can get obscured and what is made in the process indubitably is made distinctly his own.

The Development of Whitman's Long Line: A Chronology

Before turning to my topic in earnest, however, I sketch the chronological development of Whitman's long line as currently understood. The renewed attention paid to the early notebooks and poetry manuscripts—stimulated in part by the recovery in 1995 of some of the notebooks that had been lost by the Library of Congress during the Second World War[3]—has enabled scholars to see much more clearly the emergence of that line and to have a better idea of its rough chronology. Presently, the three poems published in the spring and summer of 1850—"Blood-Money,"[4] "The House of Friends,"[5]and "Resurgemus"[6]—appear to be the last poems (with line-breaks) Whitman composed prior to the trial lines found in the earliest extant notebooks, most of which date from between 1852 and 1854.[7] The break with meter in 1850 turns out to be decisive for the development of Whitman's line as it unshackles the major constraint on line-length and opens the way to using lines

---

3   A. Birney, "Missing Whitman Notebooks Returned to Library of Congress," *WWQR* 12 (1995), 217–29.

4   *New York Daily Tribune* (22 March 1850), 1, http://whitmanarchive.org/published/periodical/poems/per.00089.

5   *New York Daily Tribune* (14 June 1850), 3, http://whitmanarchive.org/published/periodical/poems/per.00442.

6   *New York Daily Tribune* (21 June 1850), 3, http://whitmanarchive.org/published/periodical/poems/per.00088.

7   The surviving notebooks are not always (easily) datable, and clearly there remains much that is missing as well. The earliest notebooks with line-breaks (e.g., *DBN III*, 773–77; *NUPM I*, 53–82, 102-12, 128–35) are conventionally dated to 1854 or a little earlier, with the "Talbot Wilson" notebook (https://whitmanarchive.org/manuscripts/notebooks/transcriptions/loc.00141.html) being the most famous (and important) of the group. For a good recent statement on the issues, see A. C. Higgins, "Wage Slavery and the Composition of Leaves of Grass: The 'Talbot Wilson' Notebook," *WWQR* 20/2 [2002], 53–77, esp. 53–61). Both J. Burroughs ("1853 and the seasons immediately following" in *Notes on Walt Whitman as Poet and Person* [New York, 1867], 83) and J. T. Trowbridge ("in that summer of 1854... he began Leaves of Grass" in *My Own Story* [Boston, 1903], 367) dates Whitman's initial work on the 1855 *Leaves* to the general period of these early notebooks.

of varying lengths according to the requirements of clause or sentence logic.[8] A majority of the lines in the three poems remain of conventional lengths. Emblematic of this is the fact that in the case of "Resurgemus," Whitman often simply combines two (or more) lines to make a single (long) line in the revised version of the poem included in the 1855 *Leaves*, e.g., "But the sweetness of mercy brewed bitter destruction,/ And frightened rulers come back:" ("Resurgemus"; eight words/ five words) => "But the sweetness of mercy brewed bitter destruction, and the frightened rulers come back:" (*LG*, 88; fourteen words).[9] Crucially, though, the lengths of the lines vary (however modestly) in these poems, and some stretch out beyond the eight-word limit that characterizes much of Whitman's earlier metered verse: "Blood-Money" has the most lines eight words in length or longer, eleven (e.g., "Where, as though Earth lifted her breast to throw him from her, and Heaven refused him," line 7; sixteen words);[10] "House of Friends" has five such lines (e.g., "The shriek of a drowned world, the appeal of women," line 28; ten words); and "Resurgemus" three (e.g., "Suddenly, out of its state and drowsy air, the air of slaves," line 1; twelve words). None of these "long" lines attain the extended reach of Whitman's longest lines in the 1855 *Leaves*, but they all fall squarely within the sweet spot for line-length in that volume, which is from eight to sixteen words per line. Lines of these lengths each occur more than a hundred times and account for 1,641 lines in total—71% of all the lines in the 1855 *Leaves* (see s. 41–42. 15). Already in these initial free-verse efforts, then, Whitman has found the lineal scale that will carry much of his verbiage in the early *Leaves*.

---

8   S. Bradley ("The Fundamental Metrical Principle in Whitman's Poetry" in *On Whitman* [eds. E. H. Cady and L. J. Budd; Durham: Duke University, 1987], 49–71 [originally published in *American Literature* 10 (1939), 437–59], 54–55) also recognizes the correlation between line-length and "predetermined metrical pattern," though he develops this insight to different ends, with different emphases.

9   I use word counts throughout as a convenient means of measurement. In doing so I do not mean to imply anything about modes of composition.

10   Significantly, lines 13 ("What will ye give me, and I will deliver this man unto you?", thirteen words) and 14 ("And they make the covenant and pay the pieces of silver," eleven words) offer a close version of Matt 26:15: "And said unto them, What will ye give me, and I will deliver him unto you? And they covenanted with him for thirty pieces of silver." The lengths of these lines, along with their sentential shaping (see below), are quite literally found in the *KJB*.

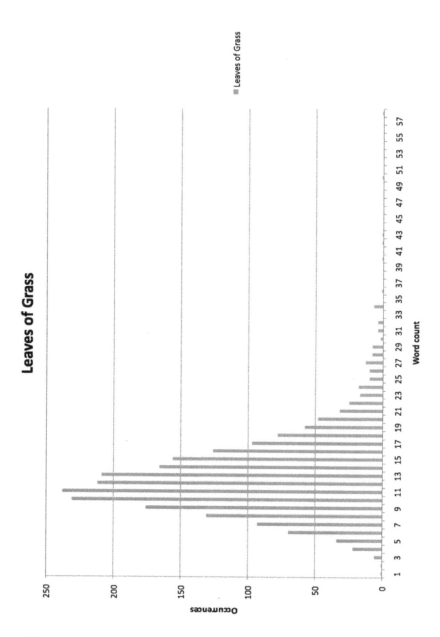

Fig. 15: Line lengths by word count for the 1855 *Leaves*. Computation and chart by Greg Murray.

In the spring of 1851 in his "Art and Artists" lecture, Whitman is still content to quote lines from "Resurgemus" as originally crafted.[11] Of the eighteen lines quoted, only one numbers more than eight words ("They live in brothers, again ready to defy you," nine words, *UPP* I, 247). In the recombined version of these lines from the 1855 *Leaves*, the overall number of lines is reduced to ten, and eight of these tally nine or more words, including the nineteen-word "Not a grave of the murdered for freedom but grows seed for freedom.... in its turn to bear seed" (*LG*, 88). The percentage of lines of conventional lengths (eight or fewer words) in the 1855 *Leaves* is still smaller, amounting to roughly 15% of the total number of lines (354 lines, see Fig. 15).

Trial verse lines appear in at least four of the pre-*Leaves* notebooks. The "med Cophósis"notebook is perhaps the earliest of these, with most dating it between 1852 and 1854.[12] Only two long leaves survive, and there is just one set of obvious verse lines, material that anticipates the opening of "Who learns my lesson complete?" (*LG*, 92–93):

My Lesson

Have you learned ~~the~~ ^my^ lesson complete:

It is well—it is ^but^ the gate to a larger lesson—and

~~And~~ that to another; ~~still~~

And ~~every one opens~~ ^each successive one^ to another still[13]

Of the four original lines started here, only the second is long, containing twelve words.[14] Whitman's deletions and additions in lines

---

11   31 March 1851. Published subsequently in the *Brooklyn Daily Advertiser* (3 April 1851). Reprinted in *UPP I*, 241–47.

12   https://whitmanarchive.org/manuscripts/notebooks/transcriptions/loc.00005. html. Miller, for example, prefers a date for this notebook later in the period, late 1853 or early 1854 (*Collage of Myself*, 15–20).

13   https://whitmanarchive.org/manuscripts/figures/loc.00005.001.jpg.

14   I assume the "—and" at the end of the line (slightly raised) was added after the line-initial "And" of line 3 was deleted. Determining which words to count in Whitman's holographs is not straightforward. My aim in making counts is heuristic, to gain a rough idea about the scale of Whitman's lines at a particular moment. For the purpose of the exercise I have counted words only in lines which could be (more or less) clearly determined to be verse. Passages of verse frequently will consist of a series of lines headed by capital letters and will feature one or more hanging indentation for excessively long lines (i.e., lines that do not

2–3 create the equivalent to the "hanging indentation" that appears in the holographs of other notebooks for rendering the continuation of long lines onto the next manuscript line. This lengthens the line to sixteen words. It also shows Whitman in the process of combining lines, much like what must be assumed, for example, to have taken place in his revisions of "Resurgemus." Interestingly, Whitman settles on a different combination in the 1855 *Leaves*, going back to the original substructure and working it out differently:

> Who learns my lesson complete?
>
> ....
>
> It is no lesson.... it lets down the bars to a good lesson,
>
> And that to another.... and every one to another still. (*LG*, 92)[15]

The last line quoted here is a combined version of lines 3–4 from the notebook fragment, stretching the line to ten words.[16] While the sample

---

fit within the narrow widths of Whitman's manuscripts). I do not count words in what are clearly incomplete lines (my aim here is to assess line-length). Further, I do not count words that have been locally deleted—such words in the holographs are normally crossed out in some manner (e.g., with strikethroughs). In contrast, I have ignored the fact that often whole passages and pages are canceled by a vertical or diagonal line drawn across the whole. My working counts were all generated manually. I do not record precise figures but rely on generalizations. The holographs are complex textual artifacts. One can easily imagine ways to sophisticate this kind of assessment. For my purpose it is enough to gain a general impression about the lengths of Whitman's lines in any one notebook or manuscript source, the chief upshot of which is that Whitman comes to his preferred line scales over time, in the process of his drafting and redrafting of verse for the first edition *of Leaves of Grass.*

15   Such "re-doings"—or as in this case an "undoing"—are not uncharacteristic of Whitman's process of composition. Another good example is the "cow crunching" line (*LG*, 34), the published version of which retrieves much from its initial trial in the "Talbot Wilson" notebook (https://whitmanarchive.org/manuscripts/figures/loc.00141.076.jpg), after experimenting with an intermediate version, of which the emendations made were ultimately abandoned (cf. E. Folsom and K. M. Price, *Re-Scripting Walt Whitman: An Introduction to His Life and Work* [Malden, MA: Blackwell, 2005], ch. 2; Miller, *Collage of Myself*, 55–59).

16   It is unsurprising that the biblicized "Have you" (the phrase "have ye" occurs eighty-three times in the *KJB* and is especially common in rhetorical questions) has been jettisoned in the published version of the opening line, viz. "Who learns my lesson complete?" (*LG*, 92).

size is statistically irrelevant, the four notebook lines share the same basic profile as found in the 1850 poems.

"I know a rich capitalist" is usually dated to 1854 like most of the remaining early notebooks.[17] Again, there is only one set of verse lines in this notebook. Of the eight lines of verse written out, only two are long (eleven and ten words in length). The profile—lines of variable lengths, mostly short and none that are really long—here, too, is suggestive of the 1850 poems.[18] Moreover, these lines were clearly culled from a passage of prose inscribed earlier in the notebook. Intriguingly, on seven occasions the clausal phrasing of the prose version is circumscribed by long dashes. One of the dashes comes at the end of the passage. Of the other six, five head material that is broken into distinct verse lines in the poetic version (Figs. 16–17). This use of dashes is most reminiscent of Whitman's long riff on Genesis 1 at the beginning of the "Art and Artists" lecture discussed in Chapter One—only here a versified version also exists.[19]

Two other early notebooks, the "Poem incarnating the mind" notebook[20] and the famous "Talbot Wilson" notebook,[21] preserve many more lines of trial verse than the two notebooks just discussed. The prevailing line profile in these notebooks is noticeably different. Short lines (eight or fewer words) and long lines (nine to sixteen words in length) appear in almost equal proportions, with long lines being slightly more numerous in each notebook. Moreover, for the first time each notebook preserves lines of seventeen words or more: "Poem incarnating the mind" has four

---

17 https://whitmanarchive.org/manuscripts/notebooks/transcriptions/nyp.00129. html. The Marble Collegiate Church of Manhattan was completed in 1854 and the first news of the wreck of the San Francisco started appearing in the New York papers in mid-January 1854. Both are referenced in this notebook.

18 Miller characterizes these free-verse lines (in passing) as "not as long" as in some of the other early notebooks (*Collage of Myself*, 22).

19 UPP I, 242. These notebook jottings show that J. Loving's conversion into verse of a similar slice of long-dash circumscribed prose material to be very much in the spirit of Whitman's own practice (*Walt Whitman: A Song of Himself* [Berkeley: University of California, 1999], 171).

20 https://whitmanarchive.org/manuscripts/notebooks/transcriptions/loc.00346.html.

21 https://whitmanarchive.org/manuscripts/notebooks/transcriptions/loc.00141. html. On the date, see esp. Birney, "Missing Whitman Notebooks," 217–29; E. Shephard, "Possible Sources of Some of Whitman's Ideas in Hermes Mercurius Trismegistus and Other Works," *MLQ* 14 (1953), 67n; E. F. Grier, "Walt Whitman's Earliest Known Notebook," *PMLA* 83 (1968), 1453–1456; Higgins, "Wage Slavery," 53–77; Miller, *Collage of Myself*, 2–5.

such lines (e.g., "And in that deadly sea waited five ^How they^ gripped close with Death ^there^ on the sea, and gave him not one inch, but held on days and nights near the helpless fogged great wreck"; twenty-two words; all canceled)[22] and "Talbot Wilson" has nine (e.g., "I will not have a single person left out.... I will ^have^ the prostitute and the thief invited.... I will make no difference between them and the rest"; twenty-seven words; all canceled).[23] And most of the short lines actually number between six and eight words in length. In fact, the majority of lines in these notebooks range between six and eighteen words in length, as also in the 1855 *Leaves* (roughly 86% of the lines in the later are of these lengths, see Fig. 15).

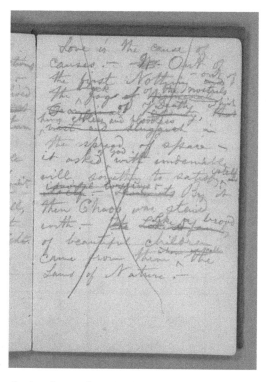

Fig. 16: Leaf 6r from the "I know a rich capitalist" notebook, https://whitmanarchive.org/manuscripts/figures/nyp.00129.011.jpg, showing the prose version of the "Love is the cause of causes" passage. Image courtesy of the Henry W. and Albert A. Berg Collection of English and American Literature, New York Public Library.

---

22   https://whitmanarchive.org/manuscripts/figures/loc_jc.01674.jpg.
23   https://whitmanarchive.org/manuscripts/figures/loc.00141.115.jpg.

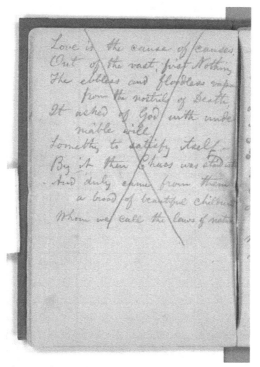

Fig. 17: Leaf 7v from the "I know a rich capitalist" notebook, https://whitmanarchive.org/manuscripts/figures/nyp.00129.014.jpg, showing the verse version of the "Love is the cause of causes" passage. Image courtesy of the Henry W. and Albert A. Berg Collection of English and American Literature, New York Public Library.

There is one last pre-*Leaves* notebook that may contain verse lines, the "Autobiographical Data" notebook.[24] The notebook appears to have been used over an extended period of time (1848–55/56).[25] Unfortunately, the original notebook itself is missing, and the passage (material set out in enumerated sections) that some identify as poetry[26]

24   https://whitmanarchive.org/manuscripts/notebooks/transcriptions/loc.05935.html.
25   Higgins, "Wage Slavery," 76, n. 35; cf. *UPP II*, 86, n. 1 ("period before 1855"); *NUPM I*, 209 (before "winter of 1855–56"); E. Folsom, "Erasing Race: The Lost Black Presence in Whitman's Manuscripts" in *Whitman Noir: Black America and the Good Gray Poet* (Iowa City: University of Iowa, 2014), 3–31, at 23.
26   E.g., A. C. Higgins, "Art and Argument: The Rise of Walt Whitman's Rhetorical Poetics, 1838–1855" (unpbl. Ph.D. diss; University of Massachusetts Amherst, 1999), 136–39—though Higgins does not argue the point but seems to assume the facticity of verse based on Holloway's transcription.

is not preserved in the extant set of (incomplete) photostats—the transcription of this material is dependent on E. Holloway's edition.[27] It is not obvious that (all of) this material is verse (e.g., Grier refers to the numbered sections as "paragraphs," *NUPM* I, 212, n. 16)[28] and the date of composition cannot be narrowed beyond the range posited for the entire notebook. If the passage is verse, it does not closely resemble "the poetry of 1855–56."[29] There could be as many as fourteen complete lines. Most range in length between seven and eighteen words; there are three longer lines of twenty-one (2x) and thirty-four words. Obviously, much uncertainty remains regarding this material.[30]

Surviving drafts of proto-versions of lines for the 1855 *Leaves* appear to stand between the early notebook trials and their published versions. For example, E. Folsom has collected a number of the holographs that anticipate "I celebrate myself" from several university collections.[31] Long lines clearly prevail in these manuscripts—more than two-thirds of the lines are long. Yet proportionately short lines still occur twice as often as they do in the 1855 *Leaves*. Not infrequently, shorter lines in these manuscripts get combined in their published version, as with the revision of "Resurgemus." The following are illustrative:

---

27 *UPP II*, 88–89; cf. *NUPM I*, 212, n. 16.
28 Holloway (followed by Grier) sets the sectioned material on separate lines, with initial capitalization, but without indentations for the continuation of longer "lines."
29 *NUPM I*, 209; cf. Higgins, "Art and Argument," 136. Both Higgins ("Wage Slavery," 60) and Folsom ("Erasing Race," 23) call attention to the material in the notebook (*NUPM I*, 215–16) that anticipates the "mashed fireman" episode in *LG*, 39.
30 Grier observes of the notebook generally, "some of the contents baffle any theory of WW's development" (*NUPM I*, 209).
31 Folsom, "Whitman." These consist of the recto or verso of single manuscript leaves and are currently being edited (along with Whitman's other poetry manuscripts) online at *WWA*. With some exceptions (e.g., "Light and Air!", see Miller, *Collage of Myself*, 60–62), most of these manuscripts "clearly date from later than the notebooks" (Folsom and Price, *Re-Scripting*, ch. 2). I counted lines in twenty-eight of the manuscripts that Folsom gathers from the University of Texas (three), Duke University (eleven), and the University of Virginia (fourteen)—several manuscripts were either entirely prose or contained lines that were indeterminable for one reason or another. I consulted the digital images for each manuscript and other transcriptions where available.

1. "Talbot Wilson":	For I take my death with the dying
	And my birth with the new-born babes [32]
"taken soon out of the laps":	
	For I take my death with the dying,
LG, 17:	I pass death with the dying, and birth with the new-washed babe…. and am not contained between my hat and boots,
2. "You there":	You there! impotent loose.. the knees! Open you ~~mouth~~ ~~send~~ bl ~~o~~ gums, my [~~illegible~~] that I ~~put~~ grit in you with ~~one~~ a [illegible]th[33]
LG, 44:	You there, impotent, loose in the knees, open your scarfed chops till I blow grit within you,
3. "Talbot Wilson":	I ~~will~~ am not to be denied—I compel; *I have stores plenty and to spare[34]
"You there":	I am not to be denied—I compel; I have stores plenty; and to spare;[35]
LG, 44:	I am not to be denied…. I compel…. I have stores plenty and to spare,
4. "You villain, Touch!":	~~190~~ You villain, Touch! what are you doing? Unloose me, ~~Touch!~~ the breath is leaving my throat; !
~~LG,~~ 44:	You there, impotent, loose in the knees, open your scarfed chops till I blow grit within you,

---

32   https://whitmanarchive.org/manuscripts/figures/loc.00141.091.jpg.
33   https://whitmanarchive.org/manuscripts/figures/uva.00263.001.jpg. The related lines from the "Talbot Wilson" notebook, though somewhat different, nevertheless still have multiple original lines that eventually are combined in the 1855 *Leaves* version.
34   https://whitmanarchive.org/manuscripts/figures/loc.00141.095.jpg.
35   http://whitmanarchive.org/manuscripts/figures/uva.00263.001.jpg.

Examples like these suggest that such combining of shorter lines to make longer lines was especially characteristic of the latest stage(s) of Whitman's composition of the first edition of *Leaves of Grass*. The lineal profile of the latter shifts yet again. Whitman's long lines in the 1855 *Leaves* continue to stretch out, and their numbers are even greater. Sometimes the expansion in length is striking, as witnessed above in Whitman's combinatory collaging of shorter lines to make long lines, and sometimes it is more incremental. A good example of the latter is the following line, which accumulates more words in each version:

> "Talbot Wilson": I tell you ~~it~~ $^{\text{I know}}$ it is ~~more~~ $^{\text{just as}}$ beautiful to die; (twelve words)[36]

> "taken soon out of the laps": I ~~tell~~ $^{\text{hasten to inform}}$ you it is just as good to die;, and I know it; (sixteen words)

> LG,17: I hasten to inform him or her it is just as lucky to die, and I know it. (eighteen words)

Almost 85% of the lines in the 1855 *Leaves* are long (65.3%) or really long (19.4%). Short lines persist, as they have from the beginning. For example, "Those corpses of young men" is among a handful of short lines from "Resurgemus" that stays unchanged (un-lengthened) from its first publication in 1850 through to the final lifetime edition of *Leaves* (*LG* 1881, 212). However, the number of such short lines decreases dramatically, accounting for just better than 15% of the lines in the 1855 *Leaves*.[37] Whitman's unpublished long poem, "Pictures," which most date to sometime around 1855,[38] mainly features long lines, with only a very few short lines (less than 5%).[39]

In sum, while Whitman's long line is birthed immediately in his break with metrical verse, the basic trajectory of line usage in the run-up to

---

36   https://whitmanarchive.org/manuscripts/figures/loc.00141.091.jpg.
37   A characteristic use to which these short lines are put in *Leaves*, as recognized by B. H. Smith, is to close runs of Whitman's otherwise more typical long lines, a form of terminal modification (*Poetic Closure: A Study of How Poems End* [Chicago: University of Chicago, 1968], 92–93). A good example is the long sentential catalogue that begins on p. 35 of the 1855 *Leaves* ("By the city's quadrangular houses.... in log-huts, or camping with lumbermen") and ends on p. 38 with a seven-word line, "I tread day and night such roads"—by far the shortest line of the catalogue (with the support of a final period as well).
38   For example, Grier: "at the earliest."
39   https://collections.library.yale.edu/catalog/2007253.

the 1855 *Leaves* is one of increasing preference for long (and really long) lines matched by decreasing dependence on short lines. The latter persist throughout but in ever decreasing numbers. Really long lines steadily increase (in number and scale), eventually overtaking the number of short lines in the 1855 *Leaves*. From the time of the "Poem incarnating the mind" and "Talbot Wilson" notebooks, lines of between nine and sixteen words in length dominate Whitman's verse exercises and published poems. Still, throughout this period Whitman's line remains strikingly variable and fluid in terms of length. In fact, though many lines settle into canonical shapes for Whitman, many others will continue to vary (and at times disappear completely) in succeeding editions. Long lines continue to be added in the next two editions of *Leaves*, though the trend towards a favoring of foreshortened lines that marks much of Whitman's poetry after 1865 already begins in these earlier editions. Whitman's "finding" of his long line on this view is decidedly processual in nature. After becoming a possibility, it emerges over time in Whitman's "many MS. doings and undoings," stretching out, reconfiguring, even contracting when needed as the poet molds his line to fit his sentences.

G. W. Allen, Parallelism, and the Biblical Poetic Line

Of the two studies that Miller recognizes as having explored the connection between Whitman's line and the Bible "perhaps most definitively," only G. W. Allen truly takes up the topic of the line, and that not without problems.[40] The engine that drives Allen's analysis is parallelism, which he takes as the first rhythmical principle of the English Bible and which he understands chiefly according to R. Lowth's system (as mediated

---

40   Miller's singling out of Bradley's "Fundamental Metrical Principle" is curious since its chief interest lies in uncovering the "true meter" of Whitman's verse, as the title implies. Neither the line *per se* (beyond how it stages the posited "periodic rhythm" of the verse) nor the Bible come in for any significant comment. Bradley recognizes the contributions made to the understanding of Whitman's prosody by the supposition of biblical influence at the beginning of his article (50) and addresses Allen's arguments a bit later only enough to make room for his own thoughts (60–61). At this point, Bradley does assert that the English translators of the Bible employ the same sort of "periodic rhythm" he posits for Whitman, which in turn inclines him more favorably toward the thesis of Whitman's debt to the Bible. Bradley seems unaware that the KJB is a prose translation and that its rhythms, though undoubtedly impacted by what is being translated, are at heart that of English prose.

by various secondary discussions).[41] This emphasis would seem to be well put, for as G. Kinnell observes, "Whitman is no doubt the greatest virtuoso of parallel structure in English poetry."[42] But in order to unravel Whitman's understanding and use of parallelism, Allen well appreciated that he had to first give attention to the line: "the line is the unit, 'the second line balancing the first, completing or supplementing its meaning.'"[43] This is Allen quoting J. H. Gardiner about biblical verse. A few pages later he turns to Whitman, making the same point: "The fact that the line in *Leaves of Grass* is also the rhythmical unit is so obvious that probably all students of Whitman have noticed it."[44] Miller, more recently, underscores just how crucial the development of his poetic line was to Whitman: "In fact his [Whitman's] notebooks suggest that it [his line] was probably the single most important factor in accelerating his development."[45] And even more emphatically a bit later: "if one event can be described as his strictly *creative* catalyst, judging from the notebooks it would seem to be his realization of new ways of composing derived from his discovery of his line."[46] What is "so obvious" for students of Whitman, or indeed students of poetry

---

41   G. W. Allen, "Biblical Analogies for Walt Whitman's Prosody," *Revue Anglo-Americaine* 6 (1933), 490–507. The biblicists he cites specifically are S. R. Driver (*Introduction to the Literature of the Old Testament* [New York, 1910], 361–62) and E. Kautzsch, *Die Poesie und die Poetischen Bücher des Alten Testaments* [Tübingen and Leipzig, 1902], 2). He also mentions Lowth's original lectures but clearly by way of the discussions of Driver and Kautzsch. In fact, it seems that Allen relies mainly on the work of literary critics for his working understanding of biblical parallelism, especially that of J. H. Gardiner (*The Bible as Literature* [New York, 1906]) and R. G. Moulton (*Modern Reader's Bible for Schools* [New York: Macmillan, 1922]). There is the problem in the latter in particular, as D. Norton recognizes (*A History of the Bible as Literature* [Cambridge: Cambridge University, 2004], 227), of simplifying Lowth's thinking to the point of distorting what he in fact says.

42   "'Strong is Your Hold': My Encounters with Whitman" in *Leaves of Grass: The Sesquicentennial Essays* (eds. S. Belasco and K. M. Price; Lincoln: University of Nebraska, 2007), 417–28.

43   Allen, "Biblical Analogies," 491–92.

44   Ibid., 493; cf. B. Erkkila, *Whitman the Political Poet* (New York/Oxford: Oxford University, 1989), 88. In *American Prosody* ([New York: American Book, 1935], 221) Allen simply uses a paraphrase of Gardiner (talking about the Bible) to characterize Whitman: "The first rhythmic principle of *Leaves of Grass* is that of parallel structure: *the line is the rhythmical unit*, each line balancing its predecessor, and completing or supplementing its meaning." Allen's fuller quotation of Gardiner in his latest statement (*New Walt Whitman Handbook* [New York: New York University, 1986 (1975)], 216) makes it clear that Gardiner is talking about the underlying Hebrew.

45   *Collage of Myself*, 2.

46   Ibid., 36.

more generally, has only rarely been noticed of biblical poetry. To date, in fact, there has been little substantive appreciation of the verse line and its significance in biblical verse—aside, that is, from issues of syntax (which is not an insignificant matter).[47] This is a considerable desideratum given that the line by most accounts is the leading differentia of verse—"the only absolute to be drawn," writes T. S. Eliot, "is that poetry is written in verse and prose is written in prose."[48] Allen's observation is astute and goes to the heart of many issues concerning biblical poetry. It warrants the attention of biblical scholars.

However, the line is also a matter Allen muddles considerably. He is very deliberate in setting up the parameters of his research. The English Bible, by which he means above all the King James Bible,[49] is the paramount focus of his comments—"I am not concerned here with the Hebrew verse."[50] This is entirely reasonable since Whitman did not know biblical Hebrew,[51] and therefore whatever sense he may have had of biblical poetics would have been mediated through translation (and whatever secondary discussions he may have encountered), above all through the KJB. But, of course, quite famously, the KJB is a *prose* translation of the Bible, including of those portions that are verse (e.g., Psalms, Proverbs, Job, etc.) and that were known to be verse by King James's translators—

---

47   On syntax and the line, see esp. M. O'Connor, *Hebrew Verse Structure* (Winona Lake: Eisenbrauns, 1980); and now on the line more generally, see F. W. Dobbs-Allsopp, "'Verse, Properly So Called': The Line in Biblical Poetry" in *On Biblical Poetry* (New York/Oxford: Oxford University, 2015), 14–94.

48   T. S. Eliot, "The Borderline of Prose," *New Statesman* 9 (1917), 158. For more general treatments, see T. V. F. Brogan, "Line" in *NPEPP*, 694; "Verse and Prose" in *NPEPP*, 1348. The distinction is a commonplace, cf. C. O. Hartman, *Free Verse: An Essay on Prosody* (Princeton: Princeton University, 1980) 11; M. Kinzie, *A Poet's Guide to Poetry* (Chicago: University of Chicago, 1999), 51, 433.

49   Clarified explicitly in the *New Walt Whitman Handbook* (215): "Possibly, as many critics have believed, he [Whitman] found such a structure in the primitive rhythms of the *King James Bible*" (my emphasis). Also in *A Reader's Guide to Walt Whitman* (Syracuse: Syracuse University, 1970), 24: "No book is more conspicuous in Walt Whitman's 'long foreground' than the *King James Bible*" (my emphasis).

50   "Biblical Analogies," 491.

51   "He was speaking; but as his language was Hebrew, we could not understand a word he uttered." This is Whitman from an 1842 editorial in which he describes his first visit to a synagogue ("A Peep at the Israelites," *New York Aurora* [28 March 1842], 2, https://whitmanarchive.org/published/periodical/journalism/tei/per.00418.html). Also in the follow-up article: "...wearied by the continuance of vocal utterance, which we could not take the meaning of, we left the place" ("Doings at the Synagogue," *New York Aurora* [29 March 1842], 2, https://whitmanarchive.org/published/periodical/journalism/tei/per.00419.html).

and indeed by scholars generally well before that period.[52] The trouble for Allen is twofold. First, the understanding of parallelism that he borrows and deploys in his analysis of Whitman and Whitman's putative use of biblical analogs is a theory derived and elaborated with the Hebrew text of the (Hebrew) Bible in view. It is, in other words, a theory about biblical *Hebrew* poetry. How well that theory may illuminate a translation of the underlying Hebrew is an open question that depends greatly on the nature of the translation and translation technique. The translation of the KJB, for example, may surely be used when illustrating the role of parallelism in biblical verse, and may even show off some aspects quite spectacularly, such as the (semantic) synonymity that often accompanies the Hebrew Bible's parallelistic poetic play—so Allen: "at least in the English translation this rhythm of thought or parallelism characterizes Biblical versification."[53] But this still has the underlying Hebrew as its ultimate target. It is a different matter altogether when the translation itself becomes the target of analysis. In other words, Allen does not pay enough attention, especially initially, to the interference and turbulence caused by translation, to the fact that translation does not offer a transparent view of the translated. There is a mismatch between his theory and the source(s) of his theory, all of which have the Hebrew in view, and his own application to an English prose translation of biblical Hebrew verse.

Symptomatic of this blindness and even more problematic for Allen is the sheer absence of lines of verse in the KJB. I repeat: the KJB, like all of its sixteenth-century English predecessors, is a prose translation.[54] Moreover, there is no formatting difference between the prose translation of the (Hebrew) Bible's prose narratives (and other non-poetic materials) and the prose translation of the (Hebrew) Bible's poetry. They both look very much the same, perhaps with only the smallest bit of extra

---

52 See esp. Norton, *History of the English Bible*, 138.
53 *New Walt Whitman Handbook*, 215.
54 I have not uncovered any comment by Whitman observing the prosaic nature of the KJB translation. However, in his tallying up of word counts on the inside cover of his "Blue Book" edition of the 1860 *Leaves* he does note that the editions he is tallying of Virgil's *Aeneid* and Dante's *Inferno* are both "prose translation[s]" (A. Golden, *Walt Whitman's Blue Book: The 1860–61 Leaves of Grass Containing His Manuscript Additions and Revision* [New York: New York Public Library, 1968], I, inside front cover [for facsimile]; II, 417 [for transcription]. Whitman does observe in his note about the number of words in the Bible, "that is assuming the whole space to be compactly filled with printed words"—which presumes a running format customary of printed prose.

whitespace in the poetic sections (see esp. Figs. 12, 18–19). This uniformity of appearance effectively levels through much of what distinguishes the underlying poetry of the Hebrew Bible from the prose, and as a consequence disposes readers to read the whole of the Bible uniformly, without a strong awareness of the variety of literary forms and genres in the Bible.[55]

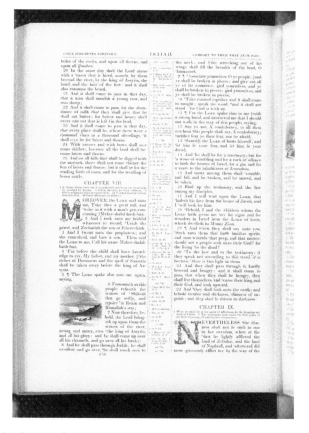

Fig. 18: Isa 7:19–9:1 from the Harper *Illuminated Bible*. In the original Hebrew, Isaiah 7–8 is prose and Isaiah 9 is poetry, but all is prose in the KJB and the page layout is the same.

---

55 For example, this is already well observed by R. G. Moulton in *The Literary Study of the Bible* (2d ed; Boston, 1899 [1895]), v–vi, 45.

Fig. 19: Isa 9:1–10:11 from the Harper *Illuminated Bible*. In the original Hebrew, Isaiah 7–8 is prose and Isaiah 9 is poetry, but all is prose in the KJB and the page layout is the same.

Though Allen is correct about the importance of the verse line to the prosodies of both biblical Hebrew verse and Whitman, it is not readily apparent what Whitman could have discerned about line structure from a prose translation lacking any formal marking of verse. This is a problem deserving of critical attention. On the strength of scholarly knowledge of the day and more crucially on Whitman's own comments, such as in "The Bible as Poetry" and also earlier in his notebooks (for discussion, see Chapter One), one may posit on Whitman's part a general awareness that the Bible contained poetry, or verse proper. But as to any more specific knowledge regarding the nature of Hebrew verse structure, that is a much more complicated and different proposition entirely, especially if we presume, as Allen does, the mediating force of the KJB. As D. Norton stresses, "It must be painfully apparent to anyone who has tried to read the poetic parts of the KJB using parallelism as a guide to the true form [i.e., line structure] that it is often no help."[56] Perhaps not surprisingly, then, Allen chooses not to use the KJB for his illustrations but instead quotes biblical passages from R. G. Moulton's "arrangement of biblical poetry in his *Modern Reader's Bible*" (see Figs. 21–22), which Allen says "in the main" has as its "basis" the "Lowth system."[57] That is, unlike in the KJB, verse in Moulton's edition is frequently lineated, following the example of the 1885 Revised Version (see Fig. 23).[58] The first of the "many evidences" of Whitman's indebtedness to the model of the "rhythmic pattern of the English Bible"[59] is the equivalence of line

---

56   *History of the English Bible*, 227. This can be done, if exceptionally, as Norton himself points out in discussing Samuel Say, who quotes Ps 78:1–2 in lines of free verse (much like the later RV): "we may say that one eighteenth-century critic was able to read the KJB's prose as verse" (200–01).

57   "Biblical Analogies," 492; *New Walt Whitman Handbook*, 347, n. 23. R. G. Moulton, *Modern Reader's Bible* (New York: Mavmillan, 1922). Moulton's edition is a bit strange. It is based on the Revised Version (Old and New Testament, 1885), which could not have influenced Whitman initially, and differs chiefly in his manner of formatting—in the case of biblical poetry, providing lineation (though this is already in RV in many instances, but not the Latter Prophets except in the most lyrical bits). However, his is not simply another edition and translation of the Bible. He tries to give the whole Old Testament, for example, a narrative shape. He relocates some poems to where he thinks they make the most narrative sense. One often has to hunt for the location of a particular poem in Moulton, since it is not guaranteed to be in canonical order. Equally frustrating, Moulton does not try to translate all biblical verse—for example, he gives only selections from the Song of Songs. And his lineations do not always reflect what contemporary scholars reconstruct as the underlying biblical Hebrew line structure—though to be sure line structure in biblical Hebrew poetry is always a matter of construal. This only adds to Allen's confusion. Not only is he foregrounding through Moulton's edition the underlying biblical Hebrew line structure, which has no transparent bearing on Whitman, but even that often gets muddled when Moulton gets things wrong, as he often does. For an overview of Moulton's project, see Norton, *History of the English Bible*, 371–76.

58   This was the first official revision to the KJB. The New Testament was completed in 1881; Old Testament in 1885; and Apocrypha in 1895. It is also the first time in an official English translation that the translation of Hebrew poetry is printed as "English poetry" (D. Daniell, *The Bible in English: Its History and Influence* [New Haven: Yale University, 2003], 696). This ultimately follows the lead of R. Lowth in his translation of Isaiah in a nonmetrical form of what has become called "free verse" (*Isaiah: A New Translation* [London: J. Nichols, 1778; reprinted in *Robert Lowth (1710–1787): The Major Works* (London: Routledge, 1995)]).

59   *American Prosody*, 220–21.

units, which Allen summarizes at the end of "Biblical Analogies" in this way:

> The first rhythmical principle of the Old Testament poetry is parallelism, or a rhythm of thought, *in which the line is the unit. The line is also the unit* in Whitman's poetry, one evidence of which is the punctuation, but conclusive evidence is the fact that the verses may be arranged in synonymous, antithetic, synthetic, and climatic "thought-groups", *just as Moulton prints the poetry of the Bible* (emphasis added).[60]

As Moulton prints the poetry of the Bible this seems self-evident. However, the KJB has no such lines of verse, a fact which the use of Moulton's edition effectively occludes (cf. Fig. 20 and contrast Figs. 21–23). F. Stovall raises the possibility of Whitman having access to verse translations of biblical poetry, such as those (of Job, Psalms, Proverbs, Song of Songs) by George R. Noyes.[61] Though possible—certainly such verse translations in English were available, most stimulated by Lowth's originary efforts in his *Isaiah: A New Translation*[62]—Stovall cannot tie Whitman to any of them. The line forms Whitman prefers are mostly enacted on a (much) larger scale (see below), and Whitman's known biblical quotations and phrasal borrowings invariably come from the KJB (see Chapter Two). Thus it is not clear that this equivalence of which Allen speaks—the line as the chief rhythmical unit—has quite the force that he imagines, at least not on his representation via Moulton's translation, as that is a formatting style that becomes most widely accessible only late in Whitman's life (in the form of the RV).[63]

---

60   "Biblical Analogies," 505.

61   *The Foreground of Leaves of Grass* (Charlottesville: University Press of Virginia, 1974), 187. Stovall does notice how Noyes's translations "arrange the poetry in verse form, and each line beginning with a capital letter and usually constituting a complete statement," recalling Whitman's practice.

62   Cf. M. Roston, *Prophet and Poet: The Bible and the Gowth of Romanticism* (Evanston: Northwestern University, 1965), 126–47.

63   Allen's later statement in the *New Walt Whitman Handbook* (215–19) is more careful about giving visibility to the underlying Hebrew, but Allen still seems to fudge the boundaries between translation and original and remains enamored by the equivalence of line units: "his [Lowth's] scheme [of parallelism] demonstrates the single line as the unit" (216) and "if parallelism is the foundation of the rhythmical style of *Leaves of Grass*, then, as we have already seen in the summary of the Lowth system, the verse must be the unit" (218).

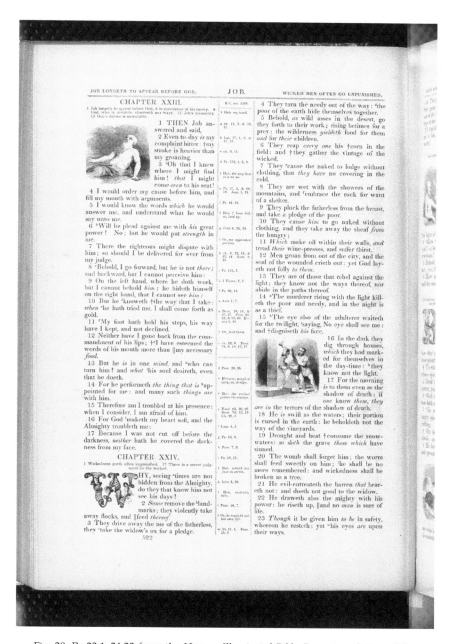

Fig. 20: Ps 23:1–24:23 from the Harper *Illuminated Bible*. Prose translation of the KJB, with no special formatting for the poetry of this psalm.

Psalms and Lyrics &

An Answer to Prayer

O LORD, rebuke me not in thine anger,
    Neither chasten me in thy hot displeasure.
Have mercy upon me, O LORD; for I am withered away;
    O LORD, heal me; for my bones are vexed:
    My soul also is sore vexed.
And thou, O LORD, how long?
    Return, O LORD, deliver my soul:
    Save me for thy lovingkindness' sake.

For in death there is no remembrance of thee:
    In Sheol who shall give thee thanks?
I am weary with my groaning;
    Every night make I my bed to swim;
    I water my couch with my tears.
Mine eye wasteth away because of grief;
    It waxeth old because of all mine adversaries.

Depart from me, all ye workers of iniquity;
    For the LORD hath heard the voice of my weeping.
The LORD hath heard my supplication;
    The LORD will receive my prayer.
All mine enemies shall be ashamed and sore vexed:
    They shall turn back, they shall be ashamed suddenly.

Under the Protection of Jehovah

The LORD is my shepherd;
I shall not want.

    He maketh me to lie down in green pastures:
    He leadeth me beside the still waters.
    He restoreth my soul:
    He guideth me in the paths of righteousness for his name's sake.

320

Fig. 21: Psalm 23 from R. G. Moulton, *Modern Reader's Bible* (New York: Mavmillan, 1922), II, 320. Public domain. Formatted as verse following the lead of the 1885 Revised Version of the Bible.

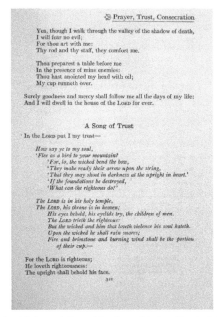

Fig. 22: Psalm 23 (cont.) from Moulton, *Modern Reader's Bible*, II, 321.

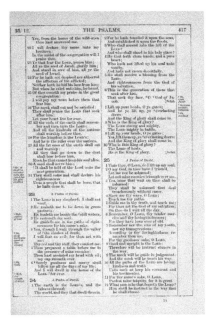

Fig. 23: Psalm 23 in the Revised Version (*The Holy Bible* [Cambridge: Cambridge University, 1885]). Public domain. First major English translation to lineate the poetry of Psalms, Proverbs, and Job as verse.

Moreover, in giving visibility to the line structure of the underlying Hebrew original through Moulton's translation what becomes strikingly apparent—and what would be obvious to any Hebraist—is just how *unalike* the two line units are. The biblical Hebrew verse line is consistently concise, while Whitman's line is famously long (and variable); and the biblical verse tradition is dominantly distichic, featuring couplets (and, less commonly, triplets), while Whitman's verse is prominently stichic. When he does group lines together, their patterns of grouping are quite dissimilar from those in the biblical Hebrew poetic corpus. These are visually apparent even on the most cursory of comparisons (see Fig. 24). Of the two, Allen senses the mismatch in the latter. In his treatment of parallelism in Whitman, he dutifully surveys parallelism involving couplets, triplets, and even quatrains, chiefly because of their prominence in the Bible. But as Allen recognizes, "the number of couplets in *Leaves of Grass* is not great;"[64] that "parallelism in the Bible does not ordinarily extend beyond the quatrain;"[65] and perhaps most astutely, that "the couplet, triplet, and quatrain are found more often in the Bible than in *Leaves of Grass*."[66] I sense in Allen's minimization of this difference—"the number of consecutive parallel verses is not particularly important"[67]—an attempt to stave off potentially troublesome worries for his thesis: for example, if Whitman was so impressed by the Bible's use of parallelism, why is not his own practice of line grouping more reflective of that of the Bible? Of course, it may be that Whitman was simply enamored of the parallelism itself and not the patterns of grouping. But Allen's own logic of exemplifying and commenting on Whitman's use of parallelistic couplets and the like suggests that Allen thinks otherwise,[68] that he intuitively feels the logic of the worry, though he mostly sweeps it deftly aside.

---

64 "Biblical Analogies," 494. Allen's added comment, "but then neither are there many [couplets] in the biblical poetry aside from *Proverbs*," is simply wrong. Biblical poetry is dominantly distichic, a fact Allen better appreciates in his later statement. By contrast, on my count, there are only 224 couplets (i.e., pairs of lines set apart spatially and punctuated as a single sentence) in the 1855 *Leaves* (on average less than three per page), and most of these are executed on a much larger scale than the typical biblical Hebrew couplet.

65 "Biblical Analogies," 495.

66 *New Walt Whitman Handbook*, 222.

67 *American Prosody*, 223.

68 J. P. Warren, who is otherwise critical of Allen's dependence on Lowth's paradigm ("'The Free Growth Of Metrical Laws': Syntactic Parallelism In 'Song Of Myself,'" *Style* 18/1 [1984], 27–42, esp. 28–32), nonetheless remains intent on comparing Whitman's two-, three-, and four-line groupings with those of the Bible (32).

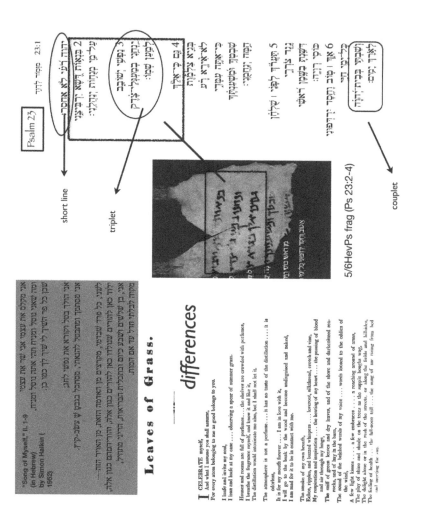

Fig. 24: A comparison of the differences between Whitman's typical poetic line and the biblical Hebrew poetic line. Image of p. 13 from the 1855 *Leaves*, public domain. Image of a 5/6HevPs fragment, showing parts of Ps 23:2–4 (Wikimedia Commons). Unpointed Hebrew translation of "Song of Myself" (lines 1–9), after Simon Halkin.

More surprising is the complete silence as to the difference in line length, which is only too apparent, at least if we are to think of the Hebrew original (usually two to four words) or Moulton's translation of that original (normally no more than eight or nine words). If the Bible is Whitman's chief inspiration, wouldn't there be more lines akin to the length of the typical biblical verse line? This is a potentially more damning worry precisely because Whitman's own lines (especially early on) are often so strikingly long with absolutely no parallels in biblical Hebrew verse. Neither worry holds substance, however. Whitman had no access to the Hebrew originals. And he probably did not have ready or ongoing access (if any access at all) to an English verse translation of the likes of Moulton's, which arranges the poetry of the Bible in lines of translated verse, grouped as couplets, triplets and the like according to Lowth's practice. That is, there is no reason to suspect that Whitman had much (if any) first-hand knowledge of either the nature of line grouping in biblical Hebrew poetry or the typical lengths of these lines (when translated into English). These are features of the biblical verse tradition that are elided in a prose translation like the KJB. It surely is not accidental that it is "chiefly the *synonymous* variety" of parallelism that Whitman picks up on and uses so pervasively throughout *Leaves of Grass*.[69] Of all linguistic elements, semantics—meaning—is the one most readily translatable. The early translators' (beginning with Tyndale) sense of a peculiar affinity between Hebrew and English idioms is spurred in part by semantics.[70] By contrast, the "core" of parallelism in the poetry of the Hebrew Bible is "syntactic," viz. the "repetition of identical or similar syntactic patterns" or frames, which when "set into equivalence" bring whatever is "filling those frames" (e.g., lexical items) "into alignment as well."[71]

The Verse Divisions of the KJB and Whitman's Line

More positively, by refocusing on the textual source that prompted Allen's interest in the first place, the KJB, and the fact that this is a specifically prose translation in distinct formats and page layouts, potential points

---

69   *New Walt Whitman Handbook*, 220–21; cf. "Biblical Analogies," 492–93; *American Prosody*, 222–23.
70   Cf. Norton, *History of the English Bible*, 11.
71   M. O'Connor, "Parallelism" in *NPEPP*, 877.

of similarity between this Bible and Whitman's line more readily resolve themselves. Besides the parallelistic play of meaning (and syntax) and the rhythm effected in part through this play, both characteristics of the biblical Hebrew verse tradition that were accessible to Whitman through translation, Whitman would have literally *seen* the verse divisions of the KJB itself. This is a point made early, though little noticed, by G. Saintsbury in his review of the 1871(–72) edition of *Leaves of Grass*: "Perhaps the likeness which is presented to the mind most strongly is that which exists between our author and the verse divisions of the English Bible, especially in the poetical books, and it is not unlikely that the latter did actually exercise some influence in molding the poet's work."[72] The "verse divisions of the English Bible" in the Old Testament correspond almost without fail to the full stop (*sôp pāsûq*) used by the Masoretes to mark the end of a biblical verse. In the narrative sections of the Hebrew Bible, the *sôp pāsûq* tends to demarcate a complete sentence, though the sentences may vary considerably in length and complexity. In "the poetical books," the *sôp pāsûq* does not demarcate the end of a single line of verse in Hebrew, but two, three, four, and sometimes even more such lines. So as in the prose sections there is variability here, too; however, it is far more constrained and regular, given the simpler clause structures and uniformly concise verse lines (see Figs. 12, 19, 20). The formatting in the KJB is the same, whether for prose or poetry, though because of the latter there is subtly more whitespace on the page in the poetic books (see Figs. 12, 18–19). Numerous aspects of Whitman's mature and signature line—viz. its variability, range of lengths, typical shapes and character, and content—become more clearly comparable to the Bible when thought through in light of Saintsbury's appreciation of the significance of the actual "verse divisions of the English Bible."

The Lengths of Lines

Most obvious, perhaps, is that the range of line-lengths in the 1855 *Leaves* is roughly equivalent to that of the verse divisions of the KJB, especially, as Saintsbury perceives, in the poetic books (e.g., Psalms, Proverbs, Job), and as significant the mix of line-lengths and the

---

72   G. Saintsbury, "[Review of *Leaves of Grass* (1871)]," *The Academy* 6 (10 Oct 1874), 398–400, https://whitmanarchive.org/criticism/reviews/lg1871/anc.00076.html.

mise-en-page that this mix effects is strikingly similar in both as well. Consider the familiar Psalm 23 (which Whitman read) lineated according to the verse divisions in the KJB (see Fig. 20):

> ¹The LORD is my shepherd; I shall not want.
>
> ²He maketh me to lie down in green pastures: he leadeth me beside the still waters.
>
> ³He restoreth my soul: he leadeth me in the paths of righteousness for his name's sake.
>
> ⁴Yea, though I walk through the valley of the shadow of death, I will fear no evil: for thou art with me; thy rod and thy staff they comfort me.
>
> ⁵Thou preparest a table before me in the presence of mine enemies: thou anointest my head with oil; my cup runneth over.
>
> ⁶Surely goodness and mercy shall follow me all the days of my life: and I will dwell in the house of the LORD for ever.

Note the overall length of the individual verse divisions and their variety. Compare this profile, first, with Moulton's version of the same psalm, which aims to follow the contours of the original Hebrew line structure,[73] resulting in much shorter lines, grouped as couplets[74]—the indentation and spacing are Moulton's invention (see Figs. 21–22):

---

73   As there is no single source for information on Hebrew line structure in biblical poems, differences in construals are common. In general, Moulton's division of lines here compares favorably to that of the NJV, for example; the division indicated by spacing in *BHS*, to take another example, is somewhat different. And the three long lines in Moulton—"He guideth me in the paths of righteousness for his name sake"; "Yea, though I walk through the valley of the shadow of death"; "Surely goodness and mercy shall follow me all the days of my life"—are too long to be individual lines of biblical verse.

74   There are likely a good many triplets in the original—according to *BHS*, vv. 1–2, 3, 4 (2x)—though Moulton misses them all.

The LORD is my shepherd;

I shall not want.

He maketh me to lie down in green pastures:

He leadeth me beside the still waters.

He restoreth my soul:

He guideth me in the paths of righteousness for his name sake.

Yea, though I walk through the valley of the shadow of death,

I will fear no evil;

For thou art with me:

Thy rod and thy staff, they comfort me.

Thou preparest a table before me

In the presence of mine enemies:

Thou hast anointed my head with oil;

My cup runneth over.

Surely goodness and mercy shall follow me all the days of my life:

And I will dwell in the house of the LORD for ever.[75]

---

75   Moulton, *Modern Reader's Bible*, II. 320–21.

Now consider a few brief selections from the 1855 *Leaves* (see Figs. 25–26):

> Trippers and askers surround me,
>
> People I meet..... the effect upon me of my early life.... of the ward and city I live in.... of the nation,
>
> The latest news.... discoveries, inventions, societies.... authors old and new,
>
> My dinner, dress, associates, looks, business, compliments, dues,
>
> The real or fancied indifference of some man or woman I love,
>
> The sickness of one of my folks—or of myself.... or ill-doing.... or loss or lack of money.... or depressions or exaltations,
>
> They come to me days and nights and go from me again,
>
> But they are not the Me myself. (*LG*, 15)

And:

> I am the hounded slave.... I wince at the bite of the dogs,
>
> Hell and despair are upon me.... crack and again crack the marksmen,
>
> I clutch the rails of the fence.... my gore dribs thinned with the ooze of my skin,
>
> I fall on the weeds and stones,
>
> The riders spur their unwilling horses and haul close,
>
> They taunt my dizzy ears.... they beat me violently over the head with their whip-stocks. (*LG*, 39)

Initially, note the typical lengths of Whitman's lines, which, with but a few exceptions (e.g., "But they are not the Me myself"; "I fall on the weeds and stones"), are much too long for a translated line of actual biblical verse but compare favorably with the verse divisions of the KJB. So:

> He maketh me to lie down in green pastures: he leadeth me beside the still waters. (Ps 23:2, KJB) [sixteen words]

I clutch the rails of the fence.... my gore dribs thinned with the ooze of
my skin, (*LG*, 39) [seventeen words]

Vs:

He maketh me to lie down in green pastures: [nine words; Hebrew:
three words]

He leadeth me beside the still waters. (Moulton) [seven words;
Hebrew: four words]

Or:

Thou preparest a table before me in the presence of mine enemies: thou
anointest my head with oil; my cup runneth over. (Ps 23:5, KJB)
[twenty-two words]

People I meet..... the effect upon me of my early life.... of the ward and
city I live in.... of the nation, (*LG*, 15) [twenty-two words]

Vs:

Thou preparest a table before me [six words; Hebrew: three words]

In the presence of mine enemies: [six words; Heb.: two words]

Thou hast anointed my head with oil; [seven words; Hebrew: three
words]

My cup runneth over. (Moulton) [four words; Heb.: two words]

Leaves of Grass.   15

As God comes a loving bedfellow and sleeps at my side all night and close on the
    peep of the day,
And leaves for me baskets covered with white towels bulging the house with their
    plenty,
Shall I postpone my acceptation and realization and scream at my eyes,
That they turn from gazing after and down the road,
And forthwith cipher and show me to a cent,
Exactly the contents of one, and exactly the contents of two, and which is ahead ?

Trippers and askers surround me,
People I meet . . . . . the effect upon me of my early life . . . . of the ward and city I
    live in . . . . of the nation,
The latest news . . . . discoveries, inventions, societies . . . . authors old and new,
My dinner, dress, associates, looks, business, compliments, dues,
The real or fancied indifference of some man or woman I love,
The sickness of one of my folks — or of myself . . . . or ill-doing . . . . or loss or lack
    of money . . . . or depressions or exaltations,
They come to me days and nights and go from me again,
But they are not the Me myself.

Apart from the pulling and hauling stands what I am,
Stands amused, complacent, compassionating, idle, unitary,
Looks down, is erect, bends an arm on an impalpable certain rest,
Looks with its sidecurved head curious what will come next,
Both in and out of the game, and watching and wondering at it.

Backward I see in my own days where I sweated through fog with linguists and
    contenders,
I have no mockings or arguments . . . . I witness and wait.

I believe in you my soul . . . . the other I am must not abase itself to you,
And you must not be abased to the other.

Loafe with me on the grass . . . . loose the stop from your throat,
Not words, not music or rhyme I want . . . . not custom or lecture, not even the best,
Only the lull I like, the hum of your valved voice.

I mind how we lay in June, such a transparent summer morning ;
You settled your head athwart my hips and gently turned over upon me,
And parted the shirt from my bosom-bone, and plunged your tongue to my barestript
    heart,
And reached till you felt my beard, and reached till you held my feet.

Swiftly arose and spread around me the peace and joy and knowledge that pass all
    the art and argument of the earth ;
And I know that the hand of God is the elderhand of my own,

Fig. 25: P. 15 from the 1855 *Leaves of Grass* (Brooklyn, NY, 1855). Public domain.

Leaves of Grass.   39

How the skipper saw the crowded and rudderless wreck of the steamship, and death
    chasing it up and down the storm,
How he knuckled tight and gave not back one inch, and was faithful of days and
    faithful of nights,
And chalked in large letters on a board, Be of good cheer, We will not desert you ;
How he saved the drifting company at last,
How the lank loose-gowned women looked when boated from the side of their
    prepared graves,
How the silent old-faced infants, and the lifted sick, and the sharp-lipped unshaved
    men ;
All this I swallow and it tastes good . . . . I like it well, and it becomes mine,
I am the man . . . . I suffered . . . . I was there.

The disdain and calmness of martyrs,
The mother condemned for a witch and burnt with dry wood, and her children
    gazing on ;
The hounded slave that flags in the race and leans by the fence, blowing and
    covered with sweat,
The twinges that sting like needles his legs and neck,
The murderous buckshot and the bullets,
All these I feel or am.

I am the hounded slave . . . . I wince at the bite of the dogs,
Hell and despair are upon me . . . . crack and again crack the marksmen,
I clutch the rails of the fence . . . . my gore dribs thinned with the ooze of my skin,
I fall on the weeds and stones,
The riders spur their unwilling horses and haul close,
They taunt my dizzy ears . . . . they beat me violently over the head with their
    whip-stocks.

Agonies are one of my changes of garments ;
I do not ask the wounded person how he feels . . . . I myself become the wounded
    person,
My hurt turns livid upon me as I lean on a cane and observe.

I am the mashed fireman with breastbone broken . . . . tumbling walls buried me in
    their debris,
Heat and smoke I inspired . . . . I heard the yelling shouts of my comrades,
I heard the distant click of their picks and shovels ;
They have cleared the beams away . . . . they tenderly lift me forth.

I lie in the night air in my red shirt . . . . the pervading hush is for my sake,
Painless after all I lie, exhausted but not so unhappy,
White and beautiful are the faces around me . . . . the heads are bared of their fire-
    caps,
The kneeling crowd fades with the light of the torches.

Fig. 26: P. 39 from the 1855 *Leaves*.

The sharp contrast in length is noticeably apparent between the lines in Whitman and in the KJB verse divisions, on the one hand, and in Moulton's versions, on the other hand. This point may be underscored to good effect by comparing the Hebrew of the latter biblical passage, Ps 23:5, with its characteristic short lines,

תַּעֲרֹךְ לְ־פָנַי ׀ שֻׁלְחָן
נֶגֶד צֹרְרָי
דִּשַּׁנְתָּ בַ־שֶּׁמֶן רֹאשׁ־ִי
כּוֹסִ־י רְוָיָה

with a set of Whitman's long lines from the beginning of "Song of Myself" in Simon Halkin's Hebrew translation:[76]

לְשׁוֹנִי כָּל פְּרָד שֶׁבְּדָמִי מְקֹרָצִים מִן הָאֲדָמָה הַזֹּאת מִן הָאֲוִיר הַזֶּה
יָלוֹד כָּאן לְהוֹרִים שֶׁנּוֹלְדוּ כָּאן לְהוֹרִים כְּגוֹן אֵלֶּה וְהוֹרֵיהֶם הֵם כְּגוֹן אֵלֶּה
אֲנִי בֶּן שְׁלֹשִׁים וְשֶׁבַע כַּיּוֹם וּבְתַכְלִית הַבְּרִיאוּת הֲרֵינִי מַתְחִיל
מְקַוֶּה לְעָבְלְתִּי חָדֹל עַד אִם הַמָּוֶת

(My tongue, every atom of my blood, form'd from this soil, this air,

Born here of parents born here from parents the same, and their parents
    the same,

I, now thirty-seven years old in perfect health begin,

Hoping to cease not till death. [*LG* 1892, 29])

Again, the contrast in line length is stark. Halkin's rendition of the first two lines of Whitman each contains more words (eleven) than in the four lines of the psalm combined (ten words). And though hardly the kind of empirical sifting that would be required to make a full case, my strong impression is that the general picture registered by these few examples holds across the board. Dip anywhere into

---

76 Cited from E. Folsom, "'Song of Myself,' Section 1, in Fifteen Languages," *WWQR* 13/1 (1995), 73–89, at 78; cf. *'Alē 'Ēsev* [Leaves of Grass] (trans. S. Halkin; Tel Aviv: Sifriat Poalim and Hakibbutz Hameuchad Publishing House Ltd, 1984 [1952]).

Whitman's 1855 *Leaves* and the poetic books of the KJB and the same
rough equivalences in lengths of lines and verse divisions appear.
The same point is made by R. Alter in a wholly different context but
in a way that is nevertheless quite telling for my own thesis. He says
of the KJB's long cherished rendering of Ps 23:4 ("Yea, though I walk
through the valley of the shadow of death, I will fear no evil: for
thou art with me; thy rod and thy staff they comfort me") that it has
"the beauty of a proto-Whitmanesque line of poetry rather than of
biblical [Hebrew] poetry."[77] Alter here, implicitly, joins the likes of
Saintsbury in recognizing the connection between Whitman and the
KJB, at least in terms of line length.

These word counts serve as a crude barometer of dis/similarity.
They cannot be pressed too literally. And yet they are also possibly
the surest means of measuring and comparing the gross scales of
Whitman's lines (in the 1855 *Leaves*) and the KJB's verse divisions.
With the aid of computerization such measures can be quantified
(to a degree; see charts in Figs. 15, 27–29).[78] Fig. 29 is perhaps the
most striking, as it shows a considerable degree of overlap between
the basic length profiles for Whitman's verse lines in the 1855 *Leaves*
and the verse divisions of the KJB in the three specially formatted (in
the Masoretic tradition) books of biblical poetry: Psalms, Proverbs,
and Job.[79] The match is not perfect, but it is incredibly close. For

---

77 R. Alter, *The Book of Psalms: A Translation with Commentary* (New York: W. W.
    Norton, 2007), xxx. The observation is made in passing, Alter simply trying to
    be descriptive in elaborating his aim to achieve a more compact rendering of the
    Hebrew of the Psalms into English. His reach for Whitman, nonetheless, is most
    appropriate. Cf. M. N. Posey, "Whitman's Debt to the Bible with Special Reference
    to the Origins of His Rhythm" (unpubl. Ph.D. dissertation, University of Texas,
    1938), 44, where the Psalms are emphasized in their import for shaping the
    pattern of Whitman's versification.

78 Gregory Murray, Director of Digital Initiatives at the Wright Library, Princeton
    Theological Seminary, is responsible for generating the computations summarized
    in the charts in Figs. 15, 27–30.

79 In the received text of the Hebrew Bible (MT) these are the only three poetic
    books that are specially formatted (in two columns instead of three, with extra
    internal spacing to mark line division). Much poetry in the Bible appears in a
    running format just like prose. See Figs. 31–32; and for a fuller discussion, see
    Dobbs-Allsopp, "'Verse, Properly So Called.'" The word counts for the three
    biblical books here do not include the prose material in Job 1–2 and 42:7–17.

example, as noted Whitman's sweet spot in terms of line-length in the 1855 edition is between eight and sixteen words, accounting for 71% of all lines in the volume. The comparable core of verse divisions in the three poetic books from the KJB contains between twelve and twenty words, accounting for roughly 76% of the verse divisions in this material (Fig. 29). This overlapping correlation in length gives substantial back-up to Saintsbury's early impressions ("especially in the poetical books"). By contrast, Fig. 30 (comparing the line lengths of Whitman's 1855 *Leaves* and the 1901 ASV [Job], which like the RV offers lineated versions of Psalms, Proverbs, and Job) shows the overall dissimilarity between Whitman's line and the average lengths of translated versions of the constrained biblical Hebrew poetic line.[80] Fig. 28, which compares Whitman's line to KJB-Pentateuch (comprised primarily of biblical prose), not surprisingly shows a good chunk of the KJB's verse divisions in this material containing more words per verse than does Whitman per line—not surprising because however prosaic Whitman's verse, it is finally verse and not prose. Importantly, however, Whitman's longest lines (forty-seven words or more) are comparable only with the verse divisions of biblical prose (see esp. Figs. 27–28)—he was reading the whole Bible.

---

80 I use the 1901 "American Standard Version" (ASV) out of convenience, since a version with the necessary XML mark-up was readily available from ebible. org. The ASV is essentially the same as the RV (Americans had been involved in the revision process since the 1870s), inclusive of numerous additions to the translation suggested by an American committee of scholars (Daniell, *Bible in English*, 696–97, 735–37). Both the RV and ASV offer verse renderings in English (formatted stichically) of some of the poetic sections of the Bible (here Psalms, Proverbs, Job) for the first time in the English translation tradition descended from the KJB. Moulton's translations used by Allen are from the RV—though formatted so "as to bring out to the eye the literary form and structure of each portion of Scripture" (*Modern Reader's Bible* I, 2).

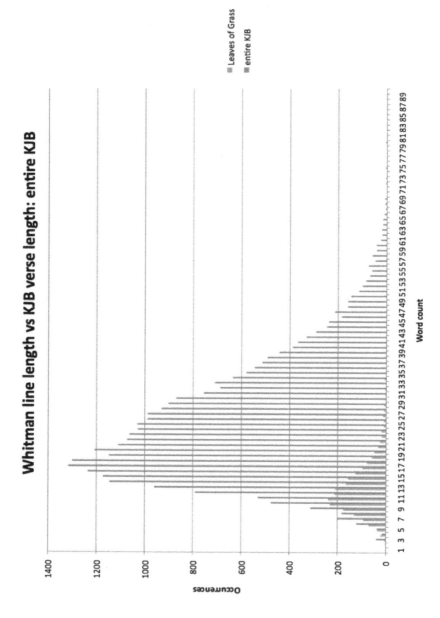

Fig. 27: Comparison by word count between the lengths of lines in the 1855 *Leaves* and the verse divisions of the entire KJB. Computation and chart by Greg Murray.

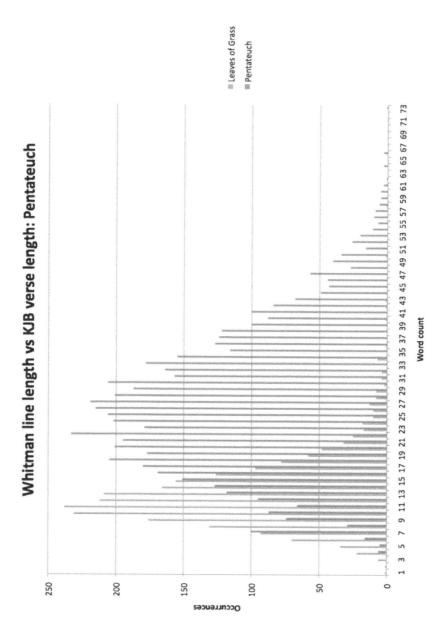

Fig. 28: Comparison by word count between the lengths of lines in the 1855 *Leaves* and the verse divisions of KJB-Pentateuch. Computation and chart by Greg Murray.

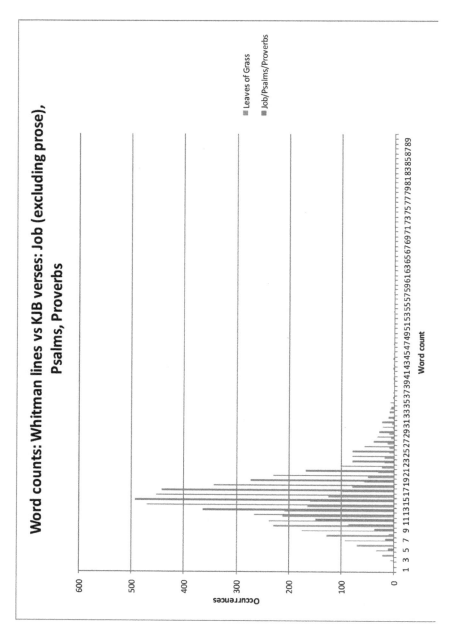

Fig. 29: Comparison by word count between the lengths of lines in the 1855 *Leaves* and the verse divisions of KJB-Job/Psalms/Proverbs. Computation and chart by Greg Murray.

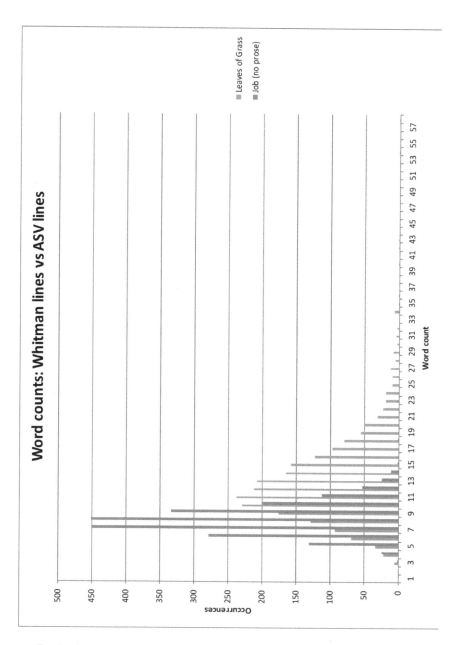

Fig. 30: Comparison by word count between the lengths of lines in the 1855 *Leaves* and the lineated translation of ASV-Job. Computation and chart by Greg Murray.

Fig. 31: B19a (Leningrad Codex), folio 423 recto (Ruth 4:13B–Song 2:5A). Freedman et al., *The Leningrad Codex*. Photograph by Bruce and Kenneth Zuckerman, West Semitic Research, in collaboration with the Ancient Biblical Manuscript Center. Courtesy Russian National Library (Saltykov-Shchedrin).

Fig. 32: B19a, folio 394 recto (Psalm 133). Freedman et al., *The Leningrad Codex*. Photograph by Bruce and Kenneth Zuckerman, West Semitic Research, in collaboration with the Ancient Biblical Manuscript Center. Courtesy Russian National Library (Saltykov-Shchedrin).

I do not postulate Whitman literally using word counts to generate his poetry or even to mimic (in some hyper-literal way) the variable lengths of the KJB's verse divisions. As Posey wryly remarks, "I suppose nobody thinks that he sat down with a psalm before him and wrote a poem laboriously fitted to the pattern."[81] Rather, the KJB and its verse divisions furnished Whitman with the model for a long(er) and highly variable line that he then fitted and honed to his own liking, as he can be seen doing in his notebooks and poetry manuscripts. This is precisely the manner of Whitman's "inspiration" when he bothers to record it, a brief animating ("spinal") idea that is then worked out over and over ("incessantly") until it is made to Whitman's liking.[82] Having said that, on at least two occasions Whitman actually counted the number of words and even letters used in (some of) his poems. Most famously, as previously noted, at the beginning of Whitman's so-called "Blue Book" edition of the 1860 *Leaves*,[83] the poet records (printer calculations of) overall word counts for *Leaves* (183,500 words, inclusive of *Drum-Taps*), the Bible, and other classic works (see Fig. 33).[84] Here one has the sense that Whitman is using the word counts to measure his poetic accomplishments to date.[85] Of equal interest is the verso of a single, 1855 manuscript leaf currently housed in the Harry Ransom Humanities Research Center of the University of Texas at Austin (Fig. 34).[86] Whitman scribbles notes on this side of the leaf about

---

81 "Whitman's Debt," 142. Although the idea that Whitman perhaps occasionally composed with the Bible open before him should not be completely discounted either—certainly the verbatim quotes in the prose writings show Whitman actively consulting a Bible.

82 See Allen, *Reader's Guide*, 159; cf. P. Zweig, *Walt Whitman: The Making of the Poet* (New York: Basic Books, 1984), 203. One of many examples comes from the "med Cophósis"notebook. Whitman jots down a note prefaced by pointing hand and the phrase "good subject Poem," https://whitmanarchive.org/manuscripts/figures/loc.00005.002.jpg, which he then follows with an initial idea: "There was a child went forth every day—and the first thing that he saw looked at with fixed love, that thing he became for the day.—". This material eventually is worked (N.B. the canceled saw already in the notebook passage) into the opening two lines of "There was a child went forth" (*LG*, 90).

83 https://whitmanarchive.org/published/1860-Blue_book/images/index.html.

84 A transcription of this leaf may be found in Golden, *Whitman's Blue Book*, II, 417; for image: I, inside front cover.

85 The introduction he was composing for this never published version of *Leaves* would seem to make this explicit, as he notices on the occasion of his forty-second birthday (May 31, 1861), "having looked over what I have accomplished" (*NUPM* IV, 1484).

86 https://whitmanarchive.org/manuscripts/figures/tex.00057.002.jpg. See E. Folsom, "Walt Whitman's Working Notes for the first Edition of Leaves of

the size of and a projected arrangement for the 1855 *Leaves* (though the latter differs markedly from the edition eventually published). In an effort to estimate the number of printed pages needed for the volume, Whitman tallies up the number of letters on average used in what he describes as "one of my closely written MS pages"—he estimates using "1,600" letters. He compares this to the number of "letters in a page of Shakespeare's poems"—"1,120" is recorded. From this he calculates that the printed *Leaves* will run to "about 127 pages"—this turns out to be a little off (the 1855 *Leaves* is 95 pages long), perhaps because of the unusually large page size ("about the size and shape of a block of typewriting paper")[87] used in the 1855 edition. Both items plainly show that literal counts of words and letters factored in Whitman's thinking about his poetry on occasion.

Fig. 33: Whitman's comparative word counts on the second leaf of the so-called "Blue Book" edition of the 1860 *Leaves*. Image courtesy of the New York Public Library.

Grass," *WWQR* 16/2 (1998), 90–95; cf. Folsom's online commentary at: Folsom, "Whitman." The date is established by the notice that Whitman had already left "5 pages MS" with the printer (so Folsom).

87 M. Cowley (ed.), *Walt Whitman's Leaves of Grass: The First (1855) Edition* (New York: Penguin Books, 1976 [1959]), vii.

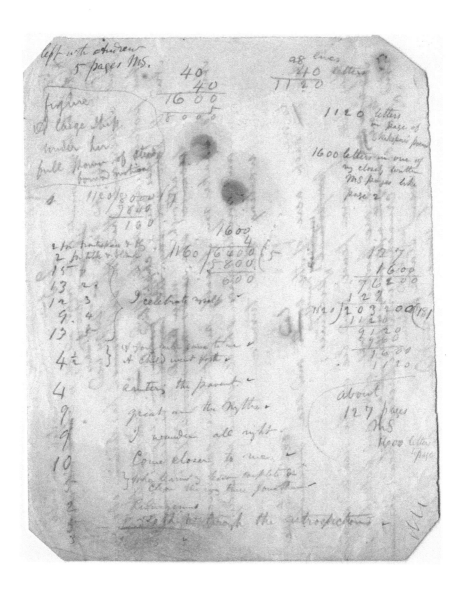

Fig. 34: Verso of "And to me every minute," https://whitmanarchive.org/manuscripts/figures/tex.00057.002.jpg. Image courtesy of the Harry Ransom Humanities Research Center of the University of Texas at Austin. Estimated average number of letters in what Whitman considers "one of my closely written MS pages," comparing to the number of "letters in page of Shakespeare's poems."

In fact, however, word (and letter) counts alone do not adequately register the expanded spatial scale of Whitman's typically long lines in the 1855 *Leaves*, especially for comparative purposes. The language material that makes up Whitman's lines and the KJB's verse divisions are dissimilar in a number of important ways. First, the KJB inherited Willian Tyndale's preference for Anglo-Saxon monosyllables, which contrasts strikingly with the many polysyllabic and compounded, often Latinate words—not to mention Whitman's fondness for foreign-derived words of all kinds—that populate Whitman's poems. So even when word counts converge (as they often do, for example, when comparing the lines of the 1855 *Leaves* with the verse divisions in KJB-Psalms, -Proverbs, and -Job), it is frequently still the case that Whitman's lines are more spatially expansive than the KJB's verse divisions—they literally are lengthier on the page. And Whitman's unconventional use of suspension points (....) and long dashes (combined with the large page format) in the first edition of *Leaves* elongates the line still further. The effect of the latter may be illustrated by comparing lines from the first edition of *Leaves* with lines from most of the succeeding editions where Whitman reverts to more conventional forms of punctuation and smaller page formats.[88] The following examples are emblematic (*LG*, 14; *LG* 1856, 7; see Figs. 35–36):

> *LG* 1855: "You shall no longer take things at second or third hand.... nor look through the eyes of the dead.... nor feed on the spectres in books"

> *LG* 1856: "You shall no longer take things at second or third hand, nor look through the eyes of the dead, nor feed on the spectres in books"

> *LG* 1855: "I have heard what the talkers were talking.... the talk of the beginning and the end"

> *LG* 1856: "I have heard what the talkers were talking, the talk of the beginning and the end"

---

88   Esp. Asselineau, *Evolution*, II, 241.

> *LG* 1855: "Always a knit of identity.... always distinction.... always a
> breed of life"

> *LG* 1856: "Always a knit of identity, always distinction, always a breed
> of life"

The extra-linguistic means (esp. suspension points) for elongating Whitman's lines, allied with their extreme lengths (by whatever count), makes clear that the poetry of the early editions of *Leaves* in particular "was a visual poetry," as Asselineau notices.[89] Whitman himself (at least late in life) recognized this as well:

> Two centuries back or so much of the poetry passed from lip to lip—was oral: was literally made to be sung: then the lilt, the formal rhythm, may have been necessary. The case is now somewhat changed: now, when the poetic work in literature is more than nineteen-twentieths of it by print, the simply tonal aids are not so necessary, or, if necessary, have considerably shifted their character.[90]

Whitman experienced the Bible chiefly visually, in print and through reading, yet the biblical traditions (even when originating in written composition) emerge out of dominantly oral environments. Almost every dimension of biblical poetry is shaped for maximal oral and aural reception, including its typically constrained verse line.[91] This is antithetical to Whitman's visually oriented poetics—as Asselineau emphasizes, "who would, without getting out of breath, declaim the first *Leaves of Grass*; some of the lines contained over sixty words."[92]

---

89   *Evolution*, II, 241.
90   *WWWC*, 1, 163; cf. Asselineau, *Evolution*, II, 240.
91   See Dobbs-Allsopp, "An Informing Orality: Biblical Poetic Style" in *On Biblical Poetry*, 233–325.
92   *Evolution*, II, 241.

14   L e a v e s   o f   G r a s s.

Have you reckoned a thousand acres much ?   Have you reckoned the earth much ?
Have you practiced so long to learn to read ?
Have you felt so proud to get at the meaning of poems ?

Stop this day and night with me and you shall possess the, origin of all poems,
You shall possess the good of the earth and sun . . . . there are millions of suns left,
You shall no longer take things at second or third hand . . . . nor look through the
    eyes of the dead . . . . nor feed on the spectres in books,
You shall not look through my eyes either, nor take things from me,
You shall listen to all sides and filter them from yourself.

I have heard what the talkers were talking . . . . the talk of the beginning and the end,
But I do not talk of the beginning or the end.

There was never any more inception than there is now,
Nor any more youth or age than there is now ;
And will never be any more perfection than there is now,
Nor any more heaven or hell than there is now.

Urge and urge and urge,
Always the procreant urge of the world.

Out of the dimness opposite equals advance . . . . Always substance and increase,
Always a knit of identity . . . . always distinction . . . . always a breed of life.

To elaborate is no avail . . . . Learned and unlearned feel that it is so.

Sure as the most certain sure . . . . plumb in the uprights, well entretied, braced in
    the beams,
Stout as a horse, affectionate, haughty, electrical,
I and this mystery here we stand.

Clear and sweet is my soul . . . . and clear and sweet is all that is not my soul.

Lack one lacks both . . . . and the unseen is proved by the seen,
Till that becomes unseen and receives proof in its turn.

Showing the best and dividing it from the worst, age vexes age,
Knowing the perfect fitness and equanimity of things, while they discuss I am silent,
    and go bathe and admire myself.

Welcome is every organ and attribute of me, and of any man hearty and clean,
Not an inch nor a particle of an inch is vile, and none shall be less familiar than the rest.

I am satisfied . . . . I see, dance, laugh, sing ;

Fig. 35: P. 14 from the 1855 Leaves, https://whitmanarchive.org/published/LG/
figures/ppp.00271.021.jpg.

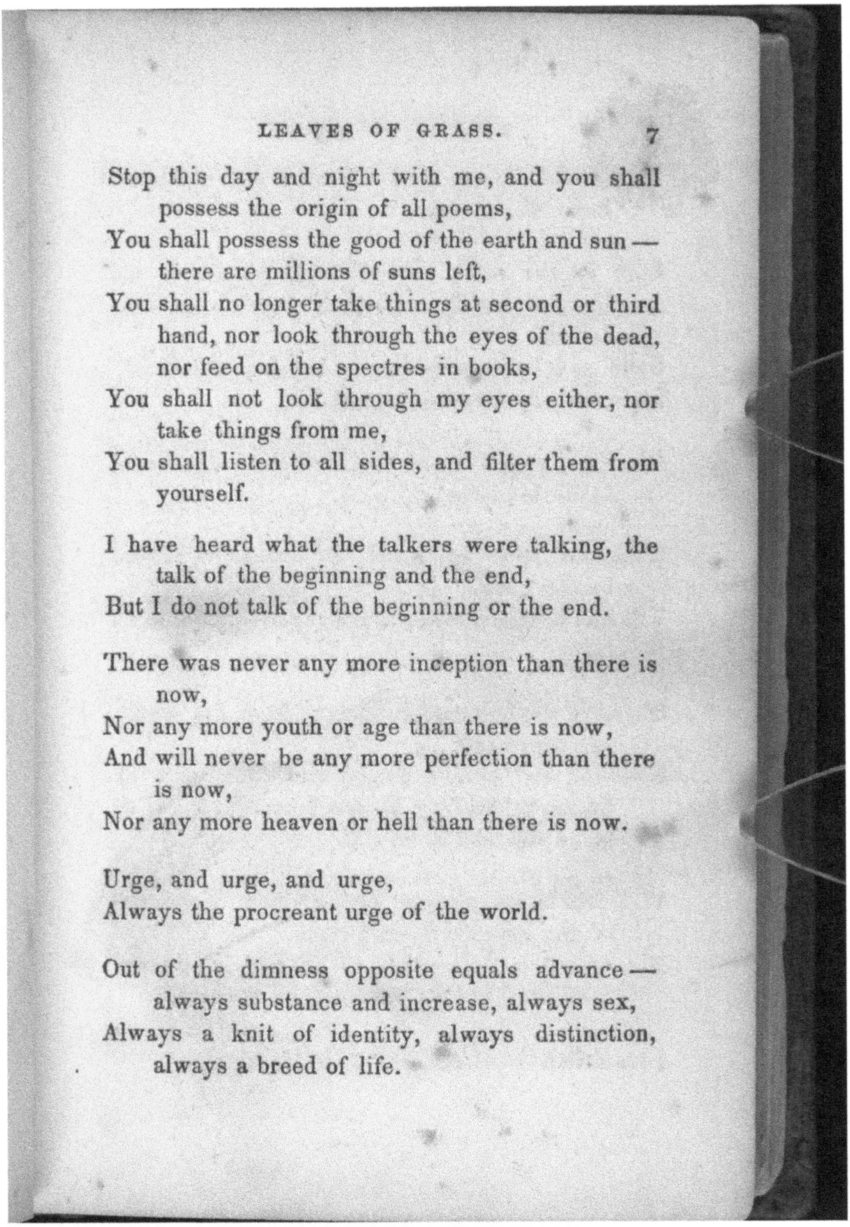

LEAVES OF GRASS. 7

Stop this day and night with me, and you shall
    possess the origin of all poems,
You shall possess the good of the earth and sun —
    there are millions of suns left,
You shall no longer take things at second or third
    hand, nor look through the eyes of the dead,
    nor feed on the spectres in books,
You shall not look through my eyes either, nor
    take things from me,
You shall listen to all sides, and filter them from
    yourself.

I have heard what the talkers were talking, the
    talk of the beginning and the end,
But I do not talk of the beginning or the end.

There was never any more inception than there is
    now,
Nor any more youth or age than there is now,
And will never be any more perfection than there
    is now,
Nor any more heaven or hell than there is now.

Urge, and urge, and urge,
Always the procreant urge of the world.

Out of the dimness opposite equals advance —
    always substance and increase, always sex,
Always a knit of identity, always distinction,
    always a breed of life.

Fig. 36: P. 7 from the 1856 *Leaves,* https://whitmanarchive.org/published/LG/
figures/ppp.00237.015.jpg. Image courtesy of the Albert and Shirley Small Special
Collections Library, University of Virginia.

Interestingly, as K. Campbell and Asselineau observe, over time Whitman's line began to shrink back down toward more conventional lengths.[93] The change already starts to appear in some instances by 1860 but begins in earnest with the (build-up to the) 1867 *Leaves*. Here is Campbell's characterization:

> In his earliest editions (1855, 1856, and 1860), there are a good many lines that run to thirty or forty words each, and a few that run as high as fifty and even sixty words. To be very specific, there are in the edition of 1856 two lines that run past sixty words each, seven that run past fifty words, sixteen that run past forty words, and forty-two that exceed thirty words each. At the same time there are no poems first published after 1870 with lines that run to as much as twenty-five words, and only one poem published in 1855 or 1856 that retained any considerable number of long lines,—namely, "Our Old Feuillage." In fact, the longest line in any of the poems first published in the eighties comprises only twenty-one words (and there are only two examples of this), whereas the average long line in the poems written after 1880 runs to about a dozen words.[94]

Whitman achieves this foreshortening or lightening (as Asselineau calls it) in a number of ways, including breaking longer lines into multiple shorter lines, reducing the number of words in long lines through revision and emendation, and sometimes simply eliminating the long line entirely. Whitman's "Blue Book" edition provides ample evidence of such revisionary practices, as it anticipates (though also differs significantly from) the 1867 edition.[95] Consider the following by way of example.[96] This fifty-four word line from "Come closer to me,"

---

93   K. Campbell, "The Evolution of Whitman as Artist," *American Literature* 6/4 (1934), 259–61; Asselineau, *Evolution*, II, 241–42.

94   "Whitman as Artist," 260; cf. Fig. 28 (above).

95   K. Price notices that "the Blue Book can be regarded as the hinge on which Whitman turns toward his late style" ("Love, War, and Revision in Whitman's Blue Book," *Huntington Library Quarterly* 73/4 [2010], 679–92, at 687); and more recently, K. M. Price, *Whitman in Washington: Becoming the National Poet in the Federal City* (Oxford: Oxford University, 2020). However, the "Blue Book" itself did not serve as the copy-text for the 1867 *Leaves*, since "many of its revisions were never implemented" (Price, "Love, War, and Revision," 683).

96   The examples themselves are identified by Asselineau (*Evolution*, II, 241–42, 371–72, nn. 13–14), though absent references to Whitman's "Blue Book" (Golden's volumes post-date the publication of Asselineau's several volumes). Cf. Campbell, "Whitman as Artist," 260–61.

> Because you are greasy or pimpled—or that you was once drunk, or a
>   thief, or diseased, or rheumatic, or a prostitute—or are so now—
>   or from frivolity or impotence—or that you are no scholar, and
>   never saw your name in print.... do you give in that you are any
>   less immortal? (*LG*, 58)

is revised in the "Blue Book" into four shorter lines, with several
cancellations:

> Because you are greasy or pimpled,
>
> Or that you was once drunk, or a thief, or diseased, ~~or rheumatic,~~ or a
>   prostitute—or are so now,
>
> ~~or from frivolity or impotence,~~ oOr that you are no scholar, and never
>   saw your name in print,
>
> Do you give in that you are any less immortal?[97]

Emendation is the method of reduction in this line from "Proto-Leaf"
(*LG* 1860, 15): "And I will show that there is no imperfection in ~~male
or female, or in the earth, or in~~ the present—and can be none in the
future." The nine canceled words in the "Blue Book" are dropped from
succeeding versions of "Starting from Paumanok" (e.g., "And I will
show that there is no imperfection in the present—and can be none
in the future," *LG* 1867, 16). And the following long line also from
"Proto-Leaf" (*LG* 1860, 21) is canceled entirely in the "Blue Book" and
does not appear in "Starting from Paumanok" in succeeding editions
of *Leaves* (e.g., section 19; *LG* 1867, 21):

---

97 Cf. Golden, *Whitman's Blue Book*, II, 145. The lines are also broken up in the
    1867 version of "To Workingmen," but slightly differently (and without the
    cancellations of the "Blue Book" version):

Because you are greasy or pimpled, or that you was once drunk, or a thief,

Or diseas'd, or rheumatic, or a prostitute, or are so now;

Or from frivolity or impotence, or that you are no scholar, and never saw your name in
    print,

Do you give in that you are any less immortal? (*LG* 1867, 241)

> See the populace, millions upon millions, handsome, tall, muscular,
> both sexes, clothed in easy and dignified clothes—teaching,
> commanding, marrying, generating, equally electing and elective.

This program of foreshortening also impacted the overall scale of the poems. New poems in the later editions are generally shorter in length.[98]

It is useful to recall that Saintsbury's appreciation of the "likeness" of Whitman's poetry to the "verse divisions of the English Bible" was articulated in a review of the 1871–72 edition of *Leaves*, an edition well evidencing the consequences of Whitman's program of lightening and trimming. There is, of course, more to the "likeness" observed than line-length (e.g., parallelism, rhythm, repetition, diction). However, it does show that the perception of lineal/divisional equivalence persists even without quantification and amidst much abbreviation on the poet's part. Here Saintsbury's specification of "especially... the poetical books" remains germane, as the verse divisions in this material only rarely approach the expanse of Whitman's lengthiest lines (Fig. 29)—Whitman hardly needed to mechanically count words or letters (which of course he could do, and on occasion did) to apprehend the force of the biblical paradigm.

Ideally, Whitman quoting a bit of biblical verse within the format of his mature line, either from the notebooks and early poetry manuscripts or in *Leaves*—akin, for example, to his close version of Matt 26:15 in "Blood-Money" (lines 12–14) would nicely cinch the observations just made. Unfortunately, so far I have not uncovered any such quotations (or seen such discussed). This makes sense, since by the early 1850s Whitman was evolving a poetic theory that forbade explicit quotations from literature like the Bible in his verse. While there are echoes of, allusions to, and even some phrasing from the Bible in *Leaves*, there are no explicit quotations or close paraphrases. And, indeed, none either in the pre-1855 notebooks or early poetry manuscripts where Whitman's long line is being worked and stretched into existence. Whitman only quotes the Bible in his prose writings—and he does that voluminously—and in his poetry from 1850 or earlier.[99] The closest I have been able to come to this sort of "catching out" is in passages where Whitman's lines have a stronger than normal resemblance to biblical material. An example was briefly discussed in Chapter Two. The line from "I celebrate myself," "Swiftly arose and

---

98   Cf. Asselineau, *Structure*, II, 244.
99   See Allen, "Biblical Echoes" and discussion in Chapter One.

spread around me the peace and joy and knowledge that pass all the art and argument of the earth" (*LG*, 15), has the shape, feel, rhythm, and some phrasing ("peace... that pass all") of Phil 4:7. The biblical material that provokes Whitman in this instance is prosaic and from the New Testament, although that the provocation is circumscribed precisely by the KJB's verse divisions is both readily apparent and significant.

Also from "I celebrate myself" is this example, where the probable biblical stimulant is poetic: "The pleasures of heaven are with me, and the pains of hell are with me" (*LG*, 26). This line does not quote or allude to a biblical passage, nor is it aiming to riff on a biblical theme. But it does borrow a phrase ("pains of hell") from Ps 116:3 and is shaped parallelistically very much like the first two-thirds of the biblical verse: "The sorrows of death compassed me, and the pains of hell gat hold upon me: I found trouble and sorrow."[100] The verse from the psalm is actually a triplet in the Hebrew original, so the final "I found trouble and sorrow" has no counterpart in Whitman's two-part line. The bipartite shape of the latter is more directly comparable to Ps 18: 5 (=2 Sam 22:6): "The sorrows of hell compassed me about: the snares of death prevented me." While the psalms' synonymous parallelism focuses two different names for the underworld ("death," Hebrew *māwet*; "hell," Hebrew *šĕʾôl*), Whitman opts for a more antithetical feel (pleasures/pains) with a biblical merism, heaven and hell (e.g., Amos 9:2; Ps 139:8; Job 11:8; Matt 11:23; Luke 10:15). Still, the sets are remarkably close in feel and form. And again the general pattern of line-length correspondences briefly sketched earlier holds. The lengths of Whitman's line (fifteen words) and of the KJB verse division of the two psalm verses (Ps 116:3, excepting the last phrase, fifteen words; Ps 18:5, thirteen words) are closely comparable, and they all contrast markedly with the consistently short biblical Hebrew poetic line. The latter are more aptly rendered in a translation such as the ASV:

> The cords of death encompassed me:
>
> And the pains of Sheol gat hold upon me;
>
> I found trouble and sorrow. (Ps 116:3)

---

100 Cf. Posey, "Whitman's Debt," 225; B. L. Bergquist, "Walt Whitman and the Bible: Language Echoes, Images, Allusions, and Ideas" (unpubl. Ph.D. dissertation, University of Nebraska, 1979), 289.

The cords of Sheol were round about me;

The snares of death came upon me. (Ps 18:5 = 2 Sam 22:6)

The component lines are half the length of the KJB verse division and Whitman's line and offer a much better approximation of the terse biblical Hebrew lines being translated, which in the Hebrew of these psalmic verses do not exceed more than three words.

Consider further this run of lines from the beginning of "I celebrate myself":

Have you reckoned a thousand acres much? Have you reckoned the earth much?

Have you practiced so long to learn to read?

Have you felt so proud to get at the meaning of poems? (*LG*, 14)

And the similar set from "To think of time":

Have you guessed you yourself would not continue? Have you dreaded those earth-beetles?

Have you feared the future would be nothing to you? (*LG*, 65)

Both have the feel and cadence of similarly phrased rhetorical questions posed to Job in the Yahweh speeches toward the end of the book of Job:

Hast thou commanded the morning since thy days; and caused the dayspring to know his place; (Job 38:12)

Hast thou entered into the springs of the sea? or hast thou walked in the search of the depth?

Have the gates of death been opened unto thee? or hast thou seen the doors of the shadow of death?

Hast thou perceived the breadth of the earth? declare if thou knowest it all. (Job 38:16–18)

Hast thou entered into the treasures of the snow? or hast thou seen the treasures of the hail, (Job 38:22)

Hast thou given the horse strength? hast thou clothed his neck with thunder? (Job 39:19)

> Hast thou an arm like God? or canst thou thunder with a voice like
> him? (Job 40:9)[101]

Whitman greatly admired Job and certainly was familiar with the
Yahweh speeches.[102] The language has been modernized (e.g., "Have
you")[103] and the subject matter is unique to Whitman,[104] but the run
itself is reminiscent of Job (esp. 38:16–18) and the two-part lines in
particular ("Have you reckoned a thousand acres much? Have you
reckoned the earth much?" [thirteen words]; "Have you guessed you
yourself would not continue? Have you dreaded those earth-beetles?"
[thirteen/fourteen words]) in pattern and length are very close to the
biblical prototype. Still, Whitman's lines do not quote or allude to Job
but rather have a biblicized feel or "flavor" about them, including their
scale.

Two final examples, one from "To think of time" and the other from
"I celebrate myself," both of which feature the archaic "he that" in
proverb-shaped sayings: "He that was President was buried, and he that
is now President shall surely be buried" (*LG*, 66; sixteen words) and
"He that by me spreads a wider breast than my own proves the width
of my own" (*LG*, 52; sixteen words). The first is shaped as a two-part,
internally parallelistic line of a kind that is especially common in the
Bible's wisdom books:

> He that is surety for a stranger shall smart for it: and he that hateth
> suretiship is sure. (Prov 11:15; eighteen words)

> He that hath a froward heart findeth no good: and he that hath a
> perverse tongue falleth into mischief. (Prov 17:20; nineteen
> words)

> He that getteth wisdom loveth his own soul: he that keepeth
> understanding shall find good. (Prov 19:8; fifteen words)

---

101 There are also runs of "Canst thou" and "Wilt thou" rhetorical questions in this
     material with a similar cadence to them, as evidenced, for example, in the second
     half of Job 40:9 ("or canst thou thunder with a voice like him?").
102 See Bergquist, "Whitman and the Bible," 301, 303.
103 The phrase "have ye" occurs some eighty-three times in the KJB, and "hast thou"
     some 147 times (both especially common in rhetorical questions.
104 Although Whitman's "Have you reckoned the earth much?" is not so very far from
     Job's "Hast thou perceived the breadth of the earth."

He that observeth the wind shall not sow; and he that regardeth the clouds shall not reap. (Eccl 11:4; seventeen words)

He that findeth his life shall lose it: and he that loseth his life for my sake shall find it. (Matt 10:39; twenty words)

This sort of saying can also be antithetically shaped:

He that walketh uprightly walketh surely: but he that perverteth his ways shall be known. (Prov 10:9; fifteen words)

He that spareth his rod hateth his son: but he that loveth him chasteneth him betimes. (Prov 13:24; sixteen words)

Although the content of Whitman's line is not overly didactic, his use of the biblical phrases "he that" (764x in KJB) and "shall surely" (65x in KJB) gives the whole a distinctly biblical feel. The usage of the archaic "he that" is all the more marked (in hindsight) as it all but drops out of modern English translations of the Bible (e.g., RSV: 36x—mostly replaced by "he who"). In fact, Whitman uses the phrase four other times in the 1855 *Leaves* (*LG* vii, 27, 75, 91) and "she that" once, in a phrase ("she that conceived," *LG*, 91) with its own biblical genealogy (Hos 2:5; cf. 1 Sam 2:5; Prov 23:25; Jer 15:9; 50:12).

The second line, much more sagacious in tone and content, also finds many biblical counterparts of similar shape and scale:

He that followeth after righteousness and mercy findeth life, righteousness, and honour. (Prov 21:21; twelve words)

He that deviseth to do evil shall be called a mischievous person. (Prov 24:8; twelve words)

He that rebuketh a man afterwards shall find more favour than he that flattereth with the tongue. (Prov 28:23; seventeen words)

He that dwelleth in the secret place of the most High shall abide under the shadow of the Almighty. (Ps 91:1; nineteen words)

Intriguingly, Martin Farquhar Tupper, a contemporary of Whitman's who was only too happy to mime biblical maxims, uses the archaic "he that" twenty-two times in his 1838 edition of *Proverbial Philosophy*, a copy of which Whitman owned and marked up (see below).[105] Most of these

---

105 (London: Joseph Rickerby, 1838). The phrase "he that" appears on the following pages: pp. 28, 48, 60, 84, 93, 100, 110, 126, 129, 130, 133, 135, 150, 155, 158, 159, 169,

are similar in shape and scale to their biblical models and to Whitman's two lines, including "He that went to comfort, is pitied; he that should rebuke, is silent" (p. 135; thirteen words) and "And he that hath more than enough, is a thief of the rights of his brother" (p. 150; sixteen words). The latter is among the four lines Whitman brackets on that page. This is quintessential Whitman as a poet-compositor, absorbing the language of others (here from the Bible) and turning it to his own ends: "The greatest poet forms the consistence of what is to be from what has been and is. He drags the dead out of their coffins and stands them again on their feet.... he says to the past, Rise and walk before me that I may realize you" (*LG*, vi; for the biblical allusion, see Luke 5:23; John 5:8; Matt 9:5; Mark 2:9; cf. John 11).[106]

Variability in Line-Length

Moreover, it is the mix of line lengths in Whitman's poetry that is also telling. Whitman's line is not monolithic, as the chronological overview offered above makes apparent. If characteristically long (especially in the early editions of *Leaves*), it is also stubbornly variable. As Allen notices, what is most consistent about it is its "clausal structure," "each verse [is] a sentence."[107] But the "sentence" can be relatively short ("I celebrate myself," *LG*, 13; three words)—Whitman, of course, started out writing metered verse with lines of conventional lengths, and these shorter lines remain a part of his lineal repertoire;[108] or really long ("If I and you and the worlds and all beneath or upon their surfaces, and all the palpable life, were this moment reduced back to a pallid float, it would not avail in the long run," *LG*, 51; thirty-six words); or most often somewhere in between ("A gigantic beauty of a stallion, fresh and responsive to my caresses," *LG*, 35; twelve words). The undoing of meter not only made possible the increased scale of Whitman's poetic line, it also opened the

---

182, 205.

106 Cf. K. M. Price, *Whitman and Tradition* (New Haven: Yale University, 1990), 67, 75—though the Bible does not figure in the literary tradition Price surveys. The language "Rise and walk" comes from the story of the paralytic, but Whitman likely had in mind one of the raising of the dead stories, such as John 11 (Lazarus).

107 *Reader's Guide*, 163.

108 In the 1855 *Leaves*, 354 lines contain eight or fewer words; only rarely does a line of Whitman's early metered verse contain more than eight words.

way to lineal variability, the capacity to shape the sentential wholes out of which Whitman's lines were normally configured as desired, without external constraints.

The Bible, too, in the familiar bi-columnar format of the KJB, is most immediately experienced as a mass of sentences of varying lengths segmented by verse (and chapter) divisions. The degree of variability and its underlying sources depends on what part of the Bible is in view. The poetic sections of the (Hebrew) Bible offer the most regularity, since the verse divisions in this material usually circumscribe groupings of two, three, four, and sometimes more poetic lines of roughly equivalent lengths. But even here variability is normative. The biblical poetic line itself, though roughly equivalent (especially within couplets and triples) and ultimately constrained, nevertheless varies in length (normally from five to twelve syllables or three to five words). And since the verse divisions distinguish groupings of this variable line, the pattern of grouping that prevails in any one corpus—sometimes more regular (as with the almost unfailing preference for couplets in Proverbs and parts of Job), sometimes less so (Psalms, Song of Songs, and much prophetic poetry, for example, feature unscripted blends of grouping strategies)—adds yet a further parameter of variability.

The magnitude of such variability increases dramatically when the underlying (Hebrew and Greek) prose portions of the Bible are considered alongside the poetic. In these sections, the verse divisions of the KJB usually reflect the sentential structure of the underlying prose. There are no (explicit) length constraints on these prose sentences, whether translated from Hebrew or Greek.[109] They can be long or short, and length considerations are not prominent in determining the overall discourse logic of a passage of prose. That is, short sentences may follow upon long ones, or not, for seemingly indiscriminate reasons. Regardless, what is presented to the English reader of the KJB, almost no matter which portions of scripture are in view, are blocks of prose sentences of varying lengths set off in verse divisions (and thus made visually

---

109 There are pragmatic constraints, however. For example, written Hebrew prose evolved out of a predominantly oral world and was engineered mainly for aural reception (e.g., "and Ezra the priest brought the law before the congregation both of men and women, and all that could hear with understanding," Neh 8:2). Hence, prose sentence lengths, though variable and unpredictable and longer on average than Hebrew poetic clausal structures, are still ultimately constrained.

uniform). Like the long lengths of Whitman's prototypical line—two, three, and often four times as long as the typical biblical Hebrew verse line (in translation)—the variety of these lengths finds a ready analog in the verse divisions in the KJB. Whitman's own image for his line play— "the [regular] recurrence of lesser and larger waves on the sea-shore, rolling in without intermission, and fitfully rising and falling"[110]—also well describes the mix of the verse divisions in the KJB, and in the poetic books in particular, and the ebb and flow of their rhythm.

That Whitman's writing should bear the imprint of both biblical poetry and biblical prose follows from various considerations. Whitman's trackable quotations, allusions, and echoes come equally from prose and poetic sources in the Bible; the whole Bible was thought of as "poetry" in the nineteenth century, as C. Beyers observes,[111] and certainly Whitman, even allowing on his part for an appreciation of the genuinely poetic parts of the Old Testament, shared this larger understanding, especially explicit "Bible as Poetry"—"all the poems of Orientalism, with the Old and New Testaments at the centre";[112] and the uniform nature of the KJB's formatting, with only the subtlest differences in whitespace to distinguish (underlying) verse from prose, would itself dispose readers to a uniform treatment of the whole Bible.[113] This double-sided impact is no small matter, since there are few sources that can match the English Bible's diversity of styles. That is, one of the key indicators of the significance of the verse divisions in the KJB for considering Whitman's line is precisely the great diversity of styles, rhythms, and the like that they enfold, composed as they are of material ultimately drawn from poetry as well as prose—and a plethora of kinds, genres, styles in both media. There are likely not many other sources available to Whitman that match his own breadth and variety.[114] As will become more apparent, the KJB does not just provide a singular point

---

110 Perry, *Walt Whitman*, 207; cf. *WWWC*, I, 414–15.
111 *A History of Free Verse* (University of Arkansas, 2001), 57 and nn. 39, 41.
112 *The Critic* 3 (February 3, 1883), 57.
113 Cf. A. McGrath, *In the Beginning: The Story of the King James Bible and How It Changed a Nation, a Language, and a Culture* (New York: Anchor, 2008), ch. 5.
114 Cf. H. Schneidau, "The Antinomian Strain: The Bible and American Poetry" in *The Bible and American Arts and Letters* (ed. G. Gunn; Philadelphia: Fortress, 1983), 11–32, at 19.

of contact with Whitman's evolving sense of a line, viz. its expanded length, but many such points, and they are diverse in nature.

Caesuras in Whitman

Beyond the gross scale of Whitman's lines, what takes place in them is also often redolent of what is found in the KJB's verse divisions, especially in the poetic books. Consider the nature of caesuras in Whitman—caesura here being understood as "syntactic juncture or pause between phrases or clauses, usually signaled by punctuation, but sometimes not," that is present in every sentence of any length.[115] Whitman's caesural division is usually marked by punctuation—"his internal commas and dashes are also often caesural pauses"[116]—as in the following handful of examples, taken from the beginning of "I celebrate myself":

> I lean and loafe at my ease.... observing a spear of summer grass.
>
> Houses and rooms are full of perfumes.... the shelves are crowded with perfumes,
>
> I breathe the fragrance myself, and know it and like it,
>
> The atmosphere is not a perfume.... it has no taste of the distillation.... it is odorless,
>
> The sniff of green leaves and dry leaves, and of the shore and darkcolored sea-rocks, and of hay in the barn, (*LG*, 13)
>
> Have you reckoned a thousand acres much? Have you reckoned the earth much?
>
> You shall no longer take things at second or third hand.... nor look through the eyes of the dead.... nor feed on the spectres in books,
>
> You shall not look through my eyes either, nor take things from me, (*LG*, 14)

---

115 T. V. F. Brogan, "Caesura" in *NPEPP*, 159. The phenomenon is usually discussed in terms of metrical verse, but is applicable to nonmetrical verse. If caesural division is not obligated by rule in nonmetrical verse, patterns of usage may nonetheless emerge for particular poets, as they do for Whitman.

116 Allen, *New Walt Whitman Handbook*, 233.

Or the absence of explicit punctuation:

Stop this day and night with me and you shall possess the origin of all
poems,

You shall listen to all sides and filter them from yourself. (*LG*, 14)

As God comes a loving bedfellow and sleeps at my side all night and
close on the peep of the day,

And leaves for me baskets covered with white towels bulging the house
with their plenty,

Shall I postpone my acceptation and realization and scream at my eyes,

Looks with its sidecurved head curious what will come next, (*LG*, 15)

One significance of Whitman's pattern of caesural division lies in its
close correspondence to the major syntactic (and phrasal) divisions,
also mostly marked through punctuation, in the larger verse divisions
of the poetic material in the KJB. Consider as but one example part of
the opening section of the Song of the Sea (Exod 15:2–8):

²The LORD is my strength and song, and he is become my salvation:
he is my God, and I will prepare him an habitation; my father's
God, and I will exalt him.

³The LORD is a man of war: the LORD is his name.

⁴Pharaoh's chariots and his host hath he cast into the sea: his chosen
captains also are drowned in the Red sea.

⁵The depths have covered them: they sank into the bottom as a stone.

⁶Thy right hand, O LORD, is become glorious in power: thy right hand,
O LORD, hath dashed in pieces the enemy.

⁷And in the greatness of thine excellency thou hast overthrown them
that rose up against thee: thou sentest forth thy wrath, which
consumed them as stubble.

⁸And with the blast of thy nostrils the waters were gathered together,
the floods stood upright as an heap, and the depths were
congealed in the heart of the sea.

These divisions are punctuated by clausal and phrasal units, typically
set off by commas, colons, and semicolons, in a manner analogous to

Whitman's caesuras—especially as regards the number of such divisions (per verse) and their characteristic length and syntactic integrity. The source of the major syntactic junctures in these verse divisions, as will be clear from the earlier discussion, is the underlying biblical Hebrew poetic line structure that gets embedded in the verse divisions of the KJB. This becomes immediately obvious, again, by either comparing the original Hebrew or a translation, such as Moulton's below,[117] that explicitly intends to show off the original verse structure:

> The LORD is my strength and song,
>
>> And he is become my salvation:
>
> This is my God, and I will praise him;
>
>> My father's God, and I will exalt him.
>
> The LORD is a man of war:
>
>> The LORD is his name.
>
> Pharaoh's chariots and his host hath he cast into the sea:
>
>> And his chosen captains are sunk in the Red sea.
>
> The deeps cover them:
>
>> They went down into the depths like a stone.
>
> Thy right hand, O LORD, is glorious in power:
>
>> Thy right hand, O LORD, dasheth in pieces the enemy.
>
> And in the greatness of thine excellency thou overthrowest them that rose up against thee:
>
>> Thou sendest forth thy wrath, it consumeth them as stubble.
>
> And with the blast of thy nostrils the waters were piled up,
>
>> The floods stood upright as an heap,
>
>> The deeps were congealed in the heart of the sea.

---

117 *Modern Reader's Bible*, II, 36.

The correspondence in length, cadence, and syntactic integrity between Whitman's caesural divisions, the major syntactic junctures in the poetic parts of the KJB, and the individual biblical Hebrew verse line (in translation) is most striking.

Not surprising, then, the caesural divisions of Whitman's longer lines may even stand on their own as singular lines. For example, the first caesural division set off by suspension points in "Or I guess the grass is itself a child.... the produced babe of the vegetation" two lines later appears as a line of its own, "Or I guess it is a uniform hieroglyphic" (*LG*, 16). Compare also the following sequence:

> Walking the path worn in the grass and beat through the leaves of the brush;
>
> Where the quail is whistling betwixt the woods and the wheatlot,
>
> Where the bat flies in the July eve.... where the great goldbug drops through the dark;
>
> Where the flails keep time on the barn floor.... (*LG*, 36)

And:

> Ever the hard and unsunk ground,
>
> Ever the eaters and drinkers.... ever the upward and downward sun.... ever the air and the
>
> ceaseless tides.... (*LG*, 47)

Allen observes similarly that "sometimes the caesura divides the parallelism and *is equivalent to the line-end pause*" (emphasis added).[118] That, in fact, Whitman thought very much along these lines is suggested by how he reshapes the 1850 "Resurgemus" into what becomes the eighth poem of the 1855 *Leaves*. Mostly his adaptation consists in relineating, in combining the shorter lines of the 1850 poem into single, longer lines in *Leaves*.[119] For example, "For many a promise sworn by royal lips/ And broken, and laughed at in the breaking" becomes the

---

118 *New Walt Whitman Handbook*, 234. t.
119 Zweig, *Walt Whitman*, 121; Miller, *Collage of Myself*, 7.

single line, "For many a promise sworn by royal lips, And[120] broken, and laughed at in the breaking" (*LG*, 88). In another example a five-line section is recombined into two long lines:

> But the sweetness of mercy brewed bitter destruction,
>
> And frightened rulers come back:
>
> Each comes in state, with his train,
>
> Hangman, priest, and tax-gatherer,
>
> Soldier, lawyer, and sycophant; ("Resurgemus")

> But the sweetness of mercy brewed bitter destruction, and the frightened rulers come back:
>
> Each comes in state with his train.... hangman, priest and tax-gatherer.... soldier, lawyer, jailer and sycophant. (*LG*, 88)

In both examples, what becomes caesural divisions in *Leaves* once stood literally as singular lines in "Resurgemus."

Line-Internal Parallelism

A related consideration arises in what Allen calls "internal parallelism." In noting dissimilarities between Whitman's and the Bible's use of parallelism, Allen observes, "As a rule it is easier to break up Whitman's long lines into shorter parallelisms ('internal', we shall call them), though this can be done with some biblical lines and cannot be done with many of Whitman's shorter lines."[121] He goes on, with some minor equivocation, to say, "Perhaps *Leaves of Grass* contains more internal parallelism than the poetry of the Bible."[122] No equivocation is necessary.

---

120 Note Whitman even retains the capitalization from the earlier version where "And" was line initial. This was normalized ("and") in 1856 and all succeeding editions.

121 "Biblical Analogies," 494; cf. *American Prosody*, 223. Cf. H. Vendler, *Poets Thinking* (Cambridge: Harvard University, 2004), 38 ("the smallest parallels in Whitman come two to a line").

122 Allen, "Biblical Analogies," 497.

While there is line internal parallelism within biblical Hebrew verse,[123] it is not nearly so prominent as in Whitman.[124] And the reason why this is so is also the telling point. Again, Allen is befuddled because he is comparing apples (mostly) and oranges, the Hebrew line of biblical verse (or a presumed translation equivalent thereof) and Whitman's line. They are not comparable. But when one recalibrates and compares, instead, Whitman's line and the verse divisions in the KJB, then the view quickly comes into focus. If the biblical Hebrew verse line only sparingly exhibits line-internal parallelism (because it often lacks the necessary scale), the verse divisions of the KJB in the poetic books are rife with it because they are themselves most often translations of sets of parallel lines. The only biblical example of line-internal parallelism that Allen quotes is Ps 19:2–4, which he lays out in the following manner:[125]

(a)   Day unto day uttereth speech, and night unto night
            sheweth knowledge,

(b);   There is no speech nor language; their voice cannot be
            heard.

(c)   Their line is gone out through all the earth, and
            their words to the end of the world.

Tellingly, this does not appear to be Moulton's rendition, which both originally and in the volume Allen claims to cite, replicates the RV, a fair English version of the underlying Hebrew line structure:

---

123 W. G. E. Watson, *Traditional Techniques in Classical Hebrew Verse* (JSOTS 170; Sheffield: Sheffield Academic, 1994), 104–91, esp. 144–62. The last line of the triplet in Ps 14:7 offers a good example of line-internal parallelism: *yāgēl yaʿăqōb* // *yiśmaḥ yiśrāʾēl* "Jacob will rejoice" // "Israel will be glad." Internal parallelism in biblical Hebrew poetry is most common in longer lines (usually containing four or more words) that can accommodate the play of matching that is at the heart of this trope.

124 Cf. B. Hrushovski, "The Theory and Practice of Rhythm in the Expressionist Po- etry of U. Z. Grinberg," *Hasifrut* 1 (Spring 1968), 176–205 (in Hebrew) (as summarized by E. Greenspan, "Whitman in Israel" in *Walt Whitman and the World* [eds. G. W. Allen and E. Folsom; Iowa City: University of Iowa, 1995], 386–95, at 393). Allen's assertion otherwise—"the biblical poets used it in abundance" ("Biblical Analogies," 497)—is simply wrong, Allen being led astray by his confusion as to what constitutes a line in biblical Hebrew verse and by inattention to translation technique in his secondary sources.

125 Allen, "Biblical analogies," 494.

Day unto day uttereth speech,

And night unto night sheweth knowledge.

There is no speech nor language;

Their voice cannot be heard.

Their line is gone out through all the earth,

And their words to the end of the world.[126]

The wording of Allen's citation is the same—whether taken from Moulton or from the RV itself—though lined according to the verse divisions of the KJB—albeit in a schematized manner:

Day unto day uttereth speech, and night unto night sheweth knowledge.

There is no speech nor language, where their voice is not heard.

Their line is gone out through all the earth, and their words to the end of the world.

Interestingly, Allen's confused version of Ps 19:2–4 shows what he claims it shows, namely, line-internal parallelism of the kind commonly found in Whitman, though admittedly not quite in the way that he imagines. The underlying Hebrew lines have no such line-internal parallelism, as Moulton's version makes clear. Rather, the source of the putative internal parallelism in this example is the verse divisions of the KJB, each containing the translation equivalent to a parallel couplet in the original Hebrew. So here, too, there is a match between the KJB (verse divisions) and Whitman's line. And as significant the trope is common in both corpuses (see Chapter Four).

Allen illustrates line-internal parallelism in Whitman by breaking up the parallel caesural divisions in the opening lines of the "Song of Myself" (with Whitman's later addition, e.g., *LG* 1881, 29) and lining them out:

---

126 R. G. Moulton, *The Modern Reader's Bible*: *The Psalms and Lamentations* (New York: Macmillan, 1898), I, 35; *Modern Reader's Bible*, II, 287).

(a)   I celebrate myself,

(a)   and sing myself,

(b)   And what I assume

(b)   you shall assume.

(c)   For every atom belonging to me

(c)   as good belongs to you.[127]

Even better is "They were purified by death.... They were taught and exalted" from "Suddenly out of its stale and drowsy lair" (*LG*, 88), which can be decomposed with confidence into the parallel lines of the 1850 "Resurgemus":

They were purified by death,

They were taught and exalted.

Such decomposition, while admirably illustrating the parallelism Allen sees, also reveals from a slightly different angle how any biblical model for Whitman's long(er) lines must be on the scale of the verse divisions of the KJB. Otherwise there would be a good deal more such sets of short(er), parallel lines, for these are the more precise equivalents to the parallelistic couple so prominent in biblical Hebrew verse, as a comparison with Moulton's rendition of Ps 19:2–4 readily reveals. And as noted above, the rough equivalence of Whitman's caesural divisions and the underlying Hebrew verse line is what may be predicted if it is the verse divisions of the KJB that have helped to inspire Whitman's typical long lines.

Internally parallelistic lines (whether of two or three parts) are extremely common in *Leaves* and are one of the surest signs of the KJB's imprint on Whitman's mature style. The parallelistic couplet and triplet are the most dominant forms of line grouping in biblical poetry. They provide the basic skeletal infrastructure for the biblical poet's art and are inevitably rendered into two and three part verses in the prose translation of the KJB. Mostly, of course, Whitman has just adopted this parallelistic substructure and fitted it out with his own language

---

127 "Biblical Analogies," 494, n. 3; *American Prosody*, 223.

material. But the substructure itself and the prominence of semantic synonymity are important markers of the biblical genealogy.[128] This is even more clear when accompanied by other biblical inflections. however. For example, the line introducing the thrush from "When Lilacs Last in the Door-yard Bloom,": "If thou wast not gifted to sing, thou would'st surely die" (*Sequel*, 4), is fitted out with archaisms ("thou wast" [50x in KJB], "thou wouldest" [29x in KJB]) and phrasing ("surely die" [22x in KJB]) redolent of the KJB, but also a conditional clause (protasis and apodosis) mapped onto the binary substructure of the underlying Hebrew couplet:

tidbaq-lĕšônî lĕḥikkî	Let my tongue cling to the roof of my mouth,
ʾim-lōʾ ʾezkĕrēkî	if I do not remember you (Ps 137:6; NRSV)
KJB:	"If I do not remember thee, let my tongue cleave to the roof of my mouth" (cf. Judg 9:15; Obad 5; Ps 66:18; 73:15; 137:5; Job 8:18; 9:23; 13:10)

I cite Ps 137:6 because Whitman uses the language from the apodosis in one of his early pieces of fiction ("His tongue cleav'd to the roof of his mouth"),[129] and thus there can be confidence of his familiarity with such poetically shaped biblical conditionals.[130] But the main point is to reveal the skeletal imprint of the underlying Hebrew pattern as it is processed through the prose translation of the KJB.

An even more spectacular example may be cited from the 1860 edition of *Leaves*. The following comes from section 34 in the new opening poem, "Proto-Leaf" (later called "Starting from Paumanok"):

³⁴ My comrade!

For you, to share with me, two greatnesses—And a third one, rising
   inclusive and more resplendent,

---

128 So also Allen: "Whitman's favorite form... is the synonymous" ("Biblical Analogies," 497)—this holds whether the focus is lineally or line internally.

129 "Death in the School-Room," *The United States Magazine and Democratic Review* 9 (August 1841), 177–81, https://whitmanarchive.org/published/fiction/shortfiction/per.00317.html (reprinted in *EPF*, 57).

130 Cf. the run of four "If they... they...." conditionals in "I celebrate myself" (*LG*, 24), and toward the end of that first poem: "If you want me again look for me under your bootsoles" (*LG*, 56).

The greatness of Love and Democracy—and the greatness of Religion.
(*LG* 1860, 13)

Such "graded number sequences" are both a commonplace in the poetry
of the Bible and distinctively biblical. Proverbs 30:18–19 is typical:

> ¹⁸ There be three things which are too wonderful for me, yea, four which
> I know not:

> ¹⁹ The way of an eagle in the air; the way of a serpent upon a rock; the
> way of a ship in the midst of the sea; and the way of a man with
> a maid. (KJB)

In both the number sequence (x// x+1) is intended to enumerate
a definite number (x+1) of items, as the items are then listed in the
following line/verse division ("Love," "Democracy," and "Religion" in
Whitman; the way of an "eagle," "serpent," ship," and "man" in Prov
30:19; cf. Ps 62:12–13; Prov 6:16–19; 30:21–23, 29–31; Job 5:19–22). What
is so distinctly biblical about the trope is how rudimentary number
knowledge (e.g., counting, basic arithmetic) is accommodated to a
parallelistic frame and biblical poetry's strong preference for couplets—
it is a dominantly distichic kind of verse. The latter comes across more
clearly in a translation, such as the ASV, which explicitly lineates
according to the underlying Hebrew—the KJB is a *prose* translation:

> *šĕlōšâ hēmmâ niplĕʾû mimmennî*
>
> *wĕʾarbaᶜ lōʾ yĕdaᶜtî*
>
> *derek hannešer aššāmayim*
>
> *derek nāḥāš ᶜălê-ṣûr*
>
> *derek-ʾŏniyyâ bĕleb-yām*
>
> *wĕderek geber bĕᶜalmâ*

> There are three things which are too wonderful for me
>
> Yea, four which I know not:
>
> The way of an eagle in the air
>
> The way of a serpent upon a rock;
>
> The way of a ship in the midst of the sea;

And the way of a man with a maiden.

The abbreviated counts attested in the graded numerical sequences in the Bible (viz. "three..."// "and four....") principally result from the shaping force of the distich, and hence one more indication of Whitman's source.[131]

Then there is the parallelism. Since Lowth,[132] parallelism has been the principal frame of reference for understanding these graded sequences of numbers in the Bible, considered by many a variety of synonymous word-pairs (A-B terms), a "peculiar" sort of "number parallelism." W. G. E. Watson's explanation is typical: "since no number can have a synonym the only way to provide a corresponding component is to use a digit which is higher in value than the original."[133] The rub—implicit in Watson's "no number can have a synonym"—is that these numbers "are clearly not synonymous," as M. O'Connor emphasizes.[134] Rather, whatever parallelism is involved in these numerical sequences is the result of the larger informing framework, and not because of any putative synonymous identity between the numbers themselves.[135] Nevertheless, the parallelism itself is another strong indicator of Whitman's source for such a trope. Whitman's language is his own, but the trope, as with the proverbial rhetoric in the "med Cophósis" notebook, is quite clearly borrowed from the Bible. In this instance, there is also the added dimension of the stanza

---

131 By way of confirmation, note a graded-number sequence from Tupper (*Proverbial Philosophy: In Four Series, Now First Complete* [London/New York: Ward, Lock and Co., 1888], 381), whose intention to mimic the Bible's proverbial wisdom is made quite obvious:
Agur the wise, the son of Yakeh, spake unto Ithiel and Ueal,
Spake to those listening disciples, in the spirit of his kinsman Solomon:
He testified of three things and of four, noting fourfold characters,
Dropping his ensamples for all others, classed by threes and fours;
As a matter may be good, or may be evil, or between-wise, or naturally neutral,
Partaking of the neither, or the both, or of each in its separate extreme:
Here Tupper all but cites Prov 30:1—and this chapter from Proverbs itself offers numerous "ensamples," as Tupper has it, of the grade-number trope, mostly "classed by threes and fours."

132 *Lectures on the Sacred Poetry of the Hebrews* (2 vols.; trans. G. Gregory; London: J. Johnson, 1787; reprinted in *Robert Lowth (1710–1787): The Major Works*, vols. 1–2 [London: Routledge, 1995]), II, 51–52; *Isaiah*, xxiii-xiv.

133 *Classical Hebrew Poetry: A Guide to Its Techniques* (London: T & T Clark, 2001 [1984]), 144.

134 *Hebrew Verse Structure*, 378; cf. J. Kugel, *The Idea of Biblical Poetry: Parallelism and Its History* (Baltimore: Johns Hopkins University, 1981), 42.

135 For details on the Hebrew phenomenon, see F. W. Dobbs-Allsopp, "So-Called 'Number Parallelism' in Biblical Poetry" in *"Like 'Ilu are you Wise": Studies in Northwest Semitic Languages and Literatures in Honor of Dennis G. Pardee* (eds, H. H. Handy et al; Chicago: University of Chicago, 2022), 205–24.

or section number (34). Whitman introduces these numbers into (many of) his longer poems in the 1860 *Leaves* in imitation of the verse numbers from the KJB. Hence, not only are the supporting language tropes borrowed from the Bible (parallelism, graded number sequence) but so is this aspect of formatting. A comparison of page images from Harper's 1846 *Illuminated Bible* (Prov 30:18–19) and from the 1860 *Leaves* (p. 13, sec. 34) offers a stunning snapshot of just how visually alike these are (Figs. 1, 37). This is perhaps as close as one can come to catching Whitman out in his act of imitation of and collation from the Bible.

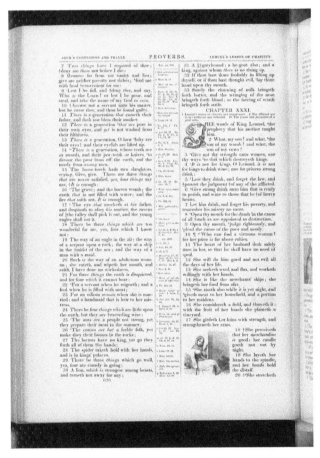

Fig. 37: Prov 30:7–31:20 from Harper's *Illuminated Bible*.

End-Stopping

Another consideration is the end-stopped nature of Whitman's lines. Early on E. C. Ross points out the structural importance of the line to Whitman's verse[136] and the fact that "a run-on line is rare in Whitman—so rare that it may be considered a 'slip.'"[137] Almost every line of Whitman's ends in a major syntactic pause, marked most frequently by commas and periods—this is Allen's "clausal structure" where "each verse [is] a sentence."[138] Allen seizes on the overwhelmingly end-stopped nature of Whitman's lines to underscore the importance of parallelism to the poet's prosody: "This [end-stopping and the line it reveals] is because parallelism is the first rhythmic principle in Whitman's verse."[139] Here Allen shows well that he understands the central force of parallelism as a phenomenon to be the iteration of the singular—in this case the singular is the lineal unit. Curiously, Allen neither notes the fact that biblical poetry is also prominently end-stopped, line-boundary normally converging with the end of discrete syntactic units, nor marshals this datum toward his larger thesis. And yet it is one of the outstanding features of biblical verse,[140] so much so that M. Kinzie in her *A Poet's Guide to Poetry* chooses the biblical tradition to exemplify how sentence logic (syntax) may be used to end a line, noting that "Hebrew poetry consists of lines that close at the ends of phrases."[141] Most of Moulton's translations cited by Allen effectively replicate in English the end-stopping that pervades Hebrew line structure. Yet Kinzie, however keen her observation, botches things roundly when it comes to illustrating her point. For this she chooses to offer selections from the KJB, lineated as I have been doing according to the verse divisions in that translation.

---

136 Later scholarship, especially in light of Whitman's notebooks, has only ramified this point. Once Whitman finds his line, it becomes the single most important structural building block in his art, see esp. Folsom and Price, *Re-Scripting Walt Whitman*, ch. 2; cf. Zweig, *Walt Whitman*, 229–30; Miller, *Collage of Myself*, 63, 81, 119–20.

137 "Whitman's Verse," *MLN* 45 (1930), 364; cf. Erkkila, *Political Poet*, 88–89.

138 *Reader's Guide*, 163.

139 "Biblical Analogies," 493; cf. *American Prosody*, 221–22; Erkkila, *Political Poet*, 88.

140 Esp. O'Connor, *Hebrew Verse Structure*, 85–86, 120–21, 129; cf. F. W. Dobbs-Allsopp, "The Enjambing Line in Lamentations: A Taxonomy (Part I)" *ZAW* 113/2 (2001), 223; *On Biblical Poetry*, 44–45, 55, 133–36, 137, 139, 285–86; Geller, "Hebrew Prosody and Poetics," 510.

141 Kinzie, *Poet's Guide*, 51.

Ps 70:2–4 (vv. 3–5 in Hebrew) is her first example, which she formats in the following manner:

> Let them be ashamed and confounded that seek after my soul: *let them be* turned backward, and put to confusion, that desire my hurt.
>
> *Let them be* turned back for a reward of their shame that say, Aha, aha.
>
> *Let all those* that seek thee rejoice and be glad in thee: *and let such* as love thy salvation say continually, *Let God be* magnified.[142]

To make matters worse she analyzes these "lines," noting in particular that they have "identical opening or closing phrases" (emphasized in the translation) and "begin with capital letters."[143] Her focus here is patently on the English. None of this—citation, like openings, capitalization—tells us anything about the end-stopped nature of the underlying Hebrew line. It is instructive nonetheless for my larger consideration of Whitman. First, however unwittingly, Kinzie provides a stunning example of a poet construing the KJB's prose rendering of biblical poetry as verse *precisely in the manner I am supposing of Whitman*. That is, the language material segmented by the verse divisions of the KJB is seen (and heard) as singular, lineal entities of verse, one (postulated) stichic unit following on another (with ainly only thematic elements available for grouping purposes)—the initial capitalization with repetitive opening or closing phrases emphasized by Kinzie's analysis also typify Whitman's lineal palette, especially in his catalogues. Another contemporary poet (and critic), J. Hollander, in his delightfully witty *Rhyme's Reason*, offers a similar kind of confirmatory example of what I imagine to be Whitman's practice. In turning to discuss and illustrate "unmeasured verse"—free verse—which he notes has existed "for ages," Hollander begins with "the verse form of the Hebrew Bible," which "as it was translated into English" is for him possibly the "most influential" form of free verse.[144] As is Hollander's practice throughout this little book, instead of citing actual examples he provides his own often very amusing and

---

142 Ibid., 51–52.
143 Ibid., 51.
144 J. Hollander, *Rhyme's Reason: A Guide to English Verse* (rev. ed.; New Haven: Yale University, 1989 [1981]), 25.

enlightening renderings. His imitation of biblical poetry in English is instructive:

> The verse of the Hebrew Bible is strange; the meter of Psalms and
>   Proverbs perplexes.
>
> It is not a matter of number, no counting of beats or syllables.
>
> Its song is a music of matching, its rhythm a kind of paralleling.
>
> One half-line makes an assertion; the other part paraphrases it;
>   sometimes a third part will vary it.
>
> An abstract statement meets with its example, yes, the way a wind runs
>   through the tree's moving leaves.
>
> One river's water is heard on another's shore; so did this Hebrew verse
>   form carry across into English.[145]

This effectively mimics biblical verse, and exactly in the manner of Kinzie's stichic construal of the verse divisions of the KJB, i.e., longer lines (corresponding to the range of lengths of the verse divisions), caesural segments that fall out according to the underlying Hebrew line structure (Hollander's "half-line"). At the same time, it is strikingly reminiscent of Whitman, whom Hollander goes on to discuss in the following paragraph. If Kinzie, by dint of her way of formatting and analyzing the KJB's versions of biblical poems, exemplifies the plausibility of assuming a similar kind of uptake on Whitman's part, then Hollander's efforts spectacularly illustrate what can result when a poet intentionally aims to emulate an Englished version of the biblical poetic tradition (as mediated by the KJB). This is the other side of the proverbial coin. Kinzie shows how the KJB verse divisions can be construed poetically and Hollander how such a construal can lead to an original poetic creation. The two together are quite intriguing for my larger thesis.

A second significance of Kinzie's understanding the KJB as a transparent rendering of the original Hebrew demonstrates how the KJB lined out according to verse divisions is also end-stopped. And the KJB is end-stopped precisely in the manner that Whitman's verse

---

145 Ibid., 26.

is end-stopped, i.e., mostly in longer segments, punctuated by caesural pauses of various kinds. Hollander's riff on biblical poetry also shows this. Indeed, he goes on in another of his made-up verse illustrations to describe the kind of end-stopped free-verse line that exemplifies both the Bible (whether in Hebrew or English) and Whitman:

Free verse is never totally "free":

It can occur in many forms,

All of them having in common one principle—

Nothing is necessarily counted or measured

(Remember biblical verse—see above).

One form—this one—makes each line a grammatical unit.

This can be a clause

Which has a subject and a predicate,

Or a phrase

Of prepositional type.[146]

End-stopped lines are prominent in biblical Hebrew poetry, but they are not so overwhelmingly dominant as in Whitman or the KJB's verse divisions. Almost a third of the lines in the biblical Hebrew corpus are enjambed, the syntax running over line boundaries—definitely not a slip.[147] But most of these run-on lines appear within couplet, triplet, and quatrain boundaries. So even in a couplet containing an enjambed line— for example, the opening couplet in Lamentations 1 ("How lonely sits the city/ that once was full of people!", NRSV)—the couplet boundary itself is almost always closed, end-stopped—syntax running over couplet or triplet boundaries in biblical verse, if not quite a slip, nonetheless is rare, e.g., "Now I would be lying down and quiet;/ I would be asleep; then I would be at rest// with kings and counselors of the earth/ who rebuild ruins for themselves," Job 3:13–14 (NRSV). The end-stopped nature of

---

146 Ibid.
147 See Dobbs-Allsopp, "Enjambing Line," 219–39; "The Effects of Enjambment in Lamentations (Part 2)," *ZAW* 113/5 (2001), 370–85; *On Biblical Poetry*, 45–48, 137, 138–39, 204,329, 330–31, 336, 507, n. 22.

the verse divisions of the KJB ultimately refracts end-stopping in the underlying Hebrew, but at the boundary of the couplet (or triplet or quatrain), not that of the line. Kinzie's larger point is on target, and if she muffs the details, she does so in a way that clarifies just how close (and closed) the KJB verse divisions are to Whitman's own lines.

This likeness is ramified when the prose portions of the Bible are considered alongside the poetry. The verse divisions of the KJB in this material, almost without exception, close at a major syntactic juncture, usually a sentence and usually marked by a period (in English translations). At base, then, the KJB, regardless of genre, presents itself as a mass of sentences set off by indentation and numbered verses. This is to emphasize the coercive nature of the verse divisions as they persistently interrupt the reading experience and divide the language material into varied sizes of sentences (or groups of sentences). Since Allen's "Biblical Analogies," scholars have pointed to the prevalence of parallelism in *Leaves* as a leading indicator of Whitman's stylistic debt to the Bible (see Chapter Four). An even more thoroughgoing marker of this debt, however, may be Whitman's predilection for a "rhythm of thought" parsed out sententially, line by end-stopped line. Certainly, the Bible in the familiar rendition of the KJB offers a ready and abundant source of such sententially versified language. In fact, the trial lines in the early notebooks appear to show Whitman primarily preoccupied with shaping his emerging line to fit his sentential mode of thought. Most of these lines, regardless of length, are composed of single thoughts. And the incidence of line-internal parallelism in these lines is remarkably low.

To recognize in the Bible a ready-made model for Whitman's predominantly end-stopped line is not to presume anything about how that model was actually encountered or accommodated. To judge by the three 1850 free-verse poems and especially the trial lines in the early notebooks and poetry manuscripts, Whitman's mode of composition is decidedly non-static, frenetic, constantly in process, doing and re-doing (and un-doing). His proclivity for lines made up of sentential wholes is evident already in the 1850 poems. A remarkable example appears in Whitman's close rendition of Matt 26:15 in "Blood-Money":

> Again goes one, saying,
>
> What will ye give me, and I will deliver this man unto you?
>
> And they make the covenant and pay the pieces of silver.

Here Whitman orchestrates his line-cuts according to the major syntactic junctures (cued by punctuation and capitalization) in the (translated) biblical passage: "And said unto them, What will ye give me, and I will deliver him unto you? And they covenanted with him for thirty pieces of silver" (Matt 26:15). The impulse toward sententially oriented lines is clearly detectable and the verse division is what holds Whitman's immediate attention. And yet run-on lines also appear in this early material, and sometimes Whitman can be seen resolving these into often larger, rounder syntactic wholes. He often achieves this through his combinatory strategy as frequently in his revisions to "Resurgemus."[148] For example, the shorter, sharper syntactic cuts in

> Not a disembodied spirit
>
> Can the weapon of tyrants let loose,
>
> But it shall stalk invisibly over the earth,
>
> Whispering, counseling, cautioning. ("Resurgemus,")

are significantly softened in their revised form in the 1855 *Leaves*:

> Not a disembodied spirit can the weapons of tyrants let loose,
>
> But it stalks invisibly over the earth . . whispering counseling
>   cautioning. (*LG*, 88)

In the latter, the inter-lineal syntactic dependencies are not totally erased, but they are eased such that the resulting two lines are more easily consumed holistically.

Another good example comes from the "I know a rich capitalist" notebook. Here what is originally conceived of as a prose sentence is broken into short(er) run-on lines of verse. Then the portion of this

---

148 Cf. Erkkila, *Political Poet*, 58. Similarly, Allen (*New Walt Whitman Handbook*, 219)
     notices the run-on lines in "Blood-Money."

material included in the 1855 *Leaves* is re-combined into a larger lineal whole:

> — Out of the first Nothing and —out of the black fogs of primeval of the nostrilsOr original Vacuity, of Death which that vast and sluggish hung ebbless and floodless in the spread of space—it asked of God with undeniable will, something to satisfy itself[149]

> Out of the vast, first Nothing

> The ebbless and floodless vapor from the nostrils of Death,

> It asked of God with undeniable will,

> Something to satisfy itself.— [150]

> Afar down I see the huge first Nothing, the vapor from the nostrils of death (*LG*, 50)

My main takeaway from such examples is to re-emphasize the processual and diachronic nature of Whitman's stylistic development as a poet and to resist the temptation to resort to stridently punctual explanations. I presume that Whitman's engagement with source material—the Bible or otherwise—is of a similar nature, that his culling of the idea for a syntactically closed line, for example, need not have been a momentary revelation nor disentangled from his compositional practice.

It is also worth stressing the centrality of the end-stopped line to Whitman's ever evolving democratic poetics. Like other elements of Whitman's style that connect with the Bible, his preference for end-stopping is invested politically. The singular, end-stopped line as it circumscribes wholeness (syntactically, ideationally, characterologically, imagistically)[151] inscribes palpable, material instantiations of particularity and individuality. And when these singularities get grouped into

---

149 https://whitmanarchive.org/manuscripts/figures/nyp.00129.011.jpg.

150 https://whitmanarchive.org/manuscripts/figures/nyp.00129.014.jpg.

151 Whitman gives what is perhaps his most revealing (though non-syntactic) description of this lineal wholeness in an early (Grier: "probably pre-1855") manuscript fragment entitled "Poem of Pictures" (anticipating the long poem "Pictures"): —"each verse presenting a picture of some scene, event, group or personage" (*NUPM* IV, 1294).

larger gatherings, as they do in Whitman's many catalogues, they
become signifiers of equality, of tolerance for difference, of unity amidst
diversity—Whitman's idea of "many in one" (*LG* 1856, 180). The long
catalogue of people at work early in "I celebrate myself" (LG, 21–23)
offers a good example. The basic lineal unit is a clausal whole of the
following kind: "The" + N(P) [actor noun, occupation] + V [present
tense, action] + DO/PP.[152] This basic syntactic template is established in
the first nine lines of the catalogues:

> The pure contralto sings in the organloft,
>
> The carpenter dresses his plank.... the tongue of his foreplane whistles
>> its wild ascending lisp,
>
> The married and unmarried children ride home to their thanksgiving
>> dinner,
>
> The pilot seizes the king-pin, he heaves down with a strong arm,
>
> The mate stands braced in the whaleboat, lance and harpoon are ready,
>
> The duck-shooter walks by silent and cautious stretches,
>
> The deacons are ordained with crossed hands at the altar,
>
> The spinning-girl retreats and advances to the hum of the big wheel,
>
> The farmer stops by the bars of a Sunday and looks at the oats and rye
>> (*LG*, 21).

Whitman occasionally varies the pattern. Sometimes he adds a second
clausal segment that expands on what the worker does or what the work
entails (as in lines 2 and 4); other times the added clause introduces a
related actor (e.g., "The pedlar sweats with his pack on his back—the
purchaser higgles about the odd cent," (*LG*, 22). At times, Whitman
extends the subject of one line into another (e.g., "The jour printer
with gray head and gaunt jaws works at his case,/ He turns his quid of
tobacco, his eyes get blurred with the manuscript," *LG*, 21). But generally
the pattern of the base lineal unit prevails repeatedly over the course of
the catalogue's sixty-nine lines. The line particularizes and individuates

---

152 For Warren's diagnosis of the clausal catalogue and for his comments on this
catalogue in particular, see "Free Growth," 27–42, esp. 31, 34.

the worker and the work. The individual in all their peculiarity is spotlighted and prized. As these similar syntactic frames are repeated and brought into alignment, the resulting parallelism both unifies and equalizes that with which the frames are filled—namely, the multitude of people—Americans all!—going about the tasks of daily, democratic existence. Erkkila describes it this way: "Presented in a sequence of separate and end-stopped images, these figures are independent and yet related" through various aspects of Whitman's "democratic poetics," including most prominently "the parallel structure of the lines."[153] Erkkila continues: "The total effect of the passage is to equalize and fuse in one chain brides and opium eaters, prostitutes and presidents, men and women, by presenting them parallelistically on a horizontal plane."[154] At the heart of Whitman's vision for American democracy is "the origin-idea of the singleness of man, individualism, asserting itself."[155] The end-stopped line is one of Whitman's primary poetic means for giving expression to this political conviction.

Prosiness

The signature length of so many of Whitman's lines—that outstanding feature of all long-line verse—makes for an expanded discursive palette onto which the poet often uncoils his thoughts in a leisurely amble otherwise so characteristic of prose. Indeed, Beyers stresses (commenting on a passage from "Song of Myself") the capacity of long-line poetry to incorporate prose and its sententious rhythms.[156] The increase in the scale of the line offers discursive possibilities that short-line verse simply cannot accommodate. Although there is more to Whitman's prosody than its prosiness, the latter has been regularly observed (positively and negatively) by readers. In fact, it is probable that "prosiness" itself (in part) led Whitman to the long line that he gradually shapes for himself. Zweig even supposes that much of the 1855 *Leaves* "was first written

---

153 *Political Poet*, 89.

154 Ibid. Cf. M. Edmundson, *Song of Ourselves: Walt Whitman and the Fight for Democracy* (Cambridge: Harvard University, 2021), Part I (Bookshare).

155 From *Democratic Vistas* (1870), *CPW*, 213. On the importance of the individual to Whitman's brand of democratic liberalism, see G. Wihl, "Politics" in *Companion to Walt Whitman*, 76–86; cf. R. Rorty, *Achieving Our Country* (Cambridge: Harvard University, 1998), 25; Edmundson, *Song of Ourselves*, Part I.

156 *History of Free Verse*, 41.

down as prose."[157] The pre-1855 notebooks are a blend of lines of verse
and prose, and, if anything, there is more prose than poetry and. As
Miller stresses, Whitman "culled more lines from the prose... than he
did from the work in lines."[158] Emblematic is the prose of "There was
a child went forth every day—and the first thing that he saw looked at
with fixed love, that thing he became for the day.—"[159] from the "med
Cophósis"notebook that Whitman turns into the initial lines of the tenth
poem of the 1855 *Leaves*, "THERE was a child went forth everyday,/
And the first object he looked upon..., that object he became" (*LG*, 90).
Whole chunks of the 1855 Preface were eventually culled in a similar
fashion and lineated to make up part of the 1856 "Poem of Many In
One" (later "By Blue Ontario's Shore"; e.g., *LG*, iv–v// *LG* 1856, 188–89
[later sec. 10]).[160] And outside of *Leaves*, Whitman would continue to
hold his prose and verse close together. There may be no more graphic
expression of this than *Two Rivulets* (1876), in which verse and prose
appear on the same page, separated by a wavy line running horizontally
across the middle of the page (Fig. 8)—"two flowing chains of prose
and verse, emanating the real and ideal."[161]

As Zweig explains, the importance of prose to the development of
Whitman's line should not be surprising:

> His most influential models were not poems at all but Carlyle's gnarled
> prose, Emerson's essays, the King James Bible, Ruskin, maybe even
> Thoreau. There was far more great prose than poetry in Whitman's
> "foreground." His achievement was to incorporate the advantages of
> prose—its flexibility, its ability to mold itself freely to an actual speaking
> voice—into a new line that was subtly accented yet never far from the
> extended rhythms of prose.[162]

Zweig's emphasis here seems to me to be very much on target. The Bible
was only one source among many in Whitman's "long foreground"
and his sources in no way fully explain his achievement; they are but
only a starting point. Still, Whitman's prosiness, especially in the 1855

---

157 *Walt Whitman*, 239.
158 *Collage of Myself*, 19.
159 https://whitmanarchive.org/manuscripts/figures/loc.00005.002.jpg.
160 https://whitmanarchive.org/published/LG/figures/ppp.00707.277.jpg. Cf. Miller,
     Collage of Myself, 19–20.
161 From a letter of Whitman's to Edward Dowden, dated 2 May 1875.
162 *Walt Whitman*, 239.

Leaves, offers (as Zweig notices) yet another point of contact with the KJB, itself the premier prose translation of the Bible (in English), and what became a revered English classic.[163] That is, not only do the lengths of the verse divisions match up well with Whitman's lines, so, too, does the prosaic nature of what takes place within the framework established by these lines, the KJB's manifest prosiness feeding the prosiness of Whitman—recall that it is above all prose (especially in his journalism) that dominates Whitman's writerly output until 1850, and indeed throughout the early 1850s in the immediate build-up to the 1855 *Leaves*. And afterwards, too. He never stops writing prose.

Line-Initial "And"

And beyond the sheer facticity of the KJB as a work of English prose, Whitman's style shows signs, as well, of having been shaped by the prose style of the Bible. This is a topic I return to in more detail in Chapter Five. Here it will suffice to point out one of the more conspicuous indicators of that style as a means of tying Whitman most specifically to the prose of the English Bible. "There was a child went forth" opens with one of Whitman's characteristic extended runs of lines beginning with "And":

> THERE was a child went forth every day,
>
> And the first object he looked upon and received with wonder or pity
> or love or dread, that object he became,
>
> And that object became part of him for the day or a certain part of the
> day.... or for many years or stretching cycles of years.
>
>
> The early lilacs became part of this child,
>
> And grass, and white and red morningglories, and white and red
> clover, and the song of the phoebe-bird,
>
> And the March-born lambs, and the sow's pink-faint litter, and
> the mare's foal, and the cow's calf, and the noisy brood of
> the barnyard or by the mire of the pond-side .. and the fish
> suspending themselves so curiously below there .. and the

---

163 Norton, *History of the English Bible*, esp 358–86.

beautiful curious liquid . . and the water-plants with their
graceful flat heads . . all became part of him.

And the field-sprouts of April and May became part of him. . . .
wintergrain sprouts, and those of

the light-yellow corn, and of the esculent roots of the garden,

And the appletrees covered with blossoms, and the fruit afterward....
and wood-berries . . and the commonest weeds by the road;

And the old drunkard staggering home from the outhouse of the tavern
whence he had lately risen,

And the schoolmistress that passed on her way to the school . . and the
friendly boys that passed . . and the quarrelsome boys . . and the
tidy an freshcheeked girls . . and the barefoot negro boy and girl,

And all the changes of city and country wherever he went. (*LG*, 90–91)

Nine of the eleven lines begin with "And." Such runs are most redolent
of the English style of the KJB, especially in the narrative passages of the
Old Testament. Consider this sample from Genesis 32 (vv. 21–32; see
Fig. 4):

²¹ So went the present over before him: and himself lodged that
night in the company.

²² And he rose up that night, and took his two wives, and his two
women servants, and his eleven sons, and passed over the ford
Jabbok.

²³ And he took them, and sent them over the brook, and sent over
that he had.

²⁴ And Jacob was left alone; and there wrestled a man with him until
the breaking of the day.

²⁵ And when he saw that he prevailed not against him, he touched
the hollow of his thigh; and the hollow of Jacob's thigh was out of
joint, as he wrestled with him.

²⁶ And he said, Let me go, for the day breaketh. And he said, I will
not let thee go, except thou bless me.

²⁷ And he said unto him, What is thy name? And he said, Jacob.

²⁸ And he said, Thy name shall be called no more Jacob, but Israel: for as a prince hast thou power with God and with men, and hast prevailed.

²⁹ And Jacob asked him, and said, Tell me, I pray thee, thy name. And he said, Wherefore is it that thou dost ask after my name? And he blessed him there.

³⁰ And Jacob called the name of the place Peniel: for I have seen God face to face, and my life is preserved.

³¹ And as he passed over Penuel the sun rose upon him, and he halted upon his thigh.

³² Therefore the children of Israel eat not of the sinew which shrank, which is upon the hollow of the thigh, unto this day: because he touched the hollow of Jacob's thigh in the sinew that shrank.

I cite enough of the passage so that the repeated "And"s at the head of each verse division may be appreciated. Biblical Hebrew is a highly paratactic language, making do with only a handful of true conjunctions. The main narrative line in classical biblical Hebrew prose is normally carried by a peculiar verbal formation known as the *waw*-consecutive or *wayyiqtol* form.[164] The form may be decomposed historically as a combination of the simple conjunction, *wa*-, and the prefix form of a verb (*yiqtol* is the paradigm form favored by Hebrew grammarians). Tyndale, the first to translate the Bible into English from its original languages (Hebrew, Greek, Aramaic), initiated the practice of translating the simple Hebrew conjunction (*wa*-) primarily with "and," and thus the *wayyiqtol* form is often rendered with "and" plus subject and a verb (usually) in the past tense, and many of those "and"s come at the beginning of a sentence:

> So went the present before him and he taried all that nyghte in the tente/ ad rose vp the same nyghte ad toke his.ij. wyves and his.ij. maydens & his.xi. sonnes/ & went ouer the foorde Iabok. And he toke them ad sent the ouer the ryuer/ ad sent ouer that he had ad taried behinde him selfe alone.

---

164 *IBHS* §§ 29, 33.

And there wrastled a man with him vnto the breakynge of the daye. And when he sawe that he coude not prevayle agaynst him/ he smote hi vnder the thye/ and the senowe of Iacobs thy shranke as he wrastled with him. And he sayde: let me goo/ for the daye breaketh. And he sayde: I will not lett the goo/ excepte thou blesse me. And he sayde vnto him: what is thy name? He answered: Iacob. And he sayde: thou shalt be called Iacob nomore/ but Israell. For thou hast wrastled with God and with men ad hast preuayled.

And Iacob asked him sainge/ tell me thi name. And he sayde/ wherfore dost thou aske after my name? and he blessed him there. And Iacob called the name of the place Peniel/ for I haue sene God face to face/ and yet is my lyfe reserved. And as he went ouer Peniel/ the sonne rose vpon him/ and he halted vpon his thye: wherfore the childern of Israell eate not of the senow that shrancke vnder the thye/ vnto this daye: because that he smote Iacob vnder the thye in the senow that shroncke.[165]

Normally the King James translators ramify this practice. However, in this instance all the verse initial "And"s are already present in Tyndale's version. Tyndale uses a plain page layout, organized in paragraphs. The look is clean, very much akin to that of a contemporary novel. Verse divisions (with accompanying indentation) do not enter English Bible translations until 1560 and the Geneva Bible (Fig. 38). The latter has a huge impact on the reading experience. In particular, they interrupt the smooth flow of sentences. Tyndale's "And"s blend in nicely with the paratactic style he fashions for his English in imitation of the underlying Hebrew. In the KJB, the verse initial "And"s stand out precisely because of the interrupting force of the verse divisions and accompanying indentations (Figs. 4, 13–14). The presentational difference between the two is helpful in isolating the KJB's impact on Whitman's style. It is not just Whitman's preference for parataxis in general, but how his line initial "And"s mirror—or better, take their inspiration from—the verse initial "And"s of the KJB.

---

165 From Tyndale's *Pentateuch*, published originally in 1530 (text from *The Bible in English* (Cambridge: Cambridge University, 1997) (last accessed: October 1, 2017).

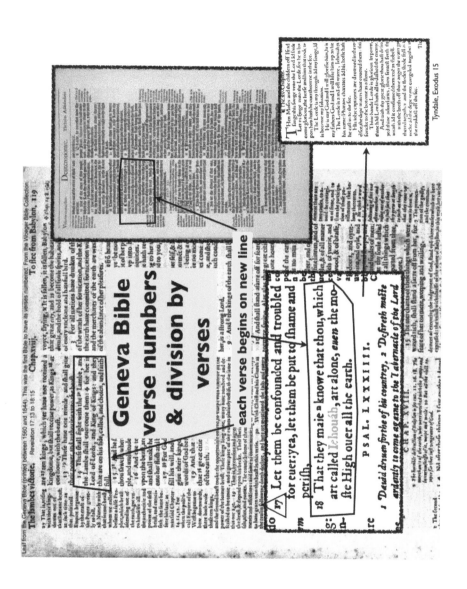

Fig. 38: Geneva Bible (1560) was the first English Bible to add verse numbers and to begin each verse on a new line.

Many runs of line-initial "And" populate the 1855 *Leaves*, beginning as early as the biblically inflected swiftly spreading of "the peace and joy and knowledge" passage from "I celebrate myself" (seven lines start with "And"; *LG*, 15-16). The opening three stanzas from "There was a child went forth" is noteworthy for several reasons. First, the slight slice of prose from the "med Cophósis"notebook out of which the first three lines are fashioned (see above) helps spotlight Whitman actively turning his prose into poetry, including in this instance promoting the sentence internal "and" to head the beginning of a line, now also capitalized: "And the first object he looked upon...." A very literal example of this kind of translation appears in "Blood-Money." Here, Whitman turns a verse internal sentence headed by "And" from Matt 26:15 ("And they covenanted with him for thirty pieces of silver") into an independent verse line, while at the same time translating the KJB's past tense into his preferred present tense: "And they make the covenant and pay the pieces of silver."[166]

This is to emphasize that such a stylistic feature is not naive or given and that the KJB by dint of its pattern of translation and page layout offers one obvious model for this practice. Also remarkable is Whitman's use of the past tense in these lines (e.g., "he looked," "object became," "all became"). This, too, is an especially marked aspect of the English biblical narrative style. Other examples of the past tense with initial "And" appear in *Leaves*, including this from "I celebrate myself":

> . . . I waited unseen and always,
>
> And slept while God carried me through the lethargic mist,
>
> And took my time.... and took no hurt from the foetid carbon. (*LG*, 50)

However, the vast majority of such "And"-initiated lines in the early *Leaves*, like so much of the rest of the poetry in the early *Leaves*, is staged as nonnarrative discourse of the moment, as if in the timeless present,

---

166 Whitman's revision of the first line taken from Matt 26:15 from "Again goes one, saying" to "And still one goes, saying" for inclusion in *Specimen Days* (*CPW*, 372) better approximates the KJB's phrasing ("And said unto them") and shows Whitman creating another "And"-initial line out of biblical language and translating from past ("said") to present ("goes, saying") tense.

and thus showing a distinct preference for the present tense (see discussion in Chapter Five).

As with many aspects of Whitman's style, this penchant for heading successive lines with "And" possesses a pre-*Leaves* genealogy. In the twenty-one poems collected by T. L. Brasher in *The Early Poems and the Fiction*,[167] lines headed by "And" appear on average about four times per poem. With the exception of several instances from "Blood-Money"[168] and "Resurgemus," these lines are always short and there are never more than three such lines in succession, and that happens only twice.[169] Of the early notebooks, the "Talbot Wilson" notebook is the one that most anticipates Whitman's use of "And"-headed lines in the 1855 *Leaves*,[170] especially in the increased lengths and usage of such lines and the runs—one leaf (38) alone has a run of four such lines on the recto[171] followed by another six on the verso.[172] In much of this material Whitman is also already translating the biblical pattern into the present tense orientation he is establishing for his verse. This selection from the "Talbot Wilson" is generally representative of this early notebook material, though distinguished specifically for showing Whitman working in the past tense (Fig. 39):

I built a nest in the ^Afar in the sky here^ was a sky nest

And my soul staid there ^flew thither^ to [st?] reconnoitre and squat, and looked long upon the universe ^out^,

And saw millions ^he journeywork of^ of suns and systems of suns,

And has known since that

And now I know that each a leaf of grass is not less than they[173]

---

167 (New York: New York University, 1963), 3–52.

168 Whitman's revisions of the poem for Collect include adding an additional line initial "And," which brings his rendition of Matt 26:15 closer to the KJB ("And still... saying"// "And said"; cf. *EPF*, 48, n. 3; third illustration after p. 170).

169 "Ambition" (https://whitmanarchive.org/published/periodical/poems/per.00148; *EPF*, 21) and "Fame's Vanity" (https://whitmanarchive.org/published/poems/per.00023; *EPF*, 23).

170 Line initial "And"s feature in the "Poem incarnating the mind" notebook as well, but they are not as conspicuous as in "Talbot Wilson."

171 https://whitmanarchive.org/manuscripts/figures/loc.00141.075.jpg.

172 https://whitmanarchive.org/manuscripts/figures/loc.00141.076.jpg.

173 https://whitmanarchive.org/manuscripts/figures/loc.00141.075.jpg.

Nine of the ten legible lines started in the "And to me each minute"
manuscript are headed by "And" (Fig. 40):

25

*tr(And to me each minute of the night and day is ~~chock with~~
~~something~~ vital and visible as ~~vital live as flesh is~~

ins in here page 34 — And I say the stars are not echoes
And I perceive that the ~~salt marsh~~ sedgy weed has ~~delicious~~
refreshing odors;
And potatoes and milk afford a ~~fit breakfast~~ dinner of state
And I ~~dare not say~~ guess the ~~the bay mare is less than I~~ chipping
bird ~~mocking bird~~ sings as well as I, ~~because~~ although she ~~reads~~
~~no newspaper,~~ never learned the gamut;

And to shake my friendly right hand governors and millionaires shall
stand all day, waiting their turns.
And ~~on~~ to me each acre of the ~~earth~~ land and sea, ~~I behold~~ exhibits ~~to~~
me ~~unending~~ marvellous pictures;
~~perpetual~~

They fill the worm-fence, and lie on the heaped stones and are hooked
to the elder and poke-   weed;

~~And to me each~~ every ~~minute of the night and day is filled with a~~
~~[illegible] joy.~~

And to me the cow crunching with depressed head ~~surpasses~~ is ~~an~~ a
every perfect and plumbed statue; ~~grouped~~

[illegible line][174]

And as observed previously (Chapter Two), "Pictures" is remarkable
precisely for its fifty-two line-initial "And"s that form the spine of this
long poem.[175]

---

174 https://whitmanarchive.org/manuscripts/figures/tex.00057.001.jpg. Cf. Folsom,
      "Working Notes," 94–95, n. 5; "Whitman."
175 The final two lines of "Pictures" appear to be revisions of lines 7 and 9 (cf. l. 1)
      from "And to me each minute"(https://whitmanarchive.org/manuscripts/figures/
      tex.00057.001.jpg):
      "And to me each every minute of the night and day is filled with a [illegible] joy."
      => "And every hour of the day and night has given deposited with me its copious
      pictures," (after *NUPM* IV, 1300)
      "And on to me each acre of the earth land and sea, I behold exhibits to
      meperpetual unending marvellous pictures;"

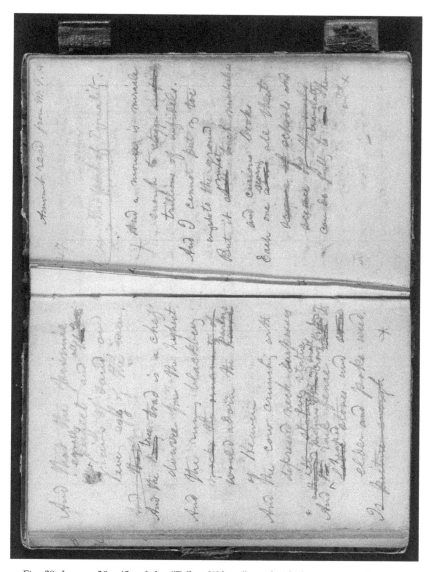

Fig. 39: Leaves 38v, 43r of the "Talbot Wilson" notebook, https://www.loc.gov/item/mss454430217. Leaf 38v shows a run of "And"-headed lines. Image courtesy od the Thomas Biggs Harned Collection of the Papers of Walt Whitman, 1842–1937, Manuscript Division, Library of Congress, Washington, D.C. MSS45443, Box 8: Notebook LC #80.

=> "And every rod of land or sea Yet still affords me, as long as I live, inimitable pictures" (after *NUPM* IV, 1300)

Fig. 40: Recto of "And to me every minute," https://whitmanarchive.org/manuscripts/figures/tex.00057.001.jpg. Image courtesy of the Harry Ransom Humanities Research Center of the University of Texas at Austin. A run of "And"-headed lines, though in a different order than the same lines appear in the 1855 *Leaves*.

The KJB Mediated Otherwise

I have noted the wide popularity of the King James Bible during the nineteenth century and endeavored to connect that Bible to Whitman, presuming (for the most part) his engagement with the printed artifact itself in one edition or another. Mine is an avowedly philological approach, motivated in part to answer Posey's call for "careful investigation and massing of evidence." My "massing" of the manifold ways in which the KJB's verse divisions are suggestive of Whitman's (long) verse line in the preceding pages is one manifestation of this philological method. Of course, the KJB in nineteenth-century America was found otherwise than in the printed pages of its many editions and its influence mediated in myriads of ways beyond readerly encounters with the biblical text itself. General and specific examples are easily identified. Very generally, for example, hymns and sermons were popular conveyors of all manner of biblical ideas, language, and imagery, the ultimate source for which was mostly the KJB. Whitman was an avid devotee of both. A lover of music broadly (e.g., opera),[176] he particularly enjoyed the "popular old camp-meeting songs,"[177] one of which he quotes from in the novella, "Jack Engle."[178] And "Pulpit oratory," as Reynolds observes, "was among his special objects of interest."[179] Abraham Lincoln provides a most specific example. Though no preacher, he used scripture with a "preacherly canniness."[180] Consequently, his speeches, as Alter shows, often bear the stylistic imprint of the KJB, especially at crucial junctures requiring a heightened sensibility of one sort or another.[181] Whitman attended Lincoln's second inauguration in person,[182]

---

176 See C. T. Skaggs, "Opera" in *Walt Whitman in Context* (eds. J. Levin and E. Whitley; Cambridge: Cambridge University, 2018), 239–56 (Google Play).

177 Reynolds, *Whitman's America*, 39; cf. 176–93.

178 "Life and Adventures of Jack Engle: An Auto-Biography," *WWQR* 34/3 (2017), 262–357, at 300—the two stanzas quoted are from "O, come my soul, and let us take" (or "Come, precious soul, and let us take" ["Calvary or Gethsemane"], see *The Revivalist: A Collection of Choice Revival Hymns and Tunes* (J. Hillman; Troy, NY: J. Hillman Publishing, 18646), hymn #23 (p. 17).

179 *Whitman's America*, 39; cf. 166–76; L. E. Eckel, "Oratory" in *Walt Whitman in Context*, 221–38.

180 *Pen of Iron: American Prose and the King James Bible* (Princeton: Princeton University, 2010), 16.

181 Ibid., 11–19.

182 For Whitman's report to the *New York Times* about Lincoln's second inauguration, see W. T. Bandy, "An Unknown 'Washington Letter' by Walt Whitman," *WWQR* 2/3 (1984), 23–27.

and therefore heard the second half of that Second Inaugural Address with its many biblical and biblicizing phrasings (e.g., "to bind up the nation's wounds," "to care... for his widow and his orphan") and cadences (e.g., the parallelism of "With malice toward none, with charity for all").[183] In hearing Lincoln that day Whitman heard language shaped to resonate (in identifiable ways) with the language of the KJB.

Such examples are offered as a reminder that Whitman will have absorbed the KJB in a multitude of ways and through various cultural practices apart from reading the Bible (or recalling its familiar figures and idioms). Whitman's world was a world suffused with the language and imagery of the KJB. Many writers influential for Whitman were also themselves influenced by the KJB (e.g., Milton, Wordsworth, Longfellow),[184] and thus their writings in turn could serve as additional (indirect) conduits of this influence. James Macpherson and Martin Farquhar Tupper were two such writers. Contemporary readers of *Leaves of Grass* most frequently associate Whitman with these poets, and both have been identified as important influences on aspects of Whitman's line.[185] Macpherson was responsible for the English "translations" of the Ossian poems.[186] These were fashioned in "emotive, rhythmic prose" and not as verse.[187] The affinities of this prose with that of the English Bible are patent, carrying a "remarkable resemblance to the style of the Old Testament," in particular, as Hugh Blair noticed in his

---

183 Alter, *Pen of Iron*, 15–19 (examples taken from p. 18).

184 Cf. Stovall, *Foreground*, 56, 121, 125–26, 128, 194, 238. 266.

185 E.g., A. C. Swinburne, "Whitmania," *Fortnightly Review* 48 (1887), 174 ("his precursors and apparent models in rhythmic structure and style" are "Mr. James Macpherson and Mr. Martin Tupper"); cf. Stovall, *Foreground*, 116–18, 255–58; Zweig, *Whitman*, 149–50; Reynolds, *Whitman's America*, 314–16; Miller, *Collage of Myself*, 25–26.

186 In 1760 Macpherson announced he had discovered poems and fragments of poems from an epic cycle about one Fingal written by Fingal's son, Ossian (putatively stemming from the third century CE). Over the next several years he published what he represented as his own English prose translations of Ossian's corpus, collected in various volumes: *Fragments of Ancient Poetry, Collected in the Highlands of Scotland, and Translated from the Garlic or Erse Language* (Edinburgh: G. Hamilton and J, Balfour, 1760); *Fingal, an Ancient Epic Poem, in Six Books: Together with Several Other Poems* (London: Becket and P. A. De Hondt, 1762); *The Works of Ossian, the Song of Fingal, in Two Volumes* (London: Becket and P. A. De Hondt, 1765). For the debate about the authenticity of the Ossian poems, see most recently the essays in H. Gaskill (ed.), *Ossian Revisited* (Edinburgh: Edinburgh University, 1991) and the *Journal of American Folklore* 114/454 (2001).

187 Reynolds, *Whitman's America*, 314.

critical dissertation on the Ossian poems.[188] Instances of overlap in content and genre obtain, but perhaps most striking is the prominence of parallelism that propels the rhythmic cadences of Macpherson's prose. And it is likely that Macpherson, who was a divinity student at King's College Aberdeen when R. Lowth's *Praelectiones* (1753) were first published, was familiar with Lowth's work and especially his theory of parallelism.[189]

Whitman routinely noted his admiration for Ossian[190] and recalled to Traubel having always owned a copy of these poems.[191] A lightly annotated 1839 edition of *The Poems of Ossian* belonging to Whitman is currently in the Feinberg Collection of the Library of Congress.[192] Most remarkable, perhaps, are the notations Whitman made about a clipping on Ossian from Margaret Fuller's "Things and Thoughts on Europe. No. V" discussed earlier (Chapter One).[193] In them, Whitman queries the

---

188 The dissertation was included in the volume of Ossian poems that Whitman owned: James Macpherson, *The Poems of Ossian* (Philadelphia: Thomas, Cowperthwait and Co., 1839), 79. Cf. Roston, *Prophet and Poet*, esp. 145–46; R. Bauman and C. Briggs, *Voices of Modernity: Language Ideologies and the Politics of Inequality* (Cambridge: Cambridge University, 2003), 155, n. 20; S. L. Sanders, *The Invention of Hebrew* (Urbana: University of Illinois, 2009), 26.

189 Cf. J. Engell, "The Other Classic: Hebrew Shapes British and American Literature and Culture" in *The Call of Classical Literature in the Romantic Age* (eds. K. P. Van Anglen and J. Engell; Edinburgh: Edinburgh University, 2017), locs. 7595–7904 (Kindle edition). It is quite certain that Blair, who actively encouraged Macpherson's work and defended the authenticity of the presumed originals (*Critical Dissertation on the Poems of Ossian* [Garland, 1765]), was very knowledgeable of Lowth—indeed, almost his entire assessment is carried out in Lowthian terms (Roston, *Prophet and Poet*, 144–46), and he even cites Lowth explicitly (on p. 114, in Whitman's copy of the *Poems of Ossian*, see below); see also Blair's summary of Lowth in "The Poetry of the Hebrews" in *Lectures on Rhetoric and Belles Lettres* (London: Thomas Tegg, 1841 [1783]), 557–70.

190 For example, in "A Backward Glance o'er Travel'd Roads" (originally published in *November Boughs* [Philadelphia: David McKay, 1888], 12–13; the essay was also included at the end of the so-called "deathbed edition" of *Leaves* (*LG* 1891-92, 425-38); cf. *NPM* V, 1808–09.

191 *WWWC* II, 17; cf. *NUPM* V, 1808. "Ossian" is listed among the books Whitman owned as of 1885 ("Walt Whitman in Camden" in *UPP* II, 61) and in a manuscript scrap (date: "between 1890 and 1892") entitled "Books of WW," http://whitmanarchive.org/manuscripts/marginalia/annotations/loc.03426.html.

192 (London: Joseph Rickerby, 1838) (PR3544.A1 1839 Feinberg Whitman Coll). Cf. Reynolds, *Whitman's America*, 314; Zweig, *Walt Whitman*, 150. The two quotations from Ossian embedded in Whitman's "An Ossianic Night—Dearest Friends," published in *Specimen Days & Collect* (*CPW*, 192) and dated by Whitman in the text to "Nov., '81," are both marked with a bracket in the margin in his copy of *Poems of Ossian* (pp. 273–74, 299; see Figs. 41–43).

193 Entitled "An Ossianic paragraph," https://whitmanarchive.org/manuscripts/marginalia/annotations/mid.00016.html. The clipping is from the *New York*

possible relationship between Ossian's poetry and the Bible: "?Can it be
a descendant of the Biblical poetry?—Is it not Isaiah, Job, the Psalms, and
so forth, transferred to the Scotch Highlands? (or to Ireland?)."[194] While
there is no actual genealogical relationship between the Bible and whatever
(written and/or oral) traditions may inform Macpherson's "freely creative"
compositions, Macpherson's prose was truly "a descendant" of the style of
prose the translators of the KJB used to render "Biblical poetry" and pretty
much as Whitman claims, "transferred" from the likes of "Isaiah, Job, the
Psalms" to "the Scotch Highlands"—articulated, incidentally, in terms of
the kind of collaging that typifies Whitman's own mode of composition in
Leaves. In fact, in the "Preface" to the edition of Ossian owned by Whitman,
Macpherson problematizes the very use of prose in his "translations."
He underscores the "novelty of cadence" in his "prose version" and the
presence of a certain "harmony" even in "the absence of the frequent
returns of rhyme."[195] He lists among the advantages of prose its "simplicity
and energy" and the "freedom and dignity of expression" it enables.[196]
Macpherson even goes so far as to offer a "Fragment of a Northern Tale,"
first rendered in the prose that typifies his "translations" of all the Ossian
poems and then in verse, with meter and rhyme—the former is easily
the more successful of the two.[197] In any event, though Whitman was not
enamored with some aspects of Macpherson's style—"(<u>Don't fall into the
Ossianic, by any chance.</u>),"[198] he does also write that "Ossian must not be
despised"[199] and would have appreciated many of those aspects of style
that Macpherson himself highlights, especially "the ~~simple [illeg.] antique~~

Tribune, 30 September 1846). See *NUPM* V, 1806–07.

194 *NUPM* V, 1807.

195 Macpherson, *Poems of Ossian*, 34. Whitman annotates the first page of the Preface
(p. 33): "Macpherson's Preface as I take it, ᵗ to the original edition 1762–63 but
the edition of 1773." And in fact the prefaces in *Fragments of Ancient Poetry* and
Fingal are very different. And *Works* never appeared with an author's preface. The
earliest edition of *Poems of Ossian* does appear to date from 1773 and with this
same Preface. Blair also praises the "measured prose" of Macpherson's translation
in the final paragraph of his "Critical Dissertation" included in Whitman's
edition of *Poems of Ossian* (122)—Whitman again annotates the first page of the
dissertation: "By Dr Hugh Blair London 1765–1773" (63); the third edition does
date to 1765, and the first, from London, to 1763.

196 Macpherson, *Poems of Ossian*, 34.

197 Ibid., 34–36. Blair emphasizes that Macpherson's prose "possesses considerable
advantages above any sort of versification he could have chosen" (122).

198 *NUPM* V, 1806—which as Grier notices is likely one of Whitman's "earliest bits of
advice to himself about style."

199 Ibid.

primitively Irish and Caledonian thought and personality in these poems"[200] and Macpherson's disparagement of meter and rhyme (highlighted by the contrasting prose and poetic versions of the trial fragment). In so far as Macpherson's style was indebted to the KJB, then, the Ossian poems provided another venue through which this style could—and surely did— impact Whitman. Indeed, not only do the Ossian poems refract biblical style but they offer Whitman a most palpable model of how that style could be fitted out with different content—"Is it not Isaiah, Job, the Psalms... transferred to the Scotch Highlands?" *Leaves of Grass* is not so dissimilar, the carrying forward "in another" of "those autochthonic bequests of Asia" such that they "still survive" and "dominate just as much as hitherto" through their "divine and primal poetic structure."[201]

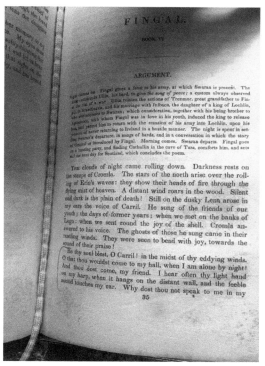

Fig. 41: P. 273 from Whitman's copy of James Macpherson, *The Poems of Ossian* (London: Joseph Rickerby, 1838) showing bracketed text. Charles E. Feinberg Collection, Rare Books and Special Collections Division, Library of Congress. Washington D. C. Photograph by Leslie Dobbs-Allsopp.

---

200 *NUPM* V, 1808.
201 Whitman, "Bible as Poetry," 57.

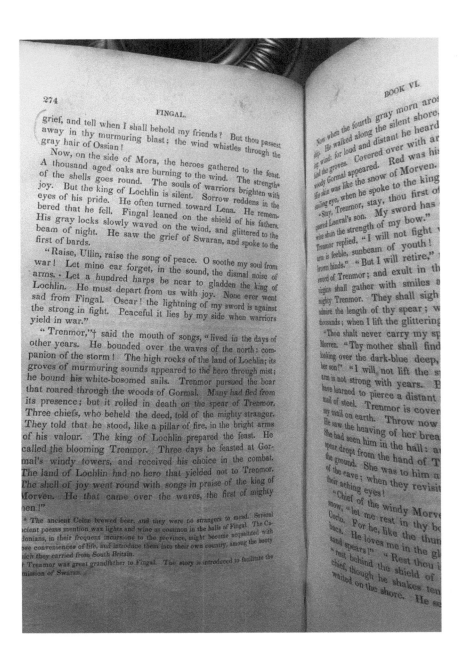

Fig. 42: P. 274 from Whitman's copy of Macpherson, *The Poems of Ossian* showing bracketed text. Photograph by Leslie Dobbs-Allsopp.

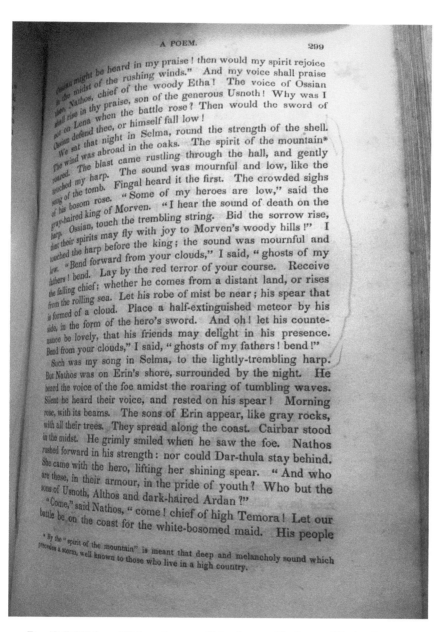

Fig. 43: P. 299 from Whitman's copy of Macpherson, *The Poems of Ossian* showing bracketed text. Photograph by Leslie Dobbs-Allsopp.

Tupper was a contemporary of Whitman's whose *Proverbial Philosophy* (issued in many editions) was wildly popular—between two and three hundred thousand copies were sold in America alone.[202] Whitman knew of Tupper. He had reviewed positively Tupper's prose work, *Probabilities: An Aid to Faith* in the *Brooklyn Daily Eagle* (20 February 1847): "the author... is one of the rare men of the time."[203] J. L. Coulombe believes it very unlikely that Whitman could have missed press coverage of Tupper's visit to the States in 1851. Stovall thinks that the only reason Whitman did not review *Proverbial Philosophy* in the *Eagle* "is that it was already too well known."[204] Several of the early reviews of *Leaves* made direct comparisons to Tupper's *Proverbial Philosophy*—"the poem [*Leaves*] is written in wild, irregular, unrhymed, almost unmetrical 'lengths,' like the measured prose of Mr. Martin Farquhar Tupper's *Proverbial Philosophy*."[205] And two of these Whitman reprinted in the second issue of the 1855 *Leaves* and again in the 1856 edition.[206] Whitman owned and annotated a copy of the 1838 edition of *Proverbial Philosophy*.[207] The annotations (consisting mostly of circles or brackets around sets of lines) are in blue pencil and appear on sixteen separate pages, including the title page which is initialed and dated in the upper righthand corner ("WW '75").[208] The latter certainly confirm that by 1875 (taking the title-page inscription at face value) Whitman had read Tupper's *Proverbial Philosophy*. J. J. Rubin argues that "even a superficial examination of Tupper's writings brings

---

202 J. L. Coulombe, "'To Destroy the Teacher': Whitman and Martin Farquhar Tupper's 1851 Trip To America," *WWQR* 4 (1996), 199–209, at 199.

203 *UPP* I, 136.

204 Coulombe, "To Destroy the Teacher," 199–209, esp. 200; Stovall, *Foreground*, 255–56.

205 George Eliot, "Transatlantic Latter-Day Poetry," *The Leader* 7 (7 June 1856), 547–48, http://whitmanarchive.org/criticism/reviews/lg1855/anc.00027.html. For details, see M. Cohen, "Martin Tupper, Walt Whitman, and the Early Revisions of *Leaves of Grass*," *WWQR* 16/1 (1998), 23–31.

206 Stovall, *Foreground*, 256; cf. Coulombe, "To Destroy the Teacher," 200–01.

207 (London: Joseph Rickerby, 1838). The copy is in the Feinberg Collection of the Library of Congress (PR5699.T5 A72 1838 Feinberg Whitman Coll). Cf. Reynolds, *Whitman's America*, 315, 620; Cohen, "Martin Tupper, Walt Whitman," 23, 30, n. 5.

208 Annotations appear on: title page, pp. 25, 33–34, 40, 41, 43, 73, 75, 113, 121, 137, 139, 150, 153, 186.

the conviction that they did contribute to the composition of *Leaves of Grass*."[209] Intriguingly, two of the seven passages Rubin cites from Tupper as suggestive of Whitman the poet himself circled or bracketed in his edition of *Proverbial Philosophy*. In the first, Rubin cites three lines from "Of Recreation" on p. 113. Whitman circles two lines on this page: "To trace the consummate skill that hath modeled the anatomy of insects" and "To learn a use in the beetle, and more than a beauty in the butterfly" (Fig. 44). The first of these comes immediately after the third line Rubin cites ("The dog at his master's feet, and the walrus anchored to the ice berg").[210] From "Of Invention," Whitman brackets the following group of lines (Fig. 45), the first two of which Rubin also cites:

And anon the cold smooth stone is warm with feathery grass,

And the light sporules of the fern are dropt by the passing wind;

The wood-pigeon, on swift wing, leaveth its crop-full of grain;

The squirrel's jealous care planteth the fir-cone and the filbert.

Years pass, and the sterile rock is rank with tangled herbage;

And the tall pine and hazel-thicket shade the rambling school boy.

Shall the rock boast of its fertility? shall it lift the head in pride?

Shall the mind of man be vain of the harvest of its thoughts?

The savage is that rock; and a million chances from without,

By little and little acting on the mind, heapeth the hot-bed of society:[211]

---

209 J. J. Rubin, "Tupper's Possible Influence on Whitman's Style," *American Notes & Queries* 1 (1941), 101.
210 Rubin, "Tupper's Possible Influence," 102; cf. Reynolds, *Whitman's America*, 316.
211 Rubin, "Tupper's Possible Influence," 102. The bracketed lines come from p. 153 of Whitman's copy of *Proverbial Philosophy*.

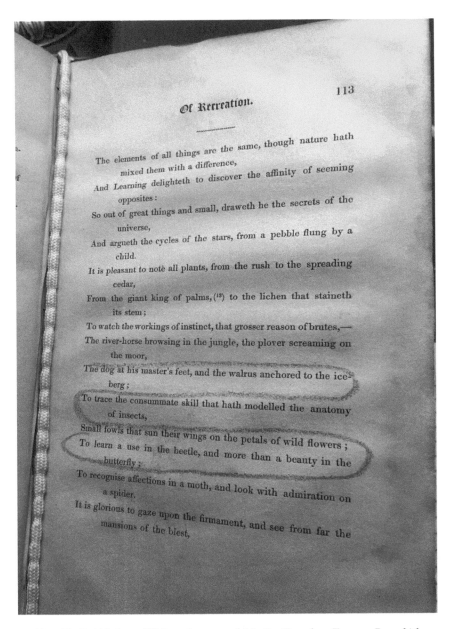

Fig. 44: P. 113 from Whitman's copy of Martin Farquhar Tupper, *Proverbial Philosophy* (London: Joseph Rickerby, 1838) showing circled text. Feinberg Collection of the Library of Congress. Photograph by Leslie Dobbs-Allsopp.

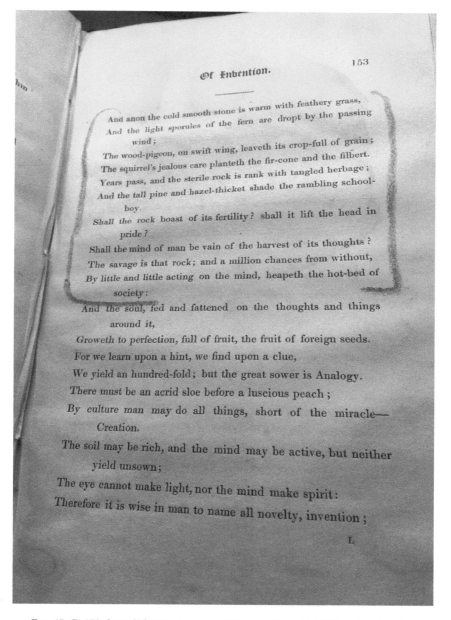

Fig. 45: P. 153 from Whitman's copy of Tupper, *Proverbial Philosophy* showing bracketed text. Photograph by Leslie Dobbs-Allsopp.

Other passages are equally suggestive of Whitman. For example, Whitman brackets material from Tupper's section "Of Memory" that is very reminiscent of parts of "Pictures," including the following:

> While wandering in the grove with Plato, and listening to Zeno in the porch?
>
> Paul have I seen, and Pythagoras, and the Stagyrite hath spoken me friendly,
>
> And His meek eye looked also upon me, standing with Peter in the palace.
>
> Athens and Rome, Persepolis and Sparta, am I not a freeman of you all?[212]

Compare these lines from "Pictures," where Whitman similarly recalls prominent people from world history:

> There is a picture of Adam in Paradise—side by side with him Eve, (the Earth's bride and the Earth's bridegroom;)
>
> There is an old Egyptian temple—and again, a Greek temple, of white marble;
>
> ....
>
> And here the divine Christ expounds ~~the~~ eternal truths—expounds the Soul,
>
> And here he ~~again~~ appears en-route to Calvary, bearing the cross—See you, the blood and sweat streaming down his face, his neck;
>
> And here, behold, a picture of once imperial Rome, full of palaces-full of masterful warriors;
>
> And here, ~~arguing,~~ the questioner, the Athenian of the classical time— Socrates, ~~this~~ in the market place,
>
> (~~O divine tongue! I too grow silent under your eclenchus;~~

---

212 Tupper, *Proverbial Philosophy*, 41. This material appears on one of the pages (p. 27) that Perry cites as containing "other interesting parallelisms with Whitman's methods" (*Walt Whitman*, 91, n.1). Perry is citing from an 1854 edition published in Boston (Phillips, Sampson, & Co.) that contains the first and second series of Tupper's *Proverbial Philosophy* (the latter was first published in 1842 and is not included in the 1838 volume that Whitman owned). The other pages Perry identifies as containing similar parallels are pp. 17 and 77 (from the first series; none of these overlap with Whitman's markings) and pp. 130, 142, 147 (from the second series)— only the passage from p. 142 is provided in the body of Perry's discussion.

O ^you with bare feet, and bulging belly! I saunter along, following you,
and obediently listen;)

And here Athens itself, ~~of~~ ─^it is a clear forenoon, ~~two thousand years~~
~~before~~ ~~These States,~~

Young men, pupils, collect in the gardens of ~~their~~ ^some a favorite master,
waiting for him,[213]

Not only do these sequences resemble one another, but Tupper's image
at the beginning of the section of the "storehouse of the mind" as a
"small cavern" or "airy chambers" whose "beams" are laid in a "strange
firmament,"[214] though conceived more biologically, nevertheless is quite
like Whitman's picture-gallery image of the mind as a "little house,"
"round" and "but a few inches" from one side to another, in which
"pictures" are hung.[215]

A last example may be cited from the final four lines in the section
"Of Wealth," which Whitman brackets and annotates ("wealth" is
written in on the bottom right hand corner of the page, immediately
under the final line of verse, see Fig. 46):

Wealth hath never given happiness, but often hastened misery:

Enough hath never caused misery, but often quickened happiness.

Enough is less than thy thought, O pampered creature of society;

And he that hath more than enough, is a thief of the rights of his brother.[216]

Compare this triplet of lines from "Great are the myths":

Wealth with the flush hand and fine clothes and hospitality:

But then the soul's wealth—which is candor and knowledge and pride
and enfolding love:

Who goes for men and women showing poverty richer than wealth?
(*LG*, 93-94)

---

213 After *NUPM* IV, 1297.
214 Tupper, *Proverbial Philosophy*, 39.
215 *NUPM* IV, 1296.
216 Tupper, *Proverbial Philosophy*, 150.

These do not seem so much to riff on or mimic Tupper's lines as respond to them with Whitman's own take on the theme.

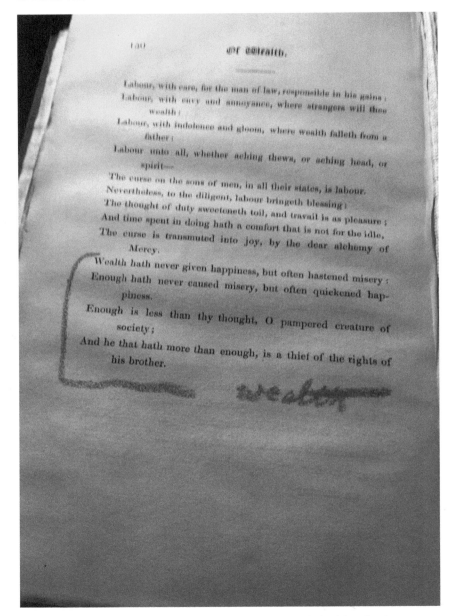

Fig. 46: P. 150 from Whitman's copy of Tupper, *Proverbial Philosophy* showing bracketed text and annotation. Photograph by Leslie Dobbs-Allsopp.

One does not have to read too far into Tupper's volume before encountering references to biblical figures (e.g., "Sirach's son," p. 6, the putative author of the biblical book of Ben Sira [or "Ecclesiasticus"]; "Wisdom" personified [pp. 9–10] as in Proverbs [e.g., Prov 8:1; 9:1]; the "Most High," p. 10; cf. Isa 14:14; Ps 82:6; 83:18 [= Hebrew ᶜ*elyôn*]) and biblicizing idioms (e.g., "dark sayings" [p. 6] ≈ "dark sentences" [as in the Prologue to Ben Sira]; "lips of Wisdom" [pp. 9, 10, 11] picking up on Wisdom's reference to her "lips" in Prov 8:6 and 7; "garden of the Lord" [p. 15] is an allusion to Eden, "the garden of God," Ezek 28:13; 31:8, 9). In fact, *Proverbial Philosophy* is filled with the kinds of "stock" biblicisms (e.g., "lo," "yea," archaisms of all sorts, including many verbs ending in "-eth") of the kind Whitman scrubbed out of the early *Leaves*. But perhaps most redolent of the KJB is Tupper's use of a two-part line patterned (largely) after the KJB's typical (prose) rendering of the underlying Hebrew parallelistic couplets that dominate in the wisdom poetry of the Bible:

> Thoughts, that have tarried in my mind, and peopled its inner chambers,
>
> The sober children of reason, or desultory train of fancy;
>
> Clear running wine of conviction, with the scum and the lees of speculation;
>
> Corn from the sheaves of science, with stubble from mine own garner;
>
>
> Searchings after Truth, that have tracked her secret lodes,
>
> And come up again to the surface-world, with a knowledge grounded deeper;
>
> Arguments of high scope, that have soared to the key-stone of heaven,
>
> And thence have swooped to their certain mark, as the falcon to its quarry;
>
> The fruits I have gathered of prudence, the ripened harvest of my musings,
>
> These commend I unto thee, O docile scholar of Wisdom,
>
> These I give to thy gentle heart, thou lover of the right.[217]

---

217 Tupper, *Proverbial Philosophy*, 6.

These are the lines that fill the first page of the "Prefatory" to Tupper's *Proverbial Philosophy*. The two-part parallelistic line prevails from the beginning. The first line is emblematic, exhibiting the synonymous form of parallelism ("Thoughts, that have tarried in my mind"// "and peopled its inner chambers") in which the subject ("Thoughts") is both fronted (note the initial comma and "that") and gapped in the second clause, all common characteristics of biblical parallelism (see Chapter Four).

Other aspects of Tupper's line beyond a fondness for internal parallelism are equally suggestive of the Bible's informing influence. For example, the lines are unmetered and unrhymed, consistently longer than lines of conventional metrical verse, and start with capital letters and are mostly end-stopped, usually ending with a major syntactic pause marked by punctuation (period, comma, colon, semi-colon, long dash). Significantly, Tupper only very rarely uses lines of more than sixteen words (e.g., "But have lost, as they ran, those apples of gold—the mind and the power to enjoy it," p. 146; eighteen words) or fewer than eight words (e.g. "Like wreathed adders crawling round his midnight conscience:", p. 29; eight words).[218] The model is quite evidently the Bible's proverbial wisdom, which in the translation of the KJB is regularly segmented into unmetered, unrhymed, and mostly closed verse divisions ranging between eight and sixteen words. And like the proverbial poetry of the biblical wisdom traditions on which *Proverbial Philosophy* is modeled, Tupper's line is not used to tell stories. His style is broadly discursive, nonnarrative.

It is above all this line that most Whitman scholars (grudgingly or not) recognize as influencing Whitman's ideas about his own line.[219] Indeed, not only do the two share the biblical-inspired attributes just outlined, but they are arranged similarly on the page. Both use

---

218 I have not attempted to quantify my counts in Tupper. My generalizations are derived from paging through and making random counts using the 1938 edition of *Proverbial Philosophy*. Stovall's characterization is similar: "long lines of ten to twenty syllables" (*Foreground*, 256).

219 E.g., Rubin, "Tupper's Possible Influence," 101; Stovall, *Foreground*, 257; C. C. Hollis, *Language and Style in Leaves of Grass* (Baton Rouge/London: Louisiana State University, 1983), 29–32 (he emphasizes Whitman's taking of "external" elements from Tupper); Reynolds, *Whitman's America*, 316; Cohen, "Martin Tupper, Walt Whitman," 25; Coulombe, "To Destroy the Teacher," 199, 205; Miller, *Collage of Myself*, 25–26.

indentation to signal the continuation of the verse line onto the next line of printed text and extra spacing to group sequences of affiliated lines. That Whitman was attentive to Tupper's line structure (at least belatedly) is made clear from the fact that the bracketing and circling in his own copy of *Proverbial Philosophy* always respect Tupper's line boundaries—and in several instances these isolate singular lines.[220] In sum, then, Tupper takes much from the Bible, including many formal features of his line (e.g., scale, prosiness, lack of meter and rhyme, parallelism, discursive style). And Whitman very "probably got ideas" about form and content from Tupper, with "the most obvious link" being the long, unrhymed, and unmetered line "in the manner of the Bible."[221] What may be emphasized with Miller and M. Cohen is that "if Whitman was influenced by Tupper's line the influence is still biblical, since 'Solomon's proverbs were the model for *Proverbial Philosophy.*'"[222]

Whitman will have found the KJB in many places in addition to its scores of printed editions. Macpherson's *Poems of Ossian* and Tupper's *Proverbial Philosophy*, copies of which Whitman owned and read, are two such places.

Conclusions

The several considerations reviewed above suggest a number of conclusions that may be drawn with respect to Whitman's line and the Bible. First, the point of comparison is between Whitman's mature line

---

220 On p. 75 ("She tricketh out her beauty like Jezebel, and is welcome in the courts of kings;") and p. 113 ("To trace the consummate skill that hath modeled the anatomy of insects," and "To learn a use in the beetle, and more than a beauty in the butterfly;").

221 The pastiche of quoted language is from Stovall (*Foreground*, 256, 257) and Cohen ("Martin Tupper, Walt Whitman," 25).

222 Miller, *Collage of Myself*, 26; cf. Cohen, "Martin Tupper, Walt Whitman," 25. Whitman's line is more variable in part because his biblical model is broader than Tupper's, consisting of the whole Bible, including especially the large swaths of biblical narrative in prose. Consistent with this hypothesis is Tupper's use of line-initial "And"s. As in Whitman these are not uncommon. However, unlike in Whitman, there are no extended runs of such lines and only rarely do these lines stretch out beyond sixteen words. Tupper's practice again is reflective of the paratactic style of the poetic wisdom books of the Bible, while Whitman's extended runs of (sometimes very long) "And"-headed lines are modeled (again, at least in part) after the Bible's narrative prose (see above).

and the verse divisions of the KJB, as originally noted by Saintsbury. Second, the central thrust of Saintbury's observation, that Whitman's line resembles the verse divisions of the KJB, appears also to be well made. I have articulated a myriad of ways in which these are alike. So much so, in fact, that it is hard to imagine, given the place of the Bible in Whitman's world and worldview (he preferred it "above all other great literature"[223]), that the KJB's verse divisions were not a major source of influence on Whitman's ideas about his line. No other proposed source has so many points of contact. The nature of the influence is likely to have been multifaceted and not simply a matter of Whitman aiming to mime biblical style. Miller raises the possibility that Whitman "chose the line he did because of the work it could do for his words" and because it "was capacious and plastic enough to involve and absorb the full range of language he had already been composing."[224] That is, when it comes to Whitman's discovery of his line, the emphasis should fall as much on the line's suitability to Whitman's own writing capabilities and temperament as on any conscious or unconscious desire to model himself after a specific style. This seems entirely reasonable to me. Models, of course, are important to all writers. But the reasons for choosing (or even happening upon) certain models and not others are never entirely naive, unmotivated, accidental. I do not think it too far-fetched to imagine that the KJB, through Whitman's repeated reading and rereading of it during his life or exposure to it through countless other means, played an important part in shaping the poet's tastes and stylistic sensibilities that eventually would lead him to his preference in line types. But this need not rule out the further possibility of the Bible, as translated and formatted in the KJB, playing a more immediate and conscious role in the formation of Whitman's signature line, a new awakening to the rich and congenial possibilities for a formal verse line informed by the KJB's verse divisions. Something shifted for Whitman between the spring and summer of 1850 and 1855 and one result was a line that in its lengths, variety, caesural rhythms, parallelistic shapes, and prosaic nature came to resemble very strongly the verse divisions of the KJB. Such an array of resemblance is not likely achieved solely by chance. Whitman's program of self-study from 1845–52 included readings

---

223 Bucke, *Walt Whitman*, 103.
224 Miller, *Collage of Myself*, 35–36; cf. Loving, *Song of Himself*, 60.

about the Bible. The evidence of Whitman's notebooks and poetry manuscripts makes clear the intentionality with which Whitman worked and reworked his verse from the very beginning. And there are the many revisings and restagings of *Leaves of Grass* over the course of Whitman's lifetime, along with the care Whitman took to promote and shape the reception of these volumes. These are the signs of a hyperly intent and intense consciousness at work. This purposefulness pertains to the language material of Whitman's poems but also to how that language material is staged, framed, formatted. Whitman the carpenter, editor, journalist, and printer had an avid "eye for form."[225] Covers, page layouts, types, titles, bindings, kinds of paper, even, all mattered to this most materialist of poets. It is difficult to imagine someone with such proclivities would just happen upon his line, no matter how loathe he was to disclose its source(s) of inspiration. The restaging of "Resurgemus" for the 1855 *Leaves* provides one concrete glimpse at this hyperly-attuned consciousness at work. The most fundamental adjustments made to the last of his 1850 pre-*Leaves* poems is to relineate it, to resize the older, shorter line forms (usually by combining multiples of them together) to accommodate his new, longer, closed-off lines.[226]

And then there is Whitman's practice of collaging and montaging of found materials, which, as Miller compellingly reveals in his study *Collage of Myself*, anticipates in remarkable ways the embrace of the readymade and found art celebrated in the work of the likes of Picasso, Braque, and Duchamp.[227] Language in many respects is perceived by Whitman as preceding his own creativity. As he explains, in reference to his own poems, "there is nothing actually new only an accumulation

---

225 I borrow the phrase from the twentieth century's foremost epigrapher of West Semitic inscriptions, Frank Moore Cross, who trained his students to be attentive to the smallest details of form, since the ability to make judgements about the development of alphabetic scripts over time often depended on such knowledge. An "eye for form" is the epigrapher's most valuable tool. For details, see Cross' collected papers on epigraphy in *Leaves from an Epigrapher's Notebook* (Winona Lake: Eisenbrauns, 2003). As it turns out, Whitman anticipates Cross. Among the things the "American poets" of Whitman's letter to Emerson are to recognize is "the eye for forms" (*LG* 1856, 355).

226 This is emblematic of Whitman's compositional practice at this period. As noted above, similar reconfigurations appear in some of the poetry manuscripts that stand between the early notebooks and the 1855 *Leaves*.

227 Esp. Miller, *Collage of Myself*, 215–50.

or fruitage or carrying out these new occasions and requirements."[228]
The allusion to Eccl 1:9 ("and there is no new thing under the sun")
is intentional, for Whitman understood his making of poems (e.g.,
a "New Bible") to include combining "all ~~those~~ that ~~has~~ belongs to
the Iliad of Homer and the ~~Jewish~~ ^{Hebrew} Canticles ~~called~~ the Bible,
and of S~~k~~hakespear's delineation of feudal heroism and personality
and would carry ^{all} the influences ~~of both~~ and all that branches from
them for thousands of years.—"[229] The recycling of the trope found
in Ecclesiastes itself enacts (emblematically) the kind of composition
by collage he is writing about. Whitman even uses the language of
the "ready-made" in his letter to Emerson: "The lists of ready-made
literature which America inherits by the mighty inheritance of the
English language—all the rich repertoire of traditions, poems, historics,
metaphysics, plays, classics, translations, have made, and still continue,
magnificent preparations for that other plainly signified literature, to
be our own" (*LG* 1856, 347). As a consequence, whether it is language,
tropes, ideas, or material matter, Whitman is only too ready to take it
up when found and carry it out; albeit in this "carrying out" he works
the found material over and over until he makes it his own and in the
process all but rubs away any sign of its finding. In effect, Miller argues,
Whitman re-conceives "poetic language as a kind of moveable type to
be constantly toyed with and restructured—to see the role of the editor
and the corresponding work of revision and visual arrangement of text
as equally as important to poetry as the immediate act of creation."[230]
The notebooks and early poetry manuscripts, with their abundant
strikethroughs and pasted-in and cut-up materials, amply attest to this
reworking. They are like photographic stills of the process, all caught in
some phase or another. The occlusion that can result has also been well
tracked (in places). Whitman's debt to Emerson, for example, has long
been appreciated, but what is especially noteworthy for my concern
is that no matter how strikingly similar the ideas, "the language is

---

228 Miller, *Collage of Myself*, 87; see *CPW* 9:12.
229 Entitled, "Poems of a nation," now in the Charles E. Feinberg Collection of the
        Papers of Walt Whitman, Library of Congress (Notes and Notebooks, 1847–1891
        mss18630, box 40; reel 25), https://www.loc.gov/item/mss1863001283.
230 *Collage of Myself*, 123.

never identical."[231] Whitman's absorption of Emerson is so thoroughly processed that the latter's ideas come out sounding just like Whitman. This is true, too, of Whitman's allusions to the Bible in *Leaves*. They are ever elusive, highly burnished, and thus mostly hidden, as Allen saw early on.[232] As with ideas and language so too with tropes. There is again no doubting Whitman's debt to the Bible when it comes to his borrowing of parallelism. Allen's central contention in "Biblical Analogies" remains unchallenged.[233] But so too does Whitman adapt the trope to suit his art, and thus whatever originating debt there is the trope in being taken up, and thus continued, is also made Whitman's own. And in so doing Whitman becomes, as Kinnell well appreciates, "the greatest virtuoso of parallel structure in English poetry"[234] (for details, see Chapter Four).

That Whitman's mature line may be another bit of his found art would not be so startling given this poet's omnivorous appetite for the readymade and his printerly eye ever attuned to the visual arrangement of text. That Whitman found his line over a period of time starting with his three free-verse poems of 1850 and continuing till the composition of the 1855 *Leaves* seems true enough. That he worked relentlessly to perfect this line and shape it also is plainly attested. And that as he worked and reworked the language material out of which his line was made Whitman scrubbed away many of the lineaments that would disclose the line's finding seems yet another empirical datum. And this too is entirely consistent with Whitman's poetic practice and theory. Was Walt Whitman's mature line "found" in the King James Bible? The many points of resemblance between this line and the verse divisions of the KJB (especially in the poetical books) make this a tantalizingly appealing thesis. Even my inability to connect (or find) all the dots in order to fully reveal Whitman's finding of his line for what I think it is seems confirming of the thesis. And yet the fact of the erasure, that

---

231 Miller, *Collage of Myself*, 82–83; cf. W. S. Kennedy, "Walt Whitman's Indebtedness to Emerson" in *An Autolycus Pack of What You Will* (West Yarmouth: Stonecraft, 1927 [1897]); Stovall, *Foreground*, 296–305.

232 Allen, "Biblical Echoes," 303; cf. Bergquist, "Walt Whitman and the Bible," 81.

233 Even for Warren, who is critical of Allen's dependence on Lowth's biblical paradigm, agrees that the Bible provides a "literary tradition" for *Leaves* and that parallelism remains critical to Whitman's nonmetrical prosody ("Free Growth," 28, 30).

234 "'Strong is Your Hold.'"

final as yet unbridgeable gap, requires at the same time that this thesis be held less tightly, more heuristically. There is much to admire in the "Perhaps" that heads Saintsbury's initial observation, albeit read ever so slightly against the grain of his intended meaning. From my vantage point it respects the data and as important the artistic temperament behind the data. The question mark at the end of my own chapter title offers "a tip of the hat" to Saintsbury and "a wink and a nod" to Whitman.

4. Parallelism: In the (Hebrew) Bible and in Whitman

Whitman no doubt is the greatest virtuoso of parallel structure in English poetry

— G. Kinnell, "'Strong is Your Hold': My Encounters with Whitman" (2007)

The Politics of Parallelism

For most of the twentieth century, the "Talbot Wilson" notebook[1]—perhaps Whitman's most important surviving notebook for understanding the initial stages of composition of the 1855 *Leaves*—was thought to date from 1847.[2] Consequently, the initial lines of verse that appear in this notebook (approximately halfway through) have attracted much scholarly attention (Fig. 47)[3]:

> I am the poet of slaves and of ^{the} masters of slaves

> I am the poet of the body
>   And I am[4]

Noting the "impress of the slavery issue" on these lines presumed to be Whitman's first that approximate the free verse of the 1855 *Leaves*, B. Erkkila writes:

---

1   https://whitmanarchive.org/manuscripts/notebooks/transcriptions/loc.00141.html
2   So most influentially E. Holloway in *UPP* II, 63.
3   https://whitmanarchive.org/manuscripts/figures/loc.00141.070.jpg
4   My lineation follows that of *NUPM* I, 67. The transcription of this notebook at *WWA* aims to show Whitman's characteristic "hanging indentation" but not construe it for what it represents, namely, the continuation of the verse line.

©2024 F. W. Dobbs-Allsopp, CC BY-NC 4.0   https://doi.org/10.11647/OBP.0357.05

The lines join or translate within the representative figure of the poet the conflicting terms of master and slave that threaten to split the Union. Essential to this process of translation are the strategies of parallelism and repetition, which, as in the democratic and free-verse poetics of *Leaves of Grass*, balance and equalize the terms of master and slave within the representative self of the poet. By balancing and reconciling the many within the one of the poet, Whitman seeks to reconcile masters and slaves within the larger figure of the E PLURIBUS UNUM that is the revolutionary seal of the American republic.[5]

This is an incisive analysis. Erkkila appreciates how thoroughly fused were this hyperly holistic poet's poetics and politics. The internally parallelistic line ("I am the poet of slaves and of [the] masters of slaves"), which Whitman collages from the King James Bible (e.g., "I am become a stranger unto my brethren, and an alien unto my mother's children," Ps 69:8; for details, see below), is essential to the "balancing and reconciling" the poet's gesture of bodily encompassment effects. By setting identical prepositional frames in equivalence ("of" + Obj // "and of" + Obj), the elements filling these frames (the prepositional objects "slaves" and "masters of slaves") "are brought into alignment as well."[6] And this "alignment" is ramified syntactically as both prepositional objects are made to modify a single nominal, "poet." Whitman's poetic response to the political dilemma is to balance ("one part does not need to be thrust above another," *LG*, vi) and join the conflicting extremes within his democratically expansive poetic-I ("I reject none, accept all, reproduce all in my own forms," *LG* 1856, 180)—the fully embodied

---

5   *Whitman the Political Poet* (New York/Oxford: Oxford University, 1989), 50. Cf. M. Klammer, *Whitman, Slavery, and the Emergence of Leaves of Grass* (University Park: The Pennsylvania State University, 1995), 50–51. More recently, A. C. Higgins has put the issue of slavery in these lines at issue, arguing forcefully in light of the contents of the "Talbot Wilson" notebook (esp. the paucity of explicit references to chattel slavery) that wage slavery is Whitman's principal referent ("Wage Slavery and the Composition of Leaves of Grass: The 'Talbot Wilson' Notebook." *WWQR* 20/2 [2002], 53–0 7). Nevertheless, the term "slavery" itself for antebellum America, on Higgins' account ("Wage Slavery," 62–63, 66–68), was ultimately grounded in the idea of chattel slavery. And by the summer of 1854 (closer to the notebook's actual time of composition) with the passage of the Kansas-Nebraska Act and the events surrounding the forced return of the escaped slave Anthony Burns Whitman began to engage the "issue of slavery"—chattel slavery—more directly. Some of Whitman's most empathetic representations of African Americans appear in the 1855 *Leaves*. The larger point for me stands, namely, that Whitman's style is deeply entangled with his politics.

6   M. O'Connor, "Parallelism" in *NPEPP*, 877–97, at 877.

nature of this "I" is underscored in the 1855 *Leaves* by the engraved daguerreotype of the poet that fronts and introduces that volume.[7]

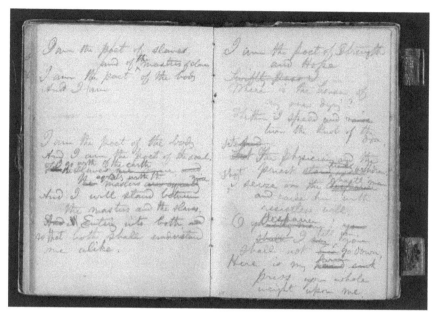

Fig. 47: Leaves 35v–36r of the "Talbot Wilson" notebook, https://www.loc.gov/item/mss454430217. Leaf 35vs is the point in the notebook Where Whitman begins experimenting with trial lines in verse. Image courtesy of the Thomas Biggs Harned Collection of the Papers of Walt Whitman, 1842–1937, Manuscript Division, Library of Congress, Washington, D.C. MSS45443, Box 8: Notebook LC #80.

The initial lines are finally canceled and Whitman begins afresh:

> I am the poet of the body
> And I am the poet of the soul
> ~~The~~ I go with the slaves of the earth ~~are mine, and the~~ equally
> with the masters ~~are equally~~ mine8
>
> And I will stand between the masters and the slaves,
> ~~And I~~ Entering into both, ~~and~~ so that both shall understand me
> alike.

---

7   https://whitmanarchive.org/multimedia/zzz.00002.html. T he engraving was by Samuel Hollyer, who also thirty plus years later (April 1888) engraved the image of Whitman on the cover of this book (based on a photograph of Whitman by Jacob Spieler at the Charles H. Spieler Studio, ca. 1876, https://whitmanarchive.org/multimedia/zzz.00045.html).

8   In the main, the transcription follows *NUPM* I, 67 and n. 84.

These lines seem to be a variation on the same strategy, and importantly parallelism continues to figure prominently. The poet asserts his embodied integrity in the famous parallelistic couplet that survives into the 1855 *Leaves* (*LG*, 26), albeit there decoupled from any slavery issue.[9] As M. Klammer observes, "Here the two sides of the divided self—body and soul—are reconciled, and that reconciliation seems to make possible the poet's egalitarian joining of himself with both slaves and masters."[10] In the 1855 Preface Whitman proclaims the poet to be "the equalizer of his age and land" (*LG*, iv). The next line originally offered another attempt to absorb parallelistically slaves and masters within the poet's holistic self: "The slaves are mine, and the masters are equally ^{mine}."[11] The line is revised. The assertion of possession ("mine") is perhaps judged inappropriate.[12] In the revision the poet (as "the equable man" to come, *LG*, iv) is imagined as going (body and soul) equally with slaves and masters. Whitman next places the poet's body (and soul) "between the masters and the slaves"—the only line not caught up in the play of parallelism. The last line on the notebook page takes a tack opposite to that of the first. Instead of absorbing masters and slaves into the poetic-I ("And I" is canceled), now the poet enters both (through his poetry?)[13] "so that" both may understand him "alike,"[14] and thus presumably become accommodated through such bodily mediation.

---

9   Higgins notes both the deemphasizing of the slavery metaphor in the notebook restart and the fact that the "poet of slaves" line does not get included in the 1855 *Leaves* ("Wage Slavery," 62, 63).

10 *Whitman, Slavery*, 51.

11 Cf. *NUPM* I, 67, n. 84.

12 For Whitman's worries about ownership broadly, see Higgins, "Wage Slavery," 65–66.

13 The 1855 Preface famously ends with a sentence that expresses Whitman's desire for such ingestion, absorption: "The proof of a poet is that his country absorbs him as affectionately as he has absorbed it" (*LG*, xiii). In the same Preface the "United States" could be imagined as "the greatest poem" (iii) with "veins full of poetical stuff" (iv) and its people as "unrhymed poetry" (iii).

14 The canceled "and" makes the parallelistic intent more obvious, although there are plenty of internally parallelistic verses in the KJB where the underlying Hebrew parataxis is translated so as to bring out the syntactic logic of clausal affiliation. For example, the KJB's rendition of Ps 106:32, "They angered him also at the waters of strife, so that it went ill with Moses for their sakes," softens ("so that") the underlying parataxis of the Hebrew original, which R. Alter captures more literally: "And they caused fury over the waters of Meribah,/ and it went

The analysis remains equally insightful and significant now that the "Talbot Wilson" notebook is more securely dated to 1854 and its first poetic lines are known not to be Whitman's first free-verse lines. Parallelism is a trope that is vital to the *democratic* and *free*-verse poetics that Whitman develops over the course of the early 1850s. In fact, though the political calculations are different, parallelism (however embryonic) already features in Whitman's very first free-verse lines, those in "Blood-Money"[15] (from the spring of 1850). Here, too, the Bible and slavery are very much in view as Whitman imagines "the Beautiful God, Jesus" (line 2), having taken on "man's form again" (line 19), as a "hunted" fugitive slave (lines 20–27):

> Thou art reviled, scourged, put into prison;
>
> Hunted from the arrogant equality of the rest:
>
> With staves and swords throng the willing servants of authority;
>
> Again they surround thee, mad with devilish spite—
>
> Toward thee stretch the hands of a multitude, like vultures' talons;
>
> The meanest spit in thy face—they smite thee with their palms;
>
> Bruised, bloody, and pinioned is thy body,
>
> More sorrowful than death is thy soul.

Parallelism in these lines does not balance or reconcile opposing sides but through its doubling movement concentrates and reiterates the abuse paid to the fugitive Christ (e.g., "throng the willing servants of authority;"// "Again they surround thee....," lines 22–23; "The meanest spit in thy face"// "they smite thee with their palms," line 25) and figures the holism of the hurt in a body-soul merism (lines 26–27) that anticipates the later lines from the "Talbot Wilson" notebook (and beyond).

---

badly for Moses because of them" (*The Book of Psalms* [New York/London: Norton & Company, 2007], 380).

15 https://whitmanarchive.org/published/periodical/poems/per.00089

Parallelism continues to figure into Whitman's political calculations on the theme in the early editions of *Leaves*. An outstanding example comes from the 1856 "Poem of Many In One":

> Slavery, the tremulous spreading of hands to shelter it—the stern
>   opposition to it, which ceases only when it ceases. (*LG* 1856, 187)

The line is culled from the prose of the 1855 Preface ("slavery and the tremulous spreading of hands to protect it, and the stern opposition to it which shall never cease till it ceases or the speaking of tongues and the moving of lips cease," *LG*, iv). It divides into two parts and is internally parallelistic. The long dash halves the line. Here Whitman exploits what in the Lowthian system of biblical parallelism is known as "antithetical parallelism," a form of parallelism in which opposites are posed (e.g., "The wicked flee when no man pursueth: but the righteous are bold as a lion," Prov 28:1[16]). Such posing can be scripted to different ends. In this instance, Whitman means to hold the opposing perspectives together without resolving their central antagonism—the holism of the trope containing the centrifugal pull of its content. After the war, Whitman's political perspective shifts. The internal parallelism of the line is exploded minus the need to contain opposing views, and the line itself morphs into two lines, both of which angrily decry the "conspiracy" to impose slavery more broadly and its consequences (of which there is no "respite"):

> Slavery—the murderous, treacherous conspiracy to raise it upon the
>   ruins of all the rest;
>
> On and on to the grapple with it—Assassin! then your life or ours be
>   the stake—and respite no more. (*LG* 1867, 9c)

The breakdown in parallelism is emblematic of the lines' prevailing sense of exhaustion and ongoing uncertainty—the trope (in this instance) can no longer conform (to) the political calculus.

---

16   Whitman cites part of this proverb, see M. N. Posey, "Whitman's Debt to the Bible with Special Reference to the Origins of His Rhythm" (unpubl. Ph.D. diss., University of Texas, 1938), 210; B. L. Bergquist, "Walt Whitman and the Bible: Language Echoes, Images, Allusions, and Ideas" (unpubl. Ph.D. diss., University of Nebraska, 1979), 280.

From the very beginning, then, Whitman's new American verse, in addition to being freed from meter and rhyme and whatever political regimes these symbolize, relies heavily on the reiterative play of a parallelism seemingly always equally posed prosodically and politically. To reflect on the place of parallelism in Whitman's poetry and its possible debt to the Bible is to reflect on part of what is foundational to Whitman's art.

* * *

In what follows I offer an explication of parallelism in three movements. In the first I review (in broad strokes) the discussion of parallelism in biblical scholarship from Robert Lowth (mid-eighteenth century) to the present. Because of the wide influence of G. W. Allen and his early essay "Biblical Analogies for Walt Whitman's Prosody,"[17] Whitman scholarship is peculiarly indebted to biblical scholarship for its understanding of parallelism. Unfortunately, Allen's own understanding of parallelism in biblical (Hebrew) poetry is both flawed and (now) dated. My ambition in reviewing the status of the question about parallelism in biblical scholarship is to give students of Whitman both updated understandings of parallelism in the biblical poetic corpus as currently conceptualized by biblical scholars and ideas for exploring Whitman's uses of the trope (prosodically and otherwise)—Biblical Studies is one discipline of textual study in which parallelism has been robustly theorized and those theorizations (multiple and contested) are eminently translatable and transferable. In the second part of the chapter I return to one of Allen's central concerns in "Biblical Analogies," namely, to indicate more precisely (now in light of a better understanding of the biblical paradigm) what in Whitman's uses of parallelism is suggestive of and/ or indebted to the Bible. My principal focus here is what Allen describes as "internal parallelism"—where "Whitman's long lines" break "into shorter parallelisms."[18] The last section is the briefest. Here I point out a number of ways in which Whitman develops his uses of parallelism beyond the models he found in the KJB. These latter observations are intentionally gestural and heuristic. Enough is said to illuminate once

---

17   *Revue Anglo-Americ aine* 6 (1933), 490–507.
18   "Biblical Analogies," 494, 497.

again how Whitman, upon finding the ready-made he is collaging (this time a trope), shapes and makes it his own. As J. P. Warren states with regard to parallelism in particular, "Whitman does not content himself with the forms of biblical poetry."[19]

Lowth's Idea of Parallelism and Its Modern Reception

The question of parallelism in Whitman's poetry since 1933 and Allen's seminal essay, "Biblical Analogies," has been deeply entangled with the idea of parallelism in biblical (Hebrew) poetry. Inspired by B. Perry's belief that Whitman's prosodic model in *Leaves* "was the rhythmical pattern of the English Bible," Allen sought, first, "to determine exactly why the rhythms of Whitman have suggested those of the Bible..., and second to see what light such an investigation throws on Whitman's sources."[20] Of these two large aims, Allen regarded the first "as more important because it should reveal the underlying laws of the poet's technique."[21] The second aim, what can be said positively of Whitman's use of the Bible as a resource, which Allen tackles most forthrightly in "Biblical Echoes," serves chiefly to provide warrant for Allen's recourse to biblical analogies as a means of elucidating Whitman's free-verse prosody.[22] In that analysis, parallelism, as understood primarily through Lowth's biblical paradigm, figures prominently—the "first rhythmic principle" of both Whitman and the poetry of the Bible.[23] Recall that at the time literary scholars were still casting around for ways to make sense of nonmetrical verse, a mostly new phenomenon (in the middle of the nineteenth century) in a poetic canon otherwise dominated since classical antiquity by meter. Allen sees in the analogy of biblical prosody the revelation of "specific principles" that enable a more perspicuous analysis and explanation of "Walt Whitman's poetic technique."[24] The analysis, though problematic in places, successfully establishes (among other things) the presence and significance of parallelism in Whitman,

---

19 "'The Free Growth Of Metrical Laws': Syntactic Parallelism In 'Song Of Myself,'" *Style* 18/1 (1984), 27–42, here 32.
20 "Biblical Analogies," 491.
21 Ibid.
22 Ibid., 490, n. 3.
23 Ibid., 505.
24 G. W. Allen, *American Prosody* (New York: American Book, 1935), 221.

especially as it bears on his underlying prosody, and the likelihood that the Bible is an important source of Whitman's knowledge of parallelism.[25] It also is important as an early effort at articulating a prosody that means to accommodate the differences of non-metrical verse.

I have detailed (some of) the confusions that attend Allen's attempt to appropriate Lowth's theory of parallelism in biblical Hebrew poetry for an understanding of parallelism in both the English Bible and in Whitman (see Chapter Three). Equally problematic, at least from a contemporary perspective, is Allen's dependence on Lowth's categorical scheme and developments thereof—to Lowth's three-way scheme of synonymous, antithetical, and synthetic parallelism, Allen adds a fourth category, climactic parallelism, as suggested by one of his primary sources for knowledge of Lowth, S. R. Driver.[26] Lowth's paradigm was already 180 years old at the time of Allen's first writing in 1933 and remained the conventional understanding of parallelism (with occasional supplementation as in Driver) in Biblical Studies for another fifty years. The late 1970s through the early 1990s saw a significant reorientation to the field's understanding of parallelism in biblical poetry.[27] Many of Lowth's insights remain vital, though his overall categorization scheme is no longer sustainable.[28]

Phenomenologically, and at its broadest, parallelism is centrally concerned with correspondence, "the quality or character of being... analogous," "correspondence or similarity between two or more things" (*OED*, meanings 1, 2), and its principal mode of manifestation (especially in the verbal arts) is through iteration or recurrence, a pattern of matching. As applied to prosody, the *OED* glosses parallelism as "correspondence, in sense or construction, of successive clauses or passages" (meaning 3). Lowth was the first to use the term with this sense, and specifically in his study of biblical Hebrew poetry (viz.

---

25 Cf. J. Engell, "Robert Lowth, Unacknowledged Legislator" in *The Committed Word: Literature and Public Values* [University Park: Pennsylvania State University, 1999], 119–40, at 124.

26 *An Introduction to the Literature of the Old Testament* (Cleveland/New York: Meridian Books, 1956 [1892]), 363–64. Allen cites a 1910 edition of the same.

27 For an especially accessible overview of these developments, see D. L. Petersen and K. H. Richards, *Interpreting Hebrew Poetry* (Minneapolis: Fortress, 1992), 21–35.

28 For an in-depth reconsideration of Lowth's idea of parallelism, see F. W. Dobbs-Allsopp, "Robert Lowth, Parallelism, and Biblical Poetry," *Journal of Hebrew Scriptures* 21 (2021), 1–36.

parallelismus membrorum "parallelism between the clauses," cf. *OED*). His analysis divides into two main parts: a general description and a threefold categorization scheme. His fullest general descriptions of parallelism are given in several places.[29] The first is the most general and appears early in *Lectures*, in Lecture III:

> In the Hebrew poetry, as I before remarked, there may be observed a certain conformation of the sentences, the nature of which is, that a complete sense is almost equally infused into every component part, and that every member constitutes an entire verse. So that as the poems divide themselves in a manner spontaneously into periods, for the most part equal; so the periods themselves are divided into verses, most commonly couplets, though frequently of greater length. This is chiefly observable in those passages which frequently occur in the Hebrew poetry, in which they treat one subject in many different ways, and dwell upon the same sentiment; when they express the same thing in different words, or different things in a similar form of words; when equals refer to equals, and opposites to opposites: and since this artifice of composition seldom fails to produce even in prose an agreeable and measured cadence, we can scarcely doubt that it must have imparted to their poetry, were we masters of the versification, an exquisite degree of beauty and grace.[30]

Parallelism will be named as such only later in the *Lectures* (esp. in Lecture XIX). Here, however, Lowth offers a first attempt to circumscribe the phenomenon. The first thing to notice is that Lowth directs his attention to the individual verse or line (the latter is the English term he will begin to use in his *Preliminary Dissertation*) and to the interlinear relations of immediately contiguous lines—"a certain conformation of the sentences."[31] The verse line in biblical poetry, Lowth observes, is typically composed of a part of a sentence or a clause, what he calls a "member"—"every member constitutes an entire verse"; and these clauses are mostly end-stopped, "a complete sense is almost

---

29 *Lectures on the Sacred Poetry of the Hebrews* (2 vols.; trans. G. Gregory; London: J. Johnson, 1787; reprinted in Reibel, *Major Works*), I, 68–69, 100; II, 34; *Isaiah: A New Translation with a Preliminary Dissertation* (London: J. Nichols, 1778; reprinted in Reibel, *Major Works*), x–xi.

30 *Lectures*, I, 68–69.

31 This is one of Lowth's crucial perceptions about Hebrew verse, which, as M. O'Connor stresses, remains "unquestioned and unquestionable" (*Hebrew Verse Structure* [Winona Lake: Eisenbrauns, 1980], 32); cf. E. L. Greenstein, "Aspects of Biblical Poetry," *Jewish Book Annual* 44 (1986–87), 33–42, at 42.

equally infused into every component part," i.e., line breaks occur at major clausal, phrasal, or sentential junctures. The poems divide into "periods" or sentences, "for the most part equal," which "are divided into verses" (composed of clauses), "most commonly couplets," but also triplets and larger groupings. This "conformation of the sentences," Lowth emphasizes later in Lecture IV, is "wholly poetical."[32] In fact, continues Lowth, there is "so strict an analogy between the structure of the sentences and the versification that when the former chances to be confused or obscured, it is scarcely possible to form a conjecture concerning the division of the lines or verses."[33]

The *OED*'s emphasis on correspondence in its definition of parallelism—"correspondence, in sense or construction, of successive clauses or passages" (meaning 3)—is essentially a gloss on Lowth's own understanding of the concept. This is most obvious in the definition given in the *Preliminary Dissertation*, viz. "the correspondence of one Verse, or Line, with another,"[34] which is the first authority cited by the *OED*.[35] What this correspondence entails is variously described by Lowth, but his emphasis is generally consistent: it "consists chiefly in a certain equality, resemblance, or parallelism between the members of each period; so that... things for the most part shall answer to things, and words to words, as if fitted to each other by a kind of rule or measure."[36] As in his other statements, the intent is to gesture to a range of correspondences that may be observed, which as he emphasizes explicitly, "has much variety and many gradations."[37] One unfortunate consequence of how Lowth goes on to categorize parallelism is to limit how these correspondences would be conceptualized by later generations of scholars. However, the impulse of his more general description of the trope (or "ornament" as Lowth calls it in Lecture IV)[38] is an expansive understanding of parallelism.

---

32 *Lectures*, I, 99.
33 Ibid.
34 *Isaiah*, x.
35 As A. Berlin emphasizes (*The Dynamics of Biblical Parallelism* [Bloomington: Indiana University, 1985], 2), the idea of correspondence is at the core of parallelism and one of Lowth's enduring insights.
36 *Lectures*, II, 34.
37 Ibid., II, 35; cf. 39.
38 Ibid., I, 100.

It is the (re)turn to linguistics by modern biblical scholars some two hundred years later that was a major stimulus for reassessing the nature of parallelism in biblical poetry. These scholars were able to expand and sophisticate Lowth's original diagnosis with a whole panoply of new tools. A. Berlin's *Dynamics of Biblical Parallelism* (1985) is paradigmatic as she, leveraging the work of R. Jakobson in particular, explores the play of parallelism beyond semantics at all levels of linguistic structure, including sound elements (phonetics), grammar (morphology and syntax), and words and their meanings (lexicon and semantics). The precision of the linguistic analysis is well advanced of what Lowth could achieve (in an era prior to the coalescence of linguistics as an academic discipline). But in this aspect the trajectory of analysis carries forward Lowth's ideas,[39] which remarkably foregrounds syntax as well as semantics, viz. "in Sense or Similar to it in the form of Grammatical Construction."[40] The place of syntax in Lowth's thinking has been underappreciated as the reception of his ideas mostly (over)emphasized semantics. Allen is emblematic when he speaks of Whitman's "thought rhythm" (his preferred gloss for parallelism, its "first principle"), a term he picked up from biblical scholarship.[41]

Berlin ultimately moves away from Lowth's tight focus on "the conformation of the sentences" as the site of parallelism and resists his privileging of syntax and semantics, though she knows well that "grammatical and semantic parallelism generally co-occur" in biblical poetry.[42] E. L. Greenstein and M. O'Connor more obviously carry forward Lowth's focus on parallelism in biblical poetry as a line-level trope. Greenstein situates the phenomenon of parallelism structurally at the interface of "one line of verse" with "the following line or lines" and foregrounds the "repetition of a syntactic pattern."[43] This twofold focus

---

39   Cf. Petersen and Richards, *Interpreting Hebrew Poetry*, 26.
40   *Isaiah*, x–xi.
41   "Biblical Analogies," 492; cf. 505; *American Prosody*, 223. Here it is likely (in part) that Allen is parroting a common idea from biblical scholarship—so H. Ewald already in the middle of the nineteenth century glosses biblical poetic parallelism as *gedankenrhythmus* "thought-rhythm" (*Die Dichter des Alten Bundes* [Göttingen: Vändenhoeck und Ruprecht, 1866], I, 111). But it also is picked up in Whitman scholarship and in discussions about free verse more broadly.
42   Berlin, *Dynamics*, 22.
43   "How Does Parallelism Mean?" in *A Sense of a Text* (JQRS; eds. S. A. Geller; Winona Lake: Eisenbrauns, 1983), 41–70; here 43, 44.

means to challenge the view that "whatever goes on between two lines" of biblical Hebrew verse is meaningfully denominated as parallelism.[44] For O'Connor, too, "the core of a [parallelism] is syntactic"—"the repetition of identical or similar syntactic patterns in adjacent phrases, clauses, and sentences."[45] He elaborates its inner workings (indebted to Jakobson's thinking), "when syntactic frames are set in equivalence by [parallelism], the elements filling those frames are brought into alignment as well," especially at the lexical level (semantics) but potentially (all) other linguistic levels may (also) be activated.[46] Greenstein, in his revision of O'Connor's entry on "Parallelism" in the newest version of *The Princeton Encyclopedia of Poetry and Poetics*, allows that while "the repeating structure is often syntactic in nature," as prototypically in biblical Hebrew verse, "the repetition may entail other ling[uistic] components" (e.g., lexicon, morphology, rhythm).[47] One of the gains, then, in the understanding of poetic parallelism in the Bible since the late 1970s is the renewed attention paid to syntax (and other levels of linguistic structure).

When a scholar such as Berlin writes that "most contemporary scholars have abandoned the models of Lowth and his successors," what she has in view most particularly is Lowth's categorization of parallelism into three "species": synonymous, antithetical, and synthetic (or constructive). The criticisms are myriad and well made, chief among which is that the schema itself (especially as articulated in the *Preliminary Dissertation*) is unnecessarily reductive. What Lowth counts as three kinds of parallelism others have numbered as many as eight.[48] The different ways of categorizing the same phenomena show that there is nothing necessarily absolute about Lowth's threefold scheme. If anything, the latter, in particular, has had the effect of obscuring the subtleties of the trope and narrowing too much how

---

44   Greenstein, "How Does Parallelism Mean?", 45. Lowth's catch-all category of "synthetic parallelism" is the main inducement for such nonchalant construals of parallelism.
45   "Parallelism," 877–97, 877.
46   Ibid.
47   E. L. Greenstein and M. O'Connor, "Parallelism" in *PEPP*, loc. 53381.
48   S. Pickett, *Words and the Word*: *Language, Poetics and Biblical Interpretation* (Cambridge: Cambridge University, 1986), 110. And more recent typologies can number even more, e.g., S. A. Geller, *Parallelism in Early Biblical Poetry* (HSM 20; Missoula: Scholars, 1979), 34–38 (twelve).

it is conceptualized.[49] And while one prominent line of discussion about parallelism following Lowth focused on supplementing and/or redescribing Lowth's categories (e.g., complete, incomplete, numerical, impressionistic, repetitive, emblematic, internal, metathetic, climactic), what has become clear is that the varieties are endless and defy any neat classification scheme (however pragmatically handy certain descriptors may be for exposition).[50]

Lowth's individual "species" are equally problematic. The "most frequent" kind of parallelism,[51] according to Lowth, is "synonymous parallelism," which he describes as that "which correspond one to another by expressing the same sense in different, but equivalent terms; when a Proposition is delivered, and is immediately repeated, in the whole or in part, the expression being varied, but the sense entirely, or nearly the same."[52] This conceptualization remains foundational for the field's understanding of parallelism. However, the emphasis on semantics, both in Lowth's denomination of the species (viz. synonymity) and in so much of his explication (though syntax, for example, is never ignored), meant that most treatments of parallelism after Lowth focused chiefly on semantic repetition,[53] with many simply glossing parallelism, as J. L. Kugel contends, as "saying the same thing twice."[54] Exact synonymity—sameness without difference—does not exist.[55] Contemporary scholarship has exposed the difference(s) that parallelism activates, revealing an infinite array of subtlety and nuance that had previously been occluded or neutralized by the emphasis on the same. Kugel and R. Alter, among others, led the way in exploring the possibilities in parallelistic play beyond likeness, from emphasizing semantic coloring, focusing, intensification, ellipsis, and antithesis to

---

49   Esp. Kugel, *Idea*, 12, 15; cf. Berlin, *Dynamics*, 64.
50   Berlin, *Dynamics*, 64–65; cf. O'Connor, *Hebrew Verse Structure*, 50; S. A. G eller, "Hebrew Prosody and Poetics, Biblical" in *PEPP*, loc. 33910.
51   In fact, it is far more common than all the other varieties combined, see O'Connor, *Hebrew Verse Structure*, 50.
52   *Isaiah*, xi; cf. *Lectures*, II, 35.
53   Greenstein, "How Does Parallelism Mean?", 44, n. 12.
54   *Idea*, 13.
55   O'Connor, *Hebrew Verse Structure*, 50–51; cf. J. Derrida, "Signature Event Context" in *The Margins of Philosophy* (trans. A. Bass; Chicago: University of Chicago, 1982), 307–30.

elaborating incipient forms of narrativity.[56] What has become of interest to biblical scholars is what takes place between the Lowthian parallel lines, or as a result of their combination, their being coupled in close adjacency. [57]

"Antithetical parallelism" is the second species of parallelism described by Lowth: "when a thing is illustrated by its contrary being opposed to it. This is not confined to any particular form: for sentiments are opposed to sentiments, words to words, singulars to singulars, plurals to plurals, &c."[58] Lowth's first example from Prov 27:6 is typical:

"The blows of a friend are faithful;

"But the kisses of an enemy are treacherous."[59]

The contemporary critique here again is not what Lowth picks out for analysis but how he conceptualizes it. As Kugel quips, it is "a distinction without a difference."[60] That is, the focus remains on semantics— contrast or opposition instead of likeness; it is "another way" for what comes afterwards "to pick up and complete" what precedes.[61] Moreover, O'Connor points out that this variety of parallelism "largely occurs" in the wisdom literature of the Bible (esp. Proverbs), making "it suspect as an independent category."[62]

The last of the Lowthian categories is "Synthetic or Constructive parallelism," wherein "the sentences answer to each other, not by the iteration of the same image or sentiment, or the opposition of their contraries, but merely by the form of construction."[63] The critique here is entirely different. If conceptualization and overemphasis on semantics

---

56   R. Alter, *The Art of Biblical Poetry* (New York: BasicBooks, 1985), 1–38; Kugel, *Idea*, 1–58.

57   For example, in Gen 49:11 the synonymous terms "wine" and "blood of grapes" are brought into adjacency not simply to restate the presence of wine, but to meld together the high esteem of wine with the violent achievement in battle so as to magnify Judah's royal trappings, epitomizing one version of the hyper-masculine image of the able Levantine ruler. For details, see Dobbs-Allsopp, "Lowth," 24–27.

58   *Lectures*, II, 45; cf. *Isaiah*, xix.

59   *Lectures*, II, 45.

60   *Idea*, 13; cf. O'Connor, "Afterword," 640 ("a notion of antonymy that is barely a notion").

61   *Idea*, 13.

62   "Parallelism," 878.

63   Lowth, *Lectures*, II, 48–49; cf. *Isaiah*, xxi.

are faulted in Lowth's characterizations of synonymous and antithetical parallelism, most contemporary scholars nonetheless agree that the underlying phenomena diagnosed are of issue, that Lowth (and his predecessors) had identified an important feature of biblical verse. The problem with the third category is phenomenological. As G. B. Gray observed early on, while Lowth's examples of synthetic parallelism "include, indeed, many couplets to which the term parallelism can with complete propriety be applied," there are other examples "in which no term in the second line is parallel to any term in the first, but in which the second line consists entirely of what is fresh and additional to the first; and in some of these examples the two lines are not even parallel to one another by the correspondence of similar grammatical terms."[64] In short, many of the lines categorized under the rubric of "synthetic parallelism" exhibit no parallelism whatsoever. The category becomes a kind of catchall: "all such as do not come within the former two classes" "may be referred" to this final class.[65] Lowth's mistake is in pressing the idea of parallelism too far, in trying to make it account for the interrelations of all sets of lines in biblical verse. But to allow parallelism to cover every possible interlinear relationship in biblical verse, even where no ostensible signs of parallelism exist, is to make the idea of parallelism itself untenable, "undeniable."[66] Rather, as Gray contends, "the study of parallelism must lead... to the conclusion that parallelism is but one of the forms of Hebrew poetry."[67] Parallelism simply is not everywhere in the biblical corpus. Conservatively estimated, as much as a third of the corpus is composed of nonparallelistic lines.[68] D. Norton, a non-biblicist, acutely draws out the logical implication of the presence

---

64 G. B. Gray, *The Forms of Hebrew Poetry* (London: Hodder and Stoughton, 1915), 49, 50.

65 Lowth, *Lectures*, II, 49.

66 O'Connor, *Hebrew Verse Structure*, 51; cf. Greenstein, "How Does Parallelism Mean?", 45; Alter, *Art of Biblical Poetry*, 19.

67 *Forms of Hebrew Poetry*, 123; so also Driver, *Introduction*, 362, s.

68 Esp. O'Connor, *Hebrew Verse Structure*, 409; see Geller, *Parallelism*, 6, 30, 295, 379; W. G. E. Watson, *Classical Hebrew Poetry: A Guide to Its Techniques* (London: T & T Clark, 2001 [1984]), 332–36; J. F. Hobbins, "Regularities in Ancient Hebrew Verse: A New Descriptive Model," *ZAW* 119/4 (2007), 573–76. For an extended treatment of the topic of "enjambment," the most prominent alternative to parallelistic lines in biblical poetry (cf. Alter, *Art of Biblical Poetry*, 19), see F. W. Dobbs-Allsopp, "The Enjambing Line in Lamentations: A Taxonomy (Part I)," *ZAW* 113/2 (2001), 219–39, and "The Effects of Enjambment in Lamentations (Part 2)," *ZAW* 113/5 (2001), 370–85.

of nonparallelistic lines that has all too often been missed even by specialists: "if there are unparallel lines, and parts of the poetry where parallelism is not apparent, it would seem that parallelism is not to be found everywhere in the poetry: consequently parallelism cannot be taken as the general system it is often thought of as being."[69]

* * *

Given the prominence of Lowth's ideas about parallelism in Allen's explication of "biblical analogies" for Whitman's prosody, the foregoing has focused principally on comprehending these ideas—especially the two main components of his understanding, his general description of the phenomenon and his classification scheme— and their modern scholarly reception. Together—Lowth's ideas and their reception—these form the bedrock of contemporary understandings of biblical parallelism. The topic continues to attract scholarly attention. One last development in the study of parallelism that deserves mention here is parallelism's rhythmic significance, especially in nonmetrical verse, like that of the Bible (and Whitman, too). Lowth could not conceptualize verse outside of a metrical framework. Even while he stresses that "nothing certain can be defined concerning the metre of the particular verses" of Hebrew poetry,[70] he continues to think it "not improbable that some regard was also paid to the numbers and feet."[71] Still, he trusts his new kind of empirically grounded close reading, noticing the "measured cadence" effected by the rough regularity of the "conformation of the sentences" and the parallelistic play it sponsors.[72] In fact, this "conformation of the sentences," he says later, "has always appeared to me a necessary concomitant of metrical composition."[73] In the end, this "measured cadence" ultimately resists strict numerical quantification. And yet in its very articulation Lowth may be seen stretching the received ideas about metricality; indeed, as J. Engell well observes, Lowth "actually ends up providing a new, different kind of poetic original... [that] could

---

69 *A History of the English Bible as Literature* (Cambridge: Cambridge University, 2004), 227.

70 *Lectures*, I, 68.

71 Ibid., II, 54.

72 *Lectures*, I, 68–69.

73 Ibid., II, 11; cf. I, 99; II, 53–54.

not be reduced, despite his own efforts, to set meters."[74] This ultimately changes how poetry is imagined in the West (especially in English language poetry) and makes possible "the unrhymed verse without strict metrical scansion" of "Blake, Smart, Cowper, Macpherson, and Whitman."[75]

Biblical scholarship more generally takes longer to absorb fully the consequences of Lowth's expanded sensibility about what counts as metrical. Not until B. Hrushovski's [Harshav's] seminal "On Free Rhythms in Modern Poetry"—which aims to account prosodically for the rhythmic achievements of the kind of not-strictly-metrical verse inspired by Lowth—is a conceptual framework articulated for understanding the rhythm of biblical poetry beyond the positing of strict numerical regularity.[76] Echoing Lowth, Hrushovski observes that "no exact regularity of any kind has been found" and thus by definition "the poetry of the Hebrew Bible" forms "a 'natural' free-rhythmic system."[77] Parallelism, in all of its variability, offers one set of parameters that may contribute to a given biblical poem's overall rhythm. For example, in poems composed predominantly of parallelistic couplets and triplets (and not all biblical poems are so composed), the forward movement of the rhythm is periodically checked by moments of felt-stasis as the balancing and repetition at the heart of parallelism—one propositional gesture instinctively triggering another of like form and meaning— enact their bilateral pulse. There may be no better description and illustration of this rhythm than that provided by J. Hollander in his delightful imitation of it in English translation, viz. "Its song is a music of matching, its rhythm a kind of paralleling."[78]

---

74   "Robert Lowth," 123.
75   Engell, "Robert Lowth" 123–25, 131; "The Other Classic: Hebrew Shapes British and American Literature and Culture" in *The Call of Classical Literature in the Romantic Age* (eds. K. P. Van Anglen and J. Engell; Edinburgh: Edinburgh University, 2017), 355–58.
76   In Style in Language (ed. T. Sebeok; New York: Technology Press of the Massachusett s Institute of Technology and John Wiley & Sons, Inc., 1960), 173–90, esp. 189–90; cf. "Prosody, Hebrew" in EcyJud (1971–72), 13: 1200–0 3; "Note on the Systems of Hebrew Versification" in The Penguin Book of Hebrew Verse (ed. T. Carmi; New York: Penguin Books, 1982), 57–72.
77   "Prosody, Hebrew," 1200; "On Free Rhythms," 189.
78   *Rhyme's Reason: A Guide to English Verse* (en gl. ed.; New Haven: Yale University, 1989), 26. Parallelism now features prominently in many accounts of free verse

Parallelism, since Lowth's celebrated analysis in the middle of the eighteenth century, is the best known characteristic of (much) biblical poetry, and, indeed, since the early 1990s, parallelism is now also the best understood feature of biblical poetry. Its many varieties and common tendencies, its basic mechanisms and informing structures, have been well researched, catalogued, and exemplified. If parallelism *per se* cannot be constitutive of biblical poetry—since there is a substantial amount of nonparallelistic lines in the biblical Hebrew poetic corpus—there is no denying its significance when present—the keen ness of Lowth's original insight continues to redound to this day.

Whitman and Biblical Parallelism: Line-Internal Parallelism

Having reviewed the question of parallelism in biblical poetry from a contemporary, post-Lowthian perspective, I want to return to a fresh consideration of the second of Allen's two main aims in "Biblical Analogies," namely, "to see what light such an investigation throws on Whitman's sources."[79] That is, what (if anything) in Whitman's use of parallelism is owed to the (English) Bible? Allen ultimately hedges some on this question. Among his main conclusions, he states: "It is certain, however, that Whitman *could* have learned (or 'absorbed') his first rhythmical principle from his extensive reading of the English Bible" (emphasis added).[80] The chief evidence, on Allen's accounting, is that as in the Bible Whitman features lines joined by synonymous, antithetical, synthetic, and climactic parallelism; and there is a great deal of line-internal parallelism as well, "which is found in the Bible almost as frequently as in *Leaves of Grass*."[81] So influential was Allen's

---

rhythm, e.g., D. Attridge, *Poetic Rhythm: An Introduction* (Cambridge: Cambridge University, 1995), 169–70.

79   "Biblical Analogies," 491.

80   Ibid., 506. Even more emphatically: "Whether or not Whitman borrowed (consciously or unconsciously) his rhythmical principle from Old Testament poetry, I am not prepared to say. That he could have done so there is no doubt" (497–98).

81   Ibid.

assessment that it became canonized in the entry on "parallelism" for the *Princeton Encyclopedia of Poetry and Poetics*.[82]

A problem with Allen's analysis is its reliance on a Lowthian inspired categorization scheme that contemporary biblical scholars no longer find compelling. This is more problematic for providing a framework for understanding Whitman's free-verse prosody than for assessing what in his use of parallelism was inspired by the Bible, as Warren notices.[83] Warren is chiefly critical of Allen's emphasis on semantics, on "thought rhythm," especially at the expense of paying attention to syntax.[84] And he cites Kugel's critique of Lowth's categorization scheme in order to bolster his own contention that Allen's "method.... for classifying Whitman's rhythmical devices does not appear to be valid."[85] The spirit of Warren's criticism is in line with the post-1970s work done by biblical scholars on parallelism. In fact, his own analysis could have been sharpened had he availed himself of more of the work reviewed above, especially those working from within an explicitly linguistic framework—Kugel is the only biblicist consulted, and he is not centrally interested in linguistic matters as they relate to parallelism. However, on the question of establishing a link between parallelism in the Bible and parallelism in Whitman, Warren thinks Allen succeeds: "By using the rhythm-producing syntax of the English Bible, Whitman connects himself with the impassioned voices of the Old Testament prophets."[86] The position, however, is more asserted than argued, with Warren seemingly content to rely on the field's long-held presumption of biblical influence on Whitman.[87]

Warren correctly underscores the limited value of the Lowthian tripartite classification paradigm for unlocking the nature of Whitman's prosody—or for that matter for simply getting a better understanding of the nature of parallelism in Whitman's poetry. The paradigm, however

---

82 R. O. Evans, "Parallelism" in *Princeton Encyclopedia of Poetry and Poetics* (eds. A. Preminger et al; engl. ed.; Princeton: Princeton University, 1974), 599.

83 "Free Growth," 28.

84 Ibid., 30.

85 Ibid.

86 Ibid., 32.

87 A gesture to the trope is made via reference to Whitman's lampoon of an "old Hebrew" prophet from 1865 (Warren, "Free Growth," 32; see discussion in Chapter Two above). See the discussion of "parataxis" in Chapter Five by way of substantiating Warren's assertion from the biblical perspective.

flawed, nevertheless does permit (with some recalibration) some initial glimpses of what Whitman takes from the Bible with regard to this trope. Synonymous parallelism is a good example. This is "Whitman's favorite form" and "no one can doubt" its presence in *Leaves*, writes Allen.[88] The vast majority of Allen's examples, in fact, involve synonymity of some kind. He even admits difficulty in distinguishing "the synonymous from the synthetic" in Whitman.[89] In part the latter difficulty arises because synthetic parallelism, as discussed above, often is used in the Lowthian paradigm to classify sets of lines that do not exhibit any kind of parallelism. In Whitman, as in the Bible, there are many nonparallelistic lines of verse (of various sorts). The large observation to make about Whitman's preference for synonymity is that semantics (meaning) is the linguistic element that most readily translates from one language into another. Putting aside Lowth's own emphasis on semantics (an emphasis then bequeathed to succeeding generations of biblical scholars and through Allen to Whitman scholars), it is the semantic element of parallelism in biblical Hebrew poetry that carries over most visibly into the English translation of the KJB—and this despite the translators' general ignorance of the phenomenon (as it later became diagnosed by Lowth). Therefore, if the Bible is one source of Whitman's knowledge of parallelism, it is not surprising that he picks up most commonly semantic reiteration and reformulation (whether synonymous, antithetical, or whatever). The challenge is to be able to identify biblicisms in Whitman's parallelistic play beyond the sheer presence of synonymity.

The likeliest place to locate a biblical genealogy for Whitman's use of parallelism is in his "long lines," which, as Allen astutely observes, often may be broken into "shorter parallelisms"—what Allen calls "internal parallelism."[90] "The smallest parallels in Whitman"—and H. Vendler says that "semantic or syntactic parallelism" is the "basic molecule of Whitmanian chemistry"—"comes two to a line."[91] These internally parallelistic lines (whether of two or three parts), as previously noted (see Chapter Three), are extremely common in *Leaves* and are one of

---

88   "Biblical Analogies," 493, 497.
89   Ibid., 493. He includes "climactic parallelism" in a similar comment in his later *The New Walt Whitman Handbook* ([New York: New York University, 1986], 221).
90   "Biblical Analogies," 494, 497.
91   H. Vendler, *Poetic Thinking* (Cambridge: Harvard University, 2004), 38.

the surest signs of the KJB's imprint on Whitman's mature style.[92] The parallelistic couplet and triplet are the most dominant forms of line grouping in biblical Hebrew verse (isolated, ungrouped, singular lines are rare) and are inevitably rendered into two- and three-part verses (i.e., verse divisions) in the prose translation of the KJB. Mostly, of course, Whitman has just adopted this parallelistic substructure and fitted it out with his own language material. Still, the substructure itself and the prominence of semantic synonymity are important markers of a biblical genealogy. I have already identified a number of examples of internally parallel lines in Whitman in which other pointers to the Bible exist as well, the most striking being Whitman's adaptation of the biblical graded number sequence ("two greatnesses—And a third") in section 34 of "Proto-Leaf" (*LG* 1860, 13; cf. Prov 30:18–19; see Chapter Three). Here I concentrate on examples of two-part, internally parallelistic lines from the 1855 *Leaves*, again highlighting those with biblical inflections of some kind.

Synonymity

I begin, however, with a selection of internally parallelistic lines featuring synonymity. I do so mainly as a reminder of the ubiquity of this line type in *Leaves*. These several examples, all taken from "I celebrate myself," could be multiplied hundreds of times over:

> "The pleasures of heaven are with me, and the pains of hell are with me" (*LG*, 26)

> "This is the meal pleasantly set.... this is the meat and drink for natural hunger" (*LG*, 25)

> "Regardless of others, ever regardful of others" (*LG*, 23)

> "The woollypates hoe in the sugarfield, the overseer views them from his saddle" (*LG*, 22)

> "Hurrah for positive science! Long live exact demonstration!" (*LG*, 28)

---

92   R. Mitchell stresses the frequency and centrality of "the two-part or two-group line" in *Leaves* ("A Prosody for Whitman?", *PMLA* 84/6 [1969], 1607). Vendler notes Whitman's closeness to the "psalmic parallel," though she mistakenly confuses (like Allen and others) the verse divisions in English translation and the Hebrew original.

The first example I discuss also in Chapter Three. I repeat it here because the closeness of its phrasing to the first two-thirds of Ps 116:3 ("The sorrows of death compassed me, and the pains of hell gat hold upon me: I found trouble and sorrow"),[93] although Ps 18:5 (= 2 Sam 22:6) brings the bipartite, parallelistic structure in Whitman more sharply into focus: "The sorrows of hell compassed me about: the snares of death prevented me." The synonymity of the psalmic verses (e.g., "sorrows"// "pains"// "snares"; "death"// "hell") contrasts with the antithesis of Whitman's line (e.g., "pleasures"/ "pains"), pointed with a well-known biblical merism, "heaven"/ "hell" (e.g., Amos 9:2; Ps 139:8; Job 11:8; Matt 11:23; Luke 10:15). The semantic upshot of Whitman's line is to signal (efficiently) the speaker's absorption of all pleasure and pain.

The second example shows Whitman working with biblical material—namely, the Lord's Supper tradition of the gospels and Paul (Matt 26:26–29; Mark 14:22–25; Luke 22:14–22: 1 Cor 11:17–34; see Chapter Three)—and shaping it into his own appositive, parallelistic phrasing. The repetition of "This is" in parallel syntactic frames holds "meal" and "meat and drink" together. The move from the abstract or general ("meal") to the more concrete ("meat and drink") is a typical semantic development activated in biblical parallelisms.[94] The prepositional phrase in the second half of the line, "for natural hunger," balances "pleasurably set" in the first half and at the same time counters the (presumed) spiritual nature of the Lord's supper tradition.

The next two examples are intended to ramify an idea I have already begun making with the first two examples, namely, that there is more to appreciating parallelism in Whitman's poetry than noting its facticity or categorizing it or even assessing its place in Whitman's prosody (which is not insignificant). Attending to what takes place as a result of setting parallel syntactic frames in equivalence is perhaps the most significant takeaway from contemporary biblical scholarship for a better understanding of the dynamics of Whitman's parallelism. In "Regardless of others, ever regardful of others" (*LG*, 23) it is the difference between "regardless" and "ever regardful" that the parallel *of*-genitives bring into alignment. The defiant "Regardless of others" is

---

93　The verse from the psalm is a triplet in the Hebrew original, so the final "I found trouble and sorrow" has no counterpart in Whitman's line.

94　See Alter, *Art of Biblical Poetry*, 15, 20, 34; Kugel, *Idea*, 7.

provided with a deep empathy by its echo in "ever regardful of others." The line "The woollypates hoe in the sugarfield, the overseer views them from his saddle" (*LG*, 22) comes amidst one of Whitman's early and long catalogues (*LG*, 21–23) in which vignettes of people at work are strung together creating a tapestry of the American worker, all of which are absorbed by Whitman's expansive "I" in the catalogue's last line, "And such as it is to be of these more or less I am" (*LG*, 23)—this is the parallelistic absorption strategy Whitman was experimenting with in the "Talbot Wilson" notebook discussed at the outset of this chapter, only now enacted on a much larger scale. Almost every line features SV word order with attendant adjuncts (e.g., objects, prepositional phrases, adverbials).[95] The vast majority of lines begins with the definite article ("The") and an actor noun. The "woollypates" line features the same syntactic structure in both halves of the line, creating the line-internal parallelism. One effect of the mirroring internal frames is to create two parts of one image, a kind of verbal diptych. What is captured is a still life of one dimension of slavery in antebellum America. The tight syntactic equivalences enhance the contrasts in the two panes: plural "woollypates" versus one "overseer"; the former are named pejoratively[96] while the "overseer" is called by his title; the slaves work while the "overseer" sits on a horse and "views them" working—the "them" (linguistically) *object*ifies the slaves, displacing the *subject*ivity that was bestowed upon "them" in the first half of the line.[97] A lot can happen in the midst of Whitman's parallelistic play.

The final example is meant as a reminder that synonymous parallelism may also serve reiterative ends. In this instance, the doubling exultation of the gains of scientific methodology and reasoning is not so differently shaped from the often iterative praise of the deity in so many of the psalms, e.g., "Praise ye the LORD. O give thanks unto the LORD" (Ps 106:1). Not infrequently this iteration at the heart of parallelism

---

95   This is what Warren describes as a "clausal catalogue" ("Free Growth," 34), and as he also notes, clausal parallelism is prominent in the Bible (32).

96   Whitman here is playing on (or offering a version of) "woolly-head," which the *OED* designates as "depreciative and offensive" and defines as "a person with woolly hair, *esp.* a black person; hence, a nickname for an abolitionist in America" (earliest citation is from 1859).

97   The addition of "As" at the head of the line beginning in the 1860 *Leaves* (40) subordinates the first clause to the second, and thus makes the displacement complete.

is ramified through what biblical scholars sometimes call "repetitive parallelism," a form of parallelism that involves verbatim repetition(s) (e.g., "Wherefore I will yet plead with you, saith the LORD, and with your children's children will I plead," Jer 2:9; "The voice of the LORD shaketh the wilderness; the LORD shaketh the wilderness of Kadesh, Ps 29:8).[98] Whitman is very fond of such internally parallel verbatim repetitions, e.g., "Have you reckoned a thousand acres much? Have you reckoned the earth much?," *LG*, 14; "Clear and sweet is my soul.... and clear and sweet is all that is not my soul," *LG*, 14; "Exactly the contents of one, and exactly the contents of two, and which is ahead?", *LG*, 15. Indeed, these kinds of verbatim repetitions are far more frequent in *Leaves* than in the Bible.

Antithesis

No matter the accuracy of the criticisms of the place of antithetical parallelism in Lowth's reductive classification scheme, it nevertheless remains the case that the kinds of semantic play organized under this rubric originally by Lowth—"when two lines correspond with one another by an Opposition of terms and sentiments; when the second is contrasted with the first, sometimes in expressions, sometimes in sense only"[99]—do in fact appear in biblical poetry, especially in the didactic verse of the wisdom tradition (Proverbs, Job, Ben Sira). A typical example cited by Lowth is Prov 10:1: "A wise son maketh a glad father: but a foolish son is the heaviness of his mother." He explains the opposing plays in this way: "Where every word hath its opposite: for the terms *father* and *mother* are, as the Logicians say, relatively opposite."[100] Such antithesis features prominently in the internally parallel lines of Martin Farquhar Tupper's *Proverbial Philosophy*,[101] a book directly inspired by the biblical wisdom tradition. Several lines may be offered to exemplify what a close emulation of the biblical form can look like:

---

98   Cf. D. Pardee, *Ugaritic and Hebrew Parallelism: A Trial Cut ('nt I and Proverbs 2)* (SuppVT 39; Leiden: Brill, 1988), 72–75, 169–70; Watson, *Classical Hebrew Poetry*, 133–34, 150, n. 1. The KJB translators sometimes substitute synonymity for such verbatim repetitions, e.g., "Who rejoice to do evil (Hebrew *rāʿ*), and delight in the frowardness of the wicked (Hebrew *rāʿ*)," Prov 2:14.

99   *Isaiah*, xix; cf. *Lectures*, II, 45.

100 *Isaiah*, xix.

101 (New York: Wiley & Putnam, 1846). For further details, see discussion in Chapter Three.

"The alchemist laboureth in folly, but catcheth chance gleams of
wisdom." (p. 13)

"And the weak hath quailed in fear, while the firm hath been glad in his
confidence." (p. 17)

"The zephyr playing with an aspen leaf,—the earthquake that rendeth a
continent;" (p. 20)

"Man liveth only in himself, but the Lord liveth in all things;" (p. 21)

"Poverty, with largeness of heat: or a full purse with a sordid spirit:" (p. 23)

Tupper is useful because he does not try to distance his own lines from
his biblical model(s); indeed, he is even willing to develop biblical
themes and ideas and feature biblical characters. Here his use of the
KJB inspired two-part line and antithetical parallelism, with his own
language slotted in, is plain to see. Whitman's collaging from the
Bible (and other sources) is often accompanied by a great deal more
processing, and thus leaves fewer signs of the collaging itself (see
Chapters Two and Three above). When he uses opposition, contrast, or
antithesis in his parallelistic play, which is not as frequently as in Tupper
or the Bible,[102] it does not have the strong oppositional and weighted
(to one side or the other) force of so many of the biblical binaries (e.g.,
wise/fool, rich/poor). Rather, Whitman's optimism and inclusivity
means that he is much more interested in using parallelism to overcome
opposing dichotomies ("It is for the wicked just the same as the
righteous," *LG*, 25), as epitomized in the line from the "Talbot Wilson"
notebook discussed above, "I am the poet of slaves and of the masters of
slaves."[103] And there is the neighboring set of lines that gets included
in *Leaves* but only belatedly massaged into a single, internally parallel
line: "I am the poet of the Body and I am the poet of the Soul" (*LG*
1881, 45)—the parallel frames ("I am the poet of") hold together the
"sharply contrasting" pair, "Body"//"Soul," thus forging a parallelistic
expression of the poet's holistic anthropology.[104]

---

102 It is difficult to discern straightforward examples of antithetical parallelism in
     Allen's discussion.

103 https://whitmanarchive.org/manuscripts/figures/loc.00141.070.jpg

104 G. Ketab, "Walt Whitman and the Culture of Democracy" in *A Political Companion
     to Walt Whitman* (ed. J. E. Seery; Lexington: University Press of Kentucky, 2011),

Whitman rarely crafts lines in which all corresponding parts are opposites (e.g., "And make short account of neuters and geldings, and favor men and women fully equipped," *LG*, 29). More commonly, Whitman's antitheses are staged amidst synonymity (Lowth's second variety of antithetical parallelism), and he is especially fond of playing on identical (or near identical) terms (see discussion of repetitive parallelism above):

> "The rest did not see her, but she saw them and loved them" (*LG*, 19)[105]

> "I hear and behold God in every object, yet I understand God not in the least" (*LG*, 54)

> "I pass so poorly with paper and types.... I must pass with the contact of bodies and souls" (*LG*, 57)

> "It is not that you should be undecided, but that you should be decided" (*LG*, 68)

> "I love the rich running day, but I do not desert her in whom I lay so long" (*LG*, 77)

> "I stay awhile away O night, but I return to you again and love you" (*LG*, 76)

> "Happiness not in another place, but this place ... not for another hour, but this hour" (*LG*, 64)

> "The welcome ugly face of some beautiful soul ... the handsome detested or despised face" (*LG*, 82)

Most of these have the classic disjunctive (with "but" or "yet" heading the second clause) shaping of biblical antithesis, as well as at least one set of opposing terms (e.g., "did not see"// "saw"; "hear and behold"//

30–57, here 35. Ketab appreciates both the complexity and fluidity of Whitman's anthropology (esp. 34–36).

105　Such chiasmus (elements repeated in reverse order) frequently features in Whitman's internally parallel lines (e.g., "I will be even with you, and you shall be even with me," *LG*, 57) as it does in biblical poetry, where "such a unit is generally a parallel couplet" and usually composed of "sub-units of the sentence, considered semantically or grammatically" (Watson, *Classical Hebrew Poetry*, 201–0 8, here 201). However, in English translation, and especially in the KJB, the tendency is to normalize the word order for English and in the process wrecking the underlying chiastic structure of the Hebrew. Though Whitman's chiasms feel biblical, they are not likely mediated by the KJB.

"understand... not"; "be undecided"// "be decided"; "day"// night (unnamed); "stay away"// "return"; "ugly face"// "handsome... face"). For the sixth example, taken from "I wander all night," compare this passage from Second Isaiah cited by Lowth in his initial discussion of antithetical parallelism: "In a little wrath I hid my face from thee for a moment; but with everlasting kindness will I have mercy on thee" (Isa 54:8).[106] Prov 11:24, "There is that scattereth, and yet increaseth; and there is that withholdeth more than is meet, but it tendeth to poverty," employs what Lowth describes as a "kind of double Antithesis": "one between the two lines themselves; and likewise a subordinate opposition between the two parts of each."[107] Whitman's line, "Happiness not in another place, but this place .. not for another hour, but this hour" (*LG*, 64), is of a similar nature, though featuring synonymity instead of antinomy between the two subparts of the lines (see also "Great is wealth and great is poverty ... great is expression and great is silence," *LG*, 93). The "subordinate opposition between the two parts of each" of the original Hebrew lines in Prov 11:24 reflects line-internal parallelism within Hebrew line structure, which as noted earlier exists but is comparatively rare because typical biblical Hebrew poetic lines are generally too short, lacking the necessary amplitude for this kind of play. Whitman's caesural divisions, as in this example, are another structural site where the poet stages parallelism with biblical antecedents. Some of these involve antithetical parallelism, e.g., "The vulgar and the refined ... what you call sin and what you call goodness ... to think how wide a difference" (*LG*, 67).

Climactic Parallelism

Following Driver, Allen isolates a fourth pattern of parallelism (beside the Lowthian triumvirate) that he believes Whitman shares with the Bible. In climactic parallelism, according to Driver, "the first line is itself incomplete, and the second line takes up words from it and completes them."[108] He then cites three examples:

---

106 *Lectures*, II, 48.
107 *Isaiah*, xix.
108 *Introduction*, 363.

Give unto the LORD, O ye sons of the mighty,

Give unto the LORD glory and strength. (Ps 29:1)

The voice of the LORD shaketh the wilderness;

The LORD shaketh the wilderness of Kadesh. (Ps 29:8)

Till thy people pass over, O LORD,

Till the people pass over, which thou hast purchased. (Exod 15:16)

Lowth treats this "variety" of parallelism in his discussion of synonymous parallelism: "The parallelism is sometimes formed by the iteration of the former member, either in the whole or in part."[109] He cites as an example Ps 94:3:

"How long shall the wicked, O Jehovah,

"How long shall the wicked triumph!"

The three examples in Exod 15:16, Ps 29:1 and Ps 94:3, all with an intervening vocative in the first lines, represent a more restrictive version of the pattern, and are now more commonly referred to as "staircase parallelism."[110] In such parallelism (involving either two or three lines of verse), typically "a sentence is started, only to be interrupted... then resumed from the beginning again, without the intervening epithet [or subject NP], to be completed in the second or third line."[111] However, with or without the intervening element, staircase or climactic, the pattern is as Driver notices, "of rare occurrence" in the Bible.[112]

Allen repeats Driver's definition and the first of his two examples from Psalm 29.[113] However, nowhere in his initial discussion, nor in

---

109 *Lectures*, II, 59.
110 Scholars began to focus attention on "staircase parallelism" after the discovery of the Ugaritic mythological texts and the recognition that the same pattern appeared in them. See S. E. Lowenstamm, "The Expanded Colon in Biblical and Ugaritic Verse," *Journal of Semitic Studies* 14 (1969), 175–96; E. L. Greenstein, "Two Variations of Grammatical Parallelism in Canaanite Poetry and Their Psycholinguistic Background," *Journal of the Ancient Near Eastern Society* 6/1 (1974), 88–105; "One More Step on the Staircase," *Ugarit-Forschungen* 9 (1977), 77–86; Watson, *Classical Hebrew Poetry*, 150–56.
111 Watson, *Classical Hebrew Poetry*, 150 (with other examples cited).
112 Driver, *Introduction*, 363.
113 "Biblical Analogies," 493.

later iterations, does he specifically identify an example of climactic (or staircase) parallelism in Whitman, and none of his cited examples are especially redolent of the proposed biblical model(s). This is not unexpected. After all, Allen admits his difficulty in differentiating in Whitman between synonymous, synthetic, and climactic parallelism.[114] In part this difficulty stems from the fact that Allen is working in translation, and is more beholden to Driver's (among others) definition, rather than appreciating the underlying Hebraic pattern and how that pattern manifests itself in English translation. Whitman is enamored with anaphora, elliptical sentences and clauses, and runs of lines whose repetitions and parallelisms build on an underlying sentential structure or logic.[115] All of these can appear to answer to Driver's definition of climactic parallelism, but they are all very different from the attested biblical paradigm. The other part of Allen's difficulty, quite simply, is that there are not many good examples of biblical climactic (or staircase) parallelism in Whitman's poetry. Allen's closest example is the first set of lines he cites from "I wander all night":[116]

> How solemn they look there, stretched and still;
>
> How quiet they breathe, the little children in their cradles. (*LG*, 70)

Variations on the three elements of staircase parallelism are present: 1) the repeated element ("How solemn they look there"// "How quiet they breathe") are more synonymous than iterative (which is likely why Allen cites the lines, i.e., as exemplifying synonymous parallelism);[117] 2) there is an intervening element ("stretched and still"), though not the vocative or subject NP of biblical exemplars; and 3) the completing element ("the little children in their cradles") supplies the referent for the fronted pronoun "they." Closer interlinear matches are these two examples from "Suddenly out of its stale and dusty lair" and "Lilacs":

> They live in other young men, O kings,

---

114 *New Walt Whitman Handbook*, 221.

115 These last usually consist of a mixture of phrases and clauses that divide "readily into well-ordered syntactic blocks or divisions" (Warren, "Free Growth," 39; cf. 36–40).

116 Allen, "Biblical Analogies," 493.

117 Synonyms sometimes show up among the repeated material in biblical examples of staircase parallelism, see Watson, *Classical Hebrew Poetry*, 153.

> They live in brothers, again ready to defy you: (*LG*, 88)
>
> Must I leave thee, lilac with heart-shaped leaves?
>
> Must I leave thee there in the door-yard, blooming, returning with
> spring? (*Sequel*, 12)

As with Allen's examples there are variations here, too—most notably the shaping of the two lines from "Lilacs" as two questions, yet the biblical staircase structure in both is readily recognizable. Also from "Suddenly out of its stale and dusty lair" appears a possible line-internal (after combination) example of the staircase structure: "Out of its robes only this.... the red robes, lifted by the arm" (*LG*, 88). The re-combined line (originally two in "Resurgemus"[118]) ultimately veers away from the biblical type, with "only this," for example, serving as the intervening element (instead of a vocative or subject NP) and the syntax carrying over into the next line (viz. "One finger pointed high over the top, like the head of a snake appears"). There is also this tantalizing example from "The bodies of men and women engirth me": "I will duly pass the day O my mother and duly return to you" (*LG*, 77)—though only "duly" is repeated from the first half. A very abbreviated version of climactic parallelism (i.e., without an intervening element) occurs late in "I celebrate myself": "I sleep.... I sleep long" (*LG*, 55). Further examples are likely to be uncovered in a thorough search of Whitman's expansive poetic corpus. Still, if staircase and climactic parallelism are rare in the Bible, they are even rarer in Whitman. The peculiarity of the form points to the Bible, but how consciously Whitman shaped his lines as a reflection of this form remains an open question.

Gapping. One of the characteristic varieties of synonymous parallelism on which Lowth remarks specifically involves the gapping (or ellipsis) of an element: "There is frequently something wanting in the latter member, which must be repeated from the former to complete the sentence."[119] The gapping commonly features the "verb" or the "Nominative Case," as Lowth observes, although verb gapping is prominent, since the verb is highly inflected and syntactically prominent in Semitic languages generally, with V(S)O word order prevailing in

---

118 https://whitmanarchive.org/published/periodical/poems/per.00088
119 *Lectures*, II, 41. Cf. O'Connor, *Hebrew Verse Structure*, 122–27; 401–0 7.

main clauses in the classical (or standard) phase of biblical Hebrew. These examples (from Lowth) feature verb gapping:

> Isa 55:7
>
> "Let-the-wicked forsake his-way;
>
> "And-the-unrighteous man his-thoughts:" (Lowth)
>
> "Let the wicked forsake his way, and the unrighteous man his thoughts" (KJB)
>
> Isa 46:3
>
> "Hearken unto-me, O-house of-Jacob;
>
> "And-all the-remnant of-the-house of-Israel." (Lowth)
>
> "Hearken unto me, O house of Jacob, and all the remnant of the house of Israel" (KJB)
>
> Prov 3:9
>
> "Honour Jehovah with-thy-riches;
>
> "And-with-the-first-fruits of-all thine-increase." (Lowth)
>
> "Honour the LORD with thy substance, and with the firstfruits of all thine increase" (KJB)

In each of these examples, the verb (forsake, hearken, honour) from the first line (or part of the verse) must be supplied in the second in order for the latter to be sensible—and in Prov 3:9 both verb and object must be supplied, i.e., "Honour Jehovah with-thy-riches"// "And-[**honour Jehovah**] with-the-first-fruits of-all thine-increase." Whitman, too, likes gapping, especially the subject (English prefers SV(O) word order and lexically explicit subjects are mostly required given the minimal nature of inflectional morphology for verbs),[120] as epitomized by the expanded opening line of the "Song of Myself," "I celebrate myself, and sing myself" (*LG* 1881, 29), in which the subject, "I," is gapped.[121] Some

---

120 By contrast, since all finite verbs in biblical Hebrew are normally inflected for person, number, and gender, explicit subjects are not always required in the surface structure of a sentence.

121 Halkin rounds out the internal parallelism by supplying the gapped first person pronoun, ʾănî "I" (*'Alē 'Ēsev*, 53) in his modern Hebrew rendering of the line.

examples from the many possibilities in the 1855 *Leaves*, include (elided elements in **bold**):

> "**They** come to me days and nights and go from me again" (*LG*, 15)

> "Not words, not music or rhyme **I want**.... not custom or lecture, not even the best" (*LG*, 15)

> "**You** settled your head athwart my hips and gently turned over upon me" (*LG*, 15)

> "And that all the men ever born **are also** my brothers.... and the women my sisters and lovers" (*LG*, 16)

> "**And mine** a word of the modern.... a word en masse" (LG, 28)

> "Through me the afflatus **surging and surging**.... through me the current and index" (*LG*, 29)

> "**Voices** of the diseased and despairing, and of thieves and dwarfs" (*LG*, 29)

> "**I do not know what it is except** that it is grand, and that it is happiness" (*LG*, 59)

> "**To thin**k of today . . and the ages continued henceforward" (LG, 65)

> "**He whom I call** answers me and takes the place of my lover" (*LG*, 72)

Many similar examples could be cited. Tyndale and the KJB, by staying close to their underlying Hebrew source, bequeath to English style a tolerance for ellipsis generally. And the prominence of ellipsis within Whitman's two-part lines is suggestive of this broad inheritance. Often as in biblical examples the gapping is compensated for—balanced— by an additional element in the second halves of lines, which can be manipulated to various (sometimes subtle) ends. For example, the gapping of the subject "You" in "You settled your head athwart my hips and gently turned over upon me" (*LG*, 15) allows Whitman to add "gently," which gives the line a tenderness it would lack were the subject repeated and the second verb left unmodified (viz. "and you turned"). In "And that all the men ever born are also my brothers.... and the women my sisters and lovers" (*LG*, 16) the elision of "are also" after the suspension points makes space for the erotic charge he adds at line-end, "and lovers."

Incipient Narrativity

The biblical poetic corpus, as previously noticed, is fundamentally nonnarrative in nature—poetry is used for all manner of things except telling tales.[122] To be sure, individual poems incorporate narrative runs and sometimes even develop characters, but for the most part these forms are restricted in scale and put mainly to nonnarrative ends (e.g., Exodus 15, Proverbs 7). Of interest here is the "propelling force" for narrative in biblical poems on a still smaller scale, namely, "the incipiently narrative momentum" that can carry over from one line to the next in the play of parallelism.[123] That is, one of the dynamics of biblical parallelism is the capacity to create a variety of small, often incremental, narrative effects (e.g., sequentiality, description, cause and effect) amidst the pulse of iteration. For example, sometimes the sequence of actions is quite explicit as in 2 Sam 22:17: "He sent from above, he took me; he drew me out of many waters." Here Yahweh is imagined as sending forth his arm from on high and takes hold of the petitioner; and in the second half of the verse he draws the speaker to safety out of the "many waters"—or better the "mighty waters" of cosmic chaos. Exod 15:10 provides another good example: "Thou didst blow with thy wind, the sea covered them: they sank as lead in the mighty waters." There is both movement in action ("sea covered them" > "they sank") and a rendering of cause ("Thou didst blow with thy wind") and effect ("they sank as lead in the mighty waters"). In Ps 106:19 ("They made a calf in Horeb, and worshipped the molten image") is subtler. There is sequential development implied thematically in the two verbs—one has to make the calf before it can be worshiped.

Whitman's internally parallel lines are filled with similar kinds of incremental narrative movement. Typical examples include:

"Loafe with me on the grass…. loose the stop from your throat" (*LG*, 15)

"You settled your head athwart my hips and gently turned over upon me,

And parted the shirt from my bosom-bone, and plunged your tongue to my barestript heart,

---

And reached till you felt my beard, and reached till you held my feet."
(*LG*, 15)

"One hand rested on his rifle.... the other hand held firmly the wrist of
the red girl" (*LG*, 19)

"And went where he sat on a log, and led him in and assured him" (*LG*, 19)

"The sun falls on his crispy hair and moustache.... falls on the black of
his polish'd and perfect limbs" (*LG*, 20)

"The carpenter dresses his plank.... the tongue of his foreplane whistles
its wild ascending lisp" (*LG*, 21)

"They have cleared the beams away.... they tenderly lift me forth" (*LG*, 39)

"I seize the descending man.... I raise him with resistless will" (*LG*, 45)

"I open my scuttle at night and see the far-sprinkled systems" (*LG*, 51)

"Washington stands inside the lines . . he stands on the entrenched hills
amid a crowd of

officers" (*LG*, 73)

"The chief encircles their necks with his arm and kisses them on the
cheek,

He kisses lightly the wet cheeks one after another.... he shakes hands
and bids goodbye to the army." (*LG*, 74)

"The coats vests and caps thrown down . . the embrace of love and
resistance,

The upperhold and underhold—the hair rumpled over and blinding the
eyes;" (*LG*, 78)

"Which the winds carry afar and re-sow, and the rains and the snows
nourish" (*LG*, 88)

"I love to look on the stars and stripes.... I hope the fifes will play
Yankee Doodle" (*LG*, 89)

"And clap the skull on top of the ribs, and clap a crown on top of the
skull" (*LG*, 90)

Detailed commentary is not required to reveal the various kinds of
incipient narrativity on display in these examples. Many involve

sequences of related actions (e.g., "parted the shirt"// "plunged your tongue"; "went where he sat"// "led him"; "I seized the descending man"// "I raised him"). The two lines from the "wrestle of wrestlers" passage (*LG*, 78) show that narrative momentum can even be projected without verbal predication. The succession of nominal phrases offers snapshots (stills) of the "two apprentice-boys" in the midst of their match. It is the succession itself, one nominal snapshot followed on by another, that creates the appearance of narrative momentum. In the content of the lines themselves Whitman is able to embellish descriptive details about the scene. For example, "the hair rumpled over and blinding the eyes" is a direct consequence of the "upperhold and underhold" (hence the long dash) and the "rumpled over" hair stands in as a metonym for the frenetic activity of wrestling. And yet what Whitman provides is a detail of the image of the wrestlers, their long hair askew and blinding them. In some of these instances, momentum can be created by using the same verb. In "And reached till you felt my beard, and reached till you held my feet" (*LG*, 15) common knowledge of human anatomy (head at the top and feet at the bottom) allows the repeated verb "reached" in immediate adjacency and sequentially to give the impression of the lover's ongoing (durative) reaching from head to feet. In "And clap the skull on top of the ribs, and clap a crown on top of the skull" (*LG*, 90) body knowledge is leveraged as well to create upward movement. The movement is provided by the noun phrases: "skull on top of ribs" > "crown on top of the skull." As in the KJB, the narrativity in question need not be actional. Sometimes the link is cause and effect, as in the line from "Clear the way there Jonathan," ("I love to look on the stars and stripes.... I hope the fifes will play Yankee Doodle," *LG*, 89), where the appearance of the flag evokes a desire to hear "Yankee Doodle" played. At other times what results is more of an enriching of details in a scene, as in the line about where Washington "stands" (*LG*, 73), or the image from the "marriage of the trapper" in which "one hand" of the trapper "rested on his rifle" and "the other hand held firmly the wrist of the red girl" (*LG*, 19)—this last, famously, is Whitman's ekphrastic rendering of an actual painting (*The Trapper's Bride* by Alfred Jacob Miller, 1845).[124]

---

124 See E. W. Todd, "Indian Pictures and Two Whitman Poems," *Huntington Library Quarterly* 19/1 (1955), 1–11; R. L. Bohan, "Walt Whitman and the Sister Arts,"

Envelope

Allen identifies the "envelope" as a figure of special import "because it shows how closely Whitman's forms resemble those of biblical poetry" and "because it is one of the most numerous of the specific parallelistic devices that Whitman used."[125] Moulton is again Allen's inspiration and source, and he uses the latter's definition of the envelope: "A series of parallels enclosed between an identical (or equivalent) opening and close."[126] Here Allen slightly misunderstands Moulton. The envelope is itself not a "specific parallelistic" device. Rather, according to Moulton, it is a figure that frames sets of parallel lines. The "opening and close" may or may not be a figure of parallelism. Unfortunately, even Moulton is mistaken about the sets of lines contained by the envelope needing to be parallelistically related. They do not. All manner of lines, however they are grouped, are so enclosed. For example, most of the lines framed by the envelope in Song 4:1 ("Behold, thou art fair, my love") and 7 ("Thou art all fair, my love") are not parallelistically related. The envelope—also known as an inclusio, ring structure, or frame—is a traditional technique for bringing the "inherent interminability" of paratactic structures to a stopping point (however momentarily) via returning to the beginning.[127] Like parallelism the envelope is a trope of repetition, viz. Moulton's "an identical... opening and close." The frames may well feature some version of parallelism (so the synonymous frame-words "city" // "gate" [a metonym for the former] in Ps 127:1, 5),[128] but most often they are exact repetitions (or plays thereon). All structural levels are made use of, including even non-linguistic material (e.g., the couplets in Job 3:3, 10 frame an unrelenting series of triplets in the first section of Job's famous curse of his birthday). Most common are envelopes made up of single lines (e.g., "Praise ye the LORD," Ps 147:1, 20) or couplets (e.g., "O LORD our Lord, how excellent is thy name in all the earth!", Ps 8:1,

---

WWQR 16 (1999), 153–60; *Looking into Walt Whitman: American Art, 1850–1920* (University Park: Pennsylvania State University, 2006), 24–26.

125 Allen, "Biblical Analogies," 495.

126 Ibid. Allen cites: R. G. Moulton, *The Literary Study of the Bible* (Chicago, 1892), 9. The definition is slightly adjusted from "parallels" to "parallel lines running to any length" in a later edition of the book ([Boston: C. Heath & Co., 1896], 53).

127 Smith, *Poetic Closure*, 101, 148–50.

128 Watson, *Classical Hebrew Poetry*, 286.

9; "O give thanks unto the LORD; for he is good: because his mercy endureth for ever," Ps 118:1, 29; "Rise up [v. 13: Arise], my love, my fair one, and come away," Song 2:10, 13). The latter is made most visible for readers (like Whitman) in the KJB as it is coextensive with the verse divisions.

Allen also draws attention to what he calls the "incomplete envelope," that is, "with either the introduction or the conclusion left off."[129] Of course, as Allen more judiciously observes later, "But of course an 'incomplete envelope' is not an envelope at all."[130] And there are no half envelopes (as such) in the Bible. Nonetheless, Allen does point to an interesting phenomenon in Whitman's poetry. These misidentified "incomplete" envelopes usually consist of short(er) lines. A common means for concluding paratactic (and other kinds of) structures is to change up the pattern(s) governing the poem (or a section of a poem) at or near the end. Smith calls this "terminal modification."[131] Given the dominance of the long(er) line in the early editions of *Leaves of Grass*, an effective means for closing a poem or section is to shift to a shorter line. It is also not uncommon for beginnings to be set off in some fashion, though this can only be experienced retrospectively by readers. Short lines introducing runs of long(er) lines in Whitman is both comprehensible and well evidenced. W. D. Snodgrass notes a common stanza form in Whitman's poetry that consists of an opening short line, progressively longer lines in the middle, and then short lines again at the close—the latter "form, with the opening lines, a syntactic and/or rhythmic envelope."[132] Here is a not untypical example from "I celebrate myself":

Trippers and askers surround me,

People I meet.... . the effect upon me of my early life.... of the ward and city I live in.... of the nation,

The latest news.... discoveries, inventions, societies.... authors old and new,

My dinner, dress, associates, looks, business, compliments, dues,

---

129 "Biblical Analogies," 496.
130 *New Walt Whitman Handbook*, 223.
131 *Poetic Closure*, 28, 43–44, 76, 92, 107.
132 *To Sound Like Yourself* (Rochester, NY: Boa Editions, 2002), 160.

> The real or fancied indifference of some man or woman I love,
>
> The sickness of one of my folks—or of myself.... or ill-doing.... or loss or lack of money....
>
> or depressions or exaltations,
>
> They come to me days and nights and go from me again,
>
> But they are not the Me myself. (*LG*, 15)

This manipulation of line length also appears commonly in biblical poetry, but the prose renderings of the KJB blur such distinctions, especially given the markedly narrower range of Hebrew line-length variation.

Conditionals

Conditional sentences (or clauses) have nothing to do with parallelism. However, because of the overwhelming binarism of the biblical poetic tradition—lines come grouped mostly as couplets—the protasis and apodosis of conditionals are often distributed to align with the couplet's component lines, and thus typically rendered in the KJB as a single, two-part verse division (e.g., "If I regard iniquity in my heart, the Lord will not hear me," Ps 66:18). Such two-part lines filled with conditionals abound in *Leaves*:

> "If I worship any particular thing it shall be some of the spread of my body" (*LG*, 30)
>
> "If they are not yours as much as mine they are nothing or next to nothing" (*LG*, 24)
>
> "If you tire, give me both burdens, and rest the chuff of your hand on my hip" (*LG*, 52)
>
> "If you would understand me go to the heights or water- shore" (*LG*, 53)
>
> "If you want me again look for me under your bootsoles" (*LG*, 56)
>
> "If you remember your foolish and outlawed deeds, do you think I cannot remember my foolish and outlawed deeds?" (*LG*, 58)

> "If you were not breathing and walking here where would they all be?"
>   (*LG*, 60)

> "If maggots and rats ended us, then suspicion and treachery and death"
>   (*LG*, 69)

> "If life and the soul are sacred the human body is sacred" (*LG*, 82)

> "If you blind your eyes with tears you will not see the President's
>   marshal" (*LG*, 89)

> "If you groan such groans you might balk the government cannon"
>   (*LG*, 89)

> "If there be equilibrium or volition there is truth . . . if there be things at
>   all upon the earth there is

>   truth" (*LG*, 94)

Several of the examples collected here have apodoses which contain questions (e.g., "...where would they all be?" *LG*, 60). There are many biblical models for these (e.g., "If the foundations be destroyed, what can the righteous do?", Ps 11:3; "If thou, LORD, shouldest mark iniquities, O Lord, who shall stand?", Ps 130:3; "If thou hast nothing to pay, why should he take away thy bed from under thee?," Prov 33:27). One example contains a compound apodosis ("If you tire, give me both burdens, and rest the chuff of your hand on my hip," *LG*, 52). Compound protases and apodoses are common in biblical poetic conditionals (e.g., "If I sin, then thou markest me, and thou wilt not acquit me from mine iniquity," Job 10:14; "If iniquity be in thine hand, put it far away, and let not wickedness dwell in thy tabernacles," Job 11:14; "If thou hast run with the footmen, and they have wearied thee, then how canst thou contend with horses?", Jer 12:5). The last example from Whitman (*LG*, 94) contains a double conditional, also found in the Bible (e.g., "If I be wicked, woe unto me; and if I be righteous, yet will I not lift up my head. I am full of confusion," Job 10:15; "If I ascend up into heaven, thou art there: if I make my bed in hell, behold, thou art there," Ps 139:8; "If thou be wise, thou shalt be wise for thyself: but if thou scornest, thou alone shalt bear it," Prov 9:12). Job 31 repeats the conditional protasis fifteen times, which is suggestive of Whitman's several runs of conditionals in the 1855 *Leaves* (*LG*, 24, 57–58).

Duple Rhythm

Whitman's two-part lines as they isolate (and iterate) syntactic units through parallelism give his verse a persistent duple rhythm that pervades the whole of the 1855 *Leaves*. Other line types ensure that this double pulse never seems too insistent or monotonous. Yet its feel and presence is periodically magnified when a number of these two-part lines are grouped together, as in this passage from "I celebrate myself":

> You settled your head athwart my hips and gently turned over upon me,
>
> And parted the shirt from my bosom-bone, and plunged your tongue to my barestript heart,
>
> And reached till you felt my beard, and reached till you held my feet. (*LG*, 15)
>
> All goes onward and outward.... and nothing collapses,... (*LG*, 17)

Or this set from "To think of time":

> How beautiful and perfect are the animals! How perfect is my soul!
>
> How perfect the earth, and the minutest thing upon it!
>
> What is called good is perfect, and what is called sin is just as perfect;
>
> The vegetables and minerals are all perfect . . and the imponderable fluids are perfect;
>
> Slowly and surely they have passed on to this, and slowly and surely they will yet pass on. (*LG*, 69)

This duple pulse mostly counterpoints the regular march of lineal (end-stopped) wholes that is the rhythmic backbone of Whitman's poetry—"internal parallelism... is one of the means Whitman employs to prevent his use of the synonymous form from becoming monotonous."[133] Occasionally, Whitman's grouping of syntactically parallel lines into couplets momentarily reinforces the doubled movement within so

---

133 Allen, "Biblical Analogies," 497. As Allen notes, "The fact that the line in *Leaves of Grass* is also the rhythmical unit is so obvious that probably all students of Whitman have noticed it" (493); cf. Mitchell, "Prosody," 1607; Warren, "Free Growth," 30.

many of his lines (e.g., "I am the poet of the body,/ And I am the poet of the soul," *LG*, 26).[134]

The role syntax plays in shaping these rhythmic effects merits underscoring, given the emphasis on syntax in more recent studies of biblical parallelism, as well as in Warren's own work on parallelism in Whitman.[135] For Warren, in fact, Whitman folds himself within the tradition of "the impassioned voices" of Hebrew prophecy specifically "by using the rhythm-producing syntax of the English Bible."[136] Like Allen, Warren is chiefly preoccupied with how parallelism structures the relationship between lines in Whitman's poetry. However, the principal elements of this "rhythm-producing syntax of the English Bible"—the coordinating structure and the parallel alignment of clauses[137]—are themselves primordially made manifest within the internally parallelistic verse divisions of the poetic books of the English Bible. While Whitman does also martial this same "rhythm-producing

---

134 Allen recognizes (*New Walt Whitman Handbook*, 222) that couplets are not as numerous in Whitman as they are in biblical (Hebrew) poetry. But they are common enough. And in this instance the fact that Whitman eventually combines this couplet into a single line ("I am the poet of the Body and I am the poet of the Soul," *LG* 1891, 45) ramifies the fact of the reinforcing effect.

135 Warren, "Free Growth," 27–42; *Walt Whitman's Language Experiment* (University Park/London: Pennsylvania State University, 1990), esp. ch. 3. The priority of syntax notwithstanding, it is crucial to keep in view the fact that parallelism, whether in the Bible or in Whitman's poetry, always comes entangled with other linguistic elements besides syntax (as Lowth already understood); indeed, its chief rhythmical effects are a consequence of this commingling of different elements, viz. "when syntactic frames are brought into equivalence... the elements filling those frames are brought into alignment as well" (O'Connor, "Parallelism," 877). This represents the core of Hrushovski's insights about "free rhythms" ("On Free Rhythms," 173–90). And in fact Hru shovski explicates Whitman's prosody in these terms in a 1968 article ("The Theory and Practice of Rhythm in the Expressionist Poetry of U. Z. Grinberg," *Hasifrut* 1 [Spring 1968], 176–205 [in Hebrew]). That the article (as well as the latter, related monograph, *The Theory and Practice of Rhythm in the Expressionist Poetry of U. Z. Greenberg* [Tel Aviv: Hakibbutz Hame'uhad, 1978] [in Hebrew]) is in Hebrew no doubt has restricted its use by Whitman scholars. E. Greenspan provides a useful page-long synthesis of pertinent parts of Hrushovski's article in his "Whitman in Israel" (in *Walt Whitman and the World* [eds. G. W. Allen and E. Folsom; Iowa City: University of Iowa, 1995], 386–95, at 393). Allen was skeptical of what he knew about Hrushovski's ideas (*New Walt Whitman Handbook* [1986], xi), though scholarship on free-verse prosody over the last thirty-plus years has demonstrated the fecundity of Hrushovski's ideas on rhythm (for details and relevant literature, see Dobbs-Allsopp, "Free Rhythms" in *On Biblical Poetry*, 95–177).

136 Warren, "Free Growth," 32.

137 Cf. Ibid., 31, 32.

syntax" as a line grouping strategy, as Warren shows, the kernel of what is taken from the "English" Bible by Whitman is most directly on display in the poet's many internally parallel lines with their distinctive duple pulse.[138]

One of Allen's main ambitions in "Biblical Analogies" is to determine "why the rhythms of Whitman have suggested those of the Bible."[139] In this instance, the doubling rhythm that courses through Whitman's many two-part lines appears to be a distinct echo of the bilateral pulse of biblical parallelism's "music of matching," which as Hollander well describes, carried over into English through translation—"One river's water is heard on another's shore; so did this Hebrew verse form carry across into English."[140] Hollander's mimicking exposition is as illuminating of Whitman as it is of the English Bible, for in Hollander we see what Whitman must have been doing as well.

Three-Part Lines

Though biblical verse is dominantly distichic, the triplet is not uncommon, often appearing at structurally or thematically pertinent places—though triplets occasionally form the basic grouping scheme in sections of a poem and even in whole poems (e.g., Ps 93; Job 3:3–10).[141] In the prose translation of the KJB, these triplets are shaped mostly into verse divisions comprised of three distinct parts (Hollander: "One half-line makes an assertion; the other part paraphrases it; sometimes a third part will vary it").[142] For example, consider Job 3:5, first in the lineated translation of the ASV and then in the prose rendering of the KJB:

> Let darkness and the shadow of death claim it for their own;

---

138 Like Allen, Warren, too, misconceives his biblical target; triangulating (and translating) between Hebrew original and English translation is critical for being able to fix on what Whitman owes to the Bible (on this and other matters).
139 "Biblical Analogies," 491.
140 *Rhyme's Reason*, 26.
141 Still larger groupings of lines (esp. the quatrain) appear in the biblical corpus, though not nearly as common as the couplet or triplet. Whitman, too, sometimes composes internally parallel lines consisting of four or more parts (e.g., "The wretched features of ennuyees, the white features of corpses, the livid faces of drunkards, the sick-gray faces of onanists," *LG*, 70).
142 Hollander, *Rhyme's Reason*, 26.

Let a cloud dwell upon it;

Let all that maketh black the day terrify it. (ASV)

Let darkness and the shadow of death stain it; let a cloud dwell upon it; let the blackness of the day terrify it. (KJB)

The three parts of the KJB's prose are marked by the two semicolons and correspond to the component lines of the underlying triplet, which the ASV's lineation makes visible (the language of the KJB and the ASV are otherwise quite close). Sometimes the underlying triplet is not apparent in translation, either because of English syntax or because the translators themselves have misunderstood the underlying line division of the Hebrew. In Ps 128:5 ("The LORD shall bless thee out of Zion: and thou shalt see the good of Jerusalem all the days of thy life") it is only the elongated second half of the verse (fourteen words as opposed to eight in the first half) that betrays the presence of a third poetic line in the underlying Hebrew (= "all the days of thy life"; ASV also misconstrues as a couplet). Whitman's verse also contains many three-part, internally parallel lines:

"A few light kisses.... a few embraces.... a reaching around of arms" (*LG*, 13)

"As God comes a loving bedfellow and sleeps at my side all night and close on the peep of the day" (*LG*, 15)

"I pass death with the dying, and birth with the new-washed babe.... and am not contained between my hat and boots" (*LG*, 17)

"The earth good, and the stars good, and their adjuncts all good" (*LG*, 17)

"The heavy omnibus, the driver with his interrogating thumb, the clank of the shod horses on the granite floor" (*LG*, 18)

"Of the builders and steerers of ships, of the wielders of axes and mauls, of the drivers of horses" (*LG*, 21)

"The floormen are laying the floor—the tinners are tinning the roof—the masons are calling for mortar," (*LG*, 23)

"The coon-seekers go now through the regions of the Red river, or through those drained by the

Tennessee, or through those of the Arkansas" (*LG*, 23)

"Evil propels me, and reform of evil propels me.... I stand indifferent" (*LG*, 28)

"This is the geologist, and this works with the scalpel, and this is a mathematician" (*LG*, 28)

"The mother condemned for a witch and burnt with dry wood, and her children gazing on" (*LG*, 39)

"Each who passes is considered, and each who stops is considered, and not a single one can it fail" (*LG*, 49)

"A show of the summer softness.... a contact of something unseen.... an amour of the light and air" (*LG*, 74)

"There swells and jets his heart.... There all passions and desires . . all reachings and aspirations (*LG*, 81)

"In them and of them natal love.... in them the divine mystery.... the same old

beautiful mystery" (*LG*, 81)

"The rope of the gibbet hangs heavily.... the bullets of princes are flying.... the creatures of power laugh aloud" (*LG*, 88)

"I cannot say to any person what I hear.... I cannot say it to myself.... it is very wonderful" (*LG*, 92)

"Yours is the muscle of life or death.... yours is the perfect science.... in you I have absolute faith" (*LG*, 93)

The three parts of the line are segmented by punctuation (whether traditional or Whitman's more idiosyncratic use of the long dash or suspension points) or a conjunction (usually "and") or a mixture of both. In several instances, the trifold segmentation may be further revealed through decomposition because Whitman forms these longer lines out of combinations of his own earlier, shorter parallel lines: "I pass death with the dying, and birth with the new-washed babe.... and am not contained between my hat and boots" (*LG*, 17) < "For I take my death with the dying/ And my birth with the new-born babes" ("Talbot Wilson"); "The rope of the gibbet hangs heavily.... the bullets of princes are flying.... the creatures of power laugh aloud" (*LG*, 88) < "The rope of the gibbet hangs heavily,/ The bullets of tyrants are flying,/ The creatures of power laugh aloud" ("Resurgemus"). Many of the varieties of parallelism discussed above with regard to Whitman's internally parallel two-part lines appear as well in the examples of three-part lines gathered above: synonymity (*LG*, 17, 21, 23, 28, 49, 74); antithesis (*LG*, 17, 28); gapping (*LG*, 15, 23, 81); incipient narrativity (*LG*, 13, 18, 39, 88). As Lowth notices, a peculiarity of many parallel triplets in the Bible is that only two of the lines "are commonly Synonymous."[143] A typical example is Hos 6:2: "After two days will he revive us: in the third day he will raise us up, and we shall live in his sight." Whitman's tripartite lines also often fall into such patterns, e.g., "Each who passes is considered, and each who stops is considered, and not a single one can it fail" (*LG*, 49); "I cannot say to any person what I hear.... I cannot say it to myself.... it is very wonderful" (*LG*, 92); "Yours is the muscle of life or death.... yours is the perfect science.... in you I have absolute faith" (*LG*, 93). These three-part, internally parallel lines, as with the more common two-part variety, lend Whitman's poetry part of its biblical patina.

A Note on Chronology

Interestingly, two- (and three-) part, internally parallel lines are not as common in the three 1850 poems or in the early notebooks and unpublished poetry manuscripts. There are some, of course. Most spectacular, perhaps, is the initial poetic line from the "notebook that was never included in a published poem: "I am the poet of slaves, and of ^{the} masters of slaves."[144] From "Blood-Money" there is this notable example (with a long dash instead of a conjunction): "The meanest spit in thy face—they smite thee with their palms" (line 25).[145] And in "Resurgemus," a poem where parallelism generally is more prominent, with the exception of the double question near poem's end ("Is the house shut? Is the master away?", line 61), the poem's parallelistic play

---

143 Lowth, *Isaiah*, xv; cf. *Lectures*, II, 42.
144 https://whitmanarchive.org/manuscripts/figures/loc.00141.070.jpg
145 Whitman's close version of Matt 26:15 also falls into a set of two two-part lines:

What will ye give me, and I will deliver this man unto you?

And they make the covenant and pay the pieces of silver. (lines 13–14)

takes place between lines and not within them. It is only when Whitman recasts and combines lines from "Resurgemus" for inclusion in the 1855 *Leaves* (sometime after the "Art and Artists" lecture of March, 1851) that the doubling movement of line-internal parallelism and the two-part line begins in earnest to inform the poem's prosody (see Chapter One). It may be that such lines, like the combining of shorter into longer lines, were mostly produced during the later phase(s) of composition for the 1855 *Leaves*. The "med Cophósis"notebook,[146] one of the earliest, datable, pre-*Leaves* notebooks (with line-breaks; ca. 1852–54), contains an early example of Whitman's combinatory practice in the deletions and additions to two verse lines found there ("It is well—it is ᵇᵘᵗ the gate to a larger lesson—and/ And that to another; still"; with gapping). However, many of the short lines from the early notebooks and poetry manuscripts only combine in the 1855 *Leaves*. Two-part lines with a simple connective are also rare in "Pictures"[147] (e.g., "There is an old Egyptian temple—and again, a Greek temple, of white marble," *NUPM* IV, 1297).[148] By the time of "Clear the way there Jonathan!", which must post-date June 2, 1854 and the return of the fugitive slave Anthony Burns to his Virginia master that the poem satirizes, Whitman is composing with two- and three-part internally parallel lines, e.g., "Way for the President' s marshal! Way for the government cannon!"; "I love to look on the stars and stripes.... I hope the fifes will play Yankee Doodle"; "What troubles you, Yankee phantoms? What is all this chattering of bare gums?"; "See how well-dressed.... see how orderly they conduct themselves "; "I will whisper it to the Mayor.... he shall send a committee to England"; "Dig out King George' s coffin.... unwrap him quick from the graveclothes.... box up his bones for a journey"; "And fetch home the roarers from Congress, and make another procession and guard it with foot and dragoons"; "And clap the skull on top of the ribs, and clap a crown on top of the skull" (*LG*, 89–90).

* * *

---

146 https://whitmanarchive.org/manuscripts/figures/loc.00005.001.jpg
147 https://collections.library.yale.edu/catalog/2007253
148 As Allen observes (*Solitary Singer*, 145), the rhythm in "Pictures" is mostly a prose rhythm "with only a slight hint" of "parallelism." This is consistent with the heavy usage of line-initial "And" in this poem, which is suggestive of biblical prose narrative and not biblical poetry.

Allen's tacit assumption is that Whitman derives his knowledge of parallelism from his reading of the Bible itself. Other mediators of this knowledge are imaginable. James Macpherson and Tupper both used in their verse biblical-styled parallelism influenced directly by the Bible (and likely knowledge of its informing Hebrew prosody in the case of Macpherson). Whitman admired the Ossian poems and was familiar with Tupper's work (see Chapter Three), and thus would have seen how both writers deployed parallelism in their work. Lineated translations of the poetic parts of the Old Testament were available, such as those produced by George R. Noyes.[149] However, only a small percentage of Whitman's parallelistic couplets, for example, are rendered on a scale equivalent to that of an English translation of a biblical couplet, e.g., "I am the poet of the body,/ And I am the poet of the soul." (*LG*, 26).

F. Stovall entertains the possibility that Whitman's knowledge of parallelism was learned from "books and articles on Hebrew poetry."[150] Whitman did read about the Bible generally, especially during his period of intense self-study in the late 1840s and early 1850s (see discussion in Chapter One). Stovall comes to no firm conclusion with regard to Whitman's reading specifically about biblical parallelism. He surveys possible secondary sources which Whitman could have accessed. Of the two premier eighteenth-century discussions, Lowth's *Lectures* and J. G. Herder's *The Spirit of Hebrew Poetry*,[151] Whitman's own aesthetic sensibilities align more naturally with Herder's, and he even references Herder appreciatively late in life: "what Herder taught to the young Goethe, that really great poetry is always (like the Homeric or Biblical canticles) the result of a national spirit, and not the privilege of a polish' d and select few."[152] But neither work is an easy read and I think it doubtful that Whitman, apparently not always the most studious of readers, would have had the patience to wade through either book, let alone distill their essential insights on parallelism—Lowth has been

---

149 E.g., *A New Translation of the Proverbs, Ecclesiastes, and the Canticles* (Boston: James Monroe and Company, 1846). For details, see. F. Stovall, *The Foreground of Leaves of Grass* (Charlottesville: University Press of Virginia, 1974), 187. See Chapter Three above. (Noyes occasionally mentions parallelism in his commentary, but he nowhere explicates its basic mechanics.)

150 *Foreground*, 185–88.

151 (2 vols; trans. J. Marsh; Burlington: Edward Smith, 1833 [1782]).

152 "A Backward Glance o'er Travel'd Roads" in *November Boughs* (Philadelphia: David McKay, 1888), 18; *LG* 1891–92, 438.

as mis-appreciated as appreciated by biblical specialists.[153] Certainly nothing in Whitman's language is suggestive of either author,[154] with perhaps one intriguing exception. Herder, addressing the place of emotions in poetry generally, asks (rhetorically): "And are these [i.e., feelings] not friendly to the parallelism?" He then elaborates with the image of waves:

> So soon as the heart gives way to its emotions, wave follows upon wave, and that is parallelism. The heart is never exhausted, it has forever something new to say. So soon as the first wave has passed away, or broken itself upon the rocks, the second swells again and returns as before. This pulsation of nature, this breathing of emotion, appears in all the language of passion, and would you not have that in poetry, which is most peculiarly the offspring of emotion.[155]

The same image is used by Whitman to describe the movement of his own lines of verse (which are often enough supercharged with emotion): "the [regular] recurrence of lesser and larger waves on the sea-shore, rolling in without intermission, and fitfully rising and falling."[156] That both writers evoke the image of waves is probably a coincidence but tantalizing just the same; it would have been an image that would have appealed to Whitman.

Stovall is unable to tie Whitman to any of the secondary sources he considers. It is more likely that if Whitman was reading about parallelism

---

153 Esp. Dobbs-Allsopp, "Lowth." With respect to the question of Herder's more general influence on Whitman, W. Grünzweig is straightforward: "The widely held assumption that Whitman was closely familiar with Herder' s writings is highly questionable" ("Herder, Johann Gottfried von (1744–1803)" in *Walt Whitman: An Encyclopedia* [eds. J.R. LeMaster and D. D. Kummings; New York/ Oxford: Routledge, 1998], 273). Whitman would have needed to absorb Herder and his ideas through others.

154 Contrast the Oxford educated Gerard Manley Hopkins, for whom parallelism is also important. He knew both Hebrew and Greek and clearly read both Lowth and Herder as he cites them and uses their language and ideas about parallelism (see M. R. Lichtmann, "'Exquisite Artifice': Parallelism in Hopkins' Poetics" in *The Contemplative Poetry of Gerard Manley Hopkins* [Princeton: Princeton University, 1989], 7–60).

155 *Spirit of Hebrew Poetry*, I, 41.

156 Perry, *Walt Whitman*, 207; cf. WWWC, I, 414–15. In a clipping from 1849, Whitman underscores a characterization of verse with this very image: "A discourse in verse resembles a billowy sea. The verses are the waves that rise and fall—to our apprehension—each by impulse, life, will of its own. *All is free*" (*WWA*). Hrushovski uses the same image ("wave after wave") to describe the rhythm of Whitman's lines (as reported in Greenspan, "Whitman in Israel," 393).

in biblical poetry, it would be from more popular, second-hand accounts, such as that recounting of F. de Sola Mendes' views on biblical Hebrew poetry that Whitman cites in the "Bible as Poetry" essay,[157] or perhaps from a "theological dictionary." Some of the latter have quite extensive entries on biblical Hebrew poetry, including descriptions (to varying degrees) of parallelism.[158] In a like vein, Engell observes that "even if Whitman never read Lowth directly," he will have likely read Hugh Blair's "hugely popular" *Lectures on Rhetoric and Belles Lettres* (1783), which includes an extended summary of Lowth's *Lectures*. This is an intriguing suggestion.[159] Blair shows up in Whitman's notetaking, but Whitman knows him most directly through his "Critical Dissertation" on the Ossian poems that was included in the volume of the latter that Whitman owned (and annotated).[160] Blair's discussion of the Ossian poems is shaped by Lowth's ideas generally, and he even cites the *Praelectiones* explicitly in a passing reference,[161] but he nowhere in that discussion explicates Lowth's ideas about parallelism, even though the trope features prominently in Macpherson's renderings. In Blair's "The Poetry of the Hebrews" the treatment of parallelism comes near the beginning of the discussion:

> The general construction of the Hebrew poetry... consists in dividing every period into correspondent, for the most part into equal members, which answer to one another, both in senseandsound. In the first member of the period a sentiment is expressed; and in the second member,

---

157 *The Critic* 3 (February 3, 1883), 57. The pasted-in clippings with the language attributed to de Sola Mendes in Whitman's original manuscript, https://www.lib. uchicago.edu/e/scrc/findingaids/view.php?eadid=ICU.SPCL.MS263.

158 E.g., R. Watson, *A Biblical and Theological Dictionary* (rev. Am. ed; New York: Lane and Scott, 1851 [1832]), 757–60; Cf. *Calmet's Dictionary of the Holy Bible* (eds. C. Taylor; E. Robinson; Rev. American ed; Boston: Crocker and Brewster, 1832), 751–54; W. Smith, *A Dictionary of the Bible* (Boston: Little, Brown, and Company, 1860), II, 893–902.

159 Engell, "Robert Lowth," 124; cf. "Other Classic," loc. 7594. A. C. Higgins is less adamant about Whitman's direct reading of Blair (and others): "As a school teacher and an aficionado of oratory, Whitman was familiar, at least indirectly, with the rhetorics of Hugh Blair and George Campbell, if not Richard Whately" ("Art and Argument: The Rise of Walt Whitman's Rhetorical Poetics, 1838–1855" [unpubl. PhD diss. University of Massachusetts Amherst, 1999], 236).

160 *CW* IX, 224; *NUPM* VI, 1140. Blair's "Critical Dissertation" appears on pp. 63–122 of James Macpherson, *The Poems of Ossian* (Philadelphia: Thomas, Cowperthwait & Co., 1839). For further discussion of this volume, see Chapter Three.

161 Macpherson, *Poems of Ossian*, 114.

the same sentiment is amplified, or is repeated in different terms, or sometimes contrasted with its opposite but in such a manner that the same structure, and nearly the same number of words, is preserved.[162]

The description is concise and straightforward, certainly easily consumable by Whitman if he saw it. However, "parallelism" is not named as such, though the phrasing as a whole leans heavily on Lowth. These latter are significant because I have not found Whitman writing specifically about "parallelism" or using anything like the language used here by Blair (*cum* Lowth). Of course, Whitman absorbs many ideas that originated with Lowth and/or Blair indirectly—for example, from Wordsworth or Emerson (e.g., the poet-prophet conceit, the equality of prose and poetry, the valuing of unrhymed and unmetered verse).[163] Perhaps the idea of parallelism is another such indirect inheritance, though so far undocumented. Or maybe Whitman's parallelistic practice is itself the practical application of what he read about parallelism, whether directly or indirectly. In the end, it is not impossible that Whitman did read about parallelism at some point. Nonetheless, his poetry itself, especially in his shaping of so many two- and three-part internally parallel lines, makes clear the importance of the English Bible (and its imitators) as one source for this knowledge.

Whitman's Parallelism

I now shift to consider (impressionistically) some of the ways in which Whitman develops his use of parallelism beyond the models the Bible (or his reading about the Bible) provided him. Whitman's practice of collage normally involves taking what he finds (here the readymade trope of parallelism) and making it his own, shaping and molding it to

---

162 *Lectures on Rhetoric and Belles Lettres* (London: Thomas Tegg, 1841 [1783]), 559.
163 For the Wordsworth connections, see Stovall, *Foreground*, 238–39, 266; R. D. Weisbuch, *Atlantic Double-Cross: American Literature and British Influence in the Age of Emerson* (Chicago: University of Chicago, 1986); R. Garvil, "A Discharged Soldier and a Runaway Slave" in *Romantic Dialogues: Anglo-American Continuities, 1776–1862* (2d rev. ed.; Penrityh: Humanities-Enools, 2015 [2000]), 283–314 (Google Play). Emerson's influence on Whitman is well documented (e.g., Stovall, *Foreground*, 282–305). Interestingly, Emerson read Lowth and Blair while at Harvard and both were impactful for Emerson's development as a thinker, see R. D. Richardson, *Emerson: The Mind on Fire* (Berkeley: University of California, 1995), 11–14.

suit his own language and to serve his larger poetic ends. Parallelism is no different. If the Bible was one source of inspiration for the use of parallelism in *Leaves*, and if there exist aspects of this use (such as the internally parallel, two-part lines) especially evocative of this source, it is also the case that there is much in Whitman's parallelistic practice that is un-biblical. Once finding the trope Whitman molds it into forms that are his own and not the Bible's. He is definitely not content to replicate forms of biblical poetry.[164]

To begin with, the biblical poetic tradition was rooted in a dominantly oral and aural world. Even when biblical poems began to be written down or composed initially in writing they still (mostly) were posed for oral performance, and thus remained beholden to the enabling technologies of oral verbal art.[165] Most distinctive, perhaps, is the lineal palette upon which parallelism enacts its art: the lines tend to be short, symmetrical and balanced, and mostly end-stopped or self-contained, and they come in limited runs, mostly of twos and threes (and sometimes more). Whitman was not so confined. His is a distinctly writerly art destined for the printed page and desirous of readers—"read these leaves in the open air every season of every year of your life" (*LG*, vi). This is not to say that Whitman did not write for the ear but to emphasize that his poetry could not exist without "the cold types and cylinder and wet paper" (*LG*, 57). In Whitman parallelism plays across a lineal palette very different from that of the (Hebrew) Bible. Whitman's lines are long, most too long for aural intake without the aid of writing. And while parallelism in Whitman does operate within couplets, triplets, and quatrains,[166] like in the Bible, such runs are not so numerous and at any rate are not basic to Whitman's prosody. His poetry is fundamentally stichic (the "single line is by necessity the stylistic unit"[167]), while that of the Bible is dominantly distichic. And occasionally Whitman's runs

---

164 Warren, "Free Growth," 32.

165 For details (with comparative literature cited throughout), see Dobbs-Allsopp, *On Biblical Poetry*, 233–325.

166 In fact, as Warren emphasizes, Whitman's parallelism most often works "in sequences of two, three, or four lines" ("Free Growth," 32), though these need not be set off as couplets, triplets, or quatrains (cf. Hrushovski as cited in Greenspan, "Whitman in Israel," 393).

167 Allen, *New Walt Whitman Handbook*, 218; cf. Warren, "Free Growth," 30.

of parallel lines can number into the forties, fifties, and higher,[168] which never occurs in the Bible. Also the shapes of his lines, internally and as grouped, are often marked by asymmetries and a lack of balance, e.g., "Not one is dissatisfied.... not one is demented with the mania of owning things" (*LG*, 34); "I loafe and invite my soul,/ I lean and loafe at my ease.... observing a spear of summer grass" (*LG*, 13); "Loafe with me on the grass.... loose the stop from your throat,/ Not words, not music or rhyme I want.... not custom or lecture, not even the best,/ Only the lull I like, the hum of your valved voice" (*LG*, 15). Such shapes and lengths (and others like them) are a commonplace in the 1855 *Leaves* but are unattested in the corpus of biblical Hebrew poetry. And even when symmetry prevails in Whitman it is usually at a scale much too expansive for a set of (translated) biblical Hebrew poetic lines, e.g., "I visit the orchards of God and look at the spheric product,/ And look at quintillions ripened, and look at quintillions green" (*LG*, 38). There are also other signs unrelated to parallelism that Whitman's poetry anticipates readers, such as the fact that his longer runs of lines and catalogues, like his couplets and triplets, are most often punctuated as single sentences, something only a *reader* of the written word on a page can track. In short, then, having found the trope of parallelism in the Bible (if that is what he did) where it is optimized for oral performance, Whitman adapts it to a print medium and for a writerly (readerly) art.

The main focus of Allen's evaluation of parallelism in Whitman is as an interlinear device, taking his cue ultimately (if indirectly) from Lowth's notion of *parallelismus membrorum*. However, as indicated above, the readiest place to assess Whitman's biblical debt with regard to parallelism is line-internally, given the place of the KJB in Whitman's world and that that translation is a prose translation with no distinctive formatting for verse. This is not to say that there was no biblical influence at the interlinear level. There was, as Allen maintains—"no one can doubt the parallelism of the synonymous form."[169] Many of the dynamics of biblical parallelism (e.g., synonymity, antithesis, gapping) noted above as characteristic of Whitman's internally parallel lines

---

168 Allen notes "strophes" with as many as sixty-two synonymously (and/or syntactically) parallel lines, "Biblical Analogies," 495.
169 "Biblical Analogies," 493.

prevail as well interlinearly between lines.[170] Yet Whitman's interlinear parallelism is also equally of his own making, a development beyond his most prominent biblical model, the KJB. Assuming the starting point for Whitman was the internally parallel verse divisions of the KJB, then Whitman's part is substantial, enlarging the dynamics of parallelism in his poetry to include interlinear relations. Yet even if Whitman received an assist from seeing lineated verse translations of Old Testament poetry, such as those of Noyes, or from reading about biblical poetry more generally, Whitman's contribution remains remarkable. He still will have adjusted the scale and evolved his own sensibilities about grouping strategies. And of course the language material itself throughout is mostly his own. Illustrative is this early set of lines from "Blood-Money" with its imagery so obviously elaborated from the passion narrative in Matthew 26–27:

> Bruised, bloody, and pinioned is thy body,
>
> More sorrowful than death is thy soul. (lines 26–27)

Here two verbal predications with the verb "to be" are juxtaposed appositionally. Semantically, the concrete images of a battered and beaten body in the first line are reformulated more abstractly in the second— perhaps reflecting the more (physically) diffuse nature of the concept of the soul. The parallelism holds together the putatively antithetical ideas of the body and the soul, a perspective which occasionally finds its way into the KJB (e.g., Isa 10:18; 51:23; Matt 10:28; 1 Thess 5:23). Isa 51:23, in the KJB's somewhat butchered rendering, is of note as it imagines the words of Israel's tormentors in ways that anticipate both the gospel story and Whitman's lines: "But I will put it into the hand of them that afflict thee; which have said to thy soul, Bow down, that we may go over: and thou hast laid thy body as the ground, and as the street, to them that went over." Regardless, I choose these lines from "Blood-Money" because they antedate the period when Whitman with regularity starts shaping his language into internally parallel lineal units, and thus showing off the poet's capacity to take the idea of parallelism, which is

---

170 This may be affirmed on the strength of the examples from Whitman's poetry cited by Allen in "Biblical Analogies" alone, even though not all of those examples are as perspicuous as might be desired and despite the infelicities that mar Allen's thinking in places.

presented quite differently in the KJB, and to adapt it as an interlinear linking device. Many such examples, of course, populate the 1855 *Leaves*.

And it is not just the fact of interlinearly parallel lines but also the runs of such lines, especially as manifested in Whitman's many catalogues. These runs (usually with a generous interweaving of word and phrase repetition)[171] commonly come in sets of twos, threes, and fours but can occur in much larger counts as well. The profile of biblical parallelism is wholly different. In the (Hebrew) Bible parallelism (of whatever type) is mostly confined to the individual couplet or triplet (with some occasional larger groupings), only rarely carrying beyond these grouping boundaries. Moreover, very few biblical poems are made up entirely of parallelistic groupings (e.g., Psalm 114), and where there is parallelism, the patterns change from couplet to couplet and triplet to triplet. This is to emphasize that like the fact of interlinear parallelism itself (not visible as such in the KJB) the nature of its deployment in *Leaves* is of Whitman's own making. Allen early on recognized the basic dynamic at work here. He associates it with Whitman's catalogues, which he thinks are "probably outgrowths of synonymous parallelism."[172] Although I prefer to understand Whitman's internally parallel lines as primordial, Allen identifies the dynamic of transposing the trope (broader, too, than synonymity) from one domain to another. Vendler describes succinctly the network of parallelistic play that results: "The basic molecule of Whitmanian chemistry," she writes, is the semantic or syntactic parallel. The smallest parallels in Whitman come two to a line: "I celebrate myself, and sing myself." When the parallels grow more complex, each requires a whole line, and we come near to the psalmic parallel, so often imitated by Whitman, in which the second verse adds something to the substance of the first. But when parallels grow too large for a single line or a couplet, they begin to require at least a stanza apiece, generating the essentially binary poem of reprise, in which the second half redoes—but in an altered fashion—the first.[173]

---

171 A. M. Wiley, "Reiterative Devices in 'Leaves of Grass,'" *American Literature* 1/2 (1929), 161–70; cf. Warren, "Free Growth," 31–32.

172 Allen, "Biblical Analogies," 497; cf. Warren, "Free Growth," 31 ("the catalogues he generates from syntactic parallelism").

173 *Poets Thinking*, 38. Incidentally, the "psalmic parallel" she must have in mind here is that which is manifested in the KJB's verse divisions.

Further, Allen reasons that the problem in differentiating the various forms of parallelism in Whitman's poetry shows that Whitman uses parallelism in a far more thoroughgoing way than does the Bible—"the rhythm of *Leaves of Grass* is more parallelistic than biblical rhythm."[174] Although the logic here seems strained to me, the final observation is very much on mark, and thus yet a further indicator of how Whitman transforms his biblical model—he uses parallelism more and at more diverse structural levels. G. Kinnell's contention that Whitman is "the greatest virtuoso of parallel structure in English poetry" may be extended to include the poetry of the English Bible.[175]

Finally, Whitman adapts the Bible's Hebraic-infused paradigm for parallelism to fit the linguistic infrastructure of English. Tyndale and the KJB translators (among others) already began this process. Because Whitman's parallelism involves his own language material and is not restricted to renderings of an underlying Hebrew original, the accommodations made to English style, lexicon, syntax, and more are noticeable, especially from a comparative perspective. Some examples by way of illustration. Biblical Hebrew does not have a singular preposition that is equivalent to the English "of," and genitive relations are mainly expressed through an adnominal construction called a "construct chain" (see discussion in Chapter Five). As a consequence, the kind of gapping with "of" (especially in genitive constructions) that Whitman often employs (e.g., "Voices of the diseased and despairing, and of thieves and dwarfs," *LG*, 29) is rare (if non-existent) in English translations of biblical poetry. This is a relatively minor detail but quite telling nonetheless, a small bit of difference that points up how Whitman engineers parallelism to suit his own language experiment. And gapping more broadly in Whitman almost always abides by the norms of English word order constraints (dominantly SVO). Again, this results in a noticeably different look than in the biblical English of the KJB. As noted earlier, for example, the subject position is gapped far more extensively in *Leaves* (esp. Whitman's "I") than in the Bible, where verb gapping dominates.

---

174 "Biblical Analogies," 493.
175 "'Strong is Your Hold': My Encounters with Whitman" in *Leaves of Grass: The Sesquicentennial Essays* (ed. S. Belesco et al; Lincoln: University of Nebraska, 2007), 417–28.

English word order norms also inform the sentential structures Whitman gives to his catalogues (and other groupings of runs of contiguous lines). Typically, these feature an end-stopped line, which can form a syntactic parallel with any number of succeeding lines, though groupings of twos, threes, and fours are most common.[176] The line is usually clausal or phrasal in nature and forms a sub-part of Whitman's long, ambling sentences. J. Longenbach describes what he calls a "parsing line" as a line, though not end-stopped, that nonetheless generally follows "the normative turns of the syntax, breaking it at predictable points rather than cutting against it."[177] This results in an additive (or supplementary) kind of syntax where main clauses are expanded in typical ways. The same kind of parsing action occurs in Whitman's catalogues, though it is managed in end-stopped chunks; that is, Whitman's line (in these instances) is an end-stopped *but* parsing line. The sentential logic holding the catalogues together is mapped and made manifest across the surface of the catalogue as a whole, one end-stopped line reiterating or extending (by normal syntactic means) the sentential logic of the preceding line. These groupings are (often) appositively structured, to use R. Holmstedt's idea.[178] Here is a characteristic example from "Crossing Brooklyn Ferry" (*LG* 1860, 381–82):

[8]I too saw the reflection of the summer sky in the water,

Had my eyes dazzled by the shimmering track of beams,

Looked at the fine centrifugal spokes of light round the shape of my head in the sun-lit water,

Looked on the haze on the hills southward and southwestward,

Looked on the vapor as it flew in fleeces tinged with violet,

Looked toward the lower bay to notice the arriving ships,

Saw their approach, saw aboard those that were near me,

Saw the white sails of schooners and sloops, saw the ships at anchor,

---

176 Warren, "Free Growth," 32.

177 *The Art of the Poetic Line* (St. Paul: Graywolf, 2008), 55.

178 "Hebrew Poetry and the Appositive Style: Parallelism, *Requiescat in pacem*," *Vetus Testamentum* (2019), 1–32.

The sailors at work in the rigging, or out astride the spars,

The round masts, the swinging motion of the hulls, the slender
    serpentine pennants,

The large and small steamers in motion, the pilots in their pilot-houses,

The white wake left by the passage, the quick tremulous whirl of the
    wheels,

The flags of all nations, the falling of them at sun-set,

The scallop-edged waves in the twilight, the ladled cups, the frolicsome
    crests and glistening,

The stretch afar growing dimmer and dimmer, the gray walls of the
    granite store-houses by the docks,

On the river the shadowy group, the big steam-tug closely flanked on
    each side by the barges—the

    hay-boat, the belated lighter,

On the neighboring shore, the fires from the foundry chimneys burning
    high and glaringly into the night,

Casting, their flicker of black, contrasted with wild red and yellow light,
    over the tops of houses, and down into the clefts of streets.

The opening line, "I too saw the reflection of the summer sky in the water," provides in miniature the base sentential structure of the short catalogue: Subject + Verb + Object + Adjuncts (Prepositional Phrase, Gerund). Intriguingly, this section of the poem appears essentially the same in the earlier "Sun-Down Poem" (*LG* 1856, 213–15), except that the first line there is punctuated as its own separate sentence, as if underscoring its function as syntactic model for the lines that follow. The subject, "I," is given only the one time in the opening line[179] and then is gapped in the next seven lines. All of the latter begin with a verb of seeing in the past tense: "Had my eyes dazzled," "Looked" (4x), and "Saw" (2x). The anaphora helps to hold the group of appositionally related verbal lines together as the speaker relates what the "I" sees on the river at sundown. Having focused in on the

---

179 The verbal phrase "I too saw" picks up on the fourfold repetition of the phrase "I
    watched/saw" in the immediately preceding section (7). The scene in section 8 has
    shifted to summer.

arriving ships, the two "Saw" lines, each containing two appositive verbal clauses ("saw" is repeated four times), concentrate the viewer's attention. Next follow seven lines each headed by the definite article ("The") and containing a nominal phrase (and often multiple nominal phrases related appositionally) that functions syntactically as the object of the verbs of seeing (explicitly "saw," since when used transitively it requires a direct object) that are now gapped along with the subject "I." The absence of verbs renders the resulting portrait slightly less dynamic, more focused as the observer concentrates on the ships, the sailors on board, the flags, the wake glistening in the last rays of light as the sun sets. Yet the stacking of object phrase after object phrase in apposition, each moving on to describe a different aspect of what is viewed makes up for some of the absence of explicitly verbalized action—the "eyes" of the "I" continue to be "dazzled" by what they take in. The two preposition-headed lines ("On the river" and "On the neighboring shore") echo the prepositional phrase at the ending of the section's first line ("in the water"), and thus intimate the section's impending close. This closural force is supported by the imagery—the light growing "dimmer and dimmer" as the last "wild red and yellow light" fleas over the housetops as night settles in—and by the gerund-fronted ("Casting") final line, which is the only line that falls outside of the strict syntax modeled in the first line, a form of terminal modification. Even here the additional adjunctive phrasal unit adds onto the main clausal unit in a way that is completely natural for English— so from section 7, "I saw them high in the air, floating with motionless wings, oscillating their bodies" (*LG* 1860, 382).

In this way, then, the sentential structure of the catalogue is facilitated by interlinear parallelism and its appositional deployment. The parallel line groups parse the sentential whole:

"I...,"

"Had my eyes dazzled...,"

"Looked...," (4x)

"Saw...," (2x)

"The" + NP (with attendant adjuncts and modifiers)..., (7x)

"On" + object phrase..., (2x)

"Casting...."

English and Hebrew are alike in their dependence on word order given the erosion of inflectional morphology in both languages, but the word order preferences differ and this is consequential for the patterns of parallelism that prevail. Whitman's favoring of a base SVO word order is not monolithic nor exceptionless. Locally, for example, he enjoys inverted syntactic structures such as his occasional chiastic shaped lines (e.g., "And these one and all tend inward to me, and I tend outward to them," *LG*, 23). And even his larger grouping patterns can partake in more convoluted syntactic structures, as Snodgrass notices.[180] The first poem in the "Enfans d'Adam" cluster is exemplary. The poem is composed of one sentence in eleven lines and the subject and main verb are withheld until the eighth line ("Existing, I peer and penetrate still," *LG* 1860, 287).[181]

A last observation may be offered about Whitman's penchant for word and phrase repetition (anaphora and the like) in his poetry. Lexical repetition (in particular) features prominently enough in the verbal art of the (Hebrew) Bible, as M. Buber famously noted.[182] But the patterns in Whitman's poetry are noticeably different. Among the several ends to which Whitman's iterative style may be disposed is supporting the syntactic core of his parallelisms. The need for such extra support follows from several factors. On the one hand, English features many irregular verbs and its inflectional morphology more generally has been severely eroded; on the other hand, Whitman, especially in the early editions of *Leaves*, favors an expansive lineal palette. As a consequence, syntax in English is more subtle in its outward appearance, especially in more expansive stretches. The syntactic frames at the core of Whitman's parallelism, shorn of their usual accompanying verbal repetitions would appear slight, less perceptible to readers. Contrast the comparable syntactic cores in biblical Hebrew poetic parallelism where verb morphology is still robustly inflected, the triconsonantal root system (for nouns and verbs) remains productive, and the poetic lines themselves are comparatively short. Here the likeness (or not) of

---

180 *Sound Like Yourself,* 153–57.

181 Ibid., 154.

182 "*Leitwort* Style in Pentateuch Narrative," in M. Buber and F. Rosenzweig, *Scripture and Translation* (trans. L. Rosenwald and E. Fox; Bloomington: Indiana University, 1994), 114–28 (the selection is excerpted from a larger lecture entitled "The Bible as Storyteller" that Buber delivered in 1927).

the adjacent syntactic frames is most conspicuous. Whitman's word and phrasal repetitions are executed to many ends, but they are crucial adaptations that enable the syntactic frames that anchor Whitman's parallelistic play to prevail in modern English.

* * *

The latter observations are only initial glimpses at some of the directions Whitman begins to evolve the play of parallelism in his poetry beyond what he found in the Bible. That the English Bible—and its many imitators—was one source from which Whitman collaged the trope seems assured. A conspicuous indicator of this particular genealogy is Whitman's favorite line type, a two-part, internally parallel line in which the second clause is headed by a simple conjunction, usually "and." The KJB's prose rendering of parallelistic couplets in the poetic books of the Old Testament has just this shape—the original Hebrew line division is leveled and the whole is formed into a single, two-part, end-stopped verse (usually with "and" joining the two parts). Allen's original insight about the prevalence of internally parallel lines in Whitman remains keen. Equally true, however, is that Whitman does not confine himself to biblically-styled parallelism (so Warren). He evolves his parallelistic play to suit his decidedly writerly art, his linguistic medium (English), and his political ambitions. As a result Whitman becomes what Kinnell proclaims him to be, "the greatest virtuoso of parallel structure in English poetry."

5. "The Divine Style": An American Prose Style Poeticized

Also no ornaments… perfect transparent clearness sanity and health

are wanted—that is the divine style—O if it can be attained—
— Walt Whitman, "In future Leaves of Grass"

In an incisive study, *Pen of Iron: American Prose and the King James Bible*,[1] R. Alter argues for the existence of an "American prose style" among major American novelists from the nineteenth through the twenty-first centuries (including Melville, Bellow, Faulkner, Hemingway, McCarthy, Robinson) that descends from the King James Bible. For Alter, style has aesthetic values and intimates a vision of reality yet also has material, linguistic manifestations. In the style that descends from the KJB, these latter include parallelism, diction and phrasing, syntactic frames, distinctive rhythms or cadences, as well as an assorted use of biblical themes, characters, imagery, and imitations. Whitman wrote lots of prose over the course of his lifetime, including some fiction, but it was as the poet of *Leaves of Grass* that he obtained real achievement as a writer. Understandably, then, Whitman does not figure in Alter's study. And yet there are ways, I want to suggest, that the style of Whitman's poetry (especially in the early editions of *Leaves*) equally descends from the prose of the KJB and shares a broad kinship with the American prose style charted by Alter, albeit in a nonnarrative mode and with a decidedly political bent—the English prose style of the Bible poeticized and politicized. For my larger thesis, recognizing the strong stylistic affinities Whitman's poetry shares with aspects of many of the novels

---

1   Robert Alter, *Pen of Iron: American Prose and the King James Bible* (Princeton: Princeton University, 2010).

©2024 F. W. Dobbs-Allsopp, CC BY-NC 4.0   https://doi.org/10.11647/OBP.0357.06

studied by Alter offers another means by which to tease out further dimensions of Whitman's debt to the KJB. And since a number of this style's leading material characteristics (e.g., parallelism) are touched on in previous chapters, viewing Whitman heuristically through Alter's lens of an American prose style provides a convenient way to reprise some of the leading features of my own argument. It also has the added benefit of confirming many of Alter's insights, not least because of the refraction the style is given in a nonnarrative mode. Lastly, the prominence of the style's prosaic bent is important for understanding both the development of Whitman's style and why he succeeds with it. Whitman mostly wrote and read prose in the run-up to the 1855 *Leaves*. It is only once he fashions a line capacious enough to accommodate his own distinctly prosaic talents and tendencies and deploys it (somewhat perversely) towards nonnarrative ends that Whitman achieves success— Chapter 19 in Whitman's novella, "Jack Engle" (from 1852),[2] offers a fabulous prosaic foretaste of this style to come. The biblical prose style poeticized was necessary for Whitman to become the poet of *Leaves of Grass*. William Tyndale (d. 1536) features prominently in my discussion as it is his commitment to plain and simple diction, clarity and accuracy, and staying close to the Hebrew and Greek originals while ultimately making sense in English that sets the norm for all succeeding English translations of the Bible, including the KJB. Whitman's self-denominated "divine style" is a rightful heir to the biblical English prose style divinely inaugurated by Tyndale.

"Plate-glassy style"

Whitman's determination to "make no mention or allusion" to classic sources like the Bible in his poetry, except "as they relate to the new, present things," was in service to the aesthetic sensibility he was evolving in the 1850s that prized above all "a perfectly transparent plate-glassy style," as he puts it in the "Rules for Composition":[3]

---

2   "Life and Adventures of Jack Engle: An Auto-Biography," *WWQR* 34/3 (2017), 262–357 (edited by Z. Turpin with an "Introduction," pp. 225–61; originally published anonymously by Whitman in six installments from March 14 to April 18, 1852 in the Manhattan newspaper, the *Sunday Dispatch*).

3   https://whitmanarchive.org/manuscripts/figures/2095_010.jpg

A perfectly transparent, plate-glassy style, artless, with no ornaments, or attempts at ornaments, for their own sake,—~they only ~~coming in where answering~~ looking well when ~~and~~ like the beauties of the person or character, by nature and intuition, ~~and~~ never lugged ⁱⁿ [illeg.] ~~in by the colla~~ to show off, which ~~founders~~ nullifies the best of them, no matter ~~under~~ when and where, ~~or under ᵒᶠ the most favorable cases.~~

....

Too much attempt at ornament is the blur upon nearly all literary styles.

Clearness, simplicity, no twistified or foggy sentences, at all—the most translucid clearness without variation.—[4]

That is, quotations of or allusion to the Bible—and "~~Mention not God at all~~" (i.e., the God of the Bible, with a capital "G")—are among the "ornaments" that Whitman judges to be a "blur upon nearly all literary styles." Also jettisoned are the many "thee"s and "thy"s and "lo"s that mark the biblical text (and its imitators, such as Martin Farquhar Tupper). And Whitman writes in a register he means to be broadly accessible— literally, democratic—and even when he is intentionally obscure ("Do I contradict myself? / Very well then.... I contradict myself," *LG*, 55) or his larger structures are at their most ambling and undulating ("the free growth of metrical laws and bud from them as unerringly and loosely as lilacs or roses on a bush," *LG*, v), his language at the lineal and sub-lineal levels remains mostly simple and clear—"I lean and loafe at my ease.... observing a spear of summer grass" (*LG*, 13). "The art of art, the glory of expression and the sunshine of the light of letters," Whitman writes in the 1855 Preface, "is simplicity" (*LG*, vi). His lines, though often long, are unfailingly end-stopped and (mostly) contain "no twistified or foggy sentences." However much this aspiration toward "clearness" and "simplicity" of style suited Whitman's temperament as a writer, he also worked hard to achieve it, as his many doings and redoings in his notebooks and poetry manuscripts amply attest. He encountered similar appreciations in the reading he did from 1845 to 1852, especially from 1848 on as his reading turned more exclusively to focus on poetry

---

4   Cf. *NUMP*, 56 ("Be simple and clear"), 132–33, 385 ("In future <u>Leaves of Grass</u>," cited as the chapter's epigraph; the manuscript is currently missing); *DBN* III, 376; *LG*, 14;.

and literature.[5] For example, in a review essay by A. De Vere in the *Edinburgh Review* from 1849, clipped and annotated by Whitman, the author's admiration for plain style is echoed by a marginal note from Whitman: "The substance is always wanted perfect—after that attend to costumes—but mind, attend to costumes."[6] Perhaps one of Whitman's earliest bits of advice to himself about style comes in an annotation to a clipping on Ossian from an article by M. Fuller from 1846.[7] After an admiring gloss on Ossian ("Ossian must not be despised"), Whitman writes more critically: "How misty, how windy, how full of diffused, only half-meaning words! —How curious a study!—(Don't fall into the Ossianic, by any chance.)." These comments are followed immediately by Whitman's query about the Ossian poems' (possible) relationship to "Biblical poetry" and his exaltation of the greatness and originality of the latter (as discussed in Chapter One). The connection between the style of the "Hebrew poems" and the style of the Ossian poems is at best implicit or subconscious, viz. the style of Ossian provoking in Whitman, first, an exhortation about his own manner of writing and, second, a reflection on the "tremendous figures and ideas of the Hebrew Poems." And yet the availability of this stylistic plainness in English is due in large part to the KJB and to the genius of William Tyndale.

Alter identifies two "great sources of stylistic counterpoint" in English, which derive respectively "from the Greco-Latin and the Anglo-Saxon components of the language."[8] The former, historically, is erudite, ornate, featuring polysyllabic words and subordinating syntax; while the latter, as Alter well describes, is "phonetically compact, often monosyllabic,

---

5   F. Stovall, *The Foreground of Leaves of Grass* (Charlottesville: University Press of Virginia, 1974), 145–49, 265–81.

6   Stovall, *Foreground*, 274–76 (quotation from p. 276). To the same end: "Of ornaments to a work nothing outre can be allowed . . but those ornaments can be allowed that conform to the perfect facts of the open air and that flow out of the nature of the work and come irrepressibly from it and are necessary to the completion of the work. Most works are most beautiful without ornament" (*LG*, ix). William Wordsworth in his own famous "Preface" to the *Lyrical Ballads* (1798, 1802) speaks of "the Poet" and advocates for a poetry "in the real language of men" and may be another mediating influence on Whitman in the Lowthian (and biblical) line.

7   "Things and Thoughts on Europe. No. V," *New York Tribune* (30 September 1846). "An Ossian P aragraph," https://whitmanarchive.org/manuscripts/marginalia/annotations/mid.00016.html. Cf. Stovall, *Foreground*, 115–17.

8   *Pen of Iron*, 34.

broadly associated with everyday speech, and usually concrete."[9] It is this latter, plain style that "by and large" pervades the KJB. And though Alter is not wrong to emphasize that "the counterpointing" of the two styles has been a possibility in "English prose since the seventeenth century"[10]—in no small part because of the wild popularity the KJB eventually obtains (especially in the nineteenth century)—in fact it is only a possibility because of Tyndale.[11] The KJB, originally conceived as "a new translation of the Bible,"[12] evolved in the end as a revision of the preceding English translations of the sixteenth century, with a 1602 edition of the Bishops' Bible (first published in 1568) serving as the base text for King James' translators.[13] Among the rules Richard Bancroft set as guidelines for the translators is the fourteenth, listing the main versions to be consulted besides the Bishops' Bible: "These translations to be used, when they agree better with the text than the Bishops' Bible, *viz.*: Tyndale's, Matthew's, Coverdale's, Whitchurch's [Great], Geneva."[14] Tyndale's inclusion in the list is both tragically ironic, he was martyred because of his translations, and strictly unnecessary, since his translations formed the foundation for all of the others, including the Bishops' Bible—and (as it turned out) the KJB. With regard to the latter the statistical data alone are telling: in the New Testament, 83% of the language is Tyndale's; and in the Old Testament where he translated (Pentateuch, Former Prophets, Jonah, and other selected passages used in the daily liturgy) Tyndale is responsible for 76% of the language used

---

9   Ibid., 34–35.

10   Ibid., 35.

11   Esp. D. Daniell, *The Bible in English: Its History and Influence* (New Haven: Yale University, 2003), 248–54.

12   W. Barlow, *The Sum and Substance of the Conference… at Hampton Court* (London, 1604), 45; cf. D. Norton, *The King James Bible: A Short History from Tyndale to Today* (Cambridge: Cambridge University, 2011), 83.

13   For details, see D. Norton, *A History of the Bible as Literature* (Cambridge: Cambridge University, 1993), I, 139–61; *A History of the English Bible as Literature* (Cambridge: Cambridge University, 2004), 56–75; *King James Bible*, esp. 81–110; Daniell, *Bible in English*, 427–50; A. McGrath, *In the Beginning: The Story of the King James Bible and How It Changed a Nation, a Language, and a Culture* (New York: Random House. 2001).

14   Norton, *King James Bible*, 86. Norton bases his modernized spelling version on MS Add. 28721 [fol. 24ʳ], one of the three surviving manuscripts in the British Library that give the instructions.

by the KJB translators.[15] The plain style that Alter associates with the KJB is largely the creation of Tyndale.

Tyndale, the first to translate from the original Hebrew, Greek, and Aramaic of the Bible into English,[16] followed Luther's lead in translating the New Testament first. A first complete edition of the latter in English appeared in 1526.[17] Upon turning his attention to the Old Testament, Tyndale discovered a linguistic congeniality between Hebrew and English:

> And the properties of the Hebrue tonge agreeth a thousande tymes moare with the englysh then with the Latyn. The maner of speaking is both one, so that in a thousande places thou neadest not but to translat it in to the englysh worde for worde when thou must seke a compase in the latyne & yet shalt haue moch worke to translate it welfauerdly, so that it haue the same grace & swetnesse sence and pure understandinge with it in the latyne as it hath in the Hebrue. A thousande partes better maye it be translated into the english then into the latyne.[18]

These observations come from Tyndale's polemical treatise, *Observations of a Christian Man* (1528), in which, among other matters, Tyndale is making a case for translating the Bible into English.[19] Tyndale here is calling attention to the fact that the syntax of both English and biblical Hebrew mostly unwinds additively in what are known as branching patterns.[20] In such patterns, as E. B. Voigt describes (for English), "modification follows in close proximity to what is modified" so that listeners are not overly taxed in remembering or anticipating referents.[21]

---

15   J. Nielson and R. Skousen, "How Much of the King James Bible is William Tyndale's?", *Reformation* 3 (1998), 49–74.

16   Whitman makes a passing reference to Tyndale's first English translation of the Bible from the original languages: "1526—first English version of Bible New Testament printed—but interdicted from the popular use by the King" (*NUPM* V, 1909; Grier: "date is 1875").

17   See D. Daniell, *William Tyndale: A Biography* (New Haven: Yale University, 1994), 134–51.

18   *Obedience of a Christian Man* (1528).

19   For details, see Daniell, *William Tyndale*, 223–49.

20   G. Hammond also emphasizes that the basis for Tyndale's assessment is "in essence, a matter of comparative syntax" (*The Making of the English Bible* [New York: Philosophical Library, 1983], 45).

21   *The Art of Syntax: Rhythm of Thought, Rhythm of Song* (Graywolf Press, 2009), 12. The language and ideas ultimately derived from Chomsky and generative grammar. For a readable overview, see S. Pinker, *The Language Instinct: the New Science of Language and Mind* (Penguin Books, 1995), esp. 83–125.

This branching pattern in part compensates for the erosion of the case system on nominals that happened in earlier stages of both languages. Without case to indicate precise grammatical function, English and biblical Hebrew make use of function words, word order, and proximity to help map syntactic relations. These are "the properties of the Hebrue tonge" that "agreeth a thousande tymes moare with the englysh then with the Latyn," a language whose rich case system is still intact (like ancient Greek), and thus is morphologically wired to tolerate more play in word order ("thou must seke a compase in the latyne") with less dependency on proximity and lexical staging. The chief upshot for Tyndale stylistically is his "willingness to be as literal as is reasonably possible within the bounds of producing a readable English version"[22]— as he says, "thou neadest not but to translat it in to the englysh worde for worde."[23] This determination to stay close to the original Hebrew of his biblical source had important implications for Tyndale's plain style, including its privileging of finite verbs, its rhythmicity, and its proclivity for variation in word orders, parataxis, short sentences, and the use of verbal and nominal redundancies (and other formulaic repetitions) and primary naming (as opposed to secondary referencing).[24] D. Daniell offers this assessment of the importance of Tyndale's discovery:

> Tyndale, and Tyndale alone... was engaged in a full-scale work of translating Hebrew into English. His discovery of the happy linguistic marriage of the two languages, though not *quite* as important as Newton's discovery of the principle of universal gravitation, was still of high significance for the history of western Christian theology, language and literature—a high claim, but not difficult to support, though the work on it has largely still to be done....[25]

---

22 Hammond, *English Bible*, 21.
23 The Israeli poet S. Shalom makes an eerily similar comment about Whitman being translated into Hebrew, "To translate him [Whitman] into Hebrew is like translating a writer back into his own language" (*New York Herald Tribune Book Review* [March 26, 1950], 3).
24 For the most perceptive analyses of Tyndale's style and its debt to underlying biblical sources (esp. Hebrew), see J. L. Lowes, "The Noblest Monument of English Prose" in *The English Bible* (ed. V. F. Storr; London: Methuen & Co., 1938), 16–42; G. Hammond, "William Tyndale's Pentateuch: Its Relation to Luther's German Bible and the Hebrew Original," *Renaissance Quarterly* 33/3 (1980), 351–85; *English Bible*, 16–67; Daniell, *William Tyndale*, 18–51, 283–315; *Bible in English*, 133–59, 248–74. W. M. Dixon stresses as well the contribution of the KJB translators ("The English Bible" in Storr, *English Bible*, 43–67).
25 Daniell, *William Tyndale*, 288–89.

Beyond the strong imprint that Hebrew narrative style in particular left on Tyndale, Tyndale's writing is marked above all by clarity, directness, and simplicity and a diction that famously every plowboy could understand—"If God spared him life, ere many years he would cause a boy that driveth the plough to know more of the Scripture than he did."[26] This set the pattern for all English translations of the Bible to follow, including the KJB.[27] Therefore, not only is there a lot of Tyndale literally in the KJB but the latter's prose style more generally is also directly indebted to Tyndale. And thus while it is undeniable that from the seventeenth century forward the KJB "introduced a new model of stylistic power to the [English] language," as Alter maintains,[28] that style originated some eighty years earlier with Tyndale. Many aspects of Whitman's plain style, as I show below, may be directly associated with stylistic elements of the KJB (as with Lincoln, Melville, and the other novelists Alter studies), making Whitman, ultimately, a rightful heir of the KJB and the KJB's foremost stylist, William Tyndale.

(Some) Biblical Elements of Whitman's Plain Style

In what follows I isolate a number of the leading material elements of Whitman's style that may be tied to the KJB. There is more to Whitman's style than a tallying of its main features. Still, these features (singularly and in aggregate) provide a concrete means of connecting this style to the prose of the KJB. In advance of his own analysis of the style of a given author (and novel under review), Alter usually establishes that author's connection to the Bible in some way (e.g., through Faulkner's title for *Absalom, Absalom!*, a modification of phrasing in 2 Sam 19:4; in Hemingway's biblical epigraph to *The Sun Also Rises*, Eccl 1:4–7). Many of the reviews of the early editions of *Leaves*, as well as Whitman's own

---

26   As recalled of Tyndale in *Foxe's Book of Martyrs* (London: William Tegg and Co., 1851), 482. And as D. Norton underscores, Thomas More's intended jibe (given the then deficiency of English vocabulary) that "'all England list now to go to school with Tyndale to learn English has turned out true: more of our English is ultimately learnt from Tyndale than from any other writer of English prose" (*English Bible as Literature*, 10).

27   Hammond, *English Bible*, 22, 25; Daniell, *William Tyndale*, 288–89; cf. Alter, *Pen of Iron*, 32–33.

28   Alter, *Pen of Iron*, 33.

(often belated) commentary (e.g., "The Great Construction of the New Bible," *NUPM* I, 353), make clear the biblical impulse of *Leaves*. And the preceding chapters of this study amply attest to Whitman's use and knowledge of the Bible more generally, and at some points even anticipate the principal topic of discussion in this chapter.

None of the authors studied by Alter fully replicates Tyndale's (or his heirs') plain prose style. Rather, they deploy elements of this style selectively and develop them to their own ends. Faulkner is emblematic. His spectacularly "flamboyant" style is often the antithesis of the simplicity and plainness of the English Bible's prose. Nevertheless, Alter points to a "thematically fraught" lexicon of biblical terms in *Absalom, Absalom!* that clarifies "how the writing in this novel is pervasively biblical even as a conspicuously unbiblical syntax and vocabulary are constantly flaunted."[29] Whitman is not different. In particular, his fondness of polysyllabic and foreign words and the expanded space of his poetic line often run counter to Tyndale and his revisers' use of Saxon monosyllabics and a spare, short prose line. And Whitman's forte is not in narrative.[30] Yet there remain multiple elements of the style Whitman fashions for his poetry in *Leaves* that he clearly found in the KJB. I review the most prominent of these here.

The Difference of Poetry

That Whitman is writing poetry in *Leaves* turns out to be consequential for what he devolves from the prose of the Bible and how. Parallelism is paradigmatic. Parallelism for Alter is a characteristic element of the prose style that descends from the KJB and features prominently throughout his study.[31] And yet because Alter's focus is on the novel, parallelism is never a pervasive stylistic feature of any of the authors he studies. Prose by its nature (viz. language organized in sentences) cannot exploit parallelism's repetitive play in anything approaching the regularity that verse (viz. language periodically interrupted) permits; and when it does

---

29 *Pen of Iron*, 86; cf. 83–86.
30 A point emphasized by H. Gross in *Sound and Form in Modern Poetry* ([Ann Arbor: University of Michigan, 1965], 87).
31 *Pen of Iron*, 17–18, 30–31, 49–52, 54, 63–64, 71–73, 80, 82, 85, 93, 133–34, 148, 153, 160, 163, 165, 170, 178, 182.

appear it is more easily sublimated by narrative's linearity, logic, and argument.[32] That is, the very medium of Whitman's writing—poetry— means that this facet of the biblically-based prose style that Alter seeks to reveal stands out as it cannot in prose. Alter rightly emphasizes the prosaic nature of the KJB as a translation and specifically its lack of "typographic indication of lines of verse for the poetry" and how this "would have encouraged Melville," for example, "as an English reader to see the biblical poetry as a loose form of elevated discourse straddling poetry and prose and hence eminently suited to his own purposes."[33] Much the same may be said of Whitman (see Chapter Three), except Whitman in *Leaves* is (mostly) not narrating a story and accommodates the underlying structure of the biblical Hebrew parallelistic couplet to his long line such that the former's shape and rhythm are not "masked" (as in Melville's prose) but accentuated (see Chapter Four). Tyndale's decision to stay as close as possible to the underlying Hebrew in his translations meant that the parallelistic structures pervading biblical literature (whether poetry or prose) were preserved and ready for Whitman (and other writers) to find and reanimate.

Whitman's line offers another example of the consequence of poetry for what Whitman inherits from the Bible. The line is the basic scaffolding for Whitman's writing, and its shapes and lengths are part of what distinguishes his style. As argued in Chapter Three, the verse divisions of the KJB likely played a role in shaping Whitman's ideas about his line. Here what is most consequential is formatting, the interrupting force of the KJB's verse divisions and accompanying indentations which Whitman transforms into lineal units—and indeed the later Whitman even reifies this move by supplying his own poem, section, and stanza numbers (beginning in the 1860 *Leaves*) in imitation of the Bible. The novelists in Alter's study, in contrast, return (unconsciously no doubt) to the plain page layout of Tyndale (Fig. 48), and thus must sublimate the persistent interruptions caused to the flow of sentences in the Bible

---

32 Cf. K. Mazur, *Poetry and Repetition: Walt Whitman, Wallace Stevens, John Ashbery* (New York/London: Routledge, 2005), 38.

33 *Pen of Iron*, 49, 50. Alter naturally focuses on the use of semantic parallelism in biblical poetry. Yet it should be emphasized that biblical narrative prose, too, exhibits parallelistic inflections, in part because it evolves out of a formal oral poetic narrative tradition in which parallelism (semantic and otherwise) was prominent.

by the verse divisions (and their enumeration). Hemingway's choice of formatting for the biblical epigraph to *The Sun Also Rises* brings this fact into relief. In his quotation of Eccl 1:4–7, he opts for a running format, eschewing the indentations and new lines for new verses, and uses ellipses instead of the verse numbers of the KJB, e.g., "One generation passeth away, and another generation cometh; but the earth abideth forever... The sun also ariseth."[34] The ellipses accommodate to the running format of Hemingway's own prose, while leaving a trace of the segmented style of the biblical source.

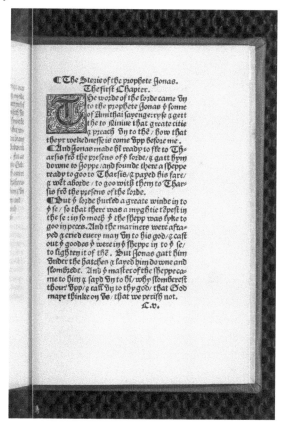

Fig. 48: A facsimile edition of William Tyndale's translation of the Book of Jonah (1863 [1531]) showing the plain page layout Tyndale used (in the then familiar "Black letter" typeface). Public domain.

---

34   The version of Eccl 1:4–5 as rendered in Ernest Hemingway , *The Sun Also Rises* (New York: Charles Scribner's Sons, 1926) [page not numbered].

Daniell emphasizes the malleability of the prose that Tyndale fashions for his Bible translations, a style that remains distinct and identifiable and yet capable of rendering a rich array of different kinds of discourses (e.g., narratives of various sorts, ritual and legal legislation, historiography, Pauline letters, some Hebrew poetry).[35] Prose in the KJB is not just for telling stories. Alter is alert to the nonnarrative dimensions of this prose as they impact the writers he surveys (e.g., semantic parallelism in *Moby-Dick*). But these dimensions, when present, are mostly intermittent in these writers and their novels. In *Leaves* the nonnarrative is primary. Like Melville and the others, Whitman absorbs the prose language of the KJB (narrative and otherwise), but he deploys it quite differently, towards nonnarrative (often explicitly lyrical) ends. This is a disposition his poetry shares with large chunks of the (English) Bible's prose, much of which, of course, is a translation of biblical Hebrew verse, itself a decidedly nonnarrative poetic tradition—"the Hebrew writers used verse for celebratory song, dirge, oracle, oratory, prophecy, reflective and didactic argument, liturgy, and often as a heightening or summarizing inset in the prose narratives—but only marginally or minimally to tell a tale."[36] The "Hebraic chant" (like that "of the ancient prophet poets") that early readers of *Leaves* heard in Whitman was mediated to English speakers through a biblical prose disposed toward nonnarrative ends.[37] Nonnarrativity itself, then, is an important aspect of (some of) the English prose of the Bible and gains sustained refraction in Whitman's verse in a way generally not met with in most novelistic fiction. Whitman's own fiction is illustrative. In Chapter 19 of his novella "Jack Engle," Whitman momentarily suspends the narrative as his young protagonist wanders among the gravestones of the old Trinity Church cemetery. Z. Turpin rightly notes how the content of the chapter "strikes similar notes" to and perhaps "hints at the geographical origins" of the various meditations on

---

35 Daniell, *Bible in English*, 136–38.
36 R. Alter, *The Art of Biblical Poetry* (New York: BasicBooks, 1985), 27.
37 The quotations are from G. Sarrazin, "Walt Whitman" (trans. H. S. Morris) in *In Re Walt Whitman* (eds. H. Traubel, R. M. Bucke, and T. Harned; Philadelphia: McKay, 1893), 159, 160 (originally published in *La Nouvelle Revue* [1 May 1888]). Some have emphasized oratorical elements in Whitman's style (e.g., C. C. Hollis, *Language and Style in* Leaves of Grass [Baton Rouge/London: Louisiana State University, 1983]). Much of the nonnarrative portions of the Bible are discourse (whether the speech of characters or the chants of prophets, psalmists, priests, or teachers of wisdom) and have the feel of spoken-ness about them.

mortality in *Leaves*.[38] Yet it is also the sentential style of this meditation, especially the expanded amplitude of so many of its sentences, pitched at an angle of non-narrativity that stands out from the rest of the novella. The opening sentence of the chapter announces the stylistic shift immediately:

> In the earliest chapter of my life, speaking of Wigglesworth, I alluded to the melancholy spectacle of old age, down at the heel, which we so often see in New York—the aged remnants of former respectability and vigor—the seedy clothes, the forlorn and half-starved aspect, the lonesome mode of life, when wealth and kindred had alike decayed or deserted.[39]

The sentence stretches out to sixty-one words, the last half of which consists of appositional elaborations frequently pocked by alliterative phrasing (e.g., "the aged remnant of former respectability," "the lonesome mode of life," "decayed or deserted"). In another example, Jack Engle, "in a musing vein," comes across a family plot of "natives of New York" and queries the human instinct to come home again to die:

> Human souls are as the dove, which went forth from the ark, and wandered far, and would repose herself at last on no spot save that whence she started. To what purpose has nature given men this instinct to die where they were born? Exists there some subtle sympathy between the thousand mental and physical essences which make up a human being, and the sources where from they are derived?[40]

The brief meditation begins with an allusion to the dove episode from the flood narrative (Gen 8:8-12), albeit read slightly against the grain—the dove returns (initially, vv. 8–9) because the earth is still covered with water and the dove "found no rest for the sole of her foot." Rhetorical questions follow. It appears to be "musing" outside of narrative that unshackles Whitman's prose in ways that anticipate the nonnarrative poetry of *Leaves*. Many similar moments occur in *Leaves*. For example, compare the latter to this passage from "I celebrate myself":

> I wish I could translate the hints about the dead young men and
> women,

---

38 "Introduction," 242–43.
39 "Jack Engle," 331.
40 Ibid., 333.

And the hints about old men and mothers, and the offspring taken soon
    out of their laps.

What do you think has become of the young and old men?

And what do you think has become of the women and children?

They are alive and well somewhere;

The smallest sprout shows there is really no death,

And if ever there was it led forward life, and does not wait at the end to
    arrest it,

And ceased the moment life appeared. (*LG*, 16–17).

Whitman's allusions to and quotations, echoes, and citations of the nonnarrative portions of the Bible show that the poet knows this prose (see Chapter Two). What I am emphasizing here is the non-narrativity itself—Whitman is chiefly a lyricist in the early editions of *Leaves of Grass*. This is perhaps a subtle point but one worth making. There are narrative runs in *Leaves*, but they are inevitably constrained and put to nonnarrative ends. What is different in Whitman (vis-a-vis the narrative artists of interest to Alter) is that all of the KJB's prose deployed for something other than telling stories—including the dialogue that dominates biblical stories—finds a ready outlet in the poet's long-line, prose-infused, nonnarrative verse.

    Emblematic of this non-narrativity is Whitman's preference for the present tense. M. Doty, commenting specifically on "I celebrate myself," perceptively observes that Whitman's "poem operates in the now"—the opening three lines "establish the poem in the present tense."[41] Doty elaborates:

> Along the way we'll hear short narratives of remembered experience, family stories, even the tale of a sea battle the speaker's heard about. But the body of the poem seems spoken in the moment of its composition, which lends the voice a living edge, and helps to account for the poem's aura of timelessness.[42]

---

41   *What is the Grass: Walt Whitman in My Life* (New York: W. W. Norton, 2020), 39.
42   Ibid.

This is the Psalms, Job, Isaiah, Song of Songs, Lamentations, and the great festival songs (e.g., Exodus 15, Judges 5, Deuteronomy 32) and the language of the present tense that Tyndale, Myles Coverdale, and the Geneva Bible and KJB translators fashioned to give expression in English to this body of decidedly nonnarrative verse. Crucially, verb morphology in biblical Hebrew does not grammaticalize tense specifically, and thus it is the necessity of rendering Hebrew into the tense-based forms of English that results in the pronounced present-tense bias of Englished versions of biblical poetry, squarely an achievement of the sixteenth- and early seventeenth-century translators.

Directly affiliated with a proclivity for non-narrativity and the present tense is what M. Miller describes as Whitman's "inclusive, declarative, broadly figured first person voice."[43] I take note of this stylistic trait here, in part, because it stands in contrast with the third person narration (mostly in past tense) that is a central preoccupation of Alter in *Pen of Iron*, and, in part, because Whitman's discovery of his voice—his "barbaric yawp"—is so dramatically on display in the early "Poem incarnating the mind"[44] notebook (especially in a section appropriately titled "The Poet"[45]) in the poet's revisions from third- to first-person address:

All this ~~he~~ ^I^ ~~drinks~~ ^swallowed^ in ~~his~~ ^my^ soul, and it becomes ~~his~~ ^mine,^ and ~~he~~ ^I^ likes it well.

~~He is~~ ^I am^ the man; ~~[illeg.] he~~ ^I^ suffered, ~~he~~ ^I^ was there:

The third person is literally canceled—struck through—and merely by a change of the pronoun, as Miller observes,[46] the first-person voice of Whitman's poetic speaker enters history. With the change, Whitman subtly but crucially shifts from writing poetry about the ideal ("greatest") poet of (his and Emerson's)[47] theory to becoming that poet—"I am the Poet."[48]

43 *Collage of Myself: Walt Whitman and the Making of Leaves of Grass* (Lincoln/London: University of Nebraska, 2010), 21.
44 https://whitmanarchive.org/manuscripts/notebooks/transcriptions/loc.00346.html
45 https://whitmanarchive.org/manuscripts/figures/loc_jc.01674.jpg
46 *Collage of Myself*, 23.
47 Cf. Stovall, *Foreground*, 296–305.
48 As in the slightly later "Talbot Wilson" notebook and eventually in the 1855 *Leaves*.

As ever with Whitman, what motivated this change is unknown.[49] C. K. Williams provocatively evokes Archilochos as a means of regrounding Whitman's all encompassing "I" in the tradition of "the lyric 'I.'"[50] I am sympathetic to the direction of Williams' gesture. But contrary to Williams, it does not all begin with Archilochos. The lyric itself is a culturally diverse phenomenon, with traditions that antedate that of ancient Greece, including those of the Hebrew Bible.[51] Whitman himself was not only well-read in the Bible but he thought "it often transcends the masterpieces of Hellas."[52] Moreover, poetry and direct discourse in the Bible share the same basic pronominal and verbal profile,[53] and thus first-person address abounds in biblical poems, including such capacious voices as the "I" of the *haggeber*—"the man"—in Lamentations 3. And it seems that Whitman himself was very much aware of the commodious nature of the Bible's own poetic speakers (including lyricists): "The finest blending of individuality with universality (in my opinion nothing out of the galaxies of the 'Iliad,' or Shakspere' s heroes, or from the Tennysonian 'Idyls,' so lofty, devoted and starlike,) typified in the songs of those old Asiatic lands."[54] In fact, the breadth and diversity of those who vocalize the "poetic I" in biblical verse (priest, prophet,

---

49   With regard to "The Poet" section of the "Poem incarnating the mind" notebook specifically (based on the wreck of the steamship *San Francisco*), a possible, contemporary, non-poetic stimulus for the shift to first person may have been the several first-person survivors' accounts that appeared in the New York papers in the aftermath of the disaster (e.g., "The Wreck of the San Francisco," New York Daily Times [16 January 1854], 4), some of which were included among the clippings Whitman made from the *New York Daily Tribune* (e.g., 14 January 1854, p. 5)—the clippings are in the Walt Whitman Papers at Duke University, https://archives.lib.duke.edu/catalog/whitmanwalt#aspace_ref1002_y9s.
50   *On Whitman* (Princeton: Princeton University, 2010), 48–53.
51   See F. W. Dobbs-Allsopp, "The Psalms and Lyric Verse" in *The Evolution of Rationality: Interdisciplinary Essays in Honor of J. Wentzel van Huyssteen* (ed. F. L. Shults; Grand Rapids: Eerdmans, 2006), 346–79; "The Idea of Lyric Poetry in the Bible" in *On Biblical Poetry* (New York/Oxford: Oxford University, 2015), 178–232.
52   "The Bible as Poetry," *The Critic* (February 3, 1883), 57.
53   See E. L. Greenstein, "Direct Discourse and Parallelism" in *Discourse, Dialogue, and Debate in the Bible: Essays in Honor of Frank H. Polak* (ed. A Brenner-Idan; Sheffield: Sheffield Phoenix, 2014), 79–92.
54   "The Bible as Poetry," 57. The parenthetical comment provides the clues to the portions of the Bible that are uppermost in mind here, as does the litany of praise in the immediately preceding paragraph, which almost unexceptionally has the Bible's poetic corpus in view (inclusive of specifically lyrical corpora, such as the Psalms or Song of Songs).

singer, ordinary women and men, God), read holistically, anticipates and no doubt in part funds Whitman's own omnivorous "poetic I."

Parallelism, Whitman's line, and the non-narrativity (often in first person, present tense) of most of the verse in the early *Leaves* illustrate to varying degrees the important difference of poetry in how and what is inherited from the prose tradition of the KJB and how that inheritance may manifest itself. What Whitman helps to illuminate, in light of Alter's identification of an American prose style devolved from the KJB, is the possibilities for that style beyond narrative fiction.

Parataxis

Parataxis, which Alter characterizes generally as "the form of syntax that strings together parallel units joined by the connective 'and,'"[55] is another hallmark of the biblical prose style that Alter traces in American fiction. The parallel units strung together in this manner tend to be "relatively short sentences" made up mostly of "phonetically compact," Anglo-Saxon monosyllables.[56] This is Tyndale's plain style: "a strong direct prose line, with Saxon vocabulary in a basic Saxon subject-verb-object syntax"—"Saxon words are short. So too are Saxon sentences, in which short phrases are joined by 'and.'"[57] It is a style that Tyndale crafted for English under the direct impress of biblical Hebrew. As G. Hammond explains: "In Hebrew biblical narrative there is little variation in the way sentence is tied to sentence and clause to clause. Ubiquitously—and by that I mean well over ninety percent of the time—the connecting link is the particle *waw*."[58] Tyndale, who never wanted "to run too far" from the underlying Hebrew, mostly translated the main (and pervasive) Hebrew coordinating conjunction (*wĕ-*) with the simple English "and"—the KJB ramifies this practice.[59] And part of the affinity Tyndale saw between English and Hebrew was how well his short native Saxon sentences matched the typically compact Hebrew prose sentences, "thou neadest

---

55 *Pen of Iron*, 47; cf. 131, 151, 163.
56 Ibid., 34–35, 151.
57 Daniell, *Bible in English*, 136, 138; cf. 248–54.
58 *English Bible*, 22; cf. Alter, *Pen of Iron*, 48, 134; G. W. Allen, *The New Walt Whitman Handbook* (New York: New York University, 1986), 215. The Hebrew particle occurs "about 50,000 times" in the Hebrew Bible (*IBHS* §39.2, n. 2).
59 Cf. Hammond, *English Bible*, 25.

not but to translat it in to the englysh worde for worde" (with but the slightest alteration of Hebrew's classic verb-(subject)-object word order).[60] Verbs are "the central verbal power" in both languages.[61]

The imprint of this paratactic style on Whitman is most obvious in the many "And"-headed lines that populate his poetry (185x in the 1855 *Leaves*), especially when they bunch together (e.g., *LG*, 15–16 [7x], 19 [5x], 20 [5x], 33 [4x], 34 [7x], 53–54 [8x], 90–91 [5x], 92–93 [7x]).[62] As noted (see Chapter Three), this is a refraction in Tyndale's English (and that of his heirs) of the peculiar Hebrew verb form (the so-called *wayyiqtol* form which has the conjunctive *waw* directly attached) that carries the main narrative line in much of the prose in the Pentateuch and Former Prophets. The verse divisions of the KJB (with attendant indentation) serve to highlight these sentence-initial "And"s. With some exceptions (e.g., "And parted the shirt from my bosom-bone, and plunged your tongue to my barestript heart,/ And reached till you felt my beard, and reached till you held my feet," *LG*, 15), the majority of these "And"-initiated lines, of course, are tuned to the present tense of Whitman's defining nonnarrative pose, viz. "And now it seems to me the beautiful uncut hair of graves" (*LG*, 16).

Parataxis pervades the Hebrew Bible beyond just this one form. Its character varies depending on medium, genre, and style. For example, Alter introduces his discussion of the paratactic style of Ernest Hemingway with a brief stylistic analysis of Eccl 1:4–7, the biblical passage which serves as an epigraph for *The Sun Also Rises* (1926): "The use of parataxis in both the original and the translation is uncompromising: a steady march of parallel clauses, with 'and' the sole connective, and the only minimal use of a subordinate clause occurring in 'from whence the rivers come'... just before the end."[63] The assessment is correct.

---

60   Although as Hammond rightly appreciates Tyndale's willingness many times to follow Hebrew word order even when it opposes English natural word order, e.g., objects fronted, verbs in initial position (*English Bible*, 49).

61   Cf. Daniell, *Bible in English*, 138.

62   J. P. Warren notices that one of the most striking features of Whitman's syntax is its "coordinating structure" and he connects this feature directly to the "rhythm-producing syntax of the English Bible" ("'The Free Growth Of Metrical Laws': Syntactic Parallelism In 'Song Of Myself,'" *Style* 18/1 [1984], 27–42, here 31, 32); cf. B. Erkkila, *Whitman the Political Poet* (New York/Oxford: Oxford University, 1989), 89.

63   *Pen of Iron*, 148 (the chapter is entitled "The World through Parataxis").

However, the language of Ecclesiastes, a relatively late book of the Bible (dating from the post-exilic period) shaped more as autobiography than straight narrative, is quite distinct from that of the earlier parts of the Old Testament that Tyndale translated. There are plenty of conjunctive *waw*s. Eight in the original Hebrew of the passage, five of which are translated with "and" in the KJB.[64] But the classic Hebrew *wayyiqtol* form never occurs and often the word order has shifted to subject-verb-(object) (e.g., *dôr* [Subj] *hōlēk* [Vb] "one generation passeth away," Eccl 1:4; *kol-hannĕḥālîm* [Subj] *hōlĕkîm* [Vb] *ʾel-hayyām* [PP] "all the rivers run to the sea," Eccl 1:7), no accommodation to English word order is needed.[65] Though still paratactic, the look and feel of the Ecclesiastes passage is subtly but significantly different from that of most narrative prose in the Pentateuch—especially note the use of the present tense in the KJB's translation:

> [4] One generation passeth away, and another generation cometh: but the earth abideth for ever.

> [5] The sun also ariseth, and the sun goeth down, and hasteth to his place where he arose.

> [6] The wind goeth toward the south, and turneth about unto the north; it whirleth about continually, and the wind returneth again according to his circuits.

> [7] All the rivers run into the sea; yet the sea is not full; unto the place from whence the rivers come, thither they return again.

The five "and"s in the translation function as clausal coordinators (as so often in the Pentateuch) but none are in verse initial position. And while "and" is the sole connective used, the "steady march of parallel clauses"

---

64   In Hebrew the same coordinating conjunction (*waw*) has a disjunctive role when it appears interclausally "before a non-verb constituent" (*IBHS* §39.2.3), which usually is rendered with "but" (or the like) in English. The final coordinating *waw* in Eccl 1:4 (*wĕhāʾāreṣ....*) is disjunctive in this way—"but the earth abideth for ever."

65   Biblical Hebrew, like all languages, changes over time. In particular, in later periods the classical *wayyiqtol* form is used far less frequently and word order in main clauses shift (see M. S. Smith, *The Origins and Development of the Waw-Consecutive: Northwest Semitic Evidence from Ugarit to Qumran* (Atlanta: Scholars, 1991); T. Givón, "The Drift from VSO to SVO in Biblical Hebrew: the Pragmatics of Tense-Aspect" in *Mechanisms of Syntactic Change* (ed. C. N. Li; Austin: University of Texas, 1977), 184–254.

often proceeds without any connecting word (e.g., "All the rivers run," v. 7)—parataxis at its base involves the "placing of propositions or clauses one after another, without indicating by connecting words the relation... between them" (*OED*). In *Leaves* lines with a similar profile of multiple line-internal, clause-initial "and"s (usually two or three) are not infrequent (e.g., "I lift the gauze and look a long time, and silently brush away flies with my hand," *LG*, 17; "Where the cheese-cloth hangs in the kitchen, and andirons straddle the hearth-slab, and cobwebs fall in festoons from the rafters," *LG*, 36). Lines headed with "And" seem also to attract line-internal "and"s (e.g., "And counselled with doctors and calculated close and found no sweeter fat than sticks to my own bones," *LG*, 26; "And lift their cunning covers and signify me with stretched arms, and resume the way," *LG*, 71). Frequently enough there are bursts of narrativity, sometimes sustained even, in the midst of *Leaves*' more typical present oriented temporality, and these are where Whitman's style can appear closest to the (past-tense) style of biblical narrative. A paradigm example is the vignette about the "runaway slave" from "I celebrate myself":

> The runaway slave came to my house and stopped outside,
>
> I heard his motions crackling the twigs of the woodpile,
>
> Through the swung half-door of the kitchen I saw him limpsey and weak,
>
> And went where he sat on a log, and led him in and assured him,
>
> And brought water and filled a tub for his sweated body and bruised feet,
>
> And gave him a room that entered from my own, and gave him some coarse clean
>
> clothes,
>
> And remember perfectly well his revolving eyes and his awkwardness,
>
> And remember putting plasters on the galls of his neck and ankles;
>
> He staid with me a week before he was recuperated and passed north,
>
> I had him sit next me at table.... my firelock leaned in the corner. (*LG*, 19)

The little narrative is evolved in a sequence of parallel clauses with and without connecting words. "And" appears fifteen times in these ten lines. Five of the lines are headed by "And." In eleven instances "and" heads a clause in which the subject is assumed and thus elided (twice the slave—"and stopped outside"; "and passed north"; nine times the "I" of the speaker) and the verb follows immediately (with or without objects), e.g., "And went... and led... and assured him." The lines themselves, and especially the individual clauses that comprise the intra-lineal caesurae, are relatively compact and feature mostly concrete, everyday vocabulary—with the occasional compound (e.g., "runaway," "half-door," "firelock") Whitman so enjoyed.[66] The vignette as a whole, as M. Klammer remarks, helps to inscribe the kind of "sympathy as measureless as its pride" (*LG*, vi) to which Whitman aspires, and the repeated use of "and" in the passage (especially at the beginning of lines) emphasizes the bond between speaker *and* slave—that is, the paratactic style itself is a manifestation of the empathy for and the receptivity to the other.[67]

On four occasions in the passage "and" functions as an item coordinator ("limpsey and weak," "his sweated body and bruised feet," "his revolving eyes and his awkwardness," "his neck and ankles"). Whitman, in fact, is very fond of this use of the simple conjunction, as is made apparent immediately in the 1855 Preface—"Here are the roughs *and* beards *and* space *and* ruggedness *and* nonchalance that the soul loves" (*LG*, iii; emphasis added). The other major role of the conjunctive

---

66   The image of the speaker bringing water and tub to wash the runaway slave's "sweated body and bruised feet" and then sitting down with him "at table" alludes to (or echoes) Jesus's famous foot-washing scene in John 13 after the last supper with the disciples, viz. "After that he poureth water into a bason, and began to wash the disciples' feet, and to wipe them with the towel wherewith he was girded" (John 13:5). Cf. T. E. Crawley, *The Structure of Leaves of Grass* (Austin: University of Texas, 1970), 227; M. C. Nussbaum, "Democratic Desire: Walt Whitman" in *A Political Companion to Walt Whitman* (ed. J. E. Seery; Lexington: University Press of Kentucky, 2011), 96–130, here 115 ("a clear reference to Christ's humility and service").

67   *Whitman, Slavery, and the Emergence of Leaves of Grass* (University Park: The Pennsylvania State University, 1995), 122–23. For the political importance of "receptivity or responsiveness... to the other" in Whitman, see G. Kateb, "Walt Whitman and the Culture of Democracy" in Seery, *Political Companion*, 19–46.

waw in biblical Hebrew is to conjoin nouns at the phrasal level.[68] This is a common use of "and" in English as well, and thus this usage is not marked as such as an indicator of possible biblical influence. Still, Whitman uses "and" very frequently to conjoin nominals. And like *Leaves* the English Bible is filled with verses containing multiple "and"s, whether conjoining clauses or individual lexemes (especially nouns), viz. "And he rose up that night, and took his two wives, and his two womenservants, and his eleven sons, and passed over the ford Jabbok" (Gen 32:22).

Parataxis pervades the biblical Hebrew poetic tradition as well but in ways that are different still from the patterning in the Bible's prose traditions. The corpus is dominantly nonnarrative. Therefore, for example, the classical *wayyiqtol* form appears more sparingly. And the speaking roles and verbal patterns that prevail are those that typify the representation of spoken discourse, whether in orally performed verbal art (which informs, for example, much biblical poetry) or in the written prose of biblical narrative. Two aspects in particular, however, bear on a consideration of parataxis in Whitman. While the conjunctive *waw* is common (especially as an item coordinator) in biblical poetry, there is also a tendency to adjoin clauses and sentences asyndetically, with no explicit conjunction—this is parataxis at its most fundamental (e.g., "The sorrows of hell compassed me about: the snares of death prevented me," Ps 18:5). That is, in the poetic sections of the Bible Whitman was confronted with runs of verses, sentences, and clauses that are conjoined contiguously without any or only minimal (often just the simple conjunction "and"—also "but," "yet," "or," "yea") indication of how these units were to be related. This is very much akin to the basic profile of Whitman's verse—"the end-stopped lines linked by parallelism, repetition, and periodic stress."[69] More specifically, as discussed in Chapters Three and Four, one of Whitman's most favored line types is a two-part, internally parallel line in which the second clause is headed by a simple conjunction, usually "and" (e.g., "Stop this day and night with me and you shall possess the origin of all poems," *LG*, 14; "I jump from the crossbeams, and seize the clover and timothy,"

---

68   *IBHS* §39.2.1b.
69   Erkkila, *Political Poet*, 86.

LG, 18).[70] There are literally hundreds of such lines populate the 1855 *Leaves*.

It is worth pausing over Whitman's use of the conjunction "and" and the parataxis it emblemizes. In the 1855 *Leaves* the conjunction appears 2,544 times (including the Preface). This is not an insubstantial number of occurrences. Such a highly paratactic style is sometimes labeled "primitive."[71] In fact, G. W. Allen explicitly links Whitman's rediscovery of such a style to the "primitive rhythms of the King James Bible," emphasizing that the "original language of the Old Testament was extremely deficient in connectives, as the numerous 'ands' of the King James translation bear witness."[72] Primitive in such usage is a literary-critical descriptor of a syntactic style (often opposed to a "sophisticated" syntax that more routinely and explicitly discriminates clausal relations of subordination, qualification, consequence, etc.).[73] The term should not be construed to imply intellectual simpleness or naiveté. In fact, Allen's comment about Whitman's "primitive" parataxis is tied directly to the poet's hyper-democratic political commitments: "such doctrines demand a form in which units are co-ordinate, distinctions eliminated, all flowing together in synonymous or 'democratic' structure. He needed a grammatical and rhetorical structure which would be cumulative in effect rather than logical or progressive."[74] "Form and style are not incidental features" of thought, as M. C. Nussbaum (among others) well explains, but themselves make claims, express "a sense of what matters," are "a part of content," and thus "an integral part... of the search for and the statement of truth."[75] That Whitman's own stylistic preferences (here his preference for parataxis) should suit his politics and even themselves bear political consequence is part and parcel of how language art works. Parataxis, no less than the high sophistication of subordinating syntax, may be disposed toward thinking. G. Deleuze's philosophical method is a case in point. It relies on a paratactic style of discourse—what he calls

---

70   R. Mitchell notices that "the two-part or two-group line is the line used most often by Whitman" ("A Prosody for Whitman?", *PMLA* 84/6 [1969], 1607).

71   E.g., Allen, *New Walt Whitman*, 215–16.

72   Ibid., 215.

73   Hammond, *English Bible*, 24.

74   Allen, *New Walt Whitman*, 215.

75   *Love's Knowledge: Essays on Philosophy and Literature* (New York/Oxford: Oxford University, 1992), 3, 5; cf. A. Shapiro, *In Praise of the Impure: Poetry and the Ethical Imagination: Essays, 1980–1991* (Northwestern University, 1993), 1.

"thinking *with* AND"—to move beyond philosophies of first principles and subordination toward a thinking through of life and world in terms of relations, fragmentation, inclusivity, and multiplicity.[76] K. Mazur has even leveraged Deleuze's ideas to sharpen the political appreciation of Whitman's formal style.[77] Parataxis, as it prescinds from predetermining connections, from privileging order, linearity, and hierarchy, making all equal, suits most congenially the poetics of democracy that Whitman crafts. And thus, as with Whitman's free verse and parallelism, the choice here of a distinct formal style—parataxis—is not simply a matter of borrowing a biblical model for the sake of that model, but the latching onto (and then developing) a style that is deployed with precise political and intellectual attention. Whitman "thinks with" the "AND" that he finds foremostly in the Bible, and thinks it toward an American democratic polity where "there can be unnumbered Supremes, and that one does not countervail another any more than one eyesight countervails another . . and that men can be good or grand only of the consciousness of their supremacy within them" (*LG*, vii).

The Periphrastic Genitive

Modern English has two genitive constructions, the *s*-genitive and the *of*-genitive.[78] The former is a clitic formation that originated in the inflectional morphology of Old English. The latter is a periphrastic and postposed construction, also present in Old English though severely restricted in use there (e.g., mostly in locatives). By the fourteenth century the *of*-genitive increasingly became the preferred adnominal genitive construction. In part this resulted from changes internal to the development of English (e.g., erosion of inflectional morphology) and in part due to the influence of French *de* after 1066. In the Early Modern period (1400–1630) the *s*-genitive again increases in frequency, though

---

76 G. Deleuze and C. Parnet, *Dialogues* (trans. H. Tomlison and B. Habberjam; New York: Columbia University, 1977), esp. 54–62.

77 *Poetry and Repetition*, 31–60, esp. 36–40; cf. Hammond, *English Bible*, 24. Parataxis *per se* is not isolated in Erkkila's otherwise incisive exposition of the political significance of Whitman's aesthetics (*Political Poet*, esp. 86–91), though it is likely subsumed in her mind with the phenomena of parallelism and repetition (and the catalogue).

78 For a convenient overview of the English genitive constructions, see A. Rosenbach, *Genitive Variation in English* (Berlin/New York: de Gruyter, 2002), esp. 177–234.

now mostly restricted to usages with highly animate (e.g., humans) and/or topical (e.g., proper names) possessors.[79] Both constructions are available to Tyndale. However, he almost exclusively uses the *of*-genitive to render the Hebrew "construct chain," the commonest means in the language for expressing a genitival relationship between two nouns. The latter consists of a head noun (in construct) followed immediately by its modifier (a noun in the absolute):[80]

Hebrew:	qĕdôš	+	yiśrāēl (2 Kgs 19:22)
	(head) noun[1]	+	(modifier) noun[2]
English:	the-Holy-One-of	+	Israel
Tyndale:	"the holy of Israel" (> KJB: "the Holy One of Israel")		

Tyndale's preference for the *of*-genitive allows him to maintain the word order of the underlying Hebrew, i.e., noun[1] + of + noun[2],[81] and imbues his prose with a distinct rhythmicity that results from the repeated use of this one genitive construction.[82] The KJB broadly retains Tyndale's pattern of usage.

The pattern of usage of the two genitives in Whitman's poetry is interesting. In the pre-1850 metrical poems the *s*-genitive is prominent.[83] This is understandable since use of the *s*-genitive provides maximum

---

79   An example is "mother's womb," which appears exclusively in the KJB (13x; a trend started by Tyndale in the 1520s and 30s, cf. Num 12:12; Luke 1:15); never "womb of a/the/his/her/my mother." So also Whitman: "the greatest poet from his birth out of his mother' s womb" (*LG*, ix; cf. Num 12:12; Judg 16:7; Job 1:21; 3:10; Luke 1:15)—the phrase appears again a little later in "A Child's Reminiscence" (1859), "Out of the boy' s mother' s womb" (l. 3), https://whitmanarchive.org/published/periodical/poems/per.00071. Whitman uses the *s*-genitive with "mother" and "mothers" eight times in the 1855 *Leaves*; and the *of*-genitive he uses only twice, including the superlative "mother of mothers" (*LG*, 81; see discussion below).

80   Historically, the modifying noun appeared in the genitive case, but the case system on nouns was lost sometime prior to the biblical period. For details about the construct formation in biblical Hebrew, see *IBHS* §9.2–7

81   As Hammond emphasizes, "any other [means of rendering the Hebrew into English] would mean either paraphrase or a reversal of the Hebrew word order" (*English Bible*, 50).

82   Hammond, *English Bible*, 49–53; cf. Daniell, *William Tyndale*, 289.

83   The *s*-genitive is also notably prevalent in the unpublished "Pictures."

flexibility in order to accommodate the constraints of meter.[84] By contrast, the s-genitive appears relatively infrequently in the 1855 *Leaves*, only a hundred times,[85] while the preposition "of" appears over 1400 times[86]— Whitman's expanded, non-metrical line making the space necessary to accommodate the lengthier, less rhythmically regular phrasing of the *of*-genitive. Less rhythmically regular, however, does not mean non-rhythmical. Indeed, the *of*-genitive is one of the oft-repeated "syntactical structures" critical to the free rhythms of Whitman's mature verse.[87] This is noticeable even at the level of the line, as in these two- and three-part lines:

> You are the gates of the body and you are the gates of the soul (*LG*, 80)

> The rope of the gibbet hangs heavily.... the bullets of princes are
>   flying.... the creatures of power laugh aloud (*LG*, 88)

In both the repeated *of*-genitive formation helps create a strong sense of parallelism in these lines and provides the lines with their basic rhythmic shape—the repeated vocabulary in the two-part line enhances this feel all the more. Increasing the scale shows what is possible when the patterned repetition is sustained over a longer stretch of lines. Consider this section from "I celebrate myself" (emphasis is mine):

> I hear *the bravuras of birds*.... *the bustle of growing wheat*.... *gossip of*
>   *flames*.... *clack of sticks cooking my meals.*

> I hear *the sound of the human voice*.... a sound I love,

> I hear all sounds as they are tuned to their uses.... *sounds of the city* and
>   sounds

>   out of the city.... *sounds of the day and night;*

---

84   Cf. O. Fischer, "Syntax" in *The Cambridge History of the English Language, vol. II, 1066–1476* (ed. N. Blake; Cambridge: Cambridge University, 1992), 226.

85   Cf. Hollis's confirming observation that the inflected genitive "is not common in *Leaves*" (contrary to his expectation as a characteristic of the stative language of journalism; *Language and Style*, 230).

86   The latter count includes usages of the preposition beyond adnominal genitival constructions.

87   Cf. Mazur, *Poetry and Repetition*, 36.

Talkative young ones to those that like them.... *the recitative of fish-pedlars*

and fruit-pedlars.... the loud laugh of workpeople at their meals,

The angry base of disjointed friendship.... the faint tones of the sick,

The judge with hands tight to the desk, his shaky lips pronouncing a
death-sentence,

The heave'e'yo of stevedores unlading ships by the wharves.... *the refrain of
the*

anchor-lifters; (*LG*, 31)

The adnominal construction itself provides a two-part cadence that then
punctuates these lines with enough regularity to be felt rhythmically. The
repetitions also help hold the section together. While more difficult to
apprehend, the rhythmical effect as the syntagma is repeated throughout
the whole of *Leaves* is not dissimilar. And it is very reminiscent of the
"rhythmic repetitiveness" that Hammond notices in Tyndale's (and by
extension the KJB's) use of the periphrastic genitive.[88]

Beyond the pattern of distribution in *Leaves*, there is also a revealing
half-line from "I wander all night" that makes clear the deliberateness
with which Whitman deploys the two genitives: "The call of the slave is
one with the master' s call" (*LG*, 76). The use of both genitives allows
Whitman to provide a chiastic (abba) shaping to the phrase: call + slave
["is one with"] master + call. The chiasm aligns slave and master in
proximate adjacency, permitting the equality of their calls at the surface
of the phrase to be ghosted by a more revolutionary equality, namely,
that "the slave is one with the master."

That the phrasing preference for the *of*-genitive is at least in part
inherited from the Bible is certain. The overall profile of genitive
usage in the 1855 *Leaves*, both in terms of the pattern of usage[89] and
the rhythmical consequences of this usage, is broadly suggestive of that
of the KJB. A few outstanding *of*-genitives in *Leaves* are lifted verbatim
from the KJB, e.g., "the hand of God" (*LG*, 15; 16x in the KJB), "the spirit
of God" (*LG*, 16; 26x in the KJB), "the pains of hell" (*LG*, 26; cf. Ps 116:3),

---

88   Hammond, *English Bible*, 49–53.
89   The proportion of *s*-genitives to the use of the preposition "of" is similar: 1:18 in
      the KJB, 1:14 in the 1855 *Leaves*.

"stars of heaven" (*LG*, 54; 11x in the KJB), "pride of man" (*LG*, 80; Ps 31:20).[90] But mostly Whitman has absorbed this pattern of phrasing and adjusted it to fit his own language. Sometimes the echoes of scriptural phrasing are readily apparent:

> "the great psalm of the republic," *LG*, iv; cf. "A Psalm of David," Ps 15; "A Psalm of Asaph," Ps 82; "A Psalm of praise," Ps 100

> "the begetters of children," *LG*, 17—here using a KJB idiom, "beget/ begat," though "begetter" or "begetters" never actually appears in the KJB

> "the mother of men," <u>*LG*, 26</u>; "~~Mother~~ ^{father} of Causes" and "~~the Father~~ a Mother _{of Causes}," "My ~~Soul~~";[91] cf. "the mother of young men," Jer 15:8; "the mother of all living," Gen 3:20; "a mother of nations," Gen 17:16; "THE MOTHER OF HARLOTS," Rev 17:5; "father of many nations," Gen 17:4)

> "A word of the faith that never balks," *LG*, 28; cf. "the word of faith, which we preach," Rom 10:8

> "in the calm and cool of the daybreak," *LG*, 31; cf. "walking in the garden in the cool of the day," Gen 3:8

> "flesh of my nose," *LG*, 37; cf. "flesh of my flesh" (Gen 2:23) and "flesh of my people" (Mic 3:3)

> "the old hills of Judea," *LG*, 37—sounds biblical in part because of the *of*-genitive but it is not

> "dimensions of Jehovah," *LG*, 45—*of*-genitive plus Jehovah (= Exod 6:3; Ps 83:18; Isa 12:2; 26:4) provides the biblical feel to the phrase

> "Soul of men," *LG*, 58; cf. "the Soul of man! the Soul of man!", *NUPM* I, 105; cf. "soul of man," Rom 2:9;

> "born of a woman and man," *LG*, 60; cf. "born of a woman," Job 14:1; 15:14; 25:4; "born of woman," *LG*, 79 (2x); cf. "born of women,"

---

90 Also: "the scope and purpose of God" ("There is no word in any tongue," https://whitmanarchive.org/manuscripts/figures/duk.00018.001.jpg; cf. Folsom, "Whitman"); cf. "the purpose of God," Rom 9:11; "servant of God" ("Rules in all addresses," https://whitmanarchive.org/manuscripts/transcriptions/loc.00163.html); 7x in KJB.

91 Folsom, "Whitman."

Matt 11:11; Luke 7:28)—not an adnominal construction but
suggestive of Whitman's penchant for adapting biblical language

"the pleasure of men with women" (*LG*, 67), cf. "the way of a man with
a maid," Prov 30:19

"Children of Adam" (*LG* 1867, 95), cf. "sons of Adam," Deut 32:8; Sir
40:1; "children of Israel," Gen 32:32; "children of Simeon," Num
1:22; "children of Levi," 1 Chron 12:26; etc.[92]

"a revelation of God," "I know as well as you";[93] cf. "revelation of Jesus
Christ," Gal 1:12; 1 Pet 1:13; Rev 1:1

Yet in at least one instance even Whitman's imitations can be directly
tied to the Bible. The Hebrew construct formation is not limited to
genitival relationships. Most notably, the superlative in biblical Hebrew
is expressed by way of a construct phrase.[94] In Deut 10:17 Israel's god
is extolled as the highest god and most superior lord through a pair
of conjoined construct phrases, *ʾĕlōhê hāʾĕlōmim* and *ʾădōnê hāʾădōnîm*,
which Tyndale renders literally, "God of goddes" and "lorde of lordes."
And this translation pattern prevails throughout the KJB (e.g., "king of
kings," Ezra 7:12; "song of songs," Song 1:1).[95] Whitman is fond of such
phrasing. An early example comes in a book notice about Harper and
Brother's *Illuminated Bible* of 1846, which he calls "the Book of Books"—
his phrasing imitating biblical English style to designate the surpassing
nature of the Bible ("It is almost useless to say that no intelligent man can
touch the Book of Books with an irreverent hand").[96] Such superlatives
abound in the early notebooks and the 1855 *Leaves*: e.g., "the nation of
nations," *LG*, iii; "the race of races," *LG*, iv; "the art of art," *LG*, vi; "the
nation of many nations," *LG*, 23 (glossed as "one of the great nations");
"the puzzle of puzzles," *LG*, 32;[97] "a compend of compends," *LG*, 33
(followed by another *of*-genitive which emphasizes the rhythmic effect:

---

92   Conventional idioms consisting of "man of," "master of," "son(s)/daughter(s)
      of," and the like are forms of the adjectival genitive that is common in biblical
      Hebrew (*IBHS* §9.5.3b). English does not use such genitives as prominently.
93   Folsom, "Whitman."
94   *IBHS* §9.5.3j.
95   Cf. W. Rosenau, *Hebraisms in the Authorized Version of the Bible* (Baltimore:
      Friedenwald, 1903), 115.
96   *UPP*, I, 127.
97   S. Halkin reinscribes a biblical flavor to his translation by using the old Hebrew
      word *ḥîdâ* "riddle" in his rendering of Whitman's superlative here, *ḥîdat-haḥîdôt*

"is the meat of a man or woman"); "the circuit of circuits," *LG*, 48; "an apex of the apices," *LG*, 49; "mother of mothers," *LG*, 81; "cause of causes" (2x), *NUPM* I, 130, 131. The biblical inspiration for this manner of phrasing is patent. There are even a handful of times where Whitman plays on the superlative construction with slight deformations, e.g., "the gripe of the gripers," *LG*, viii; "mothers of mothers," *LG*, 17;[98] "the myriads of myriads," *LG*, 49; "the mould of the moulder," *LG*, 62; "the wrestle of wrestlers," *LG*, 78; "the bids of the bidders," *LG*, 81; "offspring of his offspring," *LG*, 81.

In sum, the periphrastic *of*-genitive (i.e., the *noun+of+noun* construction) is a critical element of Whitman's style in *Leaves*. Its pervasive usage creates rhythm and coherence and its biblical lineage lends Whitman's poetry "a Biblical atmosphere" even when the content and language is decidedly un-biblical.[99] Whitman's most famous *of*-genitive is the title of the volume itself, *Leaves of Grass*, which S. Halkin's rendering as a construct phrase in (modern) Hebrew, ʿălē ʿēśeb, helpfully reifies.

Cognate Accusative

Biblical Hebrew, like other Semitic languages, has a root system in which a sequence of (usually three) consonants "stay constant in a set of nouns and verbs with meanings in some semantic field."[100] For example, Hebrew *dābār* "word," *dibbēr* "to speak," and *midbār* "mouth" all share the same three root consonants, *d-b-r*, and meanings related to "speech"—namely, the production of speech (verb "to speak"), the speech that is produced ("word"), and the place of speech production ("mouth"). The root system is relevant grammatically, rhetorically, and tropologically. A common grammatical formation is the so-called

---

(ʿAlē ʾĒsev [Leaves of Grass] trans. S. Halkin; Tel Aviv: Sifriat Poalim and Hakibbutz Hameuchad Publishing House Ltd, 1984 [952]], 86).).

98   There are biblical models for the plural deformations, e.g., "heavens of heavens," Ps 68:33; 148:4.

99   See Hammond, *English Bible*, 51. The Hebrew construct chain is routinely extended beyond only two entities (e.g., "the heart of the chief of the people of the earth," Job 12:24; cf. *IBHS* §9.3c), and Whitman commonly enough links two *of*-genitives in a row (e.g., "The sound of the belched words of my voice," *LG*, 13), and on rarer occasions even more (e.g., "with the sweet milk of the nipples of the breasts of the mother of many children," *LG*, xii).

100 J. Fox, *Semitic Noun Patterns* (Winona Lake: Eisenbrauns, 2003), 37.

"cognate accusative." This is a construction involving a verb and either an effected or internal accusative that share the same root.[101] For example, "your old men *will dream dreams* [ḥălōmôt (N) yaḥălōmûn (V), from the root ḥ-l-m "to dream"]" (Joel 2:28). This is a form of repetition that Tyndale often made sure to reproduce in his translation:[102]

> "But God plaged Pharao and his house wyth greate plages" (Gen 12:17)
>
> "wherefore hast thou rent a rent uppon the" (Gen 38:29)
>
> "the oppression, wherwith the Egiptians oppresse them" (Exod 3:2)
>
> "this people have synned a great synne" (Exod 32:31)
>
> "the Lorde slewe of the people an exceadynge myghtie slaughter" (Num 11:33)
>
> "I haue herde ye murmurynges of ye childern of Ysrael whyche they murmure agenste me" (Num 14:27)
>
> "When thou hast vowed a vowe vnto the Lorde thy God" (Deut 23:21)

And these carried through to the KJB, and the latter extended this style of translation into portions of the Bible that Tyndale did not translate.[103] One of the kinds of repetition that Whitman is enamored of consists of lexically related nouns and verbs, the ultimate model for which is the KJB and its habitual repetitive rendering (inherited from Tyndale) of the cognate accusative. A striking example comes from the 1869 poem, "The Singer in the Prison."[104] In one of the quatrains from "a quaint old hymn" that Whitman sets within the larger poem there is this line: "It was not I that sinn' d the sin." Not only does "sinn'd the sin" mimic an Englished version of the biblical cognate accusative, it does so using Tyndale's very language ("this people have synned a great synne," Exod 32:31; the combination appears dozens of times in the KJB)—the biblicism, no doubt, intended to lend the "Hymn" sung at "Christmas

101 *IBHS* §10.2.1f–g.
102 Hammond, "Tyndale's Pentateuch," 379–80; *English Bible*, 36–38—the examples are taken from Hammond's discussions.
103 Cf. Rosenau, *Hebraisms*, 113–14.
104 *Saturday Evening Visitor* (25 December 1869), https://whitmanarchive.org/published/periodical/poems/per.00079. Eventually included in *Passage to India* (cf. *LG* 1881, 292–93).

church in prison" depth and moral weight. This signature grammatical Hebraism occurs a dozen or so times already in the 1855 *Leaves*:

> "It is the medium that shall well nigh express the inexpressible" (*LG*, xii)
>
> "I do not snivel that snivel the world over" (*LG*, 25)
>
> "I chant a new chant," (*LG*, 26)
>
> "Sea breathing broad and convulsive breaths!" (*LG*, 27)
>
> "Where the laughing-gull scoots by the slappy shore and laughs her near-human laugh" (*LG*, 38)
>
> "I fly the flight" (*LG*, 38)
>
> "Bussing my body with soft and balsamic busses" (*LG*, 51)
>
> "Long enough have you dreamed contemptible dreams" (*LG*, 52; cf. Gen 37:9; 40:5; 41:11, 15; Judg 7:13; Dan 2:3)
>
> "to sing a song" (*LG*, 53; cf. Exod 15:1; Num 21:17; Ps 33:3; 96:1; 98:1; 137:3; 144:9; 149:1; Isa 5:142:10; Rev 15:3)
>
> "and songs sung" (*LG*, 60)
>
> "and named fancy names" (*LG*, 60)
>
> "I dream in my dream all the dreams of the other dreamers,/ And I become the other dreamers."(*LG*, 71)[105]
>
> "If you groan such groans you might balk the government cannon" (*LG*, 89)

The collocations "dream(ed)... dreams" and "sing a song" go back ultimately to Tyndale. The rest are not biblical phrases. Whitman has absorbed the Hebraic pattern and adapted it to his own language and needs. Whitman does not restrict his repetitive play to only verbs with direct objects. Occasionally, he extends his cognate phrasings to include verbs with prepositional objects (so also Tyndale: "sett vpp greate stones

---

105   Also from the 1859 "Live Oak, with Moss," https://whitmanarchive.org/ manuscripts/liveoak.html : "I dreamed in a dream of a city where all the men were like brothers" (IX).

and playster them with playster, and write vpo the all the wordes of this lawe," Deut 27:2):

> "Does this acknowledge liberty with audible and absolute
>   acknowledgement" (*LG*, xii)

> "stuffed with the stuff" (*LG*, 23 [2x])

> "I will certainly kiss you with my goodbye kiss" (*LG*, 52; cf. Song 1:2:
>   "Let him kiss me with the kisses of his mouth"[106]

> "but a child born of a woman and man I rate beyond all rate" (*LG*, 60)

> "I sleep close with the other sleepers" (*LG*, 71)

> "And swim with the swimmer, and wrestle with wrestlers" (*LG*, 78)

> "It attracts with fierce undeniable attraction" (*LG*, 79)

> "It is the mother of the brood that must rule the earth with the new
>   rule./The new rule shall rule as

>   the soul rules, and as the love and justice and equality that are in the
>   soul rule." (*LG*, 94)

Another Hebrew grammatical formation involving a shared root is the "paronomastic infinitive."[107] In this construction the infinitive (absolute) appears with the same root as the finite verb and adds emphasis to the verb's semantics, viz. *môt* [Inf Abs] *tāmût* [Vb] lit. "dyingly you will die" (Gen 2:17). However, with this formation Tyndale does not normally try to replicate in English the repetition of the original Hebrew but uses instead an adverb plus verb combination, usually involving "surely" (but also "certainly," "indeed," "altogether"), viz. "thou shalt surely dye" (Gen 2:17). Though involving no etymological play (in English) even here, Whitman's debt to Tyndale's biblical English is occasionally readily apparent, as in the phrase "thou would' st surely die" from "Lilacs" (*Sequel*, 4)—the paronomastic infinitive with Hebrew *m-w-t* "to die" occurs scores of times in the Hebrew Bible and inevitably appears

---

106 Halkin (*'Alē 'Ēsev*, 120) uses the cognate accusative ᵓeššāqĕkā nĕšîqâ (also echoing Song 1:2) to render "I kiss you with a good-bye kiss" (*LG* 1891–92, 74).
107 *IBHS* §35.3.1.

in the KJB with Tyndale's customary gloss ("surely die").[108] There are several points in the 1855 *Leaves* where Whitman's language takes on this biblical cadence: "it must indeed own the riches of the summer and winter" (*LG*, iii); "the purpose must surely be there" (*LG*, vi); "The coward will surely pass away" (*LG*, xii); "We should surely bring up again" and "as surely go" (*LG*, 51); "I will certainly kiss you with my goodbye kiss" (*LG*, 52);[109] "You surely come back at last" (*LG*, 63); and "he that is now President shall surely be buried" (*LG*, 66).

The peculiarity of the Hebrew root system, the strictly grammatical status of the cognate accusative and the paronomastic infinitive in biblical Hebrew, and the habituated means by which these grammatical collocations have been taken into English (following Tyndale) make identifying the (ultimate) biblical source or inspiration of some of Whitman's etymological figures certain. The root system in biblical Hebrew did not only impact the grammar of the language. It also proved a rich resource for tropological play by biblical writers and performers. The literature of the Old Testament abounds in all kinds of etymological plays, many of which, because of Tyndale's habit of keeping his English close to the underlying Hebrew, are captured in English translation:

> "What profiteth the graven image that the maker thereof hath graven it" (Hab 2:18)

> "Therefore all they that devour thee shall be devoured" (Jer 30:16)

> "a time to plant, and a time to pluck up that which is planted" (Eccl 3:2)

> "and sealed them with his seal" (1 Kgs 21:8)

> "But be ye glad and rejoice for ever in that which I create: for, behold, I create Jerusalem a rejoicing, and her people a joy." (Isa 65:18)

> "Hath he smitten him, as he smote those that smote him? or is he slain according to the slaughter of them that are slain by him?" (Isa 27:7)

---

108 Halkin renders Whitman's "thou would'st surely die" in "Lilacs" back into the old Hebrew formulation, *môt māttā* ('*Alē* 'Ēsev, 358).

109 Whitman's "goodbye kiss" here echoes the commonplace closing to several of Paul's letters, to greet one with a "holy kiss" (Rom 16:16; 1 Cor 16:20; 2 Cor 13:12; 1 Thes 5:26).

The examples are representative of a much larger phenomenon. As L. Alonso Schökel notices in his discussion of the figural significance of the root system in biblical Hebrew poetry, "the examples are extremely abundant."[110] Whitman, too, is much enamored with etymological plays of all sorts, including many that are of a kind with their biblical forerunners:

> "He judges not as the judge judges...." (*LG*, v)

> "For every atom belonging to me as good belongs to you" (*LG*, 13)

> "the plougher ploughs and the mower mows" (*LG*, 23)

> "The palpable is in its place and the impalpable is in its place" (*LG*, 24)

> "I turn the bridegroom out of bed and stay with the bride myself" (*LG*, 38; cf. 47)

> "in a framer framing a house" (*LG*, 46)

> "This printed and bound book.... but the printer and the printing-office boy?" (*LG*, 47)

> "by a look in the lookingglass" (*LG*, 61)

> "the saw and buck of the sawyer" (*LG*, 62)

> "the mould of the moulder" (*LG*, 62)

> "a bundle of rushes for rushbottoming chairs" (*LG*, 74)

> "The swimmer naked in the swimmingbath . . seen as he swims" (*LG*, 78)

> "And the glory and sweet of a man is the token of manhood untainted" (*LG*, 82)

> "he that had propelled the fatherstuff at night, and fathered him" (*LG*, 91)

> "Great is the greatest nation" (*LG*, 94)

Many, many more such plays could be cited. They are central to Whitman's style. The language, with only rare exceptions ("When the psalm sings instead of the singer," *LG*, 63; cf. Ps 98:5), is not biblical.

---

110 *A Manual of Hebrew Poetics* (SubBib 11; Roma: Editrice Pontificio Istituto Biblico, 1988), 80.

Whitman was well aware of the etymological relationships in English between verbs, nouns, adjectives, and other parts of speech.[111] And he had available to him other resources modeling the possibilities for etymological plays in English, including almost two and a half centuries of English language poetry since the KJB was first published (plus Shakespeare, of course).[112] It is not necessary to insist that the Bible was Whitman's only source of inspiration for such plays, or even his main source. But it was one resource well known to him and widely influential (stylistically). The binary pattern (e.g., "voices veiled, and I remove the veil," *LG*, 29; "I teach straying from me, yet who can stray from me?", *LG*, 53; "untouchable and untouching," *LG*, 58) in which so many of these plays are elaborated perhaps offers a vague imprint of the biblical poetic tradition in which such plays often are apportioned according to the doubling logic of much biblical poetic parallelism, whether at the level of the couplet (e.g., "and his king shall be higher than Agag, and his kingdom shall be exalted," Num 24:7) or line internally (e.g., "Heal me, O LORD, and I shall be healed," Jer 17:14). Whitman's etymological plays are not just strictly binary (e.g., "The new rule shall rule as the soul rules, and as the love and justice and equality that are in the soul rule," *LG*, 94), though many are, and often they are cast in parallelistic patterns that ghost biblical poetic line structures, e.g., "Askers embody themselves in me, and I am embodied in them" (*LG*, 43), "casting, and what is cast" (*LG*, 62), "He is the joiner . . he sees how they join" (*LG*, 86).

In sum, many of Whitman's figural plays on word formations and etymological knowledge carry forward a tradition in English that dates back to Tyndale and the KJB. In some instances, as in phrases with lexically related verbs and nominal objects (e.g., "It was not I that sinn' d the sin" from "The Singer in the Prison"; cf. Exod 32:31), the ultimate biblical genealogy is patent. Yet the main point is to suggest a broad stylistic kinship between Whitman and the prose of the English Bible with respect to these plays.

---

111 *DBN* III, 715; cf. 671, 686, 689, 671, 675–76, 678, 682, 725.
112 Stovall's research makes clear that Whitman was acquainted with an array of English language poetry, British and American (*Foreground*, esp. 231–81).

Formatting of Attributed Speech

Whitman's printerly sensibility ("I was chilled with the cold types and cylinder and wet paper between us," *LG*, 57) meant that his poetry was always infused with a strong materialist element. Formatting mattered, even stylistically.[113] For example, the use of suspension points distinguishes the poetry of the 1855 *Leaves*. Whitman introduced poem and stanza numbers to the 1860 *Leaves* in order to give his book a biblical feel. His line at times clearly mimes the verse divisions of the KJB (see Chapter Three). Another formatting element borrowed from the KJB is the practice of introducing attributed (or direct) speech with a comma followed by initial capitalization but without quotation marks:

> Whether is easier, to say, Thy sins be forgiven thee; or to say, Rise up and walk? (Luke 5:23)

> he says to the past, Rise and walk before me that I may realize you (*LG*, vi)

The Lukan passage comes from the story of Jesus' healing of the paralytic (Luke 5:17–26; Matt 9:1–8; Mark 2:1–12; cf. John 5:1–8). Whitman's language recalls Jesus' command to "Rise up and walk" (cf. "Arise, and walk," Matt 9:5; "Arise, take up thy bed, and walk," Mark 2:9; "Rise, take up thy bed, and walk," John 5:8), though Whitman likely had in mind one of the raising of the dead stories, such as that of Lazarus (John 11), since "the greatest poet" is said to drag "the dead out of their coffins and stands them again on their feet" (*LG*, vi). Regardless, it is at least clear here that Whitman borrows language from a Gospel story and formats it exactly as he found it in the KJB.[114] This formatting practice is (mostly) consistent throughout the 1855 *Leaves*:

> "He swears to his art, I will not be meddlesome...." (*LG*, vii)[115]

---

113 See G. Schmidgall's remark on how "scrupulous" was Whitman about "the physical presentation of his work" (*Intimate with Walt: Selections from Whitman's Conversations with Horace Traubel, 1888–1892* [Iowa City: University of Iowa, 2001], 89).

114 Tyndale's formatting practice in this regard is more varied, often employing a colon, e.g., "Whether is easyar to saye/ thy synnes are forgeve the/ or to saye: rise & walke?" (Luke 5:23). Although, importantly, he, too, does not use quotation marks, a formatting practice the KJB carries forward.

115 That the first singular pronoun is capitalized obscures the format here.

"The messages of great poets to each man and woman are, Come to us on equal terms" (*LG*, vii)

"It is that something in the soul which says, Rage on" (*LG*, vii)

"A child said, What is the grass?" (*LG*, 16)[116]

"Ya-honk! he says, and sounds it down to me like an invitation" (*LG*, 21)[117]

"The mocking taunt, See then whether you shall be master!" (*LG*, 30)

"It says sarcastically, Walt, you understand enough" (*LG*, 31)

"And chalked in large letters on a board, Be of good cheer, We will not desert you," (*LG*, 39)[118]

"He gasps through the clot.... Mind not me.... mind.... the entrenchments." (*LG*, 40)[119]

"...the voice of my little captain,/ We have not struck, he composedly cried, We have just begun our part of the fighting" (*LG*, 41)

"And I said to my spirit, When we become the enfolders of those orbs...." (*LG*, 52)[120]

"And I call to mankind, Be not curious about God," (*LG*, 54)

"She speaks to the limber-hip' d man near the garden pickets,

Come here, she blushingly cries.... Come nigh to me limber-hip' d man and give me your finger and thumb,

Stand at my side till I lean as high as I can upon you,

---

116 The language here is close to Isa 40:6: "The voice said, Cry. And he said, What shall I cry? All flesh is grass, and all the goodliness thereof is as the flower of the field."

117 The inverted syntax and exclamation point (the latter dropped after 1871) obscure the format. But note the comma after "says" and the capitalization. And the "Ya-honk" becomes italicized like the others in 1860.

118 Here again language and formatting is biblical: "But straightway Jesus spake unto them, saying, Be of good cheer; it is I; be not afraid" (Matt 14:27; cf. Mark 6:50; Acts 23:11).

119 The presence of suspension points before the attributed speech alters the format, i.e., no comma.

120 The comma is lacking in the corresponding notebook material from the "Talbot Wilson" notebook, https://whitmanarchive.org/manuscripts/notebooks/transcriptions/loc.00141.html (see below).

Fill me with albescent honey.... bend down to me,

Rub to me with your chafing beard . . rub to my breast and shoulders."
(*LG*, 84)

"He says indifferently and alike, How are you friend?" (*LG*, 86)

"and one representative says to another, Here is our equal appearing
and new" (*LG*, 87)

Occasionally, Whitman leaves out the comma:

"...and say Whose?" (*LG*, 16)

"Crying by day Ahoy from the rocks of the river" (*LG*, 50)

"And my spirit said No, we level that lift to pass and continue beyond."
(*LG*, 52)

"And he says Good day my brother, to Cudge that hoes in the
sugarfield;" (*LG*, 86)[121]

Quotation marks are never used.[122] This practice stands contrary
to Whitman's practice in his other writings (including his pre-1850
juvenile poetry). The last poems to have material enclosed in quotation
marks are "Blood-Money"[123] and "House of Friends."[124] Both poems are
prefaced with epigraphs containing close versions of biblical passages
enclosed in traditional quotation marks:

---

121 The phrase "he says" was not in the original prose material from the "Talbot
Wilson" notebook (see below), where the "and" continues the original
introduction, "and what says indifferently and alike," which is explicitly marked with a
comma.

122 Italics are introduced in 1860 to further distinguish attributed speech. In a
note about the "spinal idea" for "Song of the Redwood-Tree" (*LG* 1881, 165–69
[originally published in 1874]) Whitman mentions interspersing the voice of the
tree "with *italic* (first person speaking) the same as in 'Out of the Cradle endlessly
rocking'" (*LGC*, 206).

123 *New York Daily Tribune*, Supplement (22 March 1850), 1,

https://whitmanarchive.org/published/periodical/poems/per.00089.

124 *New York Daily Tribune* (14 June 1850), https://whitmanarchive.org/published/
periodical/poems/per.00442.

"Guilty of the Body and Blood of Christ" (1 Cor 11:27;
    "Blood-Money")[125]

"And one shall say unto him, What are these wounds in thy hands?
    Then he shall answer, Those with which I was wounded in the
    house of my friends."—Zechariah, xiii. 6 ("House of Friends")[126]

The quotation from Zech 13:6 contains two examples of the KJB's habitual
mode of embedding attributed speech (comma + initial capitalization,
without quotation marks), "say unto him, What...." and "Then he shall
answer, Those...." The first time Whitman uses the biblical format in the
body of a poem is in "Blood-Money" where he offers a version of Matt
26:15:

Again goes one, saying,

What will ye give me, and I will deliver this man unto you?

And they make the covenant and pay the pieces of silver. (lines 12–14)[127]

None of the poetry in the early notebooks and poetry manuscripts
contains material enclosed in quotation marks. There are in these
materials, and also in some of the prose selections from the early
notebooks, several instances of the format for introducing attributed
speech that Whitman uses in *Leaves*:

"And ~~wrote~~ chalked on a ~~great~~ board, <u>Be of good cheer, we will not
    desert you,</u> and held it up ~~as they to against the~~ and did it;"
    ("Poem incarnating the mind")[128]

"The poet seems to say to the rest of the world

Come, God and I are now here

What will you have of us." ("Poem incarnating the mind")[129]

---

125 KJB: "Wherefore whosoever shall eat this bread, and drink this cup of the Lord,
      unworthily, shall be guilty of the body and blood of the Lord."
126 KJB: "And one shall say unto him, What are these wounds in thine hands? Then he
      shall answer, Those with which I was wounded in the house of my friends."
127 KJB: "And said unto them, What will ye give me, and I will deliver him unto you?
      And they covenanted with him for thirty pieces of silver."
128 https://whitmanarchive.org/manuscripts/figures/loc_jc.01673.jpg
129 https://whitmanarchive.org/manuscripts/figures/loc.00141.038.jpg

"and ~~what~~ says ^indifferently and alike^, How are you friend? ("Talbot Wilson")[130]

"and Good day my brother, to Sambo, among the ~~black slaves~~ ^rowed^ ^hoes^ of the sugar field" ("

"~~and~~ ¹ said to my soul When we become the ~~god~~ enfolders" ("Talbot Wilson")[131]

"and the answer was No, when we fetch...." (")[132]

"and ~~it~~ ^the answer^ was, No, when I reach there...." ("Talbot Wilson")[133]

"It seems to say sternly, ~~Back~~ Do not leave me" ("Talbot Wilson")[134]

„~~they~~ each one ₛsays ~~in it down and within~~, That music!" ("The regular old followers")[135]

"Ya-honk! he says, and sounds it down to me like an invitation" ("The wild gander leads")[136]

"I simply answer, So it seems to me." ("After all is said")[137]

Whitman was aware that "punctuation marks" of all sorts "were not extant in old writings" (*DBN* III, 367),[138] and thus perhaps his motive in adopting such a format was to provide his book with the authority and

---

130 This is prose material. https://whitmanarchive.org/manuscripts/figures/loc.00141.038.jpg

131 https://whitmanarchive.org/manuscripts/figures/loc.00141.040.jpg

132 https://whitmanarchive.org/manuscripts/figures/loc.00141.040.jpg

133 https://whitmanarchive.org/manuscripts/figures/loc.00141.042.jpg

134 https://whitmanarchive.org/manuscripts/figures/loc.00141.110.jpg

135 https://whitmanarchive.org/manuscripts/figures/loc.00024.018.jpg. This is an early notebook (date: "between late 1853 and early 1855") with no obvious verse (i.e., no hanging indentations). The notebook also includes several instances in which quotation marks are used, e.g., "the poet says, 'Good day, mMy brother! good day!'" (https://whitmanarchive.org/manuscripts/figures/loc.00024.015.jpg) and "And to the great king 'How are you friend?'" (https://whitmanarchive.org/manuscripts/figures/loc.00024.015.jpg)—Grier sees these as related to the lines quoted above from "A young man came to me" (*LG*, 86); if so then the change in format in *Leaves* is remarkable.

136 Folsom, "Whitman."

137 Folsom, "Whitman." The writing in this manuscript leaf is prose, i.e., running format and no obvious hanging indentations that otherwise signal the continuation of a verse line.

138 *DBN* III, 667 [p. 432 on LC reel]. He continues: "they were commenced about (1520) three hundred years ago."

look of an old poem. Or perhaps it was simply a printerly convenience. And undoubtedly it was part and parcel of that "cleanest expression" he aspired to fashion, namely, "that which finds no sphere worthy of itself and makes one" (*LG*, vii).[139] Yet whatever the motivation, that the Bible furnished Whitman with one model for such a practice may be confidently surmised, and thus one more indicator of Whitman's biblicizing style.[140]

* * *

To summarize, I have identified a handful of elements in Whitman's style that may be directly connected to the prose style of the King James Bible. There is much more to Whitman's "divine style" than an accounting of these several elements can offer. Still, these elements do furnish a concrete means of showing where that style has been imprinted by the prose of the KJB. In particular, Whitman's use of parallelism (see also Chapter Four), parataxis of various kinds, the *of*-genitive as a superlative (e.g., "the Book of Books"), verbs with lexically related direct objects (e.g., "chant a new chant"), and the format for introducing attributed speech (comma + initial capitalization, without quotation marks) have (relatively) unambiguous biblical genealogies. These are mostly formal elements and thus devoid of positive semantic content, which made it all the easier for Whitman to take them up and shape them to his own ends; for perceptive readers he gets the biblical feel without biblical content (except what he finds congenial to his project). And while it is difficult to concretize in the same way, that the non-narrativity of so much of Whitman's poetry bears a kinship with the chunks of nonnarrative prose of the KJB, especially in the latter's present tense dominant renderings of the "Hebraic chant" of biblical Hebrew poetry, is of significance; it

---

139 In fact, Whitman's ideal of the "great poets" included the ability when necessary to work within received conventions or to turn them over—"they will be proved by their unconstraint" (*LG*, vii).

140 Cormac McCarthy, who figures among the novelists Alter treats (*Pen of Iron*, 171–80), also eschews the use of quotation marks to set apart his dialogue and instead relies on a bare convention reminiscent of that of the KJB (e.g., "Yeah, he said. You can do that," *All the Pretty Horses* [New York: Knopf, 1992], 9). Whatever McCarthy's source of inspiration, this manner of formatting dialogue is part of his lean style of writing.

brings the fact of a nonnarrative English prose style descending from the KJB into stark relief.

Prose into Poetry

The large point of the previous section is to identify elements of Whitman's poetic style that derive (ultimately) from the prose style of the KJB. In these takings from the Bible, Whitman exercises one of his most characteristic modes of composition, collage. Whitman's practice of collage has been well observed, especially in Miller's *Collage of Myself*. Often enough what is found by the poet is a readymade piece of prose (whether his own or someone else's), which he then shapes into poetry. Numerous instances of this turning of found prose into poetry have been identified or discussed in the preceding pages. When it comes to the Bible, Whitman's practice of collage is not different. A most telling (if early) example is the passage from "Blood-Money" in which the poet offers a slightly adjusted and lineated version of Matt 26:15:

> Again goes one, saying,
>
> What will ye give me, and I will deliver this man unto you?
>
> And they make the covenant and pay the pieces of silver. (ll. 12–14)

Here Whitman is quite literally culling lines from the prose of the KJB, turning major syntactic junctures into poetic lines. What changes in the immediate lead-up to the 1855 *Leaves* for Whitman is the evolution of a poetic theory that proscribes using such close renditions of traditional literature like the Bible. Some biblical content (language, imagery, ideas), whether literally, allusively, or echoically, gets into the early *Leaves* (see Chapter Two). Yet what Whitman collages far more liberally and in greater quantities from the Bible are non-semantic features of various sorts—tropes (e.g., parallelism), presentational dimensions (e.g., verse divisions), forms or kinds (e.g., lyric, non-narrativity), prosody (e.g., no meter), elements of style (e.g., parataxis, periphrastic genitive). Lacking semantic content these features do not betray their source so obviously and easily accommodate new or different content. They are readymade for reuse and recalibration. Parallelism, for example, may be fitted out with Whitman's "barbaric yawp" (instead of the "Hebraic chant" of the Bible) and its play of iteration adjusted to suit the linguistic infrastructure of English (see Chapter Four). The scale of these latter takings—to think just of Whitman's use of parallelism, the conversion of biblical verse divisions into long, end-stopped, often two-part lines, and the prominence of parataxis—is actually quite immense. Allen's contention that "no book is more conspicuous in Walt Whitman's 'long foreground' than the King James Bible" is not overstated.[141]

Not a few of the stylistic elements discussed above (e.g., plain, everyday diction, parallelism, parataxis) show up consistently in the American prose style that Alter reveals in the novelists he studies. These shared elements and their common biblical ancestry are part of why I have considered Whitman's style in light of Alter's thesis. Alter's work makes apparent the importance of prosaic style to Whitman's poetry. The place of prose in Whitman's writing, and especially in the style of poetry that he evolves for *Leaves*, is more thoroughgoing still. Prose was what Whitman read and wrote most in the years prior to the 1855 *Leaves*. This is a view that J. Loving underscores when he notices the importance of Whitman's development of the "essay form" in the 1840s writing for the *Aurora*: "It is from the essay, more than anywhere else perhaps, that Whitman's use of free verse came into being."[142] And it is the sententious style and stretched out rhythms of prose that seem to best suit his writerly temperament, leveraging, as it does, "the language of the profession he trained himself for, journalism."[143] Whitman was a writer of prose (lots of it), and ultimately in *Leaves* he became a writer of a poetry infused with pronounced prosaic inflections. The break with meter in 1850 enabled a long(er) line and the gradual shaping of that long(er) line throughout the early 1850s creates the expanded space necessary to

---

141 *A Reader's Guide to Walt Whitman* (Syracuse: Syracuse University, 1970), 24.
142 *Walt Whitman: The Song of Himself* (Berkeley: University of California, 1999), 60. The observation is made amidst discussion of Emerson's influence on Whitman. That Emerson's ideas (and some phrasing, too) influenced Whitman is undeniable. But Whitman's style is very different from Emerson's. And, notably, the later Whitman, distancing himself from Emerson, queries whether the latter "really" knows what poetry is at its highest, "as in the Bible" (*PW* II, 515–17; cf. Stovall, *Foreground*, 289). Though the criticism is unfair and not about style *per se*, nevertheless it is revealing as it identifies a real point of difference—Whitman's poetry stylistically is far closer to the style of the Bible than is Emerson's (prose or poetry).
143 Hollis, *Language and Style*, 205.

accommodate a poetic discourse injected with prosaic sensibilities—"a sort of excited prose broken into lines without any attempt at measure or regularity."[144] Therefore, not only does Whitman borrow elements of style from the prose of the (English) Bible—just like Alter's authors; but prose itself is central to his sensibility as a writer. Much of the poetry of the early *Leaves* was itself culled from prose and retains this inherited prosiness in various ways; and, as important, even the poetry that began as poetry, in lines, without obvious prosaic mediation, this poetry, too, takes advantage of the flexibility and freedom of prose and uncoils its syntax in elongated lineal stretches with leisurely patience and the extended rhythms otherwise characteristic of prose. There is perhaps no better indicator of the importance of prose to Whitman as a writer, especially early on, than the fact that the 1855 *Leaves* is itself introduced by ten pages of prose, which stylistically is so close to the poetry that follows that much of it would eventually be culled into lines for poems (e.g., "Poem of Many In One"[145] and "Poem of The Last Explanation of Prudence"[146] from the 1856 *Leaves*). Whitman may be viewed properly as participating in the "American prose" tradition that Alter identifies.

Of course, in the end Whitman's poetic style diverges, dramatically even, from that of the novelists in the tradition. Whitman's biblical inheritance and prosaic sensibilities get diverted into poetry and not narrative fiction. And the facticity of this poetry and its kind, its non-narrativity, makes a difference. Whitman only rarely tells stories in *Leaves*, and so only rarely does he exercise the "description" or "recounting of action"—*diegesis*—that is central to the *narration* that written prose makes possible.[147] The written prose narratives of the Hebrew Bible put on view an early exemplar of such diegetic narration. In this instance, the narration itself remains (mostly) lean and spare and dominated by dialogue. And it is the art of this narration as translated

---

144 *Putnam's Monthly* (September 1855), 321, https://whitmanarchive.org/criticism/reviews/lg1855/anc.00011.html. So also notably G. Eliot: "the poem [*Leaves*] is written in wild, irregular, unrhymed, almost nonmetrical 'lengths,' like the measured prose of Mr. Martin Farquhar Tupper's *Proverbial Philosophy*" ("Transatlantic Latter-Day Poetry," *The Leader* 7 [7 June 1856], 547–48, https://whitmanarchive.org/published/LG/1856/poems/45.

145 https://whitmanarchive.org/published/LG/1856/poems/8

146 https://whitmanarchive.org/published/LG/1856/poems/18

147 W. Godzich and J. Kittay, *The Emergence of Prose: An Essay in Prosaics* (Minneapolis: University of Minnesota, 1987), 22.

into (a Saxon inflected, past tense oriented) English by Tyndale and others that is of chief interest in Alter's delineation of an American prose style descending from the KJB. Thinking Whitman through Alter's paradigm reveals two additional findings. One, the prose style on view may be devolved outside of narrative proper. Alter already anticipates this by beginning his analysis with the oratory of Lincoln.[148] Whitman's nonnarrative poetry, with manifold stylistic affinities to the novels Alter studies, ramifies this fact. Two, the prose style descending from the King James Bible may be considerably broader than the tight narratival focus of Alter's study can reveal. Prose in the English Bible is used to render narration, *and everything else as well*—the dialogue in narratives, the poetry, the legal and liturgical literature, the letters, and other documentary writings. All in the KJB is prose. And it is especially the prose of the Bible outside of narration and in the present tense that suits well Whitman's writerly temperament—note H. Gross's observation that "Whitman has no narrative talent"[149]—and finds a ready outlet in the non-narrativity and present tense (of the moment) orientation of so much of the poetry in the early *Leaves*, imparting in the process its own stylistic impact. This is not to say that the novelists under review in *Pen of Iron* did not pick up stylistic elements from these other dimensions of the English Bible's prose. They plainly did (e.g., Melville's use of parallelism). Only that by dint of his modality of writing—nonnarrative poetry—Whitman could absorb and deploy such dimensions more naturally and to a far greater degree. Stylistically, then, Whitman is distinctive in part precisely because he is not writing narratives and therefore is free to channel a larger slice of the Bible's prose.

"Walt Whitman, an American"

Alter uses "American" in the subtitle of his book, *American Prose and the King James Bible*. The term serves chiefly as a descriptor of nationality and to delineate a style of written prose characteristic of novelists with this nationality. As such the term is not highly politicized. Although the delineation itself of an American literary tradition is not without

---

148 *Pen of Iron*, 11–19.
149 *Sound and Form*, 87.

political dimensions, as is made clear both in Emerson's letter of welcome to Whitman—"the most extraordinary piece of wit and wisdom that America has yet contributed" (*LG* 1856, 345)—and in Whitman's response—"the United States too are founding a literature" (*LG* 1856, 347).[150] And Alter does pointedly begin his elaboration of this American prose style with discussion of the political oratory of Abraham Lincoln, especially the latter's Second Inaugural Address (1865) which looked forward to the end of the war—a speech that becomes even more politically significant when read after Lincoln's assassination some six weeks later.[151] Alter's analysis of Lincoln's prose is fixedly literary critical. And yet the political content cannot help but spill over into Alter's text, much as he says of the writers he studies who "could scarcely ignore what the sundry biblical texts were saying about the world."[152] So both content and placement of this discussion of Lincoln lend Alter's project a light yet palpable political patina.

By contrast *Leaves of Grass* is founded in politics. Indeed, its very publication "on or about July 4, 1855," as B. Erkkila states at the very beginning of her *Whitman the Political Poet*, "was an act of revolution."[153] And for the most part *Leaves* retains its intoxicating political alchemy throughout the book's various editions. The 1855 Preface, Whitman's explication *cum* celebration of the aesthetics that underwrite the twelve poems it anticipates, is suffused with Enlightenment (revolutionary) political values—above all, liberty, equality, and freedom. It opens with "AMERICA"[154] in all caps, explicitly politicizing the book's readership. And then when the poet belatedly introduces himself part way through "I celebrate myself," it is as "an American" and "one of the roughs" (*LG*, 29), one of the "common people" in whom "the genius of the United

---

150 Whitman goes on later in that letter to iterate and elaborate, "Of course, we shall have a national character, identity"—"including literature, including poetry" (*LG* 1856, 357).

151 *Pen of Iron*, 11–19.

152 Ibid., 4. American democratic culture absorbs much from the Bible for many historical reasons and through many venues (e.g., Protestant Christianity, Rabbinic Judaism). Whitman offers a concrete example of how this happens as he emmeshes his poetry with form and content culled from the Bible and recirculates them transposed and transformed—translated—so as to serve and resource (nineteenth-century) American democracy.

153 (New York/Oxford: Oxford University, 1989), 3. Cf. E. Whitley, "The First (1855) Edition of *Leaves of Grass*" in *Companion to Walt Whitman*, 457–70.

154 https://whitmanarchive.org/published/LG/figures/ppp.00271.010.jpg

States" resides "most" (*LG*, iii).[155] Whitman's intent here is plainly to ground his democratic poetics in the lived experiences of working class Americans (hence Whitman's dress in the engraving[156] that fronts the volume). He continues by poeticizing this body politic: "The United States themselves are essentially the greatest poem" (*LG*, iii), with "veins full of poetical stuff" (*LG*, iv).[157] And that poem, as we learn, is just like the twelve ("perfect") poems that follow, "unrhymed" (*LG*, iii), "transcendent and new" and "indirect and not direct or descriptive or epic" (*LG*, iv), without "uniformity" or meter (*LG*, v), "new free forms" (*LG*, vii), and "of ornaments... nothing outré" (*LG*, viii). And then in turn Whitman politicizes the poet: he (as embodied by Whitman) "is to be commensurate with a people," "the equable man" and the "equalizer of his age and land" (*LG*, iv), whose message is one of equality ("Come to us on equal terms," *LG*, vii) and for whom "the idea of political liberty is indispensible" (*LG*, viii). Indeed, for the United States, according to Whitman, "Presidents shall not be their common referee so much as their poets shall" (*LG*, iv). This enmeshing of the political and the poetical is broadly characteristic of the 1855 Preface as a whole. As a consequence, statements about aesthetics often get elaborated as political discourse. A paradigm example is Whitman's worry about "the fluency and ornaments of the finest poems" (*LG*, v). These are clearly stylistic matters that Whitman had been problematizing during the early 1850s. The essence of his argument is that none, in fact, need worry about "ornaments or fluency" because these "greatnesses" are "not independent but dependent" on the poet's larger embodied person ("All beauty comes from beautiful blood and a beautiful brain," *LG*, v).[158] Instead of troubling oneself about "ornaments or fluency," Whitman

---

155 There is a manuscript fragment with a trial version of Whitman's self-identification. The line has been canceled by Whitman and the strikethrough mostly obscures all but the initial "W" of his last name. But otherwise the line is fairly legible: "I am Walt W[illeg.] the American" ("The spotted hawk salutes"; Folsom, "Whitman." In this preliminary version Whitman's "composite democratic persona" (Erkkila, *Political Poet*, 88) is fully identified—"I am... the American."

156 https://whitmanarchive.org/multimedia/zzz.00002.html

157 This is a move Emerson anticipates in "The Poet": "America is a poem in our eyes" (in *The Complete Essays and Other Writings of Ralf Waldo Emerson* [ed. B. Atkinson; New York: Modern Library, 1950], 338; cf. Loving, *Song of Himself*, 182).

158 The embedding of style within the embodied person of the poet is already prefigured in the "Rules for Composition" discussed at the beginning of this

urges (embodied) political action. He issues his great commandment (with its biblical overtones, see Chapter Two), consisting of thirteen imperatives, all political in nature, viz. "love the earth," "despise riches," "give alms," "stand up for the stupid and crazy," "hate tyrants"—even "read these leaves in the open air every season of every year of your life," a decidedly political act in light of Whitman's highly ritualized poetics (*LG*, v–vi). And if "you"—the implied addressee in this section morphs from poets and other artists to Whitman's readers and eventually back to the poet—"shall do" all of this, then "your very flesh shall be a great poem and have the richest fluency not only in its words but in the silent lines of its lips and face and between the lashes of your eyes and in every motion and joint of your body" (*LG*, vi). That is, whatever fluency or ornament that is appropriate—and not "outre"—for the finest poems flows from the embodied politics of the poet—"If the greatnesses are in conjunction in a man or woman it is enough" (*LG*, v). Poetics and politics are not just enmeshed for Whitman, they are enfleshed.[159]

Stovall shows that not only did Whitman collage many ideas (and some phrasing) from Emerson's essay "The Poet," but that he also translated some of these ideas into his own poetic practice.[160] The latter is emblematic of Whitman's abiding holism as thinker and artist. Similarly, the imbrication of the political in Whitman's aesthetic proves generative of stylistic practice. Whitman himself makes this connection in the Preface in terms of the new form of his unmetered and unrhymed—unconstrained—verse. Part of the "unconstraint" that marks the "greatest poets," writes Whitman, is the "silent defiance advancing from new free forms" (*LG*, vii), which echoes his earlier valorization of the "the haughty defiance of '76" (*LG*, iv)—the founding act of American political unconstraint. Here Whitman's defiance of poetic convention and his evolution of "new free forms" (rooted no less in "the free growth of metrical laws," *LG*, v) is inspired by and

---

chapter, using similar language, viz. "ornaments," "beauties of the person or character."

159 Emblematic is the twofold use to which Whitman habitually puts the term "form(s)" in the Preface: to denote either artistic form or style (e.g., "new free forms," *LG*, vii) or the "human form" (*LG*, ix).

160 Stovall, *Foreground*, 296–304.

gives expression to the political idea of freedom by which it is glossed.[161] This suggests from yet another angle that Erkkila and others are right to tease out the political provocations and entailments of Whitman's poetic style. On occasion in the previous pages I, too, have reflected briefly on the politics of Whitman's form, including elements of the prose style that he collages from the KJB, e.g., parallelism as a trope of equality and equability; singular, end-stopped lines as signifiers of particularity and individuality; parataxis as a structural modality well disposed toward democratic thinking. Style for Whitman, as for Alter, intimates a vision of the world, and that vision for Whitman is one of American democracy. As the poet culls stylistic elements from the prose of the KJB and reinscribes them in his "great psalm of the republic" (*LG*, iv), he saturates them with political "stuff" such that upon reading (and rereading) they are themselves political acts of consequence and incitements toward still other such acts.

* * *

William Tyndale, in his plain style of English prose, which was largely absorbed and emulated by the King James translators, ended up fashioning a (written and spoken) vernacular for all England, as Norton emphasizes: "more of our English is ultimately learnt from Tyndale than from any other writer of English prose."[162] Part of Alter's achievement in *Pen of Iron* is to show how the reception of that same plain, biblical style on American soil shaped an identifiable American prose style of narrative fiction. Amidst the celebration of the bicentennial of Whitman's birth (2019), P. Schjeldahl, writing for *The New Yorker*, advocated observing the occasion by sitting down with a loved one and reading aloud "Sleepers" and "Lilacs." He observed:

---

161 Emerson had already set the stage for Whitman in "The Poet" where he speaks generally about the potential political value of an "imaginative book," including the very literary "tropes" by which such a book is composed: "The poets are thus liberating gods.... They are free, and they make free. An imaginative book renders us much more service at first, by stimulating us through its tropes.... If a man is inflamed and carried away by his thought, to that degree that he forgets the authors and the public and heeds only this one dream which holds him like an insanity, let me read his paper, and you may have all the arguments and histories and criticism" (335).

162 *English Bible as Literature*, 10; cf. W. M. Dixon, "The English Bible" in Storr, *English Bible*, 43–67.

Reading Whitman silently enriches, but hearing your own or a partner's voice luxuriate in the verse's unhurried, insinuating cadences, drawn along on waves of alternately rough and delicate feeling, can quite overwhelm. That's because your voice, if you are fluent in American, is anticipated, pre-wired into the declarative but intimate, easy-flowing lines. It's as if you were a phonograph needle dropped into a vinyl groove.[163]

Presumably, here, Schjeldahl has in mind all of Whitman's "language experiment," not, of course, just what Whitman owes to the KJB. However, as I have tried to suggest in this chapter (and throughout the volume) much of the style that Whitman molds in that experiment in varied ways does devolve ultimately out of the English Bible—Schjeldahl's evocation of "the verse's unhurried, insinuating cadences" is especially redolent of this debt. Whitman not only inherits (parts of) Tyndale's plain style, but he tunes it for an American voice; it too is one of "those autochthonic bequests of Asia" (albeit mediated by England) that the poet seizes upon and adjusts "entirely to the modern."[164] One need not press Schjeldahl's evocation of a singular American vernacular too far (there are many different varieties of written and spoken American English in a twenty-first century America far more geographically expansive and culturally diverse than in Whitman's day) to appreciate nonetheless the familiarity ("if you are fluent in American") of Whitman's "barbaric yawp," some part of which is a poeticization of a prose style devolved from the King James Bible.

---

163 "How to Celebrate Walt Whitman's Two-Hundredth Birthday," *The New Yorker* (June 24, 2019). Intriguingly, the poet's own voice has been preserved, not in vinyl but in wax, reading from his late poem "America," https://whitmanarchive. org/multimedia/America.mp3. For details about the recording (from 1889 or 1890), see E. Folsom, "The Whitman Recording," *WWQR* 9 (1992), 214–16. The poem, which personifies America as a "seated Mother" (line 5), "Centre of equal daughters and equal sons" (line 1, was first published in the *New York Herald* (11 February 1888), 4, https://whitmanarchive.org/published/periodical/poems/ per.00081.html; cf. *LG* 1891–92, 387.

164 "The Bible as Poetry," *The Critic* 3 (February 3, 1883), 57.

Afterword

"No book is more conspicuous in Walt Whitman's 'long foreground' than the King James Bible"
— Gay Wilson Allen, *Reader's Guide to Walt Whitman* (1970)

In the preceding pages I have endeavored, through "careful investigation" and "massing of evidence,"[1] to reveal the fact of Walt Whitman's stylistic debt to the King James Bible and the nature and extent of this debt—G. W. Allen's estimation that the KJB is one of the "more conspicuous" books in Whitman's "long foreground" is not an exaggeration.[2] My focus throughout has been on the immediate run-up to the 1855 *Leaves* and the general period of the first three editions of Whitman's remarkable book. The intent has been to press the idea that the KJB's influence was consequential for many of the leading elements of Whitman's mature style—his long lines, unmetered rhythm, parallelism, parataxis, non-narrativity, preference for the periphrastic *of*-genitive. The style of the later period shifts dramatically in many respects. The lengths of Whitman's lines and poems atrophy, punctuation and page layout become more conventional, and some aspects of his 1850s poetic theory become relaxed, e.g., some of those "stock 'poetical' touches" once robustly eschewed appear with

---

1   "Whitman's Debt to the Bible with Special Reference to the Origins of His Rhythm" (unpubl. Ph.D. dissertation, University of Texas, 1938), 1.
2   *A Reader's Guide to Walt Whitman* (Syracuse: Syracuse University, 1970), 24.

©2024 F. W. Dobbs-Allsopp, CC BY-NC 4.0   https://doi.org/10.11647/OBP.0357.07

commonality. A full accounting of Whitman's stylistic debt to the KJB would need to consider the poetry (and other writings) of the later period. I gesture here to this fuller accounting to come with a reading of Whitman's late poem, "Death's Valley."[3]

* * *

On 28 August 1889, H. M. Alden, editor of *Harper's New Monthly Magazine*, wrote Whitman to request a poem to accompany an engraving of a painting by George Inness entitled "The Valley of the Shadow of Death"[4] (1867; see Fig. 49). Alden had "enclosed a proof" of the engraving for Whitman's use.[5] Whitman responded quickly with the requested poem by the next day's mail. [6] He asked for and received ("in a couple of days")[7] a $25 honorarium. However, *Harper's* did not publish the poem until a month after Whitman's death.[8] Although "Death's Valley" was not the last poem Whitman composed, its posthumous publication and biblically inspired provocation make the poem an especially appropriate subject for my own after-word.

---

3   https://whitmanarchive.org/published/periodical/poems/per.00028

4   http://emuseum.vassar.edu/objects/59/the-valley-of-the-shadow-of-death

5   Letter from H. M. Alder to Walt Whitman (28 August 1889, https:// whitmanarchive.org/biography/correspondence/tei/loc.04087.html. Unfortunately, H. Aspiz's treatment of the poem in his study *So Long! Walt Whitman's Poetry of Death* ([Tuscaloosa and London: University of Alabama, 2004], 241–43) contains inaccurate or misleading information, including the observation that Whitman "may never have seen the original painting" (242). Strictly speaking this is likely true. But Whitman did have the "proof" of the engraving (by W. Closson), which Alden included with his letter to Whitman and which Whitman acknowledged receiving (and perhaps returning: "illustration in text") in his return letter to Alden the next day (Letter from Walt Whitman to H. M. Alden [29 August 1889], https://whitmanarchive.org/biography/correspondence/tei/ med.00881.html). Importantly, "Death's Valley" is a poem that responds to the painting by Inness. Cf. *WWWC* 5: 470–71.

6   Letter from Walt Whitman to H. M. Alden (29 August 1889).

7   *WWWC* 5: 471.

8   *Harper's New Monthly Magazine* 84 (April 1892), 707–0 9, https://whitmanarchive. org/published/periodical/poems/per.00028.

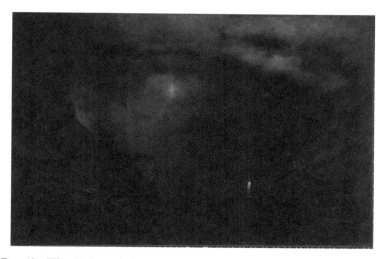

Fig. 49: "The Valley of the Shadow of Death" (1867) by George Inness. Image courtesy of the Francis Lehman Loeb Art Center, Vassar College, http://emuseum.vassar.edu/objects/59/the-valley-of-the-shadow-of-death.

The poem is in the first place a response to Inness's painting, which is as Alden requested: "on the chance that it may meet some spontaneous current of poetic movement in you... let the movement have its course & let us have the result."[9] The parenthetical comment just under the title— "(To accompany a picture; by request")—makes Whitman's ekphrastic ambition explicit. The opening (four-line) stanza is an apostrophe to the unnamed Inness (addressed only as "Thou," "thy," "thee"):

> NAY, do not dream, designer dark,
>
> Thou hast portray'd or hit thy theme entire:
>
> I, hoverer of late by this dark valley, by its confines, having glimpses of it,
>
> Here enter lists with thee, claiming my right to make a symbol too.

The painting, too, is obliquely referenced here—the "dark" of the designer's creation (line 1), that which is "portray'd" (line 2), "this dark valley" (line 3), and the other "symbol" implied by Whitman's avowal "to make a symbol too" (line 4). Later in the poem—the second (lines

---

9   Letter from H. M. Alden to Walt Whitman (28 August 1889). Cf. W. A. Pannapacker, "'Death's Valley' (1892)" in *Walt Whitman: An Encyclopedia* (eds. J. R. LeMaster and D. D. Kummings; New York: Garland Publishing, 1998).

5–11) and third (lines 12–20) stanzas are given over mostly to the making of Whitman's competing "scene" and "song" (line 13) of Death—the half-line "Nor gloom' s ravines, nor bleak, nor dark" (line 14) likely takes its initial cue from the dark, rocky crags that loom forbiddingly on either side of the valley depicted in Inness's painting. The darkness of Inness's color palette in this canvas leaves a lasting impression on viewers. The painting is also plainly in view in the poem's original opening lines that Whitman eventually rejected (after working through several drafts)—"Just as I was folding it up, the thought struck me that I was not satisfied with it—with that part and so I cut it off the sheet—let it start with the other—sent the mutilated piece":[10]

> Aye, well I know 'tis ghastly to descend that f valley:
>
> Preachers, musicians, poets, painters, always render it,
>
> Philosophs exploit—the battle-field, the ship at sea, the myriad beds, all lands,
>
> All, all the past have enter'd, the ancientest humanity we know,
>
> Syria's, India's, Egypt's, Greece's, Rome's;
>
> Till now for us under our very eyes spreading the same to-day,
>
> Grim, ready ~~for our eyes~~, for entrance, yours and mine, ~~our eyes,~~
>
> Here, here 'tis limned.
>
> #
>
> Yet[11]

Here Whitman is already intent on bending the painting's theme, alluded to in "...that f valley:/... Grim" (lines 1, 7), to his own "current of poetic movement"—here literalizing the metaphoric valley as the passageway from life to death and asserting the long history of death as a part of human existence, "all the past have enter'd." His glance at the

---

10   *WWWC* 5: 471. Aspiz (*Whitman's Poetry of Death*, 242) mistakenly asserts that "the editors chose not to print" this first set of lines.

11   "Aye, well I know 'tis ghastly to descend," https://whitmanarchive.org/ manuscripts/transcriptions/loc.00107.html. Several partial, preliminary drafts appear among the images included between pp. 242 and 243 in *WWWC* 5.

painting itself is most explicit in the final line, "Here, here 'tis limned." The primary meaning of "limn," according to Webster's *American Dictionary*, is "to draw or paint; or to paint in water-colors."[12] The deictic "here" references the extratextual "picture" the poem accompanies. Confirmation of this construal is the apostrophe to the painter that followed immediately before Whitman "cut wholly out" the first "third" of the original poem. In fact, the connection was more explicit as what became the poem's opening line ("NAY, do not dream, designer dark") originally started with "Yet," which was precisely "cut... off the sheet" (se Fig. 50).

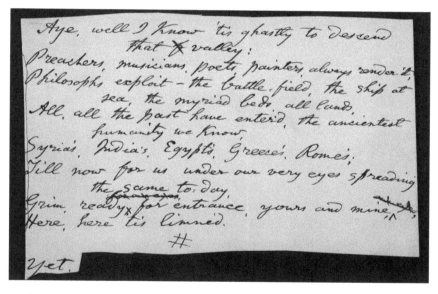

Fig. 50: "Aye, well I know 'tis ghastly to descend." Image courtesy of the Walt Whitman Papers in the Charles E. Feinberg Collection, Manuscript Division, Library of Congress, Washington, D. C. mss18630, box 26; reel 16, https://www.loc.gov/item/mss1863000626

However, "limned" also can have transferred and figurative meanings, including to describe or depict in words, a usage that the *OED* dates back to the seventeenth century (meaning 3b). Therefore, Whitman's limning "Here, here" may be intentionally doubled, pointing to Inness's

12   N. Webster, *An American Dictionary of the English Language* (Springfield: G. & C. Merriam, 1857), 666.

painting and also to his own "symbol" made of words—"And out of these and thee,/ I make a scene, a song, brief" ("Death's Valley," lines 12–13). He uses "limn" with this transferred sense in both "As a Strong Bird on Pinions Free"[13] (1872)[14] and "Had I the choice"[15] (1885). The latter poem is especially revealing because it intentionally plays on the word's base meaning, viz. "To limn their portraits, stately, beautiful, and emulate at will" (line 2) and its extended sense—the "portraits" here in view are of the "greatest bards" (Homer, Shakespeare, Tennyson) and their verbal art, "Metre or wit the best, or choice conceit to wield in perfect rhyme, delight of singers" (line 5). The speaker would "gladly barter" these poetic marvels would one wave of the sea "its trick to me transfer,/ Or breathe one breath of yours upon my verse" (lines 7–8).[16] In "Death's Valley" Whitman's "mutilated" limning in words is poised to do battle with Inness's visual art ("enter lists with thee," line 4). The "Here" that heads line 4 unmistakably points to Whitman's own poem.

The published version of "Death's Valley" consists of three stanzas, each organized sententially. The lines are irregular, ranging between four and eighteen words in length, with two of the shortest lines opening ("NAY, do not dream, designer dark," six words) and closing ("Sweet, peaceful, welcome Death," four words) the poem, forming a lineal envelope. The poem itself is "brief" (line 13)— "not a long job."[17] The small scale of the three stanzas emphasizes the syntactic connectedness of the lines, sometimes lending them an enjambed feel that contrasts with the closed feel of so many of Whitman's early end-stopped lines apportioned in long catalogues. Lines 3–4 are emblematic. The subject "I" heads line 3 and is qualified by a short series of appositional phrases ("by this dark valley, by its confines, having glimpses of it"). Line 4 completes the incomplete clause: "I.../ Here enter lists with thee." The longer second stanza (seven lines), where the speaker tallies his own experiences of death, with its receptions ("have seen" [2x], "have watch'd," "and seen"), lineal apposition (lines 8–9), three line-initial "And"s (lines 7, 9–10; cf. lines 12, 17), some interlinier parallelism (e.g.,

---

13 https://whitmanarchive.org/published/periodical/poems/per.00090
14 *New York Herald* (26 June 1872), 3.
15 https://whitmanarchive.org/published/periodical/poems/per.00003
16 "Had I the choice" was initially published as a part of the sequence "Fancies at Navesink," *The Nineteenth Century* 18 (August 1885), 234–37, 234. Cf. *LG* 1892, 389.
17 *WWWC* 5: 471.

lines 7–9; cf. lines 13–15), and even an occasional internally parallel line (e.g., "And I have watch' d the death-hours of the old; and seen the infant die," line 7; cf. line 18), gestures back to the style of the younger Whitman. And yet at the same time, all seems somehow "mutilated," to use Whitman's word for his foreshortened poem. The punctuation is conventional throughout. And Whitman has relaxed his earlier proscription of stock poetic elements, which flood this poem: "NAY" (line 1), "Thou" (line 2), "thy" (line 2), "thee" (lines 4, 11, 12, 13, 14, 18 [2x]), "hast" (line 2), elided spelling of past tense verbs ("portry'd," line2; "watch'd," line 7; "call'd," line 19), and inverted syntax (e.g., "theme entire," line 2; "a song, brief," line 13).[18]

Though provoked initially by Inness's painting, the psalm that inspired the painting is also in view for Whitman from the start.[19] The second line of the discarded opening stanza—"Preachers... always render it"—makes apparent that the biblical source of "that f valley" is as significant for Whitman as is Inness's painterly rendering of it. The speaker's doubled confession "not fear of thee" (line 13) and "for I do not fear thee" (line 14) is inspired directly from the language of Inness's theme verse, Ps 23:4: "I will fear no evil; for thou art with me." The cadence of the phrase "for I do not fear thee" mimes (and chimes with) the psalm's "for thou art with me."[20] And the line "Of the broad blessed light and perfect air, with meadows, rippling tides, and trees and flowers and grass" (line 16) is a Whitmanian elaboration of the psalm's familiar images of "green pastures" and "still waters" (v. 2)—nothing in Inness's painting answers to this beatific outburst exalting the "Rich, florid... life" (line 19) of mortal existence; hence Whitman's initial "NAY" (capitalized for emphasis). Other striking biblicisms are noticeable, e.g., "breathed my every breath" (line 10) reprises (an d repurposes) Tyndale's famous cognate coinage (not present in the Hebrew) from the

---

18 Additional stock elements from "Aye, well I know 'tis ghastly to descend" include: "Aye" (line 1), inverted syntax (e.g., "well I know," line 1; "that f valley:/... Grim," lines 1, 7), "'tis" (lines 1, 7), and elided spelling of past tense verb ("enter'd," line 4)—and perhaps the doubled "All, all" (line 4) and "Here, here" (line 7).

19 Whitman alludes to Psalm 23 a number of times elsewhere in his writings, see Posey, "Whitman's Debt," 190; B. LINE Bergquist, "Walt Whitman and the Bible: Language Echoes, Images, Allusions, and Ideas" (unpubl. Ph.D. dissertation, University of Nebraska, 1979), 98, 123, 280, 290, 308.

20 Cf. Pannapacker, "'Death's Valley' (1892)" ("'Death' s Valley' echoes the diction and cadence of the Psalms").

second creation story, "and brethed into his face the breath of lyfe" (Gen 2:7; cf. Ezek 37:9); the capitalized references to "God's" (line 17) and "Heaven" (line 18), signaling their biblical lineage; the well balanced, internally parallel line, "Thee, holiest minister of Heaven—thee, envoy, usherer, guide at last of all" (line 18), with matching biblical "thee"s and *of*-genitives ("minister of Heaven"// "guide... of all").

In the end, however, Whitman turns both painting and psalm on their proverbial heads. The psalm is a confession of trust in Yahweh, the "thou" directly addressed in vv. 4–5, and the painting Inness's Swedenborgian gloss on the Christian pilgrim's dependence on the light of "faith alone"—symbolized above all by the cross given in "place of the moon" and the dark valley's blue hues, the color of faith (for Inness).[21] The palliative consolation for the harsh reality of mortal existence implicit in the cross *cum* moon and the dark tonalities in which Inness colors the pilgrim's journey (on earth) in the shadow of death were contrary (in emphasis) to Whitman's own ideas about death—"Nor gloom's ravines, nor bleak, nor dark...,/ Nor celebrate the struggle, or contortion, or hard-tied knot" (lines 14–15).[22] Whitman's dissatisfaction with the opening stanza eventually discarded was perhaps because he realized he had already conceded too much to Inness's vision, viz. "well I know 'tis ghastly.../ Grim" (lines 1, 7). The change from "Yet" to "NAY" emphasizes Whitman's resolve to "make... a song" welcoming of death. Therefore, in contrast to Psalm 23 and Inness's painting, Whitman fixes on death itself, long a favored theme.[23] Death only comes into the psalm, and through the psalm into the painting, through that most enchanting of the KJB's mistranslations, "the valley of the shadow of death." The Hebrew is *gê' ṣalmāwet*, an adnominal genitival construction (see Chapter Five) consisting of "valley" (+ of) + "darkness." The second Hebrew noun (*ṣalmāwet*)

---

21   S. M. Promey, "The Ribband of Faith: George Inness, Color Theory, and the Swedenborgian Church," *American Art Journal* 26 (1994), 52–54. Promey emphasizes the "sharp contrast" between the painting and Whitman's (supposed) "meditation" on it.

22   For a broad characterization of these ideas, see Aspiz. *Whitman's Poetry of Death*, esp. 1–32.

23   "The Tomb-Blossoms" (1842), https://whitmanarchive.org/published/fiction/ short, in *EPF*, 94: "There have of late frequently come to me times when I do not dread the grave—when I could lie down, and pass my immortal part through the valley and shadow, as composedly as I quaff water after a tiresome walk."

signifies "an impenetrable gloom, pitch, darkness,"[24] but early on was provided with something of a folk etymology, decomposing the term as if it were a compound of *ṣēl* "shadow" and *māwet* "death" (Septuagint: *skias thanatou*; cf. Job 38:17). Whitman's title, "Death's Valley," deftly thematizes the focus of his poem. By first abbreviating the biblical phrase that Inness takes for his title, and then choosing to render the genitival relation with the apostrophe + "s" construction instead of the biblical English phrasing with an *of*-genitive,[25] the valley in question—that which "preachers, musicians, poets, painters, always render"—ceases to be a mere metaphor (a "dark valley") for danger and becomes the very place of Death's abode, a place to which "'tis ghastly to descend." The change-up from the biblical English genitive formation also allows Whitman to enclose his poem within an inclusio, "Death's" (first word of the title)//"Death" (last word of the poem)— Death literally has the first and last word. And as this inclusio encloses the lineal envelope of short opening and closing lines (lines 1, 20), Whitman fashions for his poetic "scene" a frame not unlike that which framed Inness's picture but made up entirely of words—a most literal ekphrasis.

And, importantly, Death, like the old Canaanite god Mot himself, is personified—the owner of the valley—addressed directly ("O Death," line 10), countering the psalm's opening, "The LORD is my shepherd" (v. 1). God has been demoted, all but kicked out of Whitman's poem— not unlike "Lucifer" in Isa 14:12—present only vestigially as another way of naming Death: "God' s beautiful eternal right hand,/ Thee, holiest minister of Heaven...." "Thou" and "thy" of Psalm 23 are used to address Yahweh (vv. 4–5), whereas these archaic pronouns solicit in Whitman's "song" a counterpointing use of "thee" to address Death after line 10:

> And I myself for long, O Death, have breathed my every breath
>
> Amid the nearness and the silent thought of thee.

---

24   *HALOT*, 1029. Cf. C. L. Seow, *Job 1–21* (Illuminations; Grand Rapids: Eerdmans, 2013), 341–43. So elsewhere in the KJB the phrase "shadow of death" is associated with darkness generally (Job 3:5; 10:21–22; 38:17), even where death is not at issue (e.g., Job 16:16; 24:17; 34:33; Ps 44:19; 107:10, 14; Isa 9:2; Jer 13:16; Amos 5:8).

25   The *s*-genitive, not prominent in the 1855 *Leaves*, appears three times in the published poem and five times in the rejected stanza.

And out of these and thee,

I make a scene, a song, brief (not fear of thee,

Nor gloom's ravines, nor bleak, nor dark—for I do not fear thee,

Nor celebrate the struggle, or contortion, or hard-tied knot),

Of the broad blessed light and perfect air, with meadows, rippling tides, and trees

   and flowers and grass,

And the low hum of living breeze—and in the midst God's beautiful eternal right

   hand,

Thee, holiest minister of Heaven—thee, envoy, usherer, guide at last of all,

Rich, florid, loosener of the stricture-knot call'd life,

Sweet, peaceful, welcome Death.

The line-ending "thee"s in lines 11–14 help tie the second and third stanzas together and set up the hymnic crescendo at poem's end, beginning with the internally parallel line 18 and ending by bidding "welcome" to "Death" (line 20). Within the poem these accepting "thee"s as they chime and punctuate the latter stanzas counter the disparate second person forms used in the opening, disapproving apostrophe of the painter. And it is not just the God of Psalm 23 who personified Death preempts but also the Christ symbolized in Inness's moon-like cross. Death is glossed as "God' s beautiful eternal right hand" (line 1), usurping the place the New Testament reserves for the risen Christ (Mark 16:19; Luke 22:69; Acts 2:33; 5:31; 7:55, 56; Rom 8:34; Col 3:1; Heb 10:12; 12:2; 1 Pet 3:22), whom in "Blood-Money" Whitman calls "the beautiful God, Jesus."[26] Whitman's habit of reading against the biblical grain is evident here again, as it was throughout his life.

Where Whitman reads with the psalm (and against Inness) is in his tone. His is a joy-filled song. Taking his cue from the buoyant and

---

26   *New York Daily Tribune*, Supplement (22 March 1850), 1, https://whitmanarchive. org/published/periodical/poems/per.00089.

comforting images of the psalm's iconic "green pastures" and "still waters" (v. 2), Whitman makes "a scene, a song" "Of the broad blessed light...,/ And the low hum of living breeze" (not "gloom's ravines" of Inness's devising), "and in the midst" of such a rich and ample life is "Sweet, peaceful, welcome Death." There is a way in which this attitude is fundamentally non-Hebraic. With high infant mortality rates, comparatively short average lifespans (30 years for women, 40 years for men), and deep attachments to the dead ancestors, the ancients, like Whitman, accepted death as a given part of life. Unlike Whitman, the typical pose was to lament death (and suffering), viz. "My God, my God, why hast thou forsaken me?" (Ps 22:1; cf. Mark 15:34; Matt 27:46). In the case of "Death's Valley," the adoration and trust that drive Psalm 23—a hymnic psalm that is not concerned with death (except in the KJB's mistranslation)—are taken by Whitman as found and formed into another—a final—rendition of the poet's familiar pose before death— "Sweet, peaceful, welcome."

* * *

From the vantage point of this one posthumously published poem both continuities and dissimilarities with the style of the early Whitman as it regards the Bible are noticeable. The impress of the Bible on Whitman continues, as does the poet's penchant for reading against the grain of its plain sense. Whitman's conjuring of personified Death as a means of decentering Yahweh in the biblical psalm is a striking example of the latter, lifelong tendency . Whereas the early Whitman worked assiduously to rid his poems of "stock 'poetical' touches" and all but the most necessary of second-hand allusions, in "Death's Valley" biblical stock phrasing abound ("Thou," "thy," "thee," "hast," "Heaven," elided past tense verbs, etc.) and there is no reluctance to engage the biblical psalm that inspired Inness's painting. Indeed, the later Whitman seems much less self-conscious about using language from the Bible generally. Another brief example comes in "If I Should Need to Name, O Western World!"[27] The poem was published just ahead of the presidential election of 1884 (later entitled, "Election Day, November, 1884" [*LG*

---

27   *Philadelphia Press* (25 October 1884), https://whitmanarchive.org/published/ periodical/poems/per.00010 ; cf. "If I should need to name, O Western World," https://whitmanarchive.org/manuscripts/transcriptions/loc.00203.html.

1891–92, 391]) and has as its basic conceit the scene of Elijah on the mountain waiting for Yahweh to pass by in 1 Kings 19. Famously, there is wind, an earthquake, and fired (all alluding to the episode in Exodus 19 with Moses on Mount Sinai), but Yahweh was not made manifest in any of these natural marvels. Instead, Elijah's god comes "as a still small voice" (I Kgs 19:12). According to Whitman's poem the "powerfulest scene to-day" is not America's natural wonders (paralleling those of the biblical stories) but "This seething hemisphere' s humanity, as now, I' d name—*the still small voice* preparing—America' s choosing day," (line 4). Whitman's italics signal his verbatim use of biblical language (a coinage which again goes back ultimately to Tyndale, this time from his posthumously published translation of the Former Prophets in Matthew's Bible of 1537). Not only are second-hand quotations no longer avoided; here the language is even underscored. Here, too, Whitman is happy to read against the biblical grain. His next line parenthetically notes that "(The heart of it not in the chosen—the act itself the main, the quadrennials choosing,)," which would appear to be intended to counter what the Bible's "still small voice" reveals, namely, that Elijah is to announce to the future kings of Aram and Israel that Elisha is to be Elijah's prophetic successor (I Kgs 19:15–19)—"the chosen."

One consequence of this relaxation of some of the stringencies of Whitman's earlier poetic theory is that the poet's various biblicisms in these late poems are easier to track, as they are less elusive; indeed, they are often granted semantic visibility at the surface of the poems, as is evident in both "Death's Valley" and "If I Should Need to Name."

A further noticeable difference is the reduction in typical lengths of both line and poem—the latter "mutilated" as Whitman observes. These trends toward foreshortening in the later poems have been noted more generally (see Chapter Three). This retraction in amplitude blunts the shaping force the KJB had on Whitman's early lineal palette. For example, while parallelism continues to feature prominently in Whitman's poetics, the biblical sensibilities that are so apparent in the poet's early longer, two-part, internally parallel lines seem less adamant in abbreviation.[28] However, since Whitman continues to republish the

---

28   Not surprisingly, the two most obviously internally parallel lines in the poem
     (lines 7 and 18) stretch out to biblical English proportions (14 and 13 words in
     length).

older poems intermixed with newer poems in succeeding editions of *Leaves of Grass* the overall impression of these various shifts in style may be more dispersed, less acute. In fact, somewhat counter-intuitively, the greater play of biblical language at the surface of the late poems may give an overall impression of greater biblical influence, even while the impact of the Bible on Whitman's later poetic style seems less pronounced.

These all are but initial impressions. I offer them here, alongside my closing reading of "Death's Valley," as a means of gesturing toward the ongoing need for future scholarship on the topic and of signaling an anticipation of shifts and changes amid continuities as the later Whitman continues to revise and reanimate *Leaves* with each succeeding edition.[29] Only death itself manages to thwart the poet's penchant for "doings and redoings."

---

29   The latter anticipation is acutely observed by K. M. Price in his recent *Whitman in Washington: Becoming the National Poet in the Federal City* (Oxford" Oxford University, 2022).

Selected Bibliography

For Walt Whitman's unpublished writings referenced throughout the body of this volume, see the relevant sections of the Walt Whitman Archive, https://whitmanarchive.org/ (e.g., In Whitman's Hand, https://whitmanarchive.org/manuscripts/index.html) and the various print collections of this material listed below. Here are links to some of the more important of these unpublished writings for this study:

"med Cophósis"notebook,
   https://whitmanarchive.org/manuscripts/notebooks/transcriptions/loc.00005.html

"I know a rich capitalist" notebook,
   https://whitmanarchive.org/manuscripts/notebooks/transcriptions/nyp.00129.html

"Poem incarnating the mind" notebook,
   https://whitmanarchive.org/manuscripts/notebooks/transcriptions/loc.00346.html

"Talbot Wilson" notebook,
   https://whitmanarchive.org/manuscripts/notebooks/transcriptions/loc.00141.html

"Autobiographical Data" notebook,
   https://whitmanarchive.org/manuscripts/notebooks/transcriptions/loc.05935.html

"Rules for Composition,"
   https://whitmanarchive.org/manuscripts/transcriptions/duk.00130.html

"Pictures," holograph notebook,
   https://collections.library.yale.edu/catalog/2007253

The so-called "Blueh Book" edition of the 1860 *Leaves*,
   https://whitmanarchive.org/published/1860-Blue_book/images/index.html

E. Folsom's collection of early, fragmentary manuscript drafts for "I celebrate myself,"
   http://bailiwick.lib.uiowa.edu/whitman

I. Works Published by Walt Whitman

"A Peep at the Israelites," *New York Aurora* (28 March 1842), 2,
https://whitmanarchive.org/published/periodical/journalism/tei/
per.00418.html.

"Doings at the Synagogue," *New York Aurora* (29 March 1842), 2,
https://whitmanarchive.org/published/periodical/journalism/tei/
per.00419.html.

"Shirval: A Tale of Jerusalem," *The Aristidean* (March, 1845),
https://whitmanarchive.org/published/fiction/shortfiction/per.00337.html.

"The Literary World," *The Brooklyn Daily Eagle* (12 October 1846), 2.

"Mississippi at Midnight," *New Orleans Daily Crescent* (6 March 1848), 2,
https://whitmanarchive.org/published/periodical/poems/per.00063.

"Song for Certain Congressmen," *New York Evening Post* (2 March 1850), 2,
https://whitmanarchive.org/published/periodical/poems/per.00004.

"Blood-Money," *New York Daily Tribune*, Supplement (22 March 1850), 1,
https://whitmanarchive.org/published/periodical/poems/per.00089.

"The House of Friends," *New York Daily Tribune* (14 June 1850), 3,
https://whitmanarchive.org/published/periodical/poems/per.00442.

"Resurgemus," *New York Daily Tribune* (21 June 1850), 3,
https://whitmanarchive.org/published/periodical/poems/per.00088.

"Something about Art and Brooklyn Artists," *New York Evening Post*
(1 February 1851).

"Art and Artists," *Daily Advertizer* (3 April 1851).

"Letters from Paumanok," *New York Evening Post* (27 June 1851),
http://whitmanarchive.org/published/periodical/journalism/tei/
per.00264.html.

"Letters from Paumanok," *New York Evening Post* (28 June 1851),
http://whitmanarchive.org/published/periodical/journalism/tei/
per.00265.html.

"Letters from Paumanok," *New York Evening Post* (14 August 1851),
http://whitmanarchive.org/published/periodical/journalism/tei/
per.00266.html.

"Life and Adventures of Jack Engle: An Auto-Biography," *Sunday Dispatch* (in
six installments, 14 March–18 April 1852 (ed. Z. Turpin, in *WWQR* 34/3
[2017], 262–357),
https://whitmanarchive.org/criticism/wwqr/pdf/anc.02130.pdf.

"An Afternoon Lounge About Brooklyn," *Brooklyn Evening Star* (24 May 1852), 2.

"An Hour Among the Portraits," *Brooklyn Evening Star* (7 June 1853), 2.

"A Brooklyn Daguerreotypist," *Brooklyn Daily Eagle* (27 August 1853), 2.

Leaves of Grass (Brooklyn, New York, 1855),
    https://whitmanarchive.org/published/LG/1855/whole.html.

Leaves of Grass (Brooklyn, New York, 1856),
    https://whitmanarchive.org/published/LG/1856/whole.html.

Leaves of Grass (Boston: Thayer and Eldridge, 1860–61),
    https://whitmanarchive.org/published/LG/1860/whole.html.

Drum-Taps (New-York, 1865),
    https://whitmanarchive.org/published/other/DrumTaps.html.

Drum-Taps and Sequel to Drum-Taps (New-York/Washington, 1865/1865–66),
    https://whitmanarchive.org/published/other/DrumTapsSequel.html.

Leaves of Grass (WM. E. Chapin & Co, Printers, 24 Beekman Street, New York, 1867),
    https://whitmanarchive.org/published/LG/1867/whole.html.

"The Singer in the Prison," *Saturday Evening Visitor* (25 December 1869),
    https://whitmanarchive.org/published/periodical/poems/per.00079.

Leaves of Grass (Washington D. C., 1871),
    https://whitmanarchive.org/published/LG/1871/whole.html.

Democratic Vistas (Washington, D.C., 1871).

"As a Strong Bird on Pinions Free," *New York Herald* (26 June 1872), 3,
    https://whitmanarchive.org/published/periodical/poems/per.00090.

Two Rivulets (Camden, New Jersey: Author's Edition, 1876).

"Emerson's Books, (The Shadows of Them.)," *Boston Literary World* (22 May 1880).

"The Poetry of the Future," *NAR* 132 (1881), 195–210.

Specimen Days & Collect (1882).

"The Bible as Poetry," *The Critic* 3 (3 February 1883), 57.

Leaves of Grass (Boston: James R. Osgood and Company, 1881–82),
    https://whitmanarchive.org/published/LG/1881/whole.html.

"If I Should Need to Name, O Western World!", Philadelphia Press (26 October 1884), 5,
    https://whitmanarchive.org/published/periodical/poems/per.00010;.

"Fancies at Navesink," The Nineteenth Century 18 (August 1885), 234–37,
    https://whitmanarchive.org/published/periodical/poems/per.00003.

November Boughs (Philadelphia: David McKay, 1888).

"A Backward Glance o'er Travel'd Roads" in *November Boughs*.

"America," *New York Herald* (11 February 1888), 4,
    https://whitmanarchive.org/published/periodical/poems/per.00081.

"Old Chants," *Truth* 10 (19 March 1891), 11,
    https://whitmanarchive.org/published/periodical/figures/per.00048.001.jpg.

Good-Bye My Fancy (1891)

"Death's Valley," *Harper's New Monthly Magazine* 84 (April 1892), 707–09,
    https://whitmanarchive.org/published/periodical/poems/per.00028.

Leaves of Grass. Philadelphia: David McKay, 1891–92,
    https://whitmanarchive.org/published/LG/1891/whole.html.

II. Collected Writings of Walt Whitman, Special, and Translations

Poems by Walt Whitman (ed. W. M. Rossetti; London: John Camden Hotten,
    Piccadilly, 1868),
    https://whitmanarchive.org/published/books/other/rossetti.html.

The Complete Prose Works (Philadelphia: David McKay, 1892),
    https://whitmanarchive.org/published/other/CompleteProse.html.

In Re Walt Whitman (eds. H. L. Traubel et al.; Philadelphia: David McKay,
    1893).

Notes and Fragments Left by Walt Whitman (ed. R. M. Bucke; London and
    Ontario: Talbot, 1899).

The Complete Writings of Walt Whitman (eds. R. M. Bucke, T. B. Harned, H.
    Traubel, and O. L. Triggs; New York: G. P. Putnam's Sons, 1902).

The Uncollected Poetry and Pose of Walt Whitman (ed. E. Holloway; 2 vols; Garden
    City: Doubleday, 1921).

Walt Whitman's Workshop: *A Collection of Unpublished Manuscripts* (ed. C. J.
    Furness; Cambridge, MA; 928).

A Child's Reminiscence (eds. T. O. Mabbott and R. G. Silver,; Seattle: University
    of Washington, 1930).

New York Dissected (eds. E. Holloway and R. Adimari; New York: R. R. Wilson,
    1936).

The Early Poems and the Fiction (ed. T. L. Brasher; New York: New York
    University, 1963).

Prose Works 1892 (ed. F. Stovall; 2 vols; New York: New York University,
    1963–64).

Leaves of Grass, Comprehensive Reader's Edition (eds. H. W. Blodgett and S. Bradley; New York: New York University Press, 1965).

Walt Whitman's Blue Book (ed. A. Golden; New York: New York Public Library, 1968).

Daybooks and Notebooks (ed. W. White; 3 vols; New York: New York University Press, 1978).

Walt Whitman's Leaves of Grass: The First (1855) Edition (ed. M. Cowley; New York: Penguin Books, 1976 [1959]).

'Alē 'Ēsev [Leaves of Grass] (trans. S. Halkin; Tel Aviv: Sifriat Poalim and Hakibbutz Hameuchad Publishing House Ltd, 1984 [1952]).

Notebooks and Unpublished Prose Manuscripts (ed. E. F. Grier; 6 vols; New York: New York University Press, 1984).

Song of Myself: With a Complete Commentary (eds. E. Folsom and C. Merrill; Iowa City: University of Iowa, 2016).

Leaves of Grass, 1860: The 150th Anniversary Facsimile Edition (ed. J. Stacy; Iowa City: Iowa University, 2009), https://doi.org/10.2307/j.ctt20mvcf9.4

Walt Whitman's Selected Journalism (eds. D. A. Nover and J. Stacy; Iowa City: University of Iowa, 2014), https://doi.org/10.13008/0737-0679.2248

III. Other Literature

Alexander, P.S. "Targum, Targumim" in *Anchor Bible Dictionary* (eds. D. N. Freedman et al.; New York: Doubleday, 1992), VI, 320–31.

Allen, G. W. "Biblical Analogies for Walt Whitman's Prosody," *Revue Anglo-Americaine* 6 (1933), 490–507.

_____. "Biblical Echoes in Whitman's Works," *American Literature* 6 (1934), 302–15.

_____. *American Prosody* (New York: American Book, 1935).

_____. *The Solitary Singer: A Critical Biography of Walt Whitman* (rev ed; New York: New York University, 1967 [1955]).

_____. *A Reader's Guide to Walt Whitman* (Syracuse: Syracuse University, 1970).

_____. *The New Walt Whitman Handbook* (New York: New York University, 1986)

Allen, G. W., and E. Folsom (eds.), Walt Whitman and the World (Iowa City: University of Iowa, 1995), https://whitmanarchive.org/criticism/current/pdf/anc.01049.pdf

Alonso Schökel, L. *A Manual of Hebrew Poetics* (SubBib 11; Roma: Editrice Pontificio Istituto Biblico, 1988).

Alter, R. *The Art of Biblical Poetry* (New York: Basic Books, 1985).

_____. *The Book of Psalms: A Translation with Commentary* (New York: W. W. Norton, 2007).

_____. *Pen of Iron: American Prose and the King James Bible* (Princeton: Princeton University, 2010), https://doi.org/10.1515/9781400834358

Anonymous. "Review of 1860–61 *Leaves of Grass*," *Cosmopolite* (4 August 1860).

Anonymous, "Walt Whitman, a Kosmos," *The Springfield Sunday Republican* (13 November 1881), 4.

Aspiz, H. *So Long! Walt Whitman's Poetry of Death* (Tuscaloosa and London: University of Alabama, 2004).

Asselineau, R. *The Evolution of Walt Whitman: An Expanded Edition* (Iowa City: University of Iowa, 1999 [1960, 1962]), https://whitmanarchive.org/criticism/current/pdf/anc.01050.pdf

Attridge, D. *Poetic Rhythm: An Introduction* (Cambridge: Cambridge University, 1995).

Bandy, W. T. "An Unknown 'Washington Letter' by Walt Whitman," *WWQR* 2/3 (1984), 23–27.

Barlow, W. *The Sum and Substance of the Conference... at Hampton Court* (London, 1604).

Bartel, T. G. "The Origin of Longfellow's 'The Warning,'" *Notes and Queries* 65/3 (2018), 377–78, https://doi.org/10.1093/notesj/gjy058

Bauman R., and C. Briggs, *Voices of Modernity: Language Ideologies and the Politics of Inequality* (Cambridge: Cambridge University, 2003), https://doi.org/10.1017/cbo9780511486647

Bentzon, T. "Un Poète américain, Walt Whitman; 'Muscle and Pluck Forever,'" *Revue des Deux Mondes* (1 June 1872), 565–82.

Berlin, A. *The Dynamics of Biblical Parallelism* (Bloomington: Indiana University, 1985).

Bergquist, B. L. "Walt Whitman and the Bible: Language Echoes, Images, Allusions, and Ideas" (unpubl. Ph.D. dissertation, University of Nebraska, 1979).

Beyers, C. *A History of Free Verse* (University of Arkansas, 2001), https://doi.org/10.2307/j.ctv8j72v

Birney, A. "Missing Whitman Notebooks Returned to Library of Congress," *WWQR* 12 (1995), 217–29.

Blair, H. *Critical Dissertation on the Poems of Ossian* (Garland, 1765).

_____. *Lectures on Rhetoric and Belles Lettres* (London: Thomas Tegg, 1841 [1783]).

Blémont, E. "La Poésie en Angleterre et aux Etats-Unis, III, Walt Whitman," *Renaissance Artistique et Littéraire* 7 (June 1872), 54–56; 11 (July 1872), 86–87; 12 (July 1872), 90–91.

Bloom, H. *The Anxiety of Influence: A Theory of Poetry* (New York/Oxford: Oxford University, 1997 [1973]).

Bohan, R. L. "Walt Whitman and the Sister Arts," *WWQR* 16 (1999), 153–60.

_____. *Looking into Walt Whitman: American Art, 1850–1920* (University Park: Pennsylvania State University, 2006).

Bradley, S. "The Fundamental Metrical Principle in Whitman's Poetry" in *On Whitman* (eds. E. H. Cady and L. J. Budd; Durham: Duke University, 1987), 49–71.

Brogan, T. V. F. "Caesura" in *NPEPP*.

_____. "Line" in *NPEPP*.

_____. "Verse and Prose" in *NPEPP*

Buber, M. "*Leitwort* Style in Pentateuch Narrative," in *Scripture and Translation* (eds. M. Buber and F. Rosenzweig; trans. L. Rosenwald and E. Fox; Bloomington: Indiana University, 1994), 114–28.

Buchanan, R. "Walt Whitman," *The Broadway* 1 (November 1867), 188–95.

_____. *David Gray and Other Essays* (London, 1868)

Bucke, R. M. *Walt Whitman* (Philadelphia: David McKay, 1883).

Burroughs, J. *Notes on Walt Whitman as Poet and Person* (New York, 1867).

Campbell, K. "The Evolution of Whitman as Artist," *AL* 6/4 (1934), 259–61.

Cohen, M. "Martin Tupper, Walt Whitman, and the Early Reviews of Leaves of Grass," *WWQR* 16/1 (1998), 23–31.

Cooper, G. B. "Free Verse" in *PEPP*.

Coulombe, L. "'To Destroy the Teacher': Whitman and Martin Farquhar Tupper's 1851 Trip to America," *WWQR* 4 (1996), 199–209.

Crawley, T. E. *The Structure of Leaves of Grass* (Austin: University of Texas, 1970).

Cross, F. M. *Leaves from an Epigrapher's Notebook* (Winona Lake: Eisenbrauns, 2003).

Culler, E. S. "Romanticism" in *Walt Whitman in Context* (eds. J. Levin and E. Whitley; Cambridge: Cambridge University, 2018), 654–71, https://doi.org/10.1017/9781108292443.034

Daniell, D. *William Tyndale*: *A Biography* (New Haven: Yale University, 1994).

_____. *The Bible in English*: *Its History and Influence* (New Haven: Yale University, 2003),
https://doi.org/10.12987/9780300183894

Deleuze, G., and C. Parnet, *Dialogues* (trans. H. Tomlison and B. Habberjam; New York: Columbia University, 1977).

Derrida, J. "Signature Event Context" in *The Margins of Philosophy* (trans. A. Bass; Chicago: University of Chicago, 1982), 307–30.

Dixon, W. M. "The English Bible" in Storr, *English Bible*, 43–67.

Dobbs-Allsopp, F. W. "The Enjambing Line in Lamentations: A Taxonomy (Part I)," *ZAW* 113/2 (2001), 219–39.

_____. "The Effects of Enjambment in Lamentations (Part 2)," *ZAW* 113/5 (2001), 370–85.

_____. *Lamentations* (IBC; Louisville: Westminster-John Knox, 2002).

_____. "The Psalms and Lyric Verse" in *The Evolution of Rationality*: *Interdisciplinary Essays in Honor of J. Wentzel van Huyssteen* (ed. F. L. Shults; Grand Rapids: Eerdmans, 2006), 346–79.

_____. "Poetic Discourse and Ethics" in *Dictionary of Scripture and Ethics* (eds. J. Green et al. Grand Rapids, Baker, 2011), 597–600.

_____. *On Biblical Poetry* (Oxford/New York: Oxford University, 2015),
https://doi.org/10.1093/acprof:oso/9780199766901.001.0001

_____. "Robert Lowth, Parallelism, and Biblical Poetry," *Journal of Hebrew Scriptures* 21 (2021), 1–36,
https://doi.org/10.5508/jhs29586

_____. "So-Called 'Number Parallelism' in Biblical Poetry" in *"Like 'Ilu are you Wise"*: *Studies in Northwest Semitic Languages and Literatures in Honor of Dennis G. Pardee* (eds, H. H. Handy et al.; Chicago: University of Chicago, 2022), 205–24.

Doty, M. *What is the Grass*: *Walt Whitman in My Life* (New York: W. W. Norton, 2020).

Driver, S. R. *Introduction to the Literature of the Old Testament* (New York, 1910).

Eadie, J. *Biblical Cyclopaedia* (12th. ed; London: Charles Griffin and Company, 1870 [1848]).

Edmundson, M. *Song of Ourselves*: *Walt Whitman and the Fight for Democracy* (Cambridge: Harvard University, 2021),
https://doi.org/10.4159/9780674258983

Eliot, G. "Transatlantic Latter-Day Poetry," *The Leader* 7 (7 June 1856), 547–48.

Eliot, T. S. "The Borderline of Prose," *New Statesman* 9 (1917), 157–59.

Emerson, R. W. *The Complete Essays and Other Writings of Ralph Waldo Emerson* (ed. B. A. Atkinson; New York: Modern Library, 1950).

Engell, J. "Robert Lowth, Unacknowledged Legislator" in *The Committed Word*: *Literature and Public Values* [University Park: Pennsylvania State University, 1999], 119–40.

_____. "The Other Classic: Hebrew Shapes British and American Literature and Culture" in *The Call of Classical Literature in the Romantic Age* (eds. K. P. Van Anglen and J. Engell; Edinburgh: Edinburgh University, 2017), locs. 7595–7904 (Kindle edition), https://doi.org/10.3366/edinburgh/9781474429641.003.0014

Erkkila, B. *Whitman Among the French: Poet and Myth* (Princeton: Princeton University, 1980).

_____. *Whitman the Political Poet* (New York/Oxford: Oxford University, 1989).

Evans, R. O. "Parallelism" in *Princeton Encyclopedia of Poetry and Poetics* (eds. A. Preminger et al.; engl. ed.; Princeton: Princeton University, 1974).

Ewald, H. (*Die Dichter des Alten Bundes* (Göttingen: Vändenhoeck und Ruprecht, 1866).

Fairbairn, P. *The Imperial Bible-Dictionary* (London: Blackie and Sons, 1866).

Fischer, O. "Syntax" in *The Cambridge History of the English Language, vol. II, 1066–1476* (ed. N. Blake; Cambridge: Cambridge University, 1992).

Folsom, E. "The Whitman Recording," *WWQR* 9 (1992), 214–16.

_____. "'Song of Myself,' Section 1, in Fifteen Languages," *WWQR* 13/1 (1995), 73–89.

_____. "Walt Whitman's Working Notes for the first Edition of Leaves of Grass," *WWQR* 16/2 (1998), 90–95.

_____. "Lucifer and Ethiopia: Whitman, Race, and Poetics Before the Civil War and After" in Reynolds, *Historical Guide*, 46–96.

_____. "Whitman's Notes on Emerson: An Unpublished Manuscript," *WWQR* 18/1 (2000), 60–62, https://doi.org/10.13008/2153-3695.1633

_____. "Erasing Race: The Lost Black Presence in Whitman's Manuscripts" in Wilson, *Whitman Noir*, 20–49, https://doi.org/10.2307/j.ctt20p59h7.4

_____. Whitman Making Books/Books Making Whitman: *A Catalog and Commentary* (Obermann Center for Advanced Studies; Iowa City: University of Iowa, 2005), OBP/, http:/www.whitmanarchive.org/criticism/current/anc.00150.html

Folsom, E., and K. M. Price, Re-Scripting Walt Whitman: An Introduction to his Life and Work (Blackwell, 2005), https://doi.org/10.1002/9780470774939

Fox, J. *Semitic Noun Patterns* (Winona Lake: Eisenbrauns, 2003), https://doi.org/10.1163/9789004369863

Frey, E. F. *Catalogue of the Walt Whitman Collection in the Duke Library* (Durham: Duke University Library, 1945)

Fuller, M. "Things and Thoughts on Europe. No. V," *New York Tribune* (30 September 1846)

Gardiner, J. H. *The Bible as Literature* (New York, 1906).

Gardner, T. "Modern Long Poem" in *NPEPP*.

_____. "Long Poem" in *PEPP*.

Gaskill, H. (ed.). *Ossian Revisited* (Edinburgh: Edinburgh University, 1991).

Geller, S. A. *Parallelism in Early Biblical Poetry* (HSM 20; Missoula: Scholars, 1979).

_____. "Hebrew Prosody and Poetics, Biblical" in *NPEPP*.

_____. "Hebrew Prosody and Poetics, Biblical" in *PEPP*.

G. E. M., "Whitman, Poet and Seer," *The New York Times* (22 January 1882), 4.

Givón, T. "The Drift from VSO to SVO in Biblical Hebrew: the Pragmatics of Tense-Aspect" in *Mechanisms of Syntactic Change* (ed. C. N. Li; Austin: University of Texas, 1977), 184–254.

Godzich, W., and J. Kittay, *The Emergence of Prose*: An Essay in Prosaics (Minneapolis: University of Minnesota, 1987.

Golden, A. "Walt Whitman's Blue Book" in LeMaster and Kummings, *Encyclopedia*, https://whitmanarchive.org/criticism/current/encyclopedia/entry_84.html.

Goodale, D. "Some of Walt Whitman's Borrowings," *AL* 10/2 (1938), 202–13.

Gravil, R. *Romantic Dialogues*: Anglo-American Continuities, 1776–1862 (2d rev. ed.; Penrith: Humanities-Enools, 2015 [2000]).

Gray, G. B. *The Forms of Hebrew Poetry* (London: Hodder and Stoughton, 1915).

Green, S. *A Biblical and Theological Dictionary* (London: Elliot Stock, 1867).

Greene, R. *Post-Petrarchism*: Origins and Innovations of the Western Lyric Sequence (Princeton: Princeton University, 1991).

Greenspan, E. (ed.). *The Cambridge Companion to Walt Whitman* (Cambridge: Cambridge University, 1995).

_____. "Whitman in Israel" in Allen and Folsom, *Walt Whitman and the World*, 386–95.

Greenstein, E. L. "Two Variations of Grammatical Parallelism in Canaanite Poetry and Their Psycholinguistic Background," *Journal of the Ancient Near Eastern Society* 6/1 (1974), 88-105.

_____. "One More Step on the Staircase," *Ugarit-Forschungen* 9 (1977), 77–86.

_____. "How Does Parallelism Mean?" in *A Sense of a Text* (JQRS; eds. S. A. Geller; Winona Lake: Eisenbrauns, 1983), 41–70.

_____. "Aspects of Biblical Poetry," *Jewish Book Annual* 44 (1986-87), 33–42.

_____. "Direct Discourse and Parallelism" in *Discourse, Dialogue, and Debate in the Bible*: *Essays in Honor of Frank H. Polak* (ed. A Brenner-Idan; Sheffield: Sheffield Phoenix, 2014), 79–92.

Greenstein, E. L., and M. O'Connor, "Parallelism" in *PEPP*.

Grier, E. F. "Walt Whitman's Earliest Known Notebook," *PMLA* 83 (1968), 1453–56.

Gross, H. *Sound and Form in Modern Poetry* (Ann Arbor: University of Michigan, 1965).

Grünzweig, W. "Herder, Johann Gottfried von (1744–1803)" in LeMaster and Kummings, *Encyclopedia*, 273.

Gutjahr, P. C. *An American Bible*: *A History of the Good Book in the United States, 1777–1880* (Stanford: Stanford University, 1999).

Hamlin, H. *The Bible in Shakespeare* (Oxford: Oxford University, 2013), https://doi.org/10.1093/acprof:oso/9780199677610.003.0003.

Hammond, G. "William Tyndale's Pentateuch: Its Relation to Luther's German Bible and the Hebrew Original," *Renaissance Quarterly* 33/3 (1980), 351–85.

_____. *The Making of the English Bible* (New York: Philosophical Library, 1983).

Harrison, W. "Walt Whitman's 'November Boughs'," *The Critic* n.s. 11 (19 January 1889), 25.

Hartman, C. O. *Free Verse*: *An Essay on Prosody* (Princeton: Princeton Unibrsity, 1980).

Hemingway, E. *The Sun Also Rises* (New York: Charles Scribner's Sons, 1926).

Herder, J. G. *The Spirit of Hebrew Poetry* (2 vols; trans. J. Marsh; Burlington: Edward Smith, 1833 [1782]).

Higgins, A. C. "Art and Argument: The Rise of Walt Whitman's Rhetorical Poetics, 1838–1855" (unpbl. Ph.D. diss; University of Massachusetts Amherst, 1999).

_____. "Wage Slavery and the Composition of *Leaves of Grass*: The 'Talbot Wilson' Notebook," *WWQR* 20/2 (2002), 53–77, https://doi.org/10.13008/2153-3695.1701

Hilman, J., ed. *The Revivalist: A Collection of Choice Revival Hymns and Tunes* (Troy, NY: J. Hillman Publishing, 1869.

Hindus, M. *Walt Whitman* (New York/London: Routledge, 1997).

Hobbins, J. F. "Regularities in Ancient Hebrew Verse: A New Descriptive Model," *ZAW* 119/4 (2007), 564–85, https://doi.org/10.1515/zaw.2007.040

Hollander, J. *Rhyme's Reason: A Guide to English Verse* (rev. ed.; New Haven: Yale University, 1989 [1981]).

Hollis, C. C. "Whitman and William Swinton: A Co-operative Friendship," *AL* 30 (1959), 425–49.

_____. *Language and Style in Leaves of Grass* (Baton Rouge/London: Louisiana State University, 1983).

Holmstedt, R. "Hebrew Poetry and the Appositive Style: Parallelism, *Requiescat in pacem*," *Vetus Testamentum* (2019), 1–32, https://doi.org/10.1163/15685330-12341379

Hrushovski [Harshav], B. "On Free Rhythms in Modern Poetry" in *Style in Language* (ed. T. Sebeok; New York: Wiley, 1960), 173–90.

_____. ("The Theory and Practice of Rhythm in the Expressionist Poetry of U. Z. Grinberg," *Hasifrut* 1 (Spring 1968), 176–205. (in Hebrew)

_____. "Prosody, Hebrew" in *Encyclopedia Judaica* (1971–72), 13: 1200–03.

_____. *Theory and Practice of Rhythm in the Expressionst Poetry of U. Z. Greenberg* (Tel Aviv: Hakibbutz Hame'uhad, 1978). (in Hebrew)

_____. "Note on the Systems of Hebrew Versification" in The Penguin Book of Hebrew Verse (ed. T. Carmi; New York: Penguin Books, 1982), 57–72.

Junior, J. and J. Schipper, *Black Samson: The Untold Story of an American Icon* (New York/Oxford: Oxford University, 2020), https://doi.org/10.1093/oso/9780190689780.003.0003

Kateb, G. "Walt Whitman and the Culture of Democracy" in Seery, *Political Companion*, 19–46.

Kautzsch, E. *Die Poesie und die Poetischen Bücher des Alten Testaments* (Tübingen and Leipzig, 1902).

Kennedy, W. S. "Walt Whitman's Indebtedness to Emerson" in *An Autolycus Pack of What You Will* (West Yarmouth: Stonecraft, 1927 [1897]).

Kinnell, G. "'Strong is Your Hold': My Encounters with Whitman" in *Leaves of Grass: The Sesquicentennial Essays* (eds. S. Belasco and K. M. Price; Lincoln:

University of Nebraska, 2007), 417–28,
https://doi.org/10.2307/j.ctt1djmfw7.25 .

Kinzie, M. *A Poet's Guide to Poetry* (Chicago: University of Chicago, 1999).

Klammer, M. *Whitman, Slavery, and the Emergence of Leaves of Grass* (University Park: Pennsylvania State University, 1995).

_____. "Slavery and Race" in Kummings, *Companion*, 101–21,
https://doi.org/10.1002/9780470996812.ch8

Kohl, K. M. *Rhetoric, the Bible, and the Origins of Free Verse: The Early "Hymns" of Friedrich Gottlieb Klopstock* (Berlin/New York: de Gruyter, 1990).

Kuebrich, D. "Religion and the Poet-Prophet" in Kummings, *Companion to Walt Whitman*, 197–215,
https://doi.org/10.1002/9780470996812.ch14

Kugel, J. *The Idea of Biblical Poetry: Parallelism and Its History* (Baltimore: Johns Hopkins University, 1981).

Kummings, D. D. (ed.) *A Companion to Walt Whitman* (London: Blackwell, 2006),
https://doi.org/10.1111/b.9781405120937.2005.00037.x

LeMaster, J. R. "Prophecy" in LeMaster and Kummings, *Encyclopedia*,
https://whitmanarchive.org/criticism/current/encyclopedia/entry_613.html.

LeMaster, J. R., and D. D. Kummings, eds. Walt Whitman: An Encyclopedia (New York: Garland, 1998,
https://whitmanarchive.org/criticism/current/encyclopedia/index.html

Levin, J., and E. Whitley (eds.), *Walt Whitman in Context* (Cambridge: Cambridge University, 2018),
https://doi.org/10.1017/9781108292443

Levine, H. J. "'Song of Myself' as Whitman's American Bible," *MLQ* 48/2 (1987), 145–61.

Lichtmann, M. R. "'Exquisite Artifice': Parallelism in Hopkins' Poetics" in *The Contemplative Poetry of Gerard Manley Hopkins* (Princeton: Princeton University, 1989), 7–60.

Longenbach, J. *The Art of the Poetic Line* (St. Paul: Graywolf, 2008).

Longfellow, H. W. *Poems on Slavery* (2d ed; Cambridge: John Owen, 1842).

_____. *The Poems of Henry Wadsworth Longfellow* (New York: Harper, 1846).

Loving, J. *Emerson, Whitman, and the American Muse* (Chapel Hill: University of North Carolina, 1982).

_____. *Walt Whitman: A Song of Himself* (Berkeley: University of California, 1999).

_____. "The Political Roots of *Leaves of Grass*" in Reynolds, *Historical Guide*.

Lowenstamm, S. E. "The Expanded Colon in Biblical and Ugaritic Verse," *Journal of Semitic Studies* 14 (1969), 175–96.

Lowes, J. L. "The Noblest Monument of English Prose" in Storr, *The English Bible*, 16–42.

Lowth, R. *Isaiah: A New Translation* (London: J. Nichols, 1778; reprinted in *Robert Lowth (1710–1787): The Major Works* [London: Routledge, 1995]).

_____. *Lectures on the Sacred Poetry of the Hebrews* (2 vols.; trans. G. Gregory; London: J. Johnson, 1787; reprinted in *Robert Lowth (1710–1787): The Major Works*, vols. 1–2 [London: Routledge, 1995]).

Macpherson, J. *Fragments of Ancient Poetry, Collected in the Highlands of Scotland, and Translated from the Garlic or Erse Language* (Edinburgh: G. Hamilton and J, Balfour, 1760).

_____. *Fingal, an Ancient Epic Poem, in Six Books: Together with Several Other Poems* (London: Becket and P. A. De Hondt, 1762).

_____. *The Works of Ossian, the Song of Fingal, in Two Volumes* (London: Becket and P. A. De Hondt, 1765).

_____. *The Poems of Ossian* (London: Joseph Rickerby, 1838).

_____. *The Poems of Ossian* (Philadelphia: Thomas, Cowperthwait and Co., 1839).

Mazur, K. *Poetry and Repetition: Walt Whitman, Wallace Stevens, John Ashbery* (New York/London: Routledge, 2005), https://doi.org/10.4324/9780203506547

McCarthy, C. *All the Pretty Horses* (New York: Knopf, 1992).

McGann, J. J. *Social Values and Poetic Acts: A Historical Judgment of Literary Work* (Cambridge: Harvard University, 1988).

McGrath, A. *In the Beginning: A History of the King James Bible and How It Changed a Nation, a Language, and a Culture* (New York: Anchor, 2008).

Miller, M. *Collage of Myself* (Lincoln: University of Nebraska, 2010), https://doi.org/10.2307/j.ctt1dfnr7z.

Miller, P. D., and J. J. M. Roberts, *The Hand of the Lord: A Reassessment of the "Ark Narrative" of 1 Samuel* (Baltimore: Johns Hopkins University, 1977).

Mills, A. *The Ancient Hebrews* (New York: A. S. Barnes, 1856).

Mitchell. R. ("A Prosody for Whitman?", *PMLA* 84/6 (1969), 1606–12.

Molinoff, K. *Some Notes on Whitman's Family* (Brooklyn: Comet, 1941).

Moon, M. *Disseminating Whitman: Revision and Corporality in Leaves of Grass* (Cambridge: Harvard University, 1993).

Moulton, R. G. *The Literary Study of the Bible* (2d ed; Boston, 1899 [1895]).

_____. *The Modern Reader's Bible*: *The Psalms and Lamentations* (New York: Macmillan, 1898).

_____. *Modern Reader's Bible for Schools* (New York: Macmillan, 1922).

Nielson, J., and R. Skousen, "How Much of the King James Bible is William Tyndale's?," *Reformation* 3 (1998), 49–74.

Norton, C. E. Review of *Leaves of Grass*, *Putnam's Monthly* (September 1855), 321.

Norton, D. *A History of the Bible as Literature* (2 vols; Cambridge: Cambridge University, 1993).

_____. *A History of the Bible as Literature* (Cambridge: Cambridge University, 2004), https://doi.org/10.1017/cbo9780511621390

_____. *The King James Bible*: *A Short History from Tyndale to Today* (Cambridge: Cambridge University, 2011), https://doi.org/10.1017/cbo9780511975448

Noyes, R. *A New Translation of the Proverbs, Ecclesiastes, and the Canticles* (Boston: James Monroe and Company, 1846).

Nussbaum, M. C. *Love's Knowledge*: *Essays on Philosophy and Literature* (New York/Oxford: Oxford University, 1992).

_____. "Democratic Desire: Walt Whitman" in Seery, *Political Companion*, 96–130.

O'Connor, M. *Hebrew Verse Structure* (Winona Lake: Eisenbrans, 1980).

_____. "Parallelism" in *NPEPP*.

O'Connor, W. D. "Walt Whitman," *The New York Times* (2 December 1866), 2.

_____. *The Good Gray Poet*: *A Vindication* (New York: Bunch & Huntington, 1866).

Page, H. R. *The Myth of Cosmic Rebellion*: *A Study of Its Reflexes in Ugaritic and Biblical Literature* (SVT LXV; Leiden: Brill, 1996).

Pannapacker, W. A. "'Deatj's Valley' (1892)" in LeMaster and Kummings, *Encyclopedia*, https://whitmanarchive.org/criticism/current/encyclopedia/entry_428.html.

Pardee, D. *Ugaritic and Hebrew Parallelism*: *A Trial Cut* (*'nt I and Proverbs 2*) (SuppVT 39; Leiden: Brill, 1988).

Pardes, I. *Melville's Bibles* (Berkeley: University of California, 2008), https://doi.org/10.1515/9783110815771-003

Perry, B. *Walt Whitman: His Life and Work* (New York: Houghton, Mifflin and Company, 1906).

Petersen, D. L., and K. H. Richards, *Interpreting Hebrew Poetry* (Minneapolis: Fortress, 1992).

Phillips, G. S. "Literature. Leaves of Grass—by Walt Whitman," *New York Illustrated News* 36 (26 May 1860), 429.

Pickett, S. *Words and the Word: Language, Poetics and Biblical Interpretation* (Cambridge: Cambridge University, 1986).

Pinker, P. *The Language Instinct: The New Science of Language and Mind* (Penguin Books, 1995).

Posey, M. N. "Whitman's Debt to the Bible with Special Reference to the Origins of His Rhythm" (unpubl. Ph.D. dissertation, University of Texas, 1938).

Price, K. M. *Whitman and Tradition* (New Haven: Yale University, 1990).

_____. *Walt Whitman: The Contemporary Reviews* (Cambridge: Cambridge University, 1996).

_____. "Love, War, and Revision in Whitman's Blue Book," *Huntington Library Quarterly* 73/4 (2010), 679–92,
https://doi.org/10.1525/hlq.2010.73.4.679

_____. To Walt Whitman, America (Chapel Hill: University of North Carolina, 2004),
https://whitmanarchive.org/criticism/current/anc.00151.html.

_____. *Whitman in Washington: Becoming the National Poet in the Federal City* (Oxford: Oxford University, 2022).

Promey, S. M. "The Ribband of Faith: George Inness, Color Theory, and the Swedenborgian Church," *American Art Journal* 26 (1994), 52–54.

Quick, L. "*Hêlēl ben-Šaḥar* and the Chthonic Sun: A New Suggestion for the Mythological Background of Isa 14:12–15," *Vetus Testamentum* 68 (2018), 129–48,
https://doi.org/10.1163/15685330-12341299

Rechel-White, J. A., "Longfellow's Influence on Whitman's 'Rise' from Manhattan Island," *ATQ* 6 (1992), 121–129.

_____. "Longfellow, Henry Wadsworth (1807–82)" in LeMaster and Kummings, *Encyclopedia*,
https://whitmanarchive.org/criticism/current/encyclopedia/entry_197.html.

Renner, K. "Tradition for a Time of Crisis: Whitman's Prophetic Stance" in *Poetic Prophecy in Western Literature* (eds. J. Wojcik and R.-J. Frontain; Rutherford, N.J.: Fairleigh Dickinson University, 1984), 119–30.

Reynolds, D. S. *Walt Whitman's America*: *A Cultural Biography* (Vintage, 1996).

_____. "Politics and Poetry: *Leaves of Grass* and the Social Crisis of the 1850s" in Greenspan, *Cambridge Companion*.

_____. (ed.), *A Historical Guide to Walt Whitman* (New York/Oxford: Oxford University, 2000), 225–61, https://doi.org/10.13008/0737-0679.2247

Richardson, R. D. *Emerson*: *The Mind on Fire* (Berkeley: University of California, 1995).

Robertson, M. *Worshiping Walt*: *The Whitman Disciples* (Princeton: Princeton University, 2008), https://doi.org/10.1515/9781400834037

_____. "'New-Born Bard[s] of the Holy Ghost': The American Bibles of Walt Whitman and Joseph Smith" in *Above the American Renaissance* (eds. H. K. Bush and B. Yothers; Amherst: University of Massachusetts, 2018), 140–60, https://doi.org/10.2307/j.ctv35q8p3.12

Rorty, R. *Achieving Our Country* (Cambridge: Harvard University, 1998).

Rosenau, W. *Hebraisms in the Authorized Version of the Bible* (Baltimore: Friedenwald, 1903).

Rosenbach, A. *Genitive Variation in English* (Berlin/New York: de Gruyter, 2002), https://doi.org/10.1515/9783110899818

Ross, E. C. "Whitman's Verse," *MLN* 45 (1930), 364.

Rossetti, W. M. "Prefatory Notice" in *Poems by Walt Whitman* (London: John Camden Hotten, Piccadilly, 1868).

_____. *Rossetti Papers*: *1862–1870* (London: Sands & Co., 1903).

_____. *Poems by Walt Whitman* (London: John Camden Hotten, Piccadilly, 1868).

Roston, M. *Prophet and Poet*: *The Bible and the Growth of Romanticism* (Evanston, Ill.: Northwestern University, 1965).

Rountree, T. J. "Walt Whitman's Indirect Expression and Its Application to 'Song of Myself,'" *PMLA* 73/5 (1958), 549–55.

Rubin, J. J. "Tupper's Possible Influence on Whitman's Style," *American Notes & Queries* 1 (1941), 101–02.

Saintsbury, G. "[Review of *Leaves of Grass* (1871)]," *The Academy* 6 (10 October 1874), 398–400.

Sanders, S. L. *The Invention of Hebrew* (Urbana: University of Illinois, 2009).

Schjeldahl, P. "How to Celebrate Walt Whitman's Two-Hundredth Birthday," *The New Yorker* (June 24, 2019).

Schmidgall, G. *Intimate with Walt: Selections from Whitman's Conversations with Horace Traubel, 1888–1892* (Iowa City: University of Iowa, 2001), https://doi.org/10.2307/j.ctt20q1zzr

_____. *Containing Multitudes: Walt Whitman and the British Literary Tradition* (Oxford/New York: Oxford University, 2014). https://doi.org/10.1093/acprof:oso/9780199374410.001.0001

Schneidau, H. "The Antinomian Strain: The Bible and American Poetry" in *The Bible and American Arts and Letters* (ed. G. Gunn; Philadelphia: Fortress, 1983), 11–32.

Schober, R. "Transcendentalism" in Levin and Whitley, *Walt Whitman in Context*, 388–405, https://doi.org/10.1017/9781108292443.020

Scott, C. "Vers Libre" in *NPEPP*.

Seery, J. E. (ed.) *A Political Companion to Walt Whitman* (Lexington: University Press of Kentucky, 2011).

Shalom, S. In *New York Herald Tribune Book Review* (26 March 1950), 3.

Shapiro, A. *In Praise of the Impure: Poetry and the Ethical Imagination: Essays, 1980–1991* (Northwestern University, 1993).

Shephard, E. "Possible Sources of Some of Whitman's Ideas in *Hermes Mercurius Trismegistus* and Other Works," *MLQ* 14 (1953), 60–81.

Silver, G. "Whitman in 1850: Three Uncollected Articles," *AL* 19/4 (1948), 301–17.

Skaggs, C. T. "Opera" in Levin and Whitley, *Walt Whitman in Context*, 239–56.

Smith, B. H. *Poetic Closure: A Study of How Poems End* (Chicago: University of Chicago, 1968).

Smith, M. *The Origins and Development of the Waw-Consecutive: Northwest Semitic Evidence from Ugarit to Qumran* (Atlanta: Scholars, 1991).

_____. *The Genesis of Good and Evil in the Garden of Eden* (Louisville: Westminster John Knox, 2019).

Smith, W. *A Dictionary of the Bible* (Boston: Little, Brown, and Company, 1860).

Stevenson, R. L. *Familiar Studies of Men and Books* (London: Chatto and Windus, 1882), 106, 120-21.

Storr, V. F. (ed.). *The English Bible* (London: Methuen & Co., 1938).

Stovall, F. "Notes on Whitman's Reading," *AL* 26/3 (1954), 337–62.

_____. *The Foreground of Leaves of Grass* (Charlottesville: University Press of Virginia, 1974).

Stuart, M. *A Hebrew Chrestomathy* (Andover: Codman Press, 1829).

Swinburne, A. C. "Whitmania," *Fortnightly Review* 48 (1887), 174.

Tapscott, S. J. "Leaves of Myself: Whitman's Egypt in 'Song of Myself,'" *AL* 50/1 (1978), 49–73.

Taylor, C., and E. Robinson (eds.), *Calmet's Dictionary of the Holy Bible* (Rev. American ed; Boston: Crocker and Brewster, 1832).

Todd, E. W. "Indian Pictures and Two Whitman Poems," *Huntington Library Quarterly* 19/1 (1955), 1–11.

Traubel, H. *With Walt Whitman in Camden*, 9 vols (1906–96), https://whitmanarchive.org/criticism/disciples/traubel/index.html.

Trowbridge, J. T. *My Own Story* (Boston, 1903).

Tupper, M. F. *Proverbial Philosophy* (London: Joseph Rickerby, 1838).

_____. *Proverbial Philosophy: In Four Series, Now First Complete* (London/New York: Ward, Lock and Co., 1888).

Turpin, Z. "Introduction to Walt Whitman's 'Life and Adventures of Jack Engle,'" *WWQR* 39/3 (2017), 225–61, https://doi.org/10.13008/0737-0679.2247

Tyndale, W. *Obedience of a Christian Man* (1528).

Vance, D. R. *The Question of Meter in Biblical Hebrew Poetry* (Lewiston: Edwin Mellen, 2001).

Vendler, H. *Poets Thinking* (Cambridge: Harvard University, 2004), https://doi.org/10.2307/j.ctvk12q8k

Voigt, E. B. *The Art of Syntax: Rhythm of Thought, Rhythm of Song* (Graywolf Press, 2009).

Warren, J. P. "'The Free Growth of Metrical Laws': Syntactic Parallelism in 'Song Of Myself,'" *Style* 18/1 (1984), 27–42.

_____. *Walt Whitman's Language Experiment* (University Park/London: Pennsylvania State University, 1990).

_____. "Style" in Kummings, *Companion to Walt Whitman*, 377–91, https://doi.org/10.1002/9780470996812.ch24

Watson, R. *Biblical and Theological Dictionary* (rev. Am. ed; New York: Lane and Scott, 1851 [1832]).

Watson, W. G. E. *Traditional Techniques in Classical Hebrew Verse* (JSOTS 170; Sheffield: Sheffield Academic, 1994).

_____. *Classical Hebrew Poetry: A Guide to Its Techniques* (London: T & T Clark, 2001 [1984]).

Weisbuch, R. D. *Atlantic Double-Cross: American Literature and British Influence in the Age of Emerson* (Chicago: University of Chicago, 1986).

Wesling, D., and E. Bollobás, "Free Verse" in *NPEPP*.

Whitley, E. "The First (1855) Edition of Leaves of Grass" in Companion to *Walt Whitman*, 457–70,
https://doi.org/10.1002/9780470996812.ch28

Wihl, G. "Politics" in Kummings, *Companion to Walt Whitman*, 76–86.

Wilde, O. "The Gospel According to Walt Whitman," *The Pall Mall Gazette* (25 January 1889), 3.

Wiley, A. M. "Reiterative Devices in 'Leaves of Grass,'" *AL* 1/2 (1929), 161–70.

Williams, C. K. *On Whitman* (Princeton: Princeton University, 2010),
https://doi.org/10.1515/9781400834334

Wilson, I. G. (ed.) *Whitman Noir: Black Americans and the Good Grey Poet* (Iowa City: University of Iowa, 2014),
https://whitmanarchive.org/criticism/current/pdf/anc.02128.pdf.

Yothers, B. "Nineteenth-Century Religion" in Levin and Whitley, *Walt Whitman in Context*, 524–42,
https://doi.org/10.1017/9781108292443.027

Zitter, E. S. "Songs of the Canon: *Song of Solomon* and 'Song of Myself,'" *WWQR* 5 (1987), 8–15.

Zweig, P. *Walt Whitman: The Making of the Poet* (New York: Basic Books, 1984).

List of Figures

1. P. 13 from the 1860 *Leaves of Grass* (Boston: Thayer and Eldridge, 1860–61), https://whitmanarchive.org/published/LG/figures/ppp.01500.021.jpg. Public domain. Shows section numbers in "Proto-Leaf." Section 34 also mimes the "graded number sequence" of the Bible.

2. Clipping entitled "King James' Bible" from the "Notebook Intended for an American Dictionary" (*DBN* III, 675). Courtesy of the Library of Congress. Photograph by F. W. Dobbs-Allsopp.

3. Harper and Brothers *Illuminated Bible* (1846), title page. Public domain.

4. Gen 32:21–34:1 from Harper's *Illuminated Bible*, showing bicolumnar page layout common to the KJB. Public domain.

5. Walt Whitman's Family Bible. Image courtesy of the Walt Whitman Birthplace.

6. Family Bible (published in 1867) that Whitman gave to William and Ellen O'Connor (January 1, 1871). Its translation is that of the KJB. Feinberg Collection of the Library of Congress. Photograph by Leslie Dobbs-Allsopp.

7. A copy of the edition of *Leaves of Grass* published in celebration of Whitman's 70th birthday, modeled on a little "Oxford Bible" (with thin "Oxford Bible" paper, black leather cover, wraparound flap). On display at Grolier Club, "'Poet of the Body': New York's Walt Whitman" (May 15–July 27, 2019). Photograph by Leslie Dobbs-Allsopp.

8. P. 2 (obv) of "The Bible as Poetry." Codex Ms263, https://www.lib.uchicago.edu/e/scrc/findingaids/view.php?eadid=ICU.SPCL.MS263. Shows clipping containing ideas attributed to Frederick de Sola Mendes. Image courtesy of the Hanna Holborn Gray Special Collections Research Center, University of Chicago.

9. P. 28 from *Two Rivulets* (Camden, New Jersey, 1876) showing poetry and prose divided by a wavy line running across the middle of the page. Public domain.

10. "Blood-Money," the *New York Daily Tribune* (March 22, 1850), p. 1, https://whitmanarchive.org/published/periodical/poems/per.00089.

Whitman's first nonmetrical poem. Cropped image courtesy of The Walt Whitman Archive.

11. From "Pictures," holograph notebook (leaf 38r), https://collections. library.yale.edu/catalog/2007253. Image courtesy of the Walt Whitman Collection. Yale Collection of American Literature, Beinecke Rare Book and Manuscript Library.

12. Job 2:2–3:26 from the Harper *Illuminated Bible*.

13. Gen 29:5–30:3 from the Harper *Illuminated Bible*.

14. Gen 30:4–39 from the Harper *Illuminated Bible*.

15. Line lengths by word count for the 1855 *Leaves*. Computation and chart by Greg Murray.

16. Leaf 6r from the "I know a rich capitalist" notebook," https://whitmanarchive.org/manuscripts/figures/nyp.00129.011.jpg. Showing the prose version of the "Love is the cause of causes" passage. Image courtesy of the Henry W. and Albert A. Berg Collection of English and American Literature, New York Public Library.

17. Leaf 7v from the "I know a rich capitalist" notebook," https://whitmanarchive.org/manuscripts/figures/nyp.00129.014.jpg. Showing the verse version of the "Love is the cause of causes" passage. Image courtesy of the Henry W. and Albert A. Berg Collection of English and American Literature, New York Public Library.

18. Isa 7:19–9:1 from the Harper *Illuminated Bible*. In the original Hebrew, Isaiah 7–8 is prose and Isaiah 9 is poetry, but all is prose in the KJB and the page layout is the same.

19. Isa 9:1–10:11 from the Harper *Illuminated Bible*. In the original Hebrew, Isaiah 7–8 is prose and Isaiah 9 is poetry, but all is prose in the KJB and the page layout is the same.

20. Ps 23:1–24:23 from the Harper *Illuminated Bible*.

21. Psalm 23 from R. G. Moulton, *Modern Reader's Bible* (New York: Macmillan, 1922), II, 320. Public domain.

22. Psalm 23 (cont.) from Moulton, *Modern Reader's Bible*, II, 321.

23. Psalm 23 in the Revised Version (*The Holy Bible* [Cambridge: Cambridge University, 1885]). Public domain.

24. A comparison of the differences between Whitman's typical poetic line and the biblical Hebrew poetic line. Image of p. 13 from the 1855 *Leaves*, public domain. Image of a 5/6HevPs fragment, showing parts of Ps 23:2–4 (Wikimedia Commons). Unpointed Hebrew translation of "Song of Myself" (lines 1–9), after Simon Halkin.

25. P. 15 from the 1855 *Leaves of Grass* (Brooklyn, NY, 1855), https://whitmanarchive.org/published/LG/figures/ppp.00271.022.jpg. Public domain.

26. P. 39 from the 1855 *Leaves*, https://whitmanarchive.org/published/LG/figures/ppp.00271.046.jpg.

27. Comparison by word count between the lengths of lines in the 1855 *Leaves* and the verse divisions of the entire KJB. Computation and chart by Greg Murray.

28. Comparison by word count between the lengths of lines in the 1855 *Leaves* and the verse divisions of KJB-Pentateuch. Computation and chart by Greg Murray.

29. Comparison by word count between the lengths of lines in the 1855 *Leaves* and the verse divisions of KJB-Job/Psalms/Proverbs. Computation and chart by Greg Murray.

30. Comparison by word count between the lengths of lines in the 1855 *Leaves* and the lineated translation of ASV-Job. Computation and chart by Greg Murray.

31. B19a (Leningrad Codex), folio 423 recto (Ruth 4:13B–Song 2:5A). Freedman et al., *The Leningrad Codex*. Photograph by Bruce and Kenneth Zuckerman, West Semitic Research, in collaboration with the Ancient Biblical Manuscript Center. Courtesy Russian National Library (Saltykov-Shchedrin).

32. B19a, folio 394 recto (Psalm 133). Freedman et al., *The Leningrad Codex*. Photograph by Bruce and Kenneth Zuckerman, West Semitic Research, in collaboration with the Ancient Biblical Manuscript Center. Courtesy Russian National Library (Saltykov-Shchedrin).

33. Whitman's comparative word counts on the second leaf of the so-called "Blue Book" edition of the 1860 *Leaves*, https://whitmanarchive.org/published/1860-Blue_book/images/index.html. Image courtesy of the New York Public Library.

34. Verso of "And to me every minute," https://whitmanarchive.org/manuscripts/figures/tex.00057.002.jpg. Image courtesy of the Harry Ransom Humanities Research Center of the University of Texas at Austin. Estimated average number of letters in what Whitman considers "one of my closely written MS pages," comparing to the number of "letters in page of Shakespeare's poems."

35. P. 14 from the 1855 *Leaves*, https://whitmanarchive.org/published/LG/figures/ppp.00271.021.jpg.

36. P. 7 from the 1856 *Leaves*, https://whitmanarchive.org/published/LG/figures/ppp.00237.015.jpg. Image courtesy of the Albert and Shirley Small Special Collections Library, University of Virginia.

37. Prov 30:7–31:20 from Harper's *Illuminated Bible*.

38. Geneva Bible (1560) was the first English Bible to add verse numbers and to begin each verse on a new line.

39. Leaves 38v, 43r of the "Talbot Wilson" notebook, http://hdl.loc.gov/loc. mss/ms002007.mss45443.0217. Leaf 38v shows a run of "And"-headed lines. Image courtesy of the Thomas Biggs Harned Collection of the Papers of Walt Whitman, 1842–1937, Manuscript Division, Library of Congress, Washington, D.C. MSS45443, Box 8: Notebook LC #80.

40. Recto of "And to me every minute," https://whitmanarchive.org/ manuscripts/figures/tex.00057.001.jpg. Image courtesy of the Harry Ransom Humanities Research Center of the University of Texas at Austin. A run of "And"-headed lines, though in a different order than the same lines appear in the 1855 *Leaves*.

41. P. 273 from Whitman's copy of James Macpherson, *The Poems of Ossian* (London: Joseph Rickerby, 1838) showing bracketed text. Charles E. Feinberg Collection, Rare Books and Special Collections Division, Library of Congress. Washington D. C. Photograph by Leslie Dobbs-Allsopp.

42. P. 274 from Whitman's copy of Macpherson, *The Poems of Ossian* showing bracketed text. Photograph by Leslie Dobbs-Allsopp.

43. P. 299 from Whitman's copy of Macpherson, *The Poems of Ossian* showing bracketed text. Photograph by Leslie Dobbs-Allsopp.

44. P. 113 from Whitman's copy of Martin Farquhar Tupper, *Proverbial Philosophy* (London: Joseph Rickerby, 1838) showing circled text. Feinberg Collection of the Library of Congress. Photograph by Leslie Dobbs-Allsopp.

45. P. 153 from Whitman's copy of Tupper, *Proverbial Philosophy* showing bracketed text. Photograph by Leslie Dobbs-Allsopp.

46. P. 150 from Whitman's copy of Tupper, *Proverbial Philosophy* showing bracketed text and annotation. Photograph by Leslie Dobbs-Allsopp.

47. Leaves 35v-36r of the "Talbot Wilson" notebook, http://hdl.loc.gov/loc. mss/ms002007.mss45443.0217. Leaf 35vs is the point in the notebook Where Whitman begins experimenting with trial lines in verse. Image courtesy of the Thomas Biggs Harned Collection of the Papers of Walt Whitman, 1842–1937, Manuscript Division, Library of Congress, Washington, D.C. MSS45443, Box 8: Notebook LC #80.

48. A facsimile edition of William Tyndale's translation of the Book of Jonah (1863 [1531]) showing the plain page layout Tyndale used (in the then familiar "Black letter" typeface). Public domain.

49. "The Valley of the Shadow of Death" (1867) by George Inness, http://emuseum.vassar.edu/objects/59/the-valley-of-the-shadow-of-death. Oil on canvas, 48 5/8 x 72 7/8. The Francis Lehman Loeb Art Center, Vassar College. Gift of Charles M. Pratt, 1917.1.6. Image courtesy of Art Resource.

50. "Aye, well I know 'tis ghastly to descend," http://hdl.loc.gov/loc.mss/ ms004014.mss18630.00626. Image courtesy of the Walt Whitman Papers in the Charles E. Feinberg Collection, Manuscript Division, Library of Congress, Washington, D. C. mss18630, box 26; reel 16.

Index

Alden, Henry Mills 338–339

Allen, Gay Wilson 2, 4–6, 8, 29, 37, 44, 55, 58, 60, 63–65, 75, 81, 89, 102, 105, 123–126, 128, 130, 134, 136, 166, 172–176, 181, 185, 221, 229–231, 234, 239, 241–243, 250–253, 259–260, 264–265, 270, 275, 277–278, 283, 307, 328, 337
  "Biblical Analogies for Walt Whitman's Prosody" 2, 221, 229–230
  "Biblical Echoes in Whitman's Works" 2, 230

Alonso Schökel, Luis 319

Alter, Robert 9, 144, 201, 236, 285–286, 289–290, 292–294, 296, 298–299, 301–302, 328–331, 334
  Pen of Iron: American Prose and the King James Bible 9, 285, 299, 330, 334

anthropology
  bipartite 96
  holistic 95, 248

Apocrypha
  1 Esdras (1 Esd) 92
  Ben Sira (Sir) 215, 247, 313

Archilochos 300

Asselineau, Roger 111, 156, 159

attributed speech (formatting of) 321–326

Bancroft, Richard 289

Bellow, Saul 285

Bergquist, B. L. 7, 25, 64–65, 77, 80, 98–99

Berlin, Adele 234–235
  Dynamics of Biblical Parallelism 234

Beyers, Chris 168, 189

bible(s). See also Apocrypha; See also Hebrew Bible (Old Testament); See also New Testament
  as poetry 1, 35, 36, 37, 80, 102, 127, 136, 168, 173, 178, 215, 216, 230, 240, 278. See also Hebrew poetry (biblical)
  Geneva Bible 103, 194–195, 299

Illuminated Bible (Harper and Brother's) 16, 18–19, 104, 106–107, 127–128, 131, 180, 313
  known by Whitman 14, 16–22, 64, 105
  verse divisions of 7, 13, 105, 111, 136–138, 140, 143–148, 152, 155, 161–163, 167–170, 174–176, 178, 181–186, 191, 193–194, 201, 216, 218, 221

"Black Lucifer" 56, 67–68, 101

Blair, Hugh 202, 272–273
  Lectures on Rhetoric and Belles Lettres 272

Blake, William 45, 88, 240

Bohan, Ruth 81

Braque, Georges 219

Brasher, T. L. 197
  The Early Poems and the Fiction 197

Brooklyn Daily Eagle 16, 64, 69, 208

Brooklyn Evening Star 82

Bryant, William Cullen 81

Buber, M. 282

Buchanan, Robert 45

Bucke, Richard Maurice 12, 102

Bunsen, C. K. J. 31–32, 42

Campbell, K. 159

Carlyle, Thomas 81, 86, 88, 190

cluster (of poems) 106, 282

cognate accusative 9, 314–316, 318

Cohen, Matt 217

Compromise of 1850 50, 77, 80

couplet 82, 95, 97, 134, 136, 138, 167, 175–178, 184–185, 215, 226, 232–233, 238, 240, 244, 259, 261, 263, 266, 270, 274–275, 277, 283, 294, 320

Coverdale, Myles 289, 299

Cowper, William 240

Crawley, Thomas Edward 2, 28, 63

Daniell, D. 291, 296

Dante 12, 14, 28, 126
  Inferno 14, 126

Deleuze, Gilles 307–308
democratic poetics 24, 187, 189, 287, 307, 308, 332, 334. See also political dimensions of style
De Vere, A. 288
Doty, Mark 298
Driver, S. R. 231, 250–252
Duchamp, Marcel 219

Eadie, John 33
 Biblical Cyclopaedia 33
Eliot, T. S. 125
Emerson, Ralph Waldo 1, 43, 49–51, 60, 81, 86, 88, 220, 273, 299, 331, 333
Engell, J. 239, 272
Erkkila, Betsy 56, 189, 223–224, 331, 334

Fairbairn, Patrick 33
 The Imperial Bible-Dictionary 33
Faulkner, William 285, 292–293
 Absalom, Absalom! 292
Folsom, Ed 14, 67, 69, 120
free verse (free rhythm) 5, 6, 7, 10, 11, 43, 44, 49, 52, 54, 56, 57, 60, 61, 89, 113, 117, 182, 184, 185, 221, 223, 224, 227, 230, 240, 242, 264, 308, 310, 328. See also meter (lack of); See also rhyme (lack of)
Fuller, Margaret 36, 203, 288

Gardiner, J. H. 124
Gray, G. B. 238
Greenberg, Uri Zvi 88
Green, Samuel 33
 A Biblical and Theological Dictionary 33
Greenstein, E. L. 234–235
Gross, Harvey 330
Gutjahr, Paul 16

Halkin, Simon 135, 143, 314
Hammond, Gerald 301, 311
Harper's New Monthly 338
Hebrew Bible (Old Testament)
 1 Chronicles (1 Chron) 78, 83–84, 313
 1 Kings (1 Kgs) 83–84, 87, 108, 318, 348

1 Samuel (1 Sam) 71, 83, 108, 165
2 Chronicles (2 Chron) 84, 108
2 Kings (2 Kgs) 84, 98, 309
2 Samuel (2 Sam) 71, 96, 162, 245, 256, 292
Amos 77, 162, 245
Daniel (Dan) 34, 87, 316
Deuteronomy (Deut) 71, 73, 83–85, 299, 313, 315, 317
Ecclesiastes (Eccl) 41, 91–92, 165, 220, 292, 295, 302–303, 318
Esther (Est) 84, 90
Exodus (Exod) 33–34, 84–85, 128, 170, 251, 256, 299, 312, 315–316, 320, 348
Ezekiel (Ezek) 84, 87, 98, 108, 215, 344
Ezra 84, 313
Genesis (Gen) 19, 57–58, 64, 66, 78, 81, 83, 85, 90, 98–99, 101, 105–106, 108–109, 117, 192, 297, 306, 312–313, 315–317, 344
Habakkuk (Hab) 318
Hosea (Hos) 165, 268
Isaiah (Isa) 27, 35, 37, 39, 66, 74, 82–83, 88–89, 92, 101, 104, 108, 127, 204–205, 215, 250, 254, 276, 299, 312, 316, 318, 345
Jeremiah (Jer) 165, 247, 262, 312, 318, 320
Job 12, 27, 35, 37, 39, 83, 90–91, 100, 104–105, 108, 125, 130, 133, 137, 144–145, 148–149, 155, 162–164, 167, 177–178, 184, 204–205, 245, 247, 259, 262, 265, 299, 312, 345
Joel 315
Jonah (Jon) 289, 295
Judges (Judg) 177, 299, 316
Lamentations (Lam) 39, 66, 83, 184, 299–300
Leviticus (Lev) 71
Micah (Mic) 87, 312
Nehemiah (Neh) 108
Numbers (Num) 313, 315–316, 320
Obadiah (Obad) 177
Proverbs (Prov) 60, 90, 92, 94, 125, 130, 133, 137, 144–145, 148, 155,

164–165, 167, 178, 180, 183, 215, 228, 237, 244, 247, 250, 254, 256, 262, 313
Psalms (Ps) 35, 37, 39, 92, 96, 103, 125, 130–133, 135, 137–138, 140–141, 143–145, 148, 151, 155, 162, 165, 167, 174–178, 182–183, 204–205, 215, 224, 245–247, 251, 256, 259–262, 265–266, 277, 299, 306, 311–312, 316, 319, 343–347
Revelation (Rev) 33, 84, 108, 312–313, 316
Ruth 71, 96, 150
Song of Songs/Solomon (Song) 83, 85, 93, 96, 104, 130, 150, 167, 259–260, 299, 313, 317
Zechariah (Zech) 64, 76, 324
Hebrew poetry (biblical) 6, 25, 28, 37–38, 43, 45–46, 60, 103, 125–130, 134–137, 144–145, 156, 162, 168, 171–172, 174, 176, 178, 181–184, 230–232, 234–235, 238–241, 243–244, 247, 250, 259, 261, 265, 270, 272, 274–276, 278, 282, 288, 294, 296, 299, 306, 319, 326
Hemingway, Ernest 285, 292, 295, 302
The Sun Also Rises 295, 302
Herder, Johann Gottfried 44, 88, 270–271
The Spirit of Hebrew Poetry 270
Hollander, John 182–184, 240, 265
Rhyme's Reason 182
Holloway, E. 120
Holmstedt, R. 279
Homer 12, 28, 39, 43, 91, 101, 220, 270, 342
Iliad 12, 14, 28, 39, 43, 220, 300
Horace 81
Hrushovski, B. 240
"On Free Rhythms in Modern Poetry" 240

Inness, George 10, 338–341, 343–346
"The Valley of the Shadow of Death" 10, 338–340, 342–344, 347

Jakobson, R. 234–235

Kinnell, Galway 8, 124, 221, 223, 278, 283
Kinzie, Mary 181–183, 185

A Poet's Guide to Poetry 181
Klammer, Martin 50, 80, 226, 305
Kugel, J. L. 236–237, 242

LeMaster, J. R. 88
letter(s) 20, 46, 84, 220, 331. See also Whitman, Walt (works): "Letters from New York"; See also Whitman, Walt (works): "Letters from Paumanok"
Levine, H. J 104
Lincoln, Abraham 201–202, 292, 330–331
Second Inaugural Address 202, 331
Longenbach, J. 279
Longfellow, Henry Wadsworth 68–69, 202
"Poems on Slavery" 69
"The Warning" 68–69
long poem 102–103, 105–106, 122, 198
Loving, Jerome 45, 50–52, 57–58, 328
Lowth, Robert 8, 44, 49, 60, 88, 123, 129–130, 136, 179, 203, 228–243, 247, 249–251, 253–254, 268, 270, 272–273, 275
Isaiah: A New Translation 130
Lectures on the Sacred Poetry of the Hebrews 44, 232, 272
Praelectiones 203, 272
Preliminary Dissertation 232–233, 235
Luther, Martin 43, 290
lyric (indirect or subjective expression) 5–6, 37–39, 60, 89, 102, 296, 298, 300, 327

Macpherson, James 8, 37, 202–207, 217, 240, 270
The Poems of Ossian 203, 205–207, 217
Mazur, Krystyna 308
McCarthy, Cormac 285
Melville, Herman 4, 285, 292, 294, 296, 330
Moby-Dick 296
Mendes, Frederick de Sola 25, 29–30, 35, 43, 272
Merrill, Christopher 69

meter (lack of) 7, 24–25, 43, 45–47, 49, 52, 55–57, 60, 63, 76, 101, 112, 166, 216–217, 229, 231, 273, 310, 327–328, 332–333, 337. See also free verse (free rhythm)

Michelet, Jules 1
  The Bird 1
  The People 1

Miller, Alfred Jacob 258

Miller, Matt 2, 5, 26, 28, 41–42, 99, 110–111, 123–124, 190, 217–220, 299, 327
  Collage of Myself 219, 327

Milton, John 49, 202
  Paradise Lost 14

Molinoff, Katherine 20

Moulton, R. G. 104, 129–130, 134, 136, 138, 143, 171, 174–176, 181, 259

narrativity
  incipient 237, 256–258, 268
  non-narrativity 9, 37–38, 86, 103–104, 196, 216, 256, 285–286, 296–299, 301–302, 306, 326–327, 329–330, 337

National Era 46

"New Bible" 13, 39, 70, 220, 293. See also Whitman, Walt (works): *Leaves of Grass*

New Testament
  1 Corinthians (1 Cor) 53, 69–70, 77, 84–85, 92, 245, 324
  1 Peter (1 Pet) 85, 108, 313, 346
  1 Thessalonians (1 Thess) 71, 276
  2 Corinthians (2 Cor) 85, 108
  2 Peter (2 Pet) 85
  Acts 79, 346
  Colossians (Col) 346
  Galatians (Gal) 84–85, 108, 313
  Hebrews (Heb) 107, 346
  John 56, 84, 90–91, 98–99, 166, 321
  Luke 64, 69–71, 79, 85, 92, 96, 98, 162, 166, 245, 313, 321, 346
  Mark 69–71, 79, 81, 90–91, 108, 166, 245, 321, 346–347
  Matthew (Matt) 53, 55–56, 69–72, 77, 79, 85, 87, 91–93, 108, 161–162, 165–166, 185–186, 196, 245, 276, 313, 321, 324, 327, 347
  Philippians (Phil) 96, 162
  Romans (Rom) 70, 72, 85, 109, 312, 346

New York Aurora 34, 328

New York Daily Tribune 50, 54

Norton, David 129, 238, 334

notebooks. See also Whitman, Walt (works)
  early 7, 26, 36, 47, 51–52, 54, 58, 63, 79–81, 86, 89, 92, 101, 107, 109–110, 112, 117, 185, 197, 268–269, 313, 324
  post-1856 14

Noyes, George R. 130, 270, 276

O'Connor, Michael 179, 234–235, 237

O'Connor, William Douglas 12, 21, 46

Old Testament. See Hebrew Bible (Old Testament)

originality 41–42, 288

Ossian 12, 27, 36, 202–204, 270, 272, 288. See also Macpherson, James

parallelism 5, 8, 9, 45, 49, 53, 55, 59, 82, 89, 94, 123–124, 126, 129, 130, 134, 136, 161–162, 172–179, 181, 185, 189, 202–203, 216–217, 221, 223–224, 226–242, 244–253, 256, 259, 261, 263–265, 268–271, 273, 275–278, 281–283, 285–286, 293, 296, 301, 306, 308, 310, 320, 326–328, 330, 334, 337, 342, 348. See also narrativity: incipient
  antithetical 60, 94, 228, 231, 235–237, 241, 243, 245, 247–250, 268, 275–276
  chronological development 124, 268–269
  climactic 231, 236, 241, 250–255
  conditionals 261–262
  duple rhythm 263–265
  envelope (inclusio) 259–261, 345
  gapping 253–255, 268–269, 275, 278
  interlinear 232, 238, 252, 275–277, 281
  line-internal 173–179, 185, 216, 236, 241–244, 250, 263, 269, 275
  repetitive 236, 247, 249

staircase 251–253

synonymous 60, 126, 136, 162, 177, 179, 216, 231, 235–236, 238, 241, 243–245, 247, 249–253, 259, 263, 268, 275, 277

synthetic (constructive) 231, 235, 237–238, 241, 243, 252

Whitman's 245, 273–283

parataxis 5, 9–10, 93, 193–194, 259–260, 291, 301–308, 32–328, 334, 337. See also poetic line(s): line-initial "And"

paronomastic infinitive 317–318

periphrastic genitive 9, 100, 308–314, 327

of-genitive 9, 308–314, 326, 337, 345

superlative 100, 313–314, 326

s-genitive 308–310, 345

Perry, Bliss 3, 39, 45, 230

Picasso, Pablo 219

poetic line(s). See also parallelism; See also prose style: prosiness

caesura 169–170, 172–173, 175–176, 183–184, 218, 250, 305

chronological development 7, 112–123, 166, 190

end-stopping 10, 181–187, 189, 216, 232, 263, 274, 279, 283, 287, 306, 328, 334, 342

length 7, 53, 71, 111–123, 134, 136–137, 139–169, 183, 185, 189, 191, 197, 208, 218, 232, 261, 275, 294, 310, 337, 342, 348

line-initial "And" 105, 115, 191–194, 196–200, 217, 269, 302, 304–305, 342

three-part line 244, 265–269, 273, 310

two-part line 162, 164, 215–216, 244, 248, 255, 261, 263, 265, 268–269, 273–274, 283, 306, 310–311, 328, 348

variability 7, 117, 123, 134, 137, 152, 166–168, 261

political dimensions of style 9, 55–56, 187, 189, 223–224, 227–228, 283, 285, 307–308, 331–334. See also democratic poetics

Pope, Alexander 81

Posey, M. N. 4–5, 64, 152, 201

Price, Kenneth M. 67

prophecy 88–89, 264, 296

prophet 73–74, 86–89, 98, 108, 273, 296, 300

prophetic voice 4, 37, 77, 86–89, 102

prose style

American prose style 9, 285–286, 301, 328, 330–331, 334

plain style 9, 288–293, 301, 334–335

prosiness 5, 106, 189–191, 217, 329

quotation

"no quotations" (poetic theory) 7, 63, 73–80, 87, 109, 161, 287

use of quotation 6–7, 16, 25, 63–64, 81, 85, 130, 161, 168, 287, 298, 348

Reynolds, David 38, 201

rhyme (lack of) 6, 25, 43, 45–47, 49, 50, 52, 55–57, 60, 208, 216–217, 229, 240, 273, 332–333. See also free verse (free rhythm)

Robinson, Marilynne 285

Ross, E. C. 181

Rossetti, William Michael 45–46

Rousseau, Jean-Jacques 43, 81

Rubin, J. J. 208–209

Ruskin, John 81, 190

Saintsbury, George 7, 111, 137, 144–145, 161, 218, 222

Sand, George 1

The Countess of Rudolstadt 1

Schele de Vere, M. 31–32, 42

Schjeldahl, Peter 334–335

self-study 37, 51, 80, 218, 270

Shakespeare, William 4, 12–13, 28, 43, 81, 153–154, 300, 320, 342

Shema Yisrael 73

slavery 50, 55, 60, 67, 76, 80, 223, 226–228, 246

Smart, Christopher 240

Smith, Barbara 260

Smith, William 33

Snodgrass, W. D. 260, 282

Socrates 43, 81, 101, 212

Stovall, Floyd 32, 36, 49, 60, 130, 208, 270–271, 333
Sunday Dispatch 52

Targums 72–73
Tennyson, Alfred 28, 300, 342
tense (grammatical) 32, 34, 193, 196–197, 298–299, 301–304, 326, 330, 343, 347
theological dictionary 32, 34, 272
Traubel, Horace 12, 203
triplet 82, 134, 136, 162, 176, 184–185, 213, 233, 240, 244, 259, 265–266, 268, 274–275, 277
Tupper, Martin Farquhar 8, 165, 202, 208, 210–217, 247–248, 270, 287
    Probabilities: An Aid to Faith 208
    Proverbial Philosophy 165, 208–211, 214–217
Turpin, Zachary 51, 296
Tyndale, William 9, 100, 136, 155, 193–194, 255, 278, 286, 288–296, 299, 301–303, 309, 311, 313, 315–318, 320, 330, 334–335, 343, 348
    Observations of a Christian Man 290

unpublished poetry manuscripts 7, 39, 65, 86, 102, 110, 268

Vendler, H. 243, 277
verse style. See free verse (free rhythm)
Virgil 28, 43, 126
    Aeneid 14, 126
Voigt, E. B. 290
Volney, C.-F. 31–32

Warren, James Perrin 38, 230, 242, 264–265, 283
Watson, Richard 33
    Biblical and Theological Dictionary 33
Watson, Wilfred G. E. 179
Whitman, Walt (works)
    "A Backward Glance o'er Travel'd Roads" 12, 24, 203, 270
    "A Brooklyn Daguerreotypist" 84
    "A Child's Reminiscence" 38, 309
    "After all is said" 325
    "Ambition" 197

"America" 335
"An Afternoon Lounge About Brooklyn" 82
"And to me every minute" 154, 198, 200
"An Hour Among the Portraits" 84, 102, 106
"An Ossianic Night—Dearest Friends" 203
"An Ossianic paragraph" 36–37, 203
"A Peep at the Israelites" 25, 34–35, 98, 125
"Art and Artists" 51, 57–58, 81, 115, 117, 269
"As a Strong Bird on Pinions Free" 342
"Autobiographical Data" (notebook) 26, 79, 89, 92, 119
"Aye, well I know 'tis ghastly to descend" 42, 340–341, 343
"Blood-Money" 50, 52–57, 60, 68, 76–77, 112–113, 161, 185–186, 196–197, 227, 268, 276, 323–324, 327, 346
"Books of WW" 203
"Crossing Brooklyn Ferry" 279
"Death in the School-Room" 177
"Death's Valley" 10, 42, 338, 342, 345, 347–349
Democratic Vistas 12–13, 24
"Dick Hunt" (notebook) 43, 93
Drum-Taps and Sequel to Drum-Taps 34, 152, 177, 253, 317
    "Chanting the Square Deific" 34
    "When Lilacs Last in the Dooryard Bloom" 177, 252–253, 317–318, 334
"Emerson uses the Deific" 28
"Fame's Vanity" 197
"George Walker" (notebook) 25
"Had I the choice" 342
"—How different" 28, 75
"I am a curse" 68
"I call back blunders" 107
"If I Should Need to Name, O Western World!" 347

"I know a rich capitalist" (notebook) 47, 76, 92, 100, 102, 117–119, 186

"I know as well as you" 107

"Introduction to the London Edition" 1, 29

"Is Walt Whitman's Poetry Poetical?" 1, 28

Leaves of Grass 1–7, 9–10, 13–15, 22, 28, 37–39, 41–42, 46, 50–51, 53–56, 58–60, 63–66, 70, 73–76, 78, 80–83, 85–86, 88–90, 92–93, 95–96, 98, 100–102, 107, 109, 111, 113–116, 118, 120, 122, 124, 134–137, 142, 144–149, 152–153, 155–161, 165–166, 172–173, 176–177, 180, 185–187, 189–191, 196–197, 202, 204–205, 208, 215, 219, 221, 223–226, 228, 230, 241, 243–244, 247–248, 255, 260–263, 269, 274–275, 277–278, 282, 285–286, 292, 294, 296–298, 301–302, 304, 306–307, 310–311, 313–314, 316, 318, 321, 324, 327–331, 337, 349. See also "New Bible"

   1855 edition 1, 5, 7, 9–10, 37–38, 42, 50, 53–54, 56, 59–60, 63, 73, 75–76, 78, 80–83, 86, 88, 91–93, 95–96, 98, 100–102, 107, 109, 112–116, 118, 120–123, 134–135, 137, 140, 142, 144–149, 153, 155–157, 165–166, 172, 186–187, 189–191, 196–197, 200, 208, 215, 219, 221, 223, 225–226, 228, 244, 255, 260, 262–263, 269, 275, 277, 282, 285–286, 292, 299, 301–302, 307, 309–311, 313, 316, 318, 321, 327–330, 337, 345

      "A young man came to me" 325

      "Clear the way there Jonathan" 258, 269

      "Come closer to me" 69, 159

      "Great are the myths" 213

      "I celebrate myself" 39, 47, 74, 93, 97, 100, 107, 109, 120, 161–164, 166, 169, 177,

188, 196, 244, 253, 260, 263, 297–298, 304, 310, 331

      "I wander all night" 250, 252, 311

      Preface 38, 42, 47, 57–58, 70, 73, 86, 190, 226, 228, 287, 305, 307, 331–333

      "Suddenly out of its stale and dusty lair" 59, 176, 252–253

      "The bodies of men and women engirth me" 25, 253

      "There was a child went forth every day" 152, 190–191, 196

      "To think of time" 163–164, 263

      "Who learns my lesson complete" 100, 115–116

   1856 edition 1, 5, 9, 14, 16, 37–38, 82, 92, 102, 113, 123, 156, 158, 166, 196, 208, 215, 228, 260, 282, 285, 292, 301, 327, 329–330

      "Poem of Many In One" 58, 73, 190, 228, 329

      "Poem of Salutation" 36

      "Poem of The Last Explanation of Prudence" 329

      "Sun-Down Poem" 280

   1860 edition 1, 5, 9, 13, 15, 37–39, 70, 82, 102, 113, 123, 126, 152–153, 156, 166, 177, 180, 196, 215, 228, 246, 260, 282, 285, 292, 294, 301, 321, 327, 329–330

      "Enfans d'Adam" 282

      "Proto-Leaf" 15, 160, 177, 244

   1867 edition 46, 159

      "Starting from Paumanok" 160, 177

      "To Workingmen" 160

   1871-72 edition 7, 137, 161

      "The Sleepers" 334

   1881 edition 59, 122

      "Song of Myself" 38

      "Song of the Redwood-Tree" 323

   1891-92 edition

"By Blue Ontario's Shore" 58, 190

"Song of Myself" 69–70, 74, 82, 102, 105, 135, 143, 175, 189, 254

"Blue Book" edition 14, 126, 152–153, 159–160

"Letters from New York" 83

"Letters from Paumanok" 51, 82–83

"Life and Adventures of Jack Engle: An Auto-Biography" 51, 81, 84–85, 201, 286, 296–297

"Live Oak, with Moss" 316

"Med *Cophôsis*" (notebook) 90

"Memorials" (notebook) 92

"Names. The Biblical poets" 27, 35

"Notebook Intended for an American Dictionary" (notebook) 14, 17, 26, 31

November Boughs 12, 24

"Old Chants" 12, 40, 42

"On Poems" 28

"Pictures" 67, 86, 101–102, 105, 109, 122, 187, 198, 212, 269

"Poem incarnating the mind" (notebook) 51, 68, 91, 117, 123, 197, 299–300, 324

poems from 1850 51–52, 59, 63, 73–81, 86, 101, 109, 117, 185, 268

"Poems of a nation" 39, 41, 220

"Poets—Shakespeare" 27

prose from 1850-53 80–86

"Resurgemus" 51, 53, 56, 59, 76, 78–80, 112–113, 115–116, 120, 122, 172–173, 176, 186, 197, 219, 253, 268–269

"Rules for Composition" 47, 75, 286, 332

"Shirval: A Tale of Jerusalem" 13, 98

"Sleeptalker" 51, 81

"Something about Art and Brooklyn Artists" 84

"Song for Certain Congressmen" 52–53

"Speaking of literary style" 26, 36, 75

Specimen Days & Collect 41–42, 53, 65, 88, 96, 196, 203

"Taken soon out of the laps" 121–122, 298

"Taking en-masses" 27

"Talbot Wilson" (notebook) 34, 36, 55, 93, 97, 112, 116–117, 121–123, 197, 199, 223–225, 227, 246, 248, 267, 299, 322, 325

"The Bible as Poetry" 6, 11, 23–25, 28–29, 35, 40, 43, 46, 49, 75, 128, 168, 272

"The Bible Shakespere" 28, 32

"The Egyptian Museum" 31, 95

"The florid rich" 27, 36, 75

"The House of Friends" 51, 53, 64, 76, 80, 112–113, 323–324

"The Literary World" 69

"Theological inferences" 27, 104

"There is no word in any tongue" 109, 312

"The Singer in the Prison" 315, 320

"The Tomb-Blossoms" 344

"The wild gander leads" 325

Two Rivulets 42, 47, 48, 190

"We need somebody" 86, 89

"You know how" (notebook) 92

"You there" 121

"You villain, Touch!" 121

Wilkinson, John Gardner 32
  Manners and Customs of the Ancient Egyptians 32

Williams, C. K. 300

Wordsworth, William 202, 273

Zweig, P. 11, 24, 41, 74, 76, 189, 190

About the Team

Alessandra Tosi was the managing editor for this book.

Lucy Barnes copy-edited this book.

James Hobson proof read this book.

Adèle Kreager indexed this book.

The Alt-text was created by Annie Hine.

Jeevanjot Kaur Nagpal designed the cover. The cover was produced in InDesign using the Fontin font.

Cameron Craig typeset the book in InDesign and produced the paperback and hardback editions. The text font is Tex Gyre Pagella and the heading font is Californian FB.

Cameron also produced the PDF, EPUB, and editions. The conversion was performed with open-source software and other tools freely available on our GitHub page at https://github.com/OpenBookPublishers.

This book has been anonymously peer-reviewed by experts in their field. We thank them for their invaluable help.

This book need not end here...

Share

All our books — including the one you have just read — are free to access online so that students, researchers and members of the public who can't afford a printed edition will have access to the same ideas. This title will be accessed online by hundreds of readers each month across the globe: why not share the link so that someone you know is one of them?

This book and additional content is available at:
https://doi.org/10.11647/OBP.0357

Donate

Open Book Publishers is an award-winning, scholar-led, not-for-profit press making knowledge freely available one book at a time. We don't charge authors to publish with us: instead, our work is supported by our library members and by donations from people who believe that research shouldn't be locked behind paywalls.

Why not join them in freeing knowledge by supporting us:
https://www.openbookpublishers.com/support-us

Follow @OpenBookPublish

Read more at the Open Book Publishers BLOG

You may also be interested in:

Mr. Emerson's Revolution

Jean McClure Mudge (editor)

https://doi.org/10.11647/obp.0065

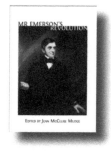

Henry James's Europe
Heritage and Transfer

Dennis Tred, Annick Duperray, and Adrian Harding (editors)

https://doi.org/10.11647/obp.0013

Romanticism and Time
Literary Temporalities

Sophie Laniel-Musitelli and Céline Sabiron (editors)

https://doi.org/10.11647/obp.0232

Milton Keynes UK
Ingram Content Group UK Ltd.
UKHW022200091223
434075UK00002B/3